Colloquial
# Turkish

## THE COLLOQUIAL SERIES
### Series Adviser: Gary King

The following languages are available in the Colloquial series:

### COLLOQUIAL 2s series: *The Next Step in Language Learning*

Colloquials are now supported by FREE AUDIO available online. All audio tracks referenced within the text are free to stream or download from www.routledge.com/cw/colloquials. If you experience any difficulties accessing the audio on the companion website, or still wish to purchase a CD, please contact our customer services team through www.routledge.com/info/contact.

# Colloquial
# Turkish

## The Complete Course for Beginners

Jeroen Aarssen and Ad Backus

Routledge
Taylor & Francis Group

LONDON AND NEW YORK

First published 2001
by Routledge
2 Park Square, Milton Park, Abingdon, Oxon, OX14 4RN

Simultaneously published in the USA and Canada
by Routledge
711 Third Avenue, New York, NY 10017

Reprinted 2003, 2004

*Routledge is an imprint of the Taylor & Francis Group, an informa business*

*British Library Cataloging in Publication Data*
A catalogue record for this book is available from the British Library

*Library of Congress Cataloging in Publication Data*
Backus, Ad.
  Colloquial Turkish : the complete course for beginners / Jeroen
Aarssen and Ad Backus.
    p. cm.
  1. Turkish language–Textbooks for foreign speakers–English.
  2. Turkish language–Self–instruction. I. Aarssen, Jeroen. II. Title.
  PL127.5E5 B33 2000
  494'.3582421-dc21                                        99–056874

ISBN: 978-1-138-95021-4 (pbk)

Typeset in Times Ten by
Florence Production, Stoodleigh, Devon.

# Contents

# Acknowledgements

This course-book of modern colloquial Turkish took quite a while to write. We are grateful to the people at Routledge for putting up with the endless delays we requested after missing yet another deadline.

Our thanks to the following companies and individuals for allowing us to use their material. To Remzi Kitabevi for the use of the recipe for 'Malzeme' from *Türk Mutfak Sanati* by Necip Usta. For the reading extract in Lesson 15, which was taken from the booklet 'Hollandaca. Yirmi milyon Hollandalı'nın ve Flaman'ın konustuğu dil' by O. Vandeputte, H. van der Heijden and J. Schipper, published in 1996 by the Flemish-Netherlands Foundation 'Stichting Ons Erfdeel', Murissonstraat 260, B8930 Rekkem (Belgium).

Special thanks go to the people who got us interested in the Turkish language, whose efforts as teachers have directly led to our enthusiasm for the language, and hence to this course. We particularly thank Rik Boeschoten in this respect. We would also like to take the opportunity to thank the folks at our workplace, at Tilburg University in Holland, for providing us with an ideal base from which to operate. Work on the book benefited from, among other things, discussions on didactic matters and the opportunity to try out bits of this material in class.

We owe a lot to the countless native speakers of Turkish who have helped us second language learners come to grips with the language's particular difficulties and perhaps most of all at steering us away from the sorts of things learners traditionally obsess about, and in the direction of true colloquial language use. Thank you, Mustafa Güleç, Asli Özyürek, İlhan Solmaz, Emel Türker, Kutlay Yağmur. We hope the end result does not offend their feel for their mother tongue.

Most of all, Saliha Şahin and Hanneke van der Heijden's help proved crucial. Their work on our behalf went far beyond what could be expected of a friend/proofreader; we are indebted to them forever.

The people at Routledge, most of all James Folan, Louise Patchett, Jane Butcher and Sophie Oliver, deserve our gratitude, not only for their patience, but also because they were reliable and efficient editors. We'd like to single out Gary King, without whom this book simply wouldn't have been possible.

Finally, we apologise to our families for spending all that time at the computer while fun could have been had.

Jeroen Aarssen
Ad Backus
Tilburg,
April 2000

# Introduction

Turkey is sometimes referred to as the bridge between Europe and Asia, since a small part of it is located in Europe (west of the Bosporus, called **Trakya** 'Thrace') and the larger part in Asia (**Anadolu** 'Anatolia'). Turkish is the official language of the Republic of Turkey, and the native language of around 55 million people (90% of the population of 64 million). Worldwide, the number of speakers is 60 million. Outside Turkey, you'll find speakers of Turkish in, for instance, Germany (1.8 million), Bulgaria (800,000), Cyprus (177,000), The Netherlands (200,000) and the UK (40,000).

The language family to which Turkish belongs is called *Turkic*. Other Turkic languages, most of them spoken in Central Asia, are Uzbek, Azerbaidjani, Turkmenian, Kazakh, Kirghiz, Uyghur and Yakut. Some believe that Turkish and Mongolian are related, although this is still somewhat controversial.

An eye-catching characteristic of Turkish is that it has long words. Turkish words are relatively long, since the language is agglutinative. In the word 'agglutinative' you can detect the English word 'glue'. In fact, Turkish has a special way of 'glueing' parts of sentences to one another. First, you have words (nouns or verbs) which you can find in a dictionary. Second, there are so-called suffixes, little parts which have a meaning, but which cannot be used on their own. These suffixes have to be 'glued' to nouns or verbs. A big challenge for you as a language learner will be to understand this process of agglutination.

## How this course works

This book is mainly organised around dialogues. Grammatical explanations are usually followed by exercises. In these exercises, you can practise newly learned information as well as information already digested in previous lessons. The key at the back of this book plays a central role (a key role, if you like). Apart from providing the right answers to the exercises, it contains additional information and explanations about specific grammatical features of Turkish. Therefore, it is essential to use the key every time you have finished an exercise.

The main focus of this course is on the colloquial spoken language. In addition, we've included a number of written texts, taken from various sources. Some of these are most likely a bit too difficult to grasp in their totality: the key is again an important instrument for tackling these texts. It will tell you exactly on which elements to focus your attention.

There is also a audio with dialogues and exercises from the textbook. Use this audio for improving your pronunciation and listening proficiency.

New words in a dialogue or an exercise are always listed below the text. If you don't know a word and it's not there, you must have seen it before but forgotten it. The thing to do in that case is to look for it in the glossary; you'll find the English translation there. Example sentences will also contain new words once in a while. As these sentences are always accompanied by a translation, you can easily find the meaning of any unfamiliar words. As a general point, we would advise you to go back a few lessons once in a while and read through dialogues and example sentences, especially if you notice there are quite a few words in the lesson you are currently working on that you were apparently supposed to know already. But even if that is not the case, reading through Turkish dialogues and sentences in previous lessons is a good way of refreshing your command of vocabulary and turns of phrase. In the process, it will probably improve your self-confidence, as you will notice that, no matter how much you're struggling with the current lesson, you have obviously learned a lot already.

From this book you will learn Turkish. You will at least be able to handle everyday situations in Turkey and to read some Turkish texts. However, there is not a single language course in the world that can teach you every aspect of a language. We therefore strongly recommend that you complement this textbook with other activities and materials:

Buy a Turkish newspaper!
Purchase a dictionary!
Get hold of a grammar book!
Go to Turkey for a holiday!

Practise your Turkish in a Turkish restaurant!

Please enjoy this course. İyi çalışmalar!

## ∩ Alphabet and pronunciation (Audio 1: 2–3)

Before the 'writing reform' of 1928 the Arabic alphabet was used. Nowadays, Turkish uses the Latin script, with a small number of modifications. It has 29 characters:

**a** as *u* in English 'truck'
**b** as *b* in English 'bus'
**c** as *j* in English 'John'
**ç** as *ch* in English 'chocolate'
**d** as *d* in English 'door'
**e** as *e* in English 'bed'
**f** as *f* in English 'find'
**g** as *g* in English 'gutter'
**ğ** **yumuşak g** or 'soft g': between vowels ğ is not pronounced; at word endings it lengthens the previous vowel
**h** as *h* in English 'help', but at word endings as *ch* in Scottish 'loch'
**ı** almost as *i* in English 'bird'. Note that the dot is always absent, to distinguish ı from i.
**i** as *ee* in English 'bee'. Even when written in capital, the i always keeps the dot: Turkey's former capital is called **İstanbul**, and not Istanbul

**j** as *j* in French '*jeune*'
**k** as *k* in English 'keeper'
**l** as *l* in English 'love'

**m** as *m* in English 'moon'
**n** as *n* in English 'noon'
**o** as *o* in English 'lot'
**ö** as *ö* in German *Wörter*, or almost as *u* in English 'blur'
**p** as *p* in English 'paper'

**r** unlike English, Turkish has a 'tongue-tip' **r**, at word endings slightly aspirated
**s** as *s* in English 'sink'
**ş** as *sh* in English 'shoe'
**t** as *t* in English 'tie'
**u** as *oo* in English 'book'

**ü** as *ü* in German *für Elise*, which is pronounced in front of the mouth, with rounded lips. You could try to imagine Peter Sellers as Inspector Clouseau pronouncing the 'oo' in 'my room'

**v** as *w* in English water

**y** as *y* in English you

**z** as *z* in English zebra

Now listen to the pronunciation of the following words on tape:

av – Avrupa – bacak – bahar – can – Cengiz – çıktı – çekirdek – duvar – düz – ellerinde – emin – foya – fuar – gittik – göl – ağır – dağ – sabah – hasret – ılık – kılıç – jeton – jandarma – kadar – keçi – leblebi – lamba – mum – melek – niye – nihayet – Orhan – otobüs – örneğin – öperim – pul – piyasa – radyo – rüya – siyaset – sandalye – şöyle – şalgam – tuvalet – tebrik – umarım – Urfa – ünlü – üzüldüm – var – vezir – yavru – yoksa – zaman – zemin

# 1 Nasılsın?

## How are you?

---

**In this lesson you will learn how to:**

- say 'hello', 'goodbye', and greet people
- say the names for family members
- understand and make simple introductions
- use the present tense
- say 'with', 'my', and make plurals

---

 **Dialogue 1** (Audio 1: 4)

## Merhaba

### Hello

*Mustafa and Ayhan run into each other at the bus station. However, they don't have all that much to say to each other*

| | |
|---|---|
| MUSTAFA: | Merhaba, Ayhan, nasılsın? |
| AYHAN: | İyidir, teşekkür ederim. Sen nasılsın? |
| MUSTAFA: | Ben de iyiyim. |
| AYHAN: | Peki, görüşürüz. |
| MUSTAFA: | *Hello, Ayhan, how are you?* |
| AYHAN: | *Fine, thank you. And you?* |
| MUSTAFA: | *I'm fine too.* |
| AYHAN: | *Well, see you.* |

## Key vocabulary

| | | | |
|---|---|---|---|
| merhaba | hello | nasılsın? | how are you? |
| iyi | good | iyidir | it is good |
| teşekkür ederim | thank you | ederim | I do |
| sen | you | ben | I |
| de | too | iyiyim | I'm fine |
| peki | OK | görüşürüz | see you |

## Language point

### Greetings

The greetings used in the dialogue above are relatively informal. They are used between friends, colleagues or acquaintances. The dialogues in this lesson are all informal. In Dialogue 2, John meets Mehmet for the first time, and greets him with **merhaba** 'hello'. However, if the situation had been more formal, for instance, if Mehmet and Cengiz hadn't known each other so well, the slightly more formal **günaydın** 'good morning/afternoon', would have been better. John takes leave with **iyi günler** 'goodbye', a little bit less informal than **görüşürüz** 'see you'. Also note how Cengiz greets his friend Mehmet: with the colloquial **ne haber?** 'what's up?' (literally 'what's the news?'), an equivalent of **merhaba**. The standard reply to **ne haber?** is **iyilik** 'I'm fine', which is based on the same word as **iyiyim** above: **iyi**, 'good'. Literally, **iyilik** means 'goodness', and **iyiyim** means 'I am good.' Mehmet answers with another informal form, which has the same meaning as **sen nasılsın: senden** 'and you?' (*literally:* 'from you?').

 **Dialogue 2** (Audio 1: 5)

## Ne haber?

### What's up?

*Cengiz has spotted Mehmet on the street and walks up to him to introduce him to John*

CENGİZ:  Merhaba, Mehmet, ne haber?

| | |
|---|---|
| MEHMET: | İyilik. Senden? |
| CENGİZ: | İyiyim, teşekkürler. Bu John. İngiliz arkadaşım. |
| JOHN: | Merhaba. |
| MEHMET: | Memnun oldum. Türkiye'yi beğeniyor musunuz? |
| JOHN: | Evet, çok seviyorum. |
| MEHMET: | Çok güzel. Cengiz, şimdi eve gidiyorum. |
| CENGİZ: | Tamam, yarın görüşürüz. |
| MEHMET: | Peki, görüşürüz. John, iyi günler. |
| JOHN: | İyi günler. |

| | |
|---|---|
| CENGİZ: | *Hello, Mehmet, how are things?* |
| MEHMET: | *Fine. How are you?* |
| CENGİZ: | *Fine, thanks. This is John. He's my English friend.* |
| JOHN: | *Hello.* |
| MEHMET: | *Nice to meet you. Are you enjoying being in Turkey?* |
| JOHN: | *Yes, I like it very much.* |
| MEHMET: | *That's good. Cengiz, I have to go home.* |
| CENGİZ: | *OK, see you tomorrow.* |
| MEHMET: | *OK, see you. John, goodbye.* |
| JOHN: | *Goodbye.* |

## Key vocabulary

| | | | |
|---|---|---|---|
| **teşekkürler** | thanks | **bu** | this |
| **İngiliz** | English | **arkadaşım** | my friend |
| **arkadaş** | friend | **Türkiye**[1] | Turkey |
| **beğenmek** | to like (something) | **beğeniyor** | he/she likes |
| **musunuz?** | do you? | **evet** | yes |
| **çok** | much, many, very | **seviyorum** | I love |
| **sevmek** | to love (something) | **güzel** | nice, beautiful, |
| **çok güzel** | that's good (*literally:* very nice) | | good |
| | | **şimdi** | now |
| **ev** | house | **gitmek** | to go |
| **tamam** | OK (similar to **peki**) | **yarın** | tomorrow |

## Exercise 1

Rearrange the words on the right to match the English translations on the left.

1 The **-yi** ending indicates that **Türkiye** is a direct object. The ending is discussed in Lesson 6.

| thanks | görüşürüz |
|---|---|
| hello | nasılsın? |
| yes | iyiyim |
| goodbye | teşekkürler |
| what's up? | tamam |
| how are you? | memnun oldum |
| see you | ne haber? |
| OK | iyi günler |
| pleased to meet you | evet |
| I'm fine | merhaba |

## Language point

### Introducing people

In the dialogue above, Cengiz uses **bu** 'this' to introduce John to his friend. Note that the phrase he uses simply consists of **bu** and the name **John**. Turkish does not use a word for 'is' in these types of sentences. In the last of the examples below, the word **öğretmen** 'teacher' is followed by the ending **-im**, which means 'I am'. It can also mean 'my', so that **öğretmenim** can mean both 'I'm a teacher' and 'my teacher'. In **arkadaşım** and **adım**, the ending **-ım** indeed means 'my'. It is stuck on to the nouns **arkadaş** 'friend' and **ad** 'name'. The word **benim** also means 'my'. The two meanings of the ending **-im** will be explained more fully later on, starting in this lesson.

| **Ben Cem.** | I am Cem. |
|---|---|
| **Adım Cem.** | My name is Cem. |
| **Bu benim arkadaşım.** | This is my friend. |
| **Öğretmenim.** | I'm a teacher. |

## Dialogue 3

## Bu babam ve annem

### This is my mum and dad

*John now introduces his family members to Cengiz*

| | |
|---|---|
| CENGİZ: | Merhaba, dostum, nasılsın. Beni ailenle tanıştırır mısın? |
| JOHN: | İşte, bu babam. *Dad, this is Cengiz.* |
| CENGİZ: | Hoş geldiniz, beyefendi. |
| JOHN: | *You are supposed to say 'Hoş bulduk' now, dad.* Evet, bu da annem. *Mum, Cengiz.* |
| CENGİZ: | Hoş geldiniz, hanımefendi. |
| JOHN'S MUM: | Hoş bulduk (*to John:* I heard that!) |
| JOHN: | Bu gençler kardeşlerim: Jimmy ve Eileen. |
| CENGİZ: | Siz de hoş geldiniz. |

NB: In the following translation, '(...)' stands for the things that are said in English in this dialogue.

| | |
|---|---|
| CENGİZ: | *Hello, my friend, how are you? Won't you introduce me to your family?* |
| JOHN: | *Well, this is my dad. (...)* |
| CENGİZ: | *Welcome, sir.* |
| JOHN: | *(...) Yes, and this is my mother. (...)* |
| CENGİZ: | *Welcome, madam.* |
| JOHN'S MUM: | *The pleasure's mine. (...)* |
| JOHN: | *Those young people are my brother and sister: Jimmy and Eileen.* |
| CENGİZ: | *And welcome to you, too.* |

## Key vocabulary

| | | | |
|---|---|---|---|
| **dost** | friend | **dostum** | my friend |
| **beni** | me | **aile** | family |
| **ailenle** | with your family | **tanıştırmak** | to introduce |
| **tanıştırır** | introduce | **mısın?** | do you? |
| **işte** | well | **baba** | father |
| **babam** | my father | **hoş geldiniz** | welcome |
| **beyefendi** | sir | **hoş bulduk** | (*answer to* **hoş geldiniz**) |
| **da** | too, and (*same as* **de**) | **anne** | mother |
| **annem** | my mother | **hanımefendi** | Madam |
| **genç** | young | **gençler** | young people |
| **kardeş** | brother or sister | **kardeşlerim** | (*here:*) my brother and sister |
| **ve** | and | | |
| **siz** | you (*plural*) | | |

## Language point

### Endings

You may have noticed that phrases that mean 'my . . .' all end in
**-m**, e.g. **babam** or **annem**. This is because Turkish uses an ending,
attached to the noun, to indicate possession. The **-m**, plus sometimes the preceding vowel, means 'my'. In fact, Turkish uses such
endings for practically every grammatical function. You will
encounter the pattern time and time again, when we will discuss
case endings, verb tenses and many more.
The structure of the possessive nouns is as follows. In **babam**,
the root word meaning 'father' is **baba**. The ending is **-m**. In
**dostum**, the basic word is **dost**, 'friend'. Here the ending is **-um**.
Both **-m** in **babam** and **-um** in **dostum** mean 'my'. When the
preceding vowel is used and when not, depends on the last sound
of the basic word. If it ends in a vowel, only **-m** is used. Note that
the vowel of the suffix is not always the same. It is a **u** in **dostum**
and an **i** in **kardeşim**. This is because of another typical feature of
Turkish, called vowel harmony (see page 12). For now, study the
following examples:

**dost** friend          **dostum** my friend
**gün** day            **günüm** my day
**kardeş** sibling      **kardeşim** my brother *or* my sister
**arkadaş** friend     **arkadaşım** my friend

**Dost** is a more intimate word for 'friend' than an **arkadaş**. You
will use **arkadaş**, a more neutral word, most of the time and **dost**
for close friends.
The dictionary forms of verbs contain an ending, too, the infinitive ending **-mek/-mak**. Whether the vowel is an **e** or an **a** again
depends on vowel harmony. When you look up 'to go' in a dictionary, you will find the infinitive **gitmek**, consisting of the stem **git-**
and the ending **-mek**.

### Exercise 2

Many of the words in the dialogue above contain endings. The following is a list of word stems. Go through the dialogue and identify
the endings these words carry. Make a list of these and see if you
can identify the meaning of each one on the basis of the translation.
The stems are: **dost, nasıl, aile, baba, gel, bul, anne, kardeş**.

## Exercise 3

Pretend you're travelling to Turkey with your family to show them what a great country it is, and you are met at the airport by a friend who you will all be staying with. Introduce everyone, using the words given below (you may have to choose between the last two). The word **erkek** means 'male', **kız** stands for 'female'. Start each sentence with **bu**, and remember that there is no word that expresses 'is'.

my husband – **kocam**; my wife – **eşim**; my brother – **erkek kardeşim**; my sister – **kız kardeşim**; my boyfriend – **erkek arkadaşım**; my girlfriend – **kız arkadaşım**

NB: **eşim** is given here as translating 'my wife', but it can actually be used for 'my husband' as well.

## Dialogue 4 (Audio 1: 6)

## Ailem

## My family

*John and his family have arrived at Cengiz's house. The latter introduces his relatives to his guests*

JOHN:    Cengiz, ailemi tanıyorsun. Ama onlar da senin ailenle tanışmak istiyorlar.

CENGİZ:    Tamam. Bu Ahmet Bey, babam. Bu kız kardeşim Müjgan. İngilizce biliyor, yani önemli bir kişi. Bu beyefendi, onun kocası, adı Mustafa.

JOHN:    Oğlan kim?

CENGİZ:    O Orhan, Ali'nin çocuğu.

JOHN:    Erkek kardeşin nerede?

CENGİZ:    Ali şimdi İngiltere'de. Bu da annem, Nursen Hanım.

JOHN:    *Well, Cengiz, you know my family. But they would like to get to know yours too.*

CENGİZ:    *OK. This is Ahmet Bey, my father. This girl is Müjgan, my sister. She speaks English, so she's an important person. This man is her husband, his name is Mustafa.*

JOHN:    *Who's the boy?*

CENGİZ:    *That's Orhan, Ali's boy.*

JOHN:    *Where is your brother?*

CENGİZ: *Ali is in Britain right now. And here is my mum, Nursen Hanım.*

## Key vocabulary

| | | | |
|---|---|---|---|
| **ailem**[2] | my family | **tanıyorsun** | you know |
| **tanımak** | to know (someone) | **ama** | but |
| **onlar** | they | **senin** | your |
| **ailen** | your family | **-le** | with |
| **tanışmak** | to get to know | **istemek** | to want |
| **istiyorlar** | they want | **İngilizce** | English (the language) |
| **biliyor** | she knows | **bilmek** | to know (something) |
| **yani** | so | **önemli** | important |
| **bir** | one | **kişi** | person |
| **onun** | her | **kocası** | her husband |
| **koca** | husband | **adı** | his name |
| **ad** | name | **oğlan** | boy |
| **kim** | who | **o** | that |
| **çocuk** | child | **Ali'nin** | Ali's |
| **çocuğu** | his child | **nerede** | where |
| **İngiltere** | England | **İngiltere'de** | in England |

## Language points

### Articles

Turkish has no articles. That means that a simple noun, such as **şehir**, can mean 'town', and 'the town' as well as 'a town'. The context will usually provide abundant clues as to how such a noun has to be translated exactly. Having said that, the numeral **bir** ('one') sometimes means 'a'. You have encountered **bir** in the dialogue above, when Cengiz mentioned that his sister is **önemli bir kişi**.

###  Vowel harmony (Audio 1: 7)

Turkish has a specific feature in word endings, which is called vowel harmony. The vowels of these endings may change, depending on

2 For **-i**, see footnote 1. It indicates a direct object: **ailemi**.

the last syllable of the preceding noun or verb stem. There are in fact two types of vowel harmony: two-fold endings can have **e-** or **a-** forms. The vowels in four-fold endings are either **i, ı, u** or **ü**. It all has to do with place of articulation in the mouth.

It all may seem ridiculously complicated right now, but the experience of most learners of Turkish (or other languages with vowel harmony) is that it soon becomes second nature. This is for two reasons. First, the harmony is based on very natural sounds. Second, many of the relevant suffixes are so frequent that they appear in virtually every sentence. This way of course you get ample opportunity for practice. For the time being the following overview is sufficient:

| Two-fold (**e** or **a**) | after **e, i, ü, ö** > | **e** |
| | after **a, ı, u, o** > | **a** |
| Four-fold (**i, ı, ü, u**) | after **e, i** > | **i** |
| | after **a, ı** > | **ı** |
| | after **ü, ö** > | **ü** |
| | after **u, o** > | **u** |

The vowel that decides what form the ending is going to take is the last vowel in the stem.

Examples:  the suffix **-im** 'my' is four-fold, so it can appear as **-im, -ım, -üm** or **-um**.
the suffix **-le** 'with' is two-fold, so it can appear as **-le** or **-la**.
the suffix **-ler** (plural) is two-fold, so it can appear as **-ler** or **-lar**.

| | |
|---|---|
| **kardeş-im-le** | with my brother |
| **arkadaş-ım-la** | with my friend |
| **kardeş-ler-im** | my brothers |
| **arkadaş-lar-ım** | my friends |
| **kardeş-ler-im-le** | with my brothers |
| **arkadaş-lar-ım-la** | with my friends |

Note that when the noun that **-im** is suffixed to ends in a vowel, only an **-m** is added, so that in these combinations vowel harmony plays no role. Examples are **ailem** 'my family' and **arabam** 'my car', as well as of course **babam** and **annem**. Some more examples:

**Arkadaşlarımla Almanya'ya gidiyoruz.**
We're going to Germany with my friends.

**Bu yeni evim.**
This is my new house.

 **Exercise 4** (Audio 1: 8)

Fill in the correct form of the ending. The first one has been done already.

| | | |
|---|---|---|
| 1 | **aileml__** | with my family **ailemle** (as the last vowel in **ailem** is 'e') |
| 2 | **kadın__** | women (**kadın** 'woman') |
| 3 | **arkadaş__** | with a friend |
| 4 | **kişi__** | persons |
| 5 | **dost__** | with my friend |
| 6 | **ev__** | my house |
| 7 | **adam__** | with men (**adam** 'man') |
| 8 | **Türk__** | Turks |
| 9 | **ad__** | my name |
| 10 | **öğretmen__** | with my teachers |

*Exercise 5*

Re-read the first two dialogues carefully, and pay special attention to the greetings. Then try to fill in the right forms below, without consulting the dialogues again.

CENGİZ: Merhaba John, _____?
JOHN: İyiyim, _____ ederim. Sen _____?
CENGİZ: Ben de _____. Türkiye'yi beğeniyor musun?
JOHN: Çok beğeniyorum. Şimdi eve gidiyorum.
CENGİZ: Tamam, yarın _____.

## Language points

### Verb endings

In the dialogues for this lesson you have met several sentences of the type 'This is . . .' and 'I am' . . . When you compare the sentences beginning **Bu John** and **İyiyim,** you will notice that they both contain a form of 'to be' in the translation. You may notice as well that of the Turkish sentences, the one that has a third person subject (*this* is) has no ending, while the one with a first person subject

(*I* am) does: the **-yim** in **iyiyim.** Unlike English, Turkish does not use separate pronouns (such as *I, you* or *we*) but verb endings instead. Except, that is, for third person subjects, in which case there is neither ending nor pronoun. For 'He is a good friend' you say **İyi bir arkadaş,** while 'You're a good friend' is **İyi bir arkadaşsın.** In the first of these sentences, **arkadaş** has no ending. Note that no pronouns are used to translate 'he' and 'you'.

You have already met a few of these endings, and you will meet them over and over again, as practically every sentence in Turkish contains one of them. So you don't need to learn them by heart, as they will become second nature to you before you know it. Still, in order to provide a clear picture of the endings, consider the following, in which the verb stem **yap-** 'to do', is followed by the present tense ending **-iyor** and the person endings:

| | | | |
|---|---|---|---|
| **yapıyorum** | I do | **yapıyoruz** | we do |
| **yapıyorsun** | you do | **yapıyorsunuz** | you do (*plural*) |
| **yapıyor** | she/he does | **yapıyorlar** | they do |

The relevant endings are **-um** for first person singular (the same as for 'my'), **-sun** for second person singular, **-uz** for first person plural, **-sunuz** for second person plural and **-lar** for third person plural. For third person singular, there is no ending. Some more examples:

| | |
|---|---|
| **Türkçe öğreniyorum.** | I'm learning Turkish. |
| **Güzel Türkçe konuşuyorsun.** | You're speaking Turkish very well. |
| **Kız kardeşin güzel Türkçe konuşuyor.** | Your sister speaks good Turkish. |
| **Türkçe öğreniyoruz.** | We're learning Turkish. |

So in forming a Turkish sentence, you should proceed as follows. If the subject would be a pronoun in English, do not use one. Remember that the subject will be expressed through the verb ending: **-im** for 'I', **-sin** for 'you' etc. If you want to say 'I'm learning', you need to start out with the verb 'learn'. This is **öğren-**, then you add **-iyor**, the present tense indicator. For the 'I' part, you then add the ending **-um**, so that you end up with **öğreniyorum.**

You might be wondering why the translations of the example sentences sometimes contain a progressive verb form (e.g., *learning*) and sometimes a simple present tense form (e.g., *speaks*).

The present tense of **-iyor** is the basic present tense in Turkish and covers both English tenses. (However, there is another present tense in Turkish, which you have encountered already in the formulaic phrases **teşekkür ederim** and **görüşürüz**, but we won't discuss that until Lesson 8.)

Finally, it should be mentioned that the difference between **-sin** and **-siniz** is not just that of singular and plural. As in many other languages, the plural form of the second person is also used as the *polite* form of address. Strangers in Turkey will usually address you with **-siniz**.

##  Dialogue 5 (Audio 1: 9)

## Türkçe öğreniyorum

### I'm learning Turkish

*In a corner, John's sister Eileen and Cengiz's sister Müjgan have struck up a conversation. Eileen has learned some basic Turkish, and is practising it right away*

EILEEN: Biraz Türkçe konuşuyorum.
MÜJGAN: Ah, çok güzel konuşuyorsun. Nerede öğrendin?
EILEEN: Teşekkür ederim. Evde öğrendim.
MÜJGAN: Burada mutlaka daha da çok öğreneceksin. Ben sana yardım edeceğim.
EILEEN: Affedersin, anlamadım. Tekrarlar mısın?
MÜJGAN: Ben sana yardım edeceğim. 'I will help you' demek.

EILEEN: *I speak a bit of Turkish.*
MÜJGAN: *Oh, you speak it very well. Where did you learn it?*
EILEEN: *Thanks. I've learnt it at home.*
MÜJGAN: *Here you'll surely learn more. I'll help you.*
EILEEN: *Sorry, I didn't get that. Can you repeat it?*
MÜJGAN: *Ben sana yardım edeceğim. That means 'I will help you'.*

## Key vocabulary

| | | | |
|---|---|---|---|
| **biraz** | a little, a bit | **konuşuyorum** | I speak |
| **konuşmak** | to talk, to speak | **öğrendin** | you learned |
| **öğrenmek** | to learn | **evde** | at home |

| burada | here | mutlaka | surely, definitely |
|---|---|---|---|
| daha | more | öğreneceksin | you will learn |
| sana | you (literally: to you) | yardım edeceğim | I will help you |
| affedersin | sorry, excuse me | anlamadım | I didn't understand |
| anlamak | to understand | tekrarlar mısın? | can you repeat (it)? |
| tekrarlamak | to repeat | demek | to say (here: it means) |

## Exercise 6

Fill in the correct ending.

| 1 Öğretmen_____ | I am a teacher |
|---|---|
| 2 Dost_____ | my friend |
| 3 Bil_____ | we know |
| 4 Tanıştırıyor_____ | he's introducing |
| 5 Aile_____ | my family |
| 6 Konuşuyor_____ | you (pl.) are talking/speaking |
| 7 Öğreniyor_____ | they are learning |
| 8 Yardım ediyor_____ | I'm helping |

## How to find words in the dictionary

As a general rule, pay attention to the beginning of words if you want to know the meaning of the noun or verb stem. If there is a discrepancy between what you find in the glossary at the end of the book, or in a dictionary, and the word as it appears in the text, it is likely that there is a suffix attached to the word in the text. It won't take long before you will start to spot the more frequent suffixes. In fact, you may already have developed a feel for not only **-im** ('my'), **-ler** (plural) and **-le** ('with'), but also for **-iyor** (present tense), **-de** ('in', 'at'), **-e** or **-ye** ('to') and **-di** (past tense).

## Reading text (Audio 1: 10)

Try to read the following, difficult text. It is not important to understand every single detail of it. Could you try to answer the questions that follow, without looking at the translation in the Key?

*Cengiz and his sister Müjgan are waiting for a plane at Esenboğa airport in Ankara. Their brother Ali, coming back from a holiday in Britain, may arrive any minute. Suddenly, Cengiz hears a familiar voice. It's Uncle Halil*

| | |
|---|---|
| HALİL: | Tesadüfe bak! |
| CENGİZ: | Merhaba, Halil Amca, nasılsınız? |
| HALİL: | Vallahi, iyiyim, sağ ol. Sen nasılsın? |
| CENGİZ: | Fena değil, amca, teşekkür ederim. |
| HALİL: | Ya annen ve baban nasıl? |
| CENGİZ: | Annem iyi. Babam biraz rahatsız. |
| HALİL: | Geçmiş olsun. Kardeşlerin iyi mi? |
| CENGİZ: | İyiler. Aslında Ali'yi bekliyoruz. Birazdan gelecek. |
| HALİL: | Öyle mi? O zaman beraber bekleyelim. Yaklaşık bir senedir görmedim onu. Şey, bu güzel kız kim? |
| CENGİZ: | Tanımıyor musunuz? Bu Müjgan, benim kız kardeşim! |
| HALİL: | Öyle mi? Çok büyümüş! |

*At that moment Ali arrives at the scene*

Uncle Halil first says **bak** 'look here', and refers to a **tesadüf**. Can you guess what this word means? **Vallahi** 'I swear' is used here as an intensifier of **iyiyim**. **Sağ ol** is more informal than **teşekkür ederim**, but means the same. Halil asks Cengiz how he's doing. If we tell you that **değil** means 'not', what would Cengiz's answer **Fena değil** mean? Cengiz's father is **biraz rahatsız**, and when Halil hears this news, he uses the idiom **geçmiş olsun** 'May it be past'. So, what is **biraz rahatsız**? If we tell you that **-ecek** expresses future ('shall'/'will'), what would **birazdan gelecek** mean (considering the reason why they are at the airport)? Note the ending **-elim**, in **beraber bekleyelim** 'let's wait together', which in this case indicates a proposal. **Yaklaşık bir senedir** means 'For a year or so'. Halil does not seem to recognise Müjgan. Cengiz asks **Tanımıyor musunuz** 'Don't you recognise her?' Apparently, Müjgan has **büyümüş** a lot. Can you guess why Halil does not recognise her at first?

## A short history of Turkey

The territory of modern day **Türkiye** 'Turkey' is divided between the small European part **Trakya** 'Trace' (West of the **Boğaziçi** 'Bosporus') and the larger Asian part **Anadolu** 'Anatolia'. This area has continuously been playing an important role in the **tarih** 'history' of both the **Orta Doğu** 'Middle East' and **Avrupa** 'Europe'.

One reason was the significance of the Bosporus, a narrow strait, the only gateway to the **Kara Deniz** 'Black Sea'. As early as 7500 BC, civilisations were present in Anatolia. Traces of these early inhabitants can still be seen in the **Anadolu Medeniyetleri Müzesi** 'The museum of Anatolian Civilisations' in Ankara, or at the site of Çatal Höyük. Many **yüzyıllar** 'centuries' later, around 2000 BC, the Hittites came to the area and developed the great Hittite Empire. Some small kingdoms on the western coast (such as the city of Troy) challenged the Hittite dominance, but Troy itself was attacked by the Greeks (the Trojan War, as depicted by Homer, took place near the small **köy** 'village' of Truva). After the Hittites, Greek warriors came and conquered parts of Asia Minor; later on the Greeks were defeated by the Persians, who in turn were driven off by **Büyük İskender** 'Alexander the Great'. Later, the Roman Empire also had its impact on **sanat** 'art' and **mimarlık** 'architecture' of the region. After the decline of Rome, the city of Byzantium, (later called Constantinople, now **İstanbul**) became the capital of the East Roman, or Byzantine, Empire. Gradually, Turkish tribes came to Anatolia, and founded small kingdoms. The **Selcuk** 'Seljuk' Turks decisively defeated the Byzantines and forced them to retreat to Constantinople. Much later again, in 1453, the **Osmanlı** 'Ottoman' Sultan **Fatih Mehmet** 'Mehmet the Conqueror' was able to conquer Constantinople. From that day, the Ottomans considered themselves to be the legitimate heirs of the Roman legacy.

# til yapıyoruz

## We're on holiday

---

**In this lesson you will learn how to:**

- say something about yourself and your present situation
- tell people what you've done recently

---

## 🎧 Dialogue 1 (Audio 1: 11)

## Ankara'da

### In Ankara

*Müjgan is showing Eileen around in Ankara. She is trying to find out what her guest is interested in doing*

MÜJGAN: Nereleri görmek istiyorsun?
EILEEN: Bakalım, bir dakika, oradaki bina ne?
MÜJGAN: İşte bu, ünlü etnoğrafya müzesi.
EILEEN: Biraz dolaşalım. Vaktim çok. Sonra, bazı yerlere daha gideceğim. Güzel bir park var mı buralarda?
MÜJGAN: Var, birkaç sokak ileride Gençlik Parkı var.
EILEEN: Ah, güzel. Gidelim.

MÜJGAN: *What places would you like to see?*
EILEEN: *Let's see, just a minute, what's that building over there?*
MÜJGAN: *Well, that's the famous ethnographic museum.*
EILEEN: *Let's just walk around a bit. I have plenty of time. I'll go to some more places later. Is there a nice park somewhere around here?*
MÜJGAN: *Yes, a few streets ahead there's the Gençlik Park.*
EILEEN: *Ah, good. Let's go.*

# Key vocabulary

| | | | |
|---|---|---|---|
| nereleri | what places | sonra | later |
| görmek | to see | bazı | some |
| istiyorsun | you want, you like | yerlere | to places |
| bakalım | let's see | yer | place |
| bir dakika | (just) a minute | gideceğim | I'll go |
| oradaki | over there, yonder | var | there is |
| bina | building | var mı | is there? |
| ne | what | buralarda | around here |
| işte | well | birkaç | some, a few |
| ünlü | famous | sokak | street |
| dolaşalım | let's walk around | ileride | ahead |
| dolaşmak | to walk around | Gençlik | Youth |
| vaktim çok | I have plenty of time | gidelim | let's go |
| | (see below) | | |

## Three remarks:

1 The construction **vaktim çok** 'I have plenty of time' contains the word **vaktim** (= **vakit** 'time' + **-im** 'my'). (More in Unit 4.) Some words in which the second syllable contains an **-i-** lose it when it is followed by a suffix starting with a vowel. So, it is not *vakitim* but **vaktim**. Likewise, the word for 'city' is **şehir**. 'My city' is **şehrim**, not *şehirim*.

2 You may wonder where the verb 'to be' is in Turkish, e.g. in **oradaki bina ne?** 'What is that building over there?' Well, in Turkish 'to be' is in fact not a full-fledged verb, but merely a personal ending. Remember **iyiyim** 'I am fine' and **Bu John** 'This is John' in Unit 1. The first example shows that 'I am' is **-yim**; the latter shows that the third person singular form of 'to be' ('he/she/it/John is' in English) has in fact no ending. There's more on 'to be' in Lesson 4.

3 Note that in her last sentence, Müjgan says **var** 'there is' twice. When a question contains **var** and the answer is positive, you can simply reply **var**, in which case it means 'yes'.

**Dialogue 2** (Audio 1: 12)

## Parkta piknik

## A picnic in the park

*The two women have found a nice place to have a picnic. Müjgan asks Eileen about her life in Britain*

MÜJGAN: Nerede oturuyorsun, Eileen?
EILEEN: Londra'da oturuyorum. Oraya hiç gittin mi?
MÜJGAN: Gitmedim. Anlatsana biraz, evin nasıl, güzel mi?
EILEEN: Evet, tam merkezde. Oldukça büyük, ve bahçesi var. Büyüklüğü benim için yeterli.
MÜJGAN: Güzel. Yalnız mı oturuyorsun?
EILEEN: Evet. Erkek arkadaşım var, ama o Oxford'da oturuyor. Maalesef.
MÜJGAN: Sizinle gelmedi mi?
EILEEN: Gelmedi. Çalışıyor.
MÜJGAN: Ne iş yapıyor?
EILEEN: Öğretmen. Fransızca dersi veriyor.

MÜJGAN: *Where do you live, Eileen?*
EILEEN: *I live in London. Did you ever go there?*
MÜJGAN: *No, I didn't (literally: I did not go). Tell me, how's your house, is it nice?*
EILEEN: *Yes, it's right in the centre. It's fairly big, and it has a garden. The size is enough for me.*
MÜJGAN: *Nice. Do you live by yourself?*
EILEEN: *Yes. I have a boyfriend, but he lives in Oxford. Unfortunately.*
MÜJGAN: *He didn't come with you?*
EILEEN: *No, he didn't (literally: he did not come). He is working.*
MÜJGAN: *What kind of job does he do?*
EILEEN: *He's a teacher. He teaches French lessons.*

## Key vocabulary

| | | | |
|---|---|---|---|
| **oturyorsun** | you live | **hiç** | ever |
| **oturmak** | to live, to sit | **gittin mi?** | did you go? |
| **oturuyorum** | I live | **gitmedim** | I did not go |
| **oraya** | to there | **anlatsana** | tell me |

| | | | |
|---|---|---|---|
| **anlatmak** | to tell | **yalnız** | alone |
| **evin nasıl?** | how's your house? | **sizinle** | with you |
| **nasıl** | how, what kind of | **maalesef** | unfortunately |
| **tam** | right, precisely | **gelmedi** | he did not come |
| **merkezde** | in the centre | **gelmek** | to come |
| **merkez** | centre | **çalışıyor** | he works, he is |
| **oldukça** | fairly | | working |
| **büyük** | big | **çalışmak** | to work |
| **bahçesi var** | it has a garden | **iş** | job |
| **bahçe** | garden | **ders** | lesson |
| **büyüklük** | size | **Fransızca dersi** | French lessons |
| **için** | for | **veriyor** | he gives |
| **yeterli** | enough | **vermek** | to give |

## Language point

### Verbs

In order to produce even the simplest sentences you need to know something about verb tenses. For example, if you want to say when you arrived, you need to put the verb in the .past tense, as in 'I came yesterday', because you did the arriving sometime in the (recent) past. Similarly, if you want to say what line of work you're in, you will want to use the present tense, because you are describing something that is still going on. All this is true for Turkish as it is for any other language.

It is important to learn at least the two basic forms of present and past tenses right away. These are the endings **-iyor,** the present tense ending and **-di**, the past tense ending.

But remember that where you would use forms of 'to be' in English, such as *I am* sick, *are you* a teacher? etc., you do not need **-iyor**. A personal ending (I, you, they, etc.) on the noun or adjective is enough. In the past tense, **-di** is needed, however.

### Exercise 1

Without translating, say whether you need a verb with **-iyor** or **-di** in the translations of the following sentences or whether you should only use one of the personal suffixes.

| | |
|---|---|
| 1 The food is ready. | 6 Did you know that? |
| 2 They came early. | 7 She's not going. |
| 3 Where do you work? | 8 I like it very much. |
| 4 It's a nice day. | 9 Where is she? |
| 5 They came early! | 10 He's a young man. |

 **Dialogue 3** (Audio 1: 13)

## Buyurun

**There you are/ What can I get you**

*Bülent and Sabahat have arrived in Antalya for a weekend at the beach. They are sitting at an outdoor cafe and are about to order*

GARSON: Hoş geldiniz. Buyurun.
SABAHAT: Hoş bulduk.
GARSON: Ne içersiniz?
SABAHAT: Bir kola ve bir bira lütfen.
GARSON: Hemen getireyim.

(*The waiter returns*)

GARSON: Buyurun, bir kola ve bir bira.
SABAHAT: Teşekkürler.
GARSON: Bir şey değil.

(*The waiter hangs around*)

GARSON: Buraya ilk defa mı geliyorsunuz?
SABAHAT: Evet, ilk defa. Geçen yıllarda hep İzmir'e gittik.
GARSON: Kaç gün kalacaksınız?
SABAHAT: Bu hafta sonu Antalya'da kalıyoruz. Ondan sonra biraz gezmek istiyoruz.
GARSON: Ne zaman döneceksiniz?
SABAHAT: Gelecek hafta gideceğiz.
GARSON: İyi tatiller.
SABAHAT: Teşekkürler.

GARSON: *Welcome. What can I get you?*
SABAHAT: *Thank you.*
GARSON: *What would you like to drink?*
SABAHAT: *A coke and a beer, please.*

| GARSON: | Let me bring that right away. |
| | There we are, one coke and one beer. |
| SABAHAT: | Thank you. |
| GARSON: | You're welcome. |
| | Is this your first time here? |
| SABAHAT: | Yes, it's the first time. In previous years, we've always gone to İzmir. |
| GARSON: | How many days will you be staying? |
| SABAHAT: | We're staying in Antalya for the weekend. After that we want to travel around a bit. |
| GARSON: | When will you return? |
| SABAHAT: | We'll go next week. |
| GARSON: | Have a nice holiday. |
| SABAHAT: | Thank you. |

## Key vocabulary

| | | | |
|---|---|---|---|
| içersiniz | you (plural) drink | gittik | we went, we have gone |
| içmek | to drink | | |
| lütfen | please | kaç | how many |
| hemen | right away, immediately | gün | day |
| | | kalacaksınız | you (plural) will stay |
| getireyim | let me bring | | |
| getirmek | to bring | kalmak | to stay |
| bir şey değil | you're welcome (literally: it's nothing) | hafta sonu | weekend |
| | | hafta | week |
| | | son | end |
| değil | not | kalıyoruz | we stay |
| ilk | first | gezmek | travel/walk/drive around |
| defa | time | | |
| geliyorsunuz | you (plural) come | ne zaman | when |
| buraya | to here | döneceksiniz | you will return |
| geçen | last, previous | gelecek | next, coming |
| yıl | year | gideceğiz | we'll go |
| geçen yıllarda | in previous years | tatil | vacation, holiday |
| hep | always, all | iyi tatiller | have a nice holiday |
| İzmir'e | to Izmir | | |

# Language points

## Forming the present tense

You first take the verb stem and add **-iyor** to it. Then you add the personal ending. (Remember that this ending is necessary because in Turkish you do not usually use words meaning 'I', 'you', 'we' etc.) So, the steps you need to make in order to say 'I give a book' are:

1 Find the verb stem. In a dictionary you will usually find **vermek** 'to give'. The **-mek** part is the infinitive ending, so the stem is **ver-**.
2 Add **-iyor** to give **veriyor-**.
3 Add the personal ending. For 'I' that is **-im** or a variant of it (which form exactly depends on vowel harmony). After **-iyor**, the vowel is always **u**, because the **o** in **-iyor** never changes. In our example, this gives us **veriyorum** 'I give'.
4 Now you need to make clear that it is *a book* you give: **bir kitap veriyorum.** Note that the verb comes last.

## Forming the past tense

You follow the same steps if you want to say that you gave a book some time ago, i.e. in the past. Only now you use **-di**.

1 Find the verb stem **ver-**.
2 Add **-di**: **verdi-**.
3 Add the personal ending **-m**: **verdim**.
4 Put the other words you need before the verb: **bir kitap verdim.**

With these two endings you will have what you need, as far as grammar goes, to say most of the basic things you would want to say in the early stages of language learning. In this and the other early lessons, you will encounter most of the more frequently used verbs.

## The endings: the present tense with -iyor

Since Turkish uses personal *endings* (not personal *pronouns* such as 'I', 'you' etc.), the verb endings change to show who the subject is. In the case of **-iyor** (see p 15) they are:

| | |
|---|---|
| **-iyorum** | I |
| **-iyorsun** | you |

| -iyor | he/she/it |
|-------|-----------|
| -iyoruz | we |
| -iyorsunuz | you (pl.) |
| -iyor or -iyorlar | they |

All these of course attach to a verb stem, and each of these forms has four slightly different versions which have to do with the rules of vowel harmony. (See Lesson 1 to refresh your memory.) If the vowel in the last syllable of the stem is an 'i' or an 'e', for example, the first vowel in the -iyor suffix will be -i.

The form can be -iyor, -ıyor, -uyor or -üyor, depending on the final vowel of the stem:

after **e, i** > **i**   e.g. **bekliyor** he waits, **gidiyor** she goes
after **a, ı** > **ı**   e.g. **bakıyor** she looks, **kırıyor** it breaks
after **ü, ö** > **ü**   e.g. **büyüyor** she grows, **dönüyor** he returns
after **u, o** > **u**   e.g. **oturuyor** he lives, **oluyor** it becomes

Remember that the -iyor tense can be translated with either the English progressive or simple present.

| | *gelmek* 'to come' | *yapmak* 'to do' | *büyümek* 'to grow' | *oturmak* 'to live'/'to sit' |
|---|---|---|---|---|
| I | **geliyorum** I come/I am coming | **yapıyorum** I do/I am doing | **büyüyorum** I grow/I am growing | **oturuyorum** I live/I am living |
| you (*sg.*) | **geliyorsun** | **yapıyorsun** | **büyüyorsun** | **oturuyorsun** |
| he/she/it | **geliyor** | **yapıyor** | **büyüyor** | **oturuyor** |
| we | **geliyoruz** | **yapıyoruz** | **büyüyoruz** | **oturuyoruz** |
| you (*pl.*) | **geliyorsunuz** | **yapıyorsunuz** | **büyüyorsunuz** | **oturuyorsunuz** |
| they | **geliyorlar** | **yapıyorlar** | **büyüyorlar** | **oturuyorlar** |

## The past tense with -di

Again, the exact form of the past tense depends upon the subject, and on vowel harmony. The different forms are:

| *Final vowel of the stem:* | **e, i** | **a, ı** | **ü, ö** | **u, o** |
|---|---|---|---|---|
| I (1st sg.) | **-dim** | **-dım** | **-düm** | **-dum** |
| you (*sg.*) (2nd sg.) | **-din** | **-dın** | **-dün** | **-dun** |
| he/she/it (3rd sg.) | **-di** | **-dı** | **-dü** | **-du** |

| *Final vowel of* *the stem:* | | *e, i* | *a, ı* | *ü, ö* | *u, o* |
|---|---|---|---|---|---|
| we | (1ˢᵗ pl.) | -dik | -dık | -dük | -duk |
| you (*pl.*) | (2ⁿᵈ pl.) | -diniz | -dınız | -dünüz | -dunuz |
| they | (3ʳᵈ pl.) | -di *or* -diler | -dı *or* -dılar | -dü *or* -düler | -du *or* -dular |

Note that there are a couple of surprises here. The personal endings are not exactly the same as for the present tense. The **-uz** of the first person plural (in **-iyoruz** 'we') is replaced by **-k** and the **-sunuz** of the second person plural (in **-iyorsunuz** 'you' (pl.), 'you all', etc.) is replaced by **-niz/-nız/-nuz/-nüz**.

Again, these endings, indicating both past tense and subject, attach to verb stems and are subject to vowel harmony. As you can see in the list above, the vowel of the past tense suffix can be an **i**, **ı**, **u** or **ü**.

In addition, the **-d-**, with which the past tense suffix starts, is sometimes changed into **-t-**. This depends on the last sound of the stem: if it is a **ç**, **f**, **h**, **k**, **p**, **s**, **ş** or **t**, the **-d** becomes a **-t**. (The process of consonants changing under the influence of preceding consonants is called 'assimilation'.) That means that there are even more possibilities:

| *Final vowel of* *the stem:* | | *e, i* | *a, ı* | *ü, ö* | *u, o* |
|---|---|---|---|---|---|
| I | (1ˢᵗ sg.) | -tim | -tım | -tüm | -tum |
| you (*sg.*) | (2ⁿᵈ sg.) | -tin | -tın | -tün | -tun |
| he/she/it | (3ʳᵈ sg.) | -ti | -tı | -tü | -tu |
| we | (1ˢᵗ pl.) | -tik | -tık | -tük | -tuk |
| you (*pl.*) | (2ⁿᵈ pl.) | -tiniz | -tınız | -tünüz | -tunuz |
| they | (3ʳᵈ pl.) | -ti *or* -tiler | -tı *or* -tılar | -tü *or* -tüler | -tu *or* -tular |

These sounds (**ç**, **f**, **h**, **k**, **p**, **s**, **ş** and **t**) are the so-called 'voiceless' consonants, as opposed to their 'voiced' counterparts (**c**, **v**, **ğ**, **b**, **z** and **d**, as well as **l**, **m**, **n** and **r**). Don't worry about learning this list by heart, as in running speech you won't have time to decide whether the suffix should start with a **-d** or a **-t**. As with vowel harmony, it is better to let the principle slowly but surely become part of your expanding 'feel' for the language. It'll be second nature before you know it.

Here are some examples of the past tense with **-di**:

| | gelmek | yapmak | büyümek | oturmak |
|---|---|---|---|---|
| I | geldim | yaptım | büyüdüm | oturdum |
| | I came | I did | I grew up | I lived |
| you (*sg.*) | geldin | yaptın | büyüdün | oturdun |
| he/she/it | geldi | yaptı | büyüdü | oturdu |
| we | geldik | yaptık | büyüdük | oturduk |
| you (*pl.*) | geldiniz | yaptınız | büyüdünüz | oturdunuz |
| they | geldi/ | yaptı/ | büyüdü/ | oturdu/ |
| | geldiler | yaptılar | büyüdüler | oturdular |

**Dün gece televizyonda güzel bir programı <u>seyrettim</u>.**
<u>I saw</u> a good programme on TV last night.

**Bu sabah kaçta <u>kalktın</u>?**
What time <u>did you get up</u> this morning?

**Onun için Türkiye'yi <u>seçtik</u>.**
That's why <u>we chose</u> Turkey.

## Exercise 2

Find out the dictionary forms (the infinitives) of the following verb forms and look them up in the Glossary to find their meanings. Dictionary forms consist of the verb stem plus the infinitive suffix **-mak** or **-mek**; try to supply the right alternative before looking up the verb's meaning. Then work out exactly what each verb form means. The first one has been done as an example.

1 yazdı        yaz- + -dı  >>  yaz + mak  >>  yazmak  to write
                                                  >> yazdı    he wrote
2 geliyorsun
3 kaldık
4 seçiyorsunuz
5 gitti
6 veriyorlar
7 satıyoruz
8 çıktın
9 vardınız
10 yardım ediyoruz

## Exercise 3

Fill in the right vowel in the sentences below. Remind yourself first of the rules for vowel harmony and of which one of the two types you need to use for the **-iyor** and **-di** tenses. Don't be put off by any unfamiliar verbs in the example sentences. You don't need to know them, as the focus of the exercise is on getting a feel for the vowel harmony rules. Translations of the sentences, which contain many useful new words, are given in the Key.

1  Ona bir mektup yazd..m.
2  Bu sene sonbahar hangi gün başl..yor?
3  Ali bulutlu ve soğuk hava çok sev..yor
4  Trenin kaçta kalk..yor?
5  Yürüd..n mü?
6  Dün akşam hep dans ett..k.
7  Sana söyled..m ya!
8  Çarşıdan ne ald..nız?
9  Saat onda buluş..yoruz.
10 Kalabalık bir lokantada yemek yed..k.

 **Exercise 4** (Audio 1: 14)

Many of the sentences you learn to say in this lesson will often be used to answer questions like 'Where did you learn Turkish?', 'Are you enjoying your stay?' and 'What are your plans for the next few days?'. Obviously, you will need to learn how to understand these questions before you can answer them. Several questions are used in the dialogues of this lesson, and in Lesson 3 we will look into them in detail.

You will also want to know how to give negative answers, such as 'I don't speak Turkish very well yet.' The same thing holds true as for questions: some examples are used here, but actual discussion will follow later.

Nevertheless, you may have already developed a bit of a feel for how questions and negative answers are formed in Turkish on the basis of examples in the dialogues. To test these intuitions, try to translate the following little dialogue.

| | |
|---|---|
| Nerede oturuyorsunuz? | New York'ta oturuyorum. |
| Ne zaman geldiniz? | Bu sabah geldim. |
| Türkiye'yi beğeniyor musun? | Çok beğeniyorum. |
| Buraya tatil için mi geldiniz? | Evet, tatil için. |

Türkçeyi iyi konuşuyorsunuz? Teşekkür ederim, ama henüz
iyi konuşamıyorum.

## Exercise 5

Go back to the verbs given in Exercise 2, and change their tense
from **-iyor** into **-di** and vice versa. The first one has been done:

1 **yazdı** = stem **yaz** plus past tense **-dı**, subject = he/she/it >>
present tense **yaz** + **-iyor** >> **yazıyor** he/she/it is writing

A final remark: the main difference you should focus on right now
is between sentences where you do need to use **-iyor** or **-di** and
those where you don't, i.e. where the personal ending is enough,
as practised in Exercise 1 above. The rule is that the **-iyor** and **-di**
endings apply to verbs only, never to nouns or adjectives. This is
why in sentences like 'I'm a banker' (**bankacıyım**), there is no need
for **-iyor**. Using a personal ending (here **-yım**) is enough.

## Language points

### Adverbs of time

Tenses often go hand in hand with time words. An example is
'yesterday', which always occurs with a past tense marking on the
verb. A word like 'now' on the other hand, is typically associated
with the present tense. Here are some of the most important of
those words related to time:

| | | | |
|---|---|---|---|
| **şimdi** | now | **saat** | hour |
| **bugün** | today | **gün** | day |
| **dün** | yesterday | **hafta** | week |
| **yarın** | tomorrow | **ay** | month |
| **dakika** | minute | **yıl, sene** | year |
| **erken** | early | **geç** | late |
| **sık sık** | often | | |

In order to say things like 'last week' and 'next month' the words
**geçen** 'last' and **gelecek** or **önümüzdeki** 'next', 'coming' are important.

| | | | |
|---|---|---|---|
| **geçen gün** | the other day | **gelecek/önümüzdeki** | next/the |
| **geçen hafta** | last week | **hafta** | coming week |
| **haftaya** | next week | | |

Often you will need to say things like 'tomorrow morning' or 'last night', for which you need to know the words for the parts of the day:

| | | | |
|---|---|---|---|
| **sabah** | morning | **akşam** | evening |
| **öğleden sonra** | afternoon | **gece** | night |

If you want to say something like 'in the mornings, evenings', etc., you use the form **-ları.**

**Sabahları erken kalkıyorum.** In the mornings, I get up early.

Easy-to-handle combinations give you **dün akşam** for 'yesterday evening' and **bu öğleden sonra** for 'this afternoon'. In these kinds of time expressions you also need to know what the days of the week are called (the word **günü** 'day' is optional):

| | |
|---|---|
| **pazar (günü)** | Sunday |
| **pazartesi (günü)** | Monday |
| **salı (günü)** | Tuesday |
| **çarşamba (günü)** | Wednesday |
| **perşembe (günü)** | Thursday |
| **cuma (günü)** | Friday |
| **cumartesi (günü)** | Saturday |

**Çarşamba günü buraya geldik.**
We arrived here on Wednesday.

**Sizinle cuma günü buluşuyoruz.**
We'll meet you on Friday.

### Exercise 6

The following sentences all contain a time adverb. The verb has not been given the proper tense ending yet. Your job is to supply it. Choose between **-iyor** and **-di**, and make sure you use the right form of those, as has been done for the first sentence.

1 **Her yaz Türkiye'ye dön_____** (Every summer we return to Turkey) her yaz >> **-iyor** >> **dönüyor** (+ we) >> **dönüyoruz**

2 **Dün büyük bir hata yap_____** (Yesterday I made a big mistake)

3 **Gelecek hafta Liverpool'a gi_____** (Next week they go to Liverpool)

4 **Arkadaşlarım dün akşam gel_____** (My friends came yesterday evening)
5 **Bugün çok çalış_____** (You worked a lot today)
6 **O filmi geçen ay gör_____** (I saw that film last month)
7 **Şimdi bir şey yemek ist_____** (Now I want to eat something)
8 **Ona bir hediye ver_____** (He gives her a present)
9 **Tamam, şimdi yap_____** (Okay, we'll do it now)
10 **Geçen hafta sonu ne yap_____** (What did you do last weekend?)

| | | | |
|---|---|---|---|
| **yaz** | summer | **film** | movie |
| **dönmek** | to return | **yemek** | food, to eat |
| **hata** | mistake | **hediye** | present, gift |
| **o filmi görmek** | to see that movie | | |

## Exercise 7

Translate:

1 I went home early.
2 You speak good Turkish. (You is plural here!)
3 He gave me a present.
4 She goes to school in the evenings.
5 We live in Newcastle.
6 I did it yesterday.
7 I work for a bank.
8 They came late yesterday evening.

| | |
|---|---|
| **okul** | school |
| **bankada** | for a bank |

## Exercise 8

The first page of the **Ankara kültür ve sanat haritası**, the Ankara culture and arts map, is on page 34 and contains the Table of Contents, the **içindekiler**.

You can probably guess most of these words without knowing any Turkish. Now for the other ones: on pp 36–37 are sample entries under **sergi**, **söyleşi**, **gezi** and **kitap**. Can you work out what these words are?

içindekiler ■

**kütüphane**      library

## Spelling

You may have noticed that the spelling of verbs which have a stem that ends in a vowel and are marked with the present tense suffix is not predictable. Taking **istemek** 'to want' as an example, it is not so obvious why 'she wants' would be **İstiyor** and not '*isteyor*' or even '*isteiyor*'. The last option is impossible in the Turkish spelling system, as the combination of two vowels in a row is simply ruled out. The other option, '*isteyor*', is not possible either. This is because **-iyor** 'absorbs' the last vowel of the stem. This is not a universal rule; in other cases, the vowel of the suffix is lost (e.g. the possessive in words like **baba-m**, which could have been, but isn't, **bab-ım**), and in yet others the two vowels are separated by an extra consonant (e.g. in **iyi-y-im**). But be that as it may, **-iyor** absorbs the last vowel of a verb stem if that stem ends in one.

Vowel harmony with the last vowel before that one, **i** in the case of **istemek**, then decides the actual form of the **-iyor** suffix, giving us **istiyor.**

So, when you have the time (and in writing you usually do), think of the following rule: if the stem ends in a vowel, lop off that vowel and make sure the first vowel of **-iyor** harmonises with what is now the last vowel of the stem. Remember to apply the correct vowel harmony rules:

final vowel in stem = **e, i**   >   **iyor**
final vowel in stem = **a, ı**   >   **ıyor**
final vowel in stem = **ü, ö**   >   **üyor**
final vowel in stem = **u, o**   >   **uyor**

For example:

**istemek – ist – istiyor**
**oynamak – oyn – oynuyor**
**anlamak – anl – anlıyor**
**ödemek – öd – ödüyor**

The last two verbs mean 'to understand' and 'to pay', respectively.

## ∩ Reading text (Audio 1: 15)

*Cengiz and his sister Müjgan listen to their brother Ali's travel experiences*

MÜJGAN:  Hadi, abi, anlatsana!
ALI:  Peki. İngiltere'ye geldiğimde, araba kiraladım ve Londra'ya gittim. Fakat hemen şaşakaldım.
CENGIZ:  Niye abi?
ALI:  Hayret! Arabalar hep sol taraftan gider! Az kalsın trafik kazası oluyordu!
CENGIZ:  Allaha şükür, kazasız belasız döndün!
MÜJGAN:  Londra güzel mi?
ALI:  Çok, şahane bir yer. Bir sürü eski binalar var. Tower Köprüsü, Saint Paul Katedrali. Hem de Buckingham Sarayı.
CENGIZ:  Kraliçeyi filan gördün mü?
ALI:  Yoo, beni çaya davet etti de, vaktim yoktu.

*All three start to laugh*

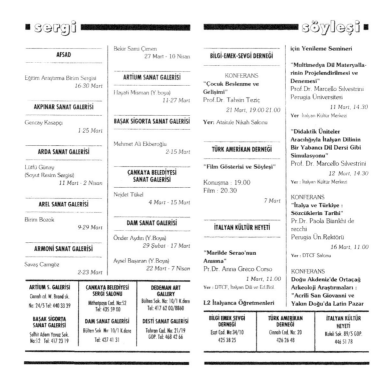

**sergi**

| AFSAD | Bekir Sami Çimen 27 Mart - 10 Nisan | BİLGİ-EMEK-SEVGİ DERNEĞİ |
| --- | --- | --- |

Eğitim Araştırma Birim Sergisi
16-30 Mart

**ARTİUM SANAT GALERİSİ**
Hayati Misman (Y.boya)
11-27 Mart

**AKPINAR SANAT GALERİSİ**

Gencay Kasapçı
1.25 Mart

**BAŞAK SİGORTA SANAT GALERİSİ**

Mehmet Ali Ekberoğlu
2-15 Mart

**ARDA SANAT GALERİSİ**

Lütfü Günay
(Soyut Resim Sergisi)
11 Mart - 2 Nisan

**ÇANKAYA BELEDİYESİ SANAT GALERİSİ**

Nejdet Tükel
4 Mart - 15 Mart

**AREL SANAT GALERİSİ**

Birim Bozok
9-29 Mart

**DAM SANAT GALERİSİ**

Önder Aydın (Y.Boya)
29 Şubat - 17 Mart

**ARMONİ SANAT GALERİSİ**

Savaş Camgöz
2-23 Mart

Aysel Başaran (Y.Boya)
22 Mart - 7 Nisan

**KONFERANS**
"Çocuk Beslenme ve Gelişimi"
Prof.Dr. Tahsin Teziç
21 Mart, 19.00-21.00
Yer: Ataküle Nikah Salonu

**TÜRK AMERİKAN DERNEĞİ**
"Film Gösterisi ve Söyleşi"
Konuşma : 19.00
Film : 20.30
7 Mart

**İTALYAN KÜLTÜR HEYETİ**
"Marilde Serao'nun Anısına"
Pr.Dr. Anna Greco Corso
1 Mart, 11.00
Yer : DTCF, İtalyan Dili ve Ed.Bol.
I.2 İtalyanca Öğretmenleri

**söyleşi**

için Yenileme Semineri
"Multimedya Dil Materyallarinin Projelendirilmesi ve Denemesi"
Prof.Dr. Marcello Silvestrini
Perugia Üniversitesi
11 Mart, 14.30
Yer : İtalyan Kültür Merkezi

"Didaktik Üniteler Aracılığıyla İtalyan Dilinin Bir Yabancı Dil Dersi Gibi Simulasyonu"
Prof. Dr. Marcello Silvestrini
12 Mart, 14.30
Yer : İtalyan Kültür Merkezi

KONFERANS
"İtalya ve Türkiye : Sözcüklerin Tarihi"
Pr.Dr. Paola Biankhi de recchi
Perugia Ün.Rektörü
16 Mart, 11.00
Yer : DTCF Salonu

KONFERANS
Doğu Akdeniz'de Ortaçağ Arkeoloji Araştırmaları :
"Acrili San Giovanni ve Yakın Doğu'da Latin Pazar

| ARTİUM S. GALERİSİ Cinnah cd. W. Brand sk. No: 24/5 Tel: 440 33 39 | CANKAYA BELEDİYESİ SERGİ SALONU Mithatpaşa Cad. No:52 Tel: 435 59 00 | DEDEMAN ART GALLERY Bülten Sok. No: 10/1 K.dere Tel: 417 62 00/8860 |
| --- | --- | --- |
| BAŞAK SİGORTA SANAT GALERİSİ Selhit Adem Yavuz Sok. No:12 Tel: 417 23 19 | DAM SANAT GALERİSİ Bülten Sok No: 10/1 K.dere Tel: 427 41 31 | DESTİ SANAT GALERİSİ Tahran Cad. No: 21/19 GOP. Tel: 468 42 66 |

| BİLGİ EMEK SEVGİ DERNEĞİ Esat Cad. No:34/10 425 38 25 | TÜRK AMERİKAN DERNEĞİ Cinnah Cad. No: 20 426 26 48 | İTALYAN KÜLTÜR HEYETİ Kuleli Sok. 89/5 GOP. 446 51 78 |
| --- | --- | --- |

Müjgan urges Ali to start his story about his trip to **İngiltere**, by saying **hadi anlatsana** 'come on, tell us about it'. Müjgan addresses Ali with **abi**. Try to figure out what this means. Ali rented a car (**araba kiraladım**). You may guess the meaning now of **İngiltere**'ye **geldiğimde**, especially when we tell you that the last part, **-diğimde** means 'when I . . .'. Since you know that **gittim** means 'I went', the **-ya** part in **Londra**'ya is easy to understand. Ali says **fakat hemen saşakaldım** 'but immediately I was astonished'. After Cengiz asks him **niye** 'why', Ali explains that **arabalar hep sol taraftan gider** (an alternative to **gidiyor**). Now, the word **hayret** expresses surprise, and **trafik kazası** means 'traffic accident'. So why was Ali flabbergasted? Luckily, there was no **trafik kazası**, as can be derived from **az kalsın** 'almost'. Cengiz thanks God (**Allaha şükür**) that Ali returned (**döndün**) home **kazasız belasız**. How did Ali return home? Müjgan asks whether London is a nice city. Ali starts his answer by saying **Çok**, colloquial for 'Yes, very!'. London has many

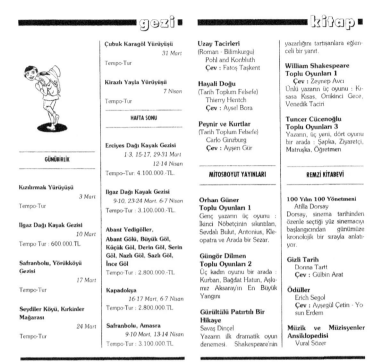

**gezi**

**GÜNÜBİRLİK**

Çubuk Karagöl Yürüyüşü
31 Mart
Tempo-Tur

Kirazlı Yayla Yürüyüşü
7 Nisan
Tempo-Tur

HAFTA SONU

Erciyes Dağı Kayak Gezisi
1-3, 15-17, 29-31 Mart
12-14 Nisan
Tempo-Tur: 4.100.000.-TL.

Kızılırmak Yürüyüşü
3 Mart
Tempo-Tur

Ilgaz Dağı Kayak Gezisi
10 Mart
Tempo-Tur: 600.000.TL

Safranbolu, Yörükköyü Gezisi
17 Mart
Tempo-Tur

Seydiler Köyü, Kırkinler Mağarası
24 Mart
Tempo-Tur

Ilgaz Dağı Kayak Gezisi
9-10, 23-24 Mart. 6-7 Nisan
Tempo-Tur: 3.100.000.-TL.

Abant Yedigöller,
Abant Gölü, Büyük Göl,
Küçük Göl, Derin Göl, Serin
Göl, Nazlı Göl, Sazlı Göl,
İnce Göl
Tempo-Tur: 2.800.000.-TL

Kapadokya
16-17 Mart, 6-7 Nisan
Tempo-Tur: 2.800.000.TL

Safranbolu, Amasra
9-10 Mart, 13-14 Nisan
Tempo-Tur: 3.100.000.TL

**kitap**

Uzay Tacirleri
(Roman - Bilimkurgu)
Pohl and Konbluth
Çev : Fatoş Taşkent

Hayali Doğu
(Tarih Toplum Felsefe)
Thierry Hentch
Çev : Aysel Bora

Peynir ve Kurtlar
(Tarih Toplum Felsefe)
Carlo Ginzburg
Çev : Ayşen Gür

MİTOSBOYUT YAYINLARI

Orhan Güner
Toplu Oyunları 1
Genç yazarın üç oyunu :
İkinci Nöbetçinin sıkıntıları,
Sevdalı Bulut, Antonius, Kle-
opatra ve Arada bir Sezar.

Güngör Dilmen
Toplu Oyunları 2
Üç kadın oyunu bir arada :
Kurban, Bağdat Hatun, Aşkı-
mız Aksaray'ın En Büyük
Yangını

Gürültülü Patırtılı Bir
Hikaye
Savaş Dinçel
Yazarın ilk dramatik oyun
denemesi. Shakespeare'nin

yazarlığını tartışanlara eğlen-
celi bir yanıt.

William Shakespeare
Toplu Oyunları 1
Çev : Zeynep Avcı
Ünlü yazarın üç oyunu : Kı-
sasa Kısas, Onikinci Gece,
Venedik Taciri

Tuncer Cücenoğlu
Toplu Oyunları 3
Yazarın, üç yeni, dört oyunu
bir arada : Şapka, Ziyaretçi,
Matruşka, Öğretmen

REMZİ KİTABEVİ

100 Yılın 100 Yönetmeni
Atilla Dorsay
Dorsay, sinema tarihinden
özenle seçtiği yüz sinemacıyı
başlangıcından günümüze
kronolojik bir sırayla anlatı-
yor.

Gizli Tarih
Donna Tartt
Çev : Gülbin Arat

Ödüller
Erich Segol
Çev : Ayşegül Çetin - Yo-
sun Erdem

Müzik ve Müzisyenler
Ansiklopedisi
Vural Sözer

---

**eski binalar** which make the place not just **güzel**, but **şahane**! What are those **eski binalar** which seem to fascinate Ali? He mentions a few: **Tower Köprüsü**, **Saint Paul Katedrali** and **Buckingham Sarayı**. There you have three new words to add to your vocabulary! When Ali mentions **Buckingham Sarayı**, Cengiz asks whether he saw the **kraliçe**. Who would that be? Ali answers **yoo**, which is colloquial for **hayır** 'no'. He says he was invited (**beni davet etti** 'she invited me') to **çay** 'tea'. Alas, he could not accept the invitation because **vaktim yoktu**, he had no time.

## A short history of the Turks

Since the fall of communist **Sovyet Birliği** 'Soviet Union', contacts between Turkey and former **Sovyet Cumhuriyetleri** 'Soviet Republics' have intensified. The interest of the Turks in Central

Asia is not strange, considering that, for instance, the Uzbek, Kazakh and Kirghiz people speak a language that is quite similar to Turkish. A generic term for all these people and their languages is 'Turkic'. Anatolia has not always been the area where Turkish (or rather, Turkic) people lived. In fact, Turkic tribes originate from the Altai region (which is situated where the **sınırlar** 'borders' of **Moğolistan** 'Mongolia', **Çin** 'China' and **Rusya** 'Russia' meet). The need to find new **çayır** 'pasture' grounds for their **sürü** 'flock' of **koyun** 'sheep', **at** 'horses' and other animals was the cause of several westward **göç** 'migration' waves. This was a gradual process that took centuries, but **arasıra** 'from time to time' one of these tribes left their traces in **Avrupa tarihi** 'European history', such as the Huns and their leader Attila.

The Seljuks in Persia were Turkic as well. Their influence on **sanat** 'art' and **mimarlık** 'architecture' in Persia, modern day Iran, was great. A branch of these Seljuks were among the first Turks to arrive in Anatolia. In 1071, in the decisive Battle of **Malazgırt** 'Manzikert', the Turkish-Seljuk army defeated the **Bizanslılar** 'Byzantines' and the road towards Anatolia lay open to them. The Seljuk Sultanate of Rum was overrun by Mongol hordes, but especially the city of Konya preserves many good examples of Seljuk buildings. The Mongols drove the Turks to the West (being driven westward seems to be a recurrent theme in Turkish history), where they settled and established several small **beylikler** 'principalities'.

One of these developed into the **Osmanlı Emperatorluğu** 'Ottoman Empire', named after the founder, Osman. The Ottomans ambitiously developed their Empire and were strong enough to beat the Byzantines. Under the reign of **Muhteşem Sultan Süleyman** 'Sultan Süleyman the Magnificent', also called **Kanuni** 'the Lawgiver', the Ottoman Empire was at the very height of its glory. Süleyman brought the Ottoman **ordu** 'army' to the gates of **Viyana** 'Vienna', and he conquered large parts of **Kuzey Afrika** 'Northern Africa'. After Süleyman, however, the Empire lost power and its **çöküş** 'fall' came slowly, but inevitably. Reforms of later sultans, efforts to modernise and westernise, were in vain and could not prevent the decline of the once mighty empire. In those days, its nickname was 'the sick man of Europe'. In the beginning of the twentieth century, the Ottoman Empire came to its end, and was replaced by the **Türkiye Cumhuriyeti** 'Republic of Turkey'.

# 3 Nerede?

## Where?

##  Dialogue 1 (Audio 1: 16)

# O kim?

## Who's that?

| | |
|---|---|
| CEM: | O kim? |
| ÖZLEM: | Emel. |
| CEM: | Nerede oturuyor? |
| ÖZLEM: | Ankara'da oturuyor. |
| CEM: | Çalışıyor mu? |
| ÖZLEM: | Hayır, Ankara Üniversitesinde okuyor. |
| | |
| CEM: | *Who is that?* |
| ÖZLEM: | *That's Emel.* |
| CEM: | *Where does she live?* |
| ÖZLEM: | *She lives in Ankara.* |
| CEM: | *Does she work?* |
| ÖZLEM: | *No, she is studying at Ankara University.* |

## Key vocabulary

| o | that | Ankara'da | in Ankara |
|---|------|-----------|-----------|
| okumak | to study | hayır | no |
| mu | does she? | | |

NB: Note that the simple answer **Emel** is enough to express 'That's Emel'.

## Language point

###  Asking questions (Audio 1: 17)

There are two types of questions in this conversation. The first type uses question words like 'where', 'how' and 'what' (interrogative pronouns). In the first question, **kim** 'who' is used, and **nerede** 'where' in the second. The second type of question involves 'yes/no' answers. It is used in Cem's last question.

The major question words are:

| **ne?** | what? | **ne kadar?** | how much? |
|---------|-------|---------------|-----------|
| **nasıl?** | how? | **nerede?** | where? |
| **ne zaman?** | when? | **nereli?** | from where? |
| **neden?** | why? | **kaç?** | how many? |
| **niye?** | why? | **kim?** | where? |
| **niçin?** | why? | **hangi?** | which? |

In **-iyor** and **-di** sentences, question words appear either at the beginning of a sentence, or right before the verb:

| **Ne yaptın?** | What did you do? |
|----------------|------------------|
| **Nerede oturuyorsun?** | Where do you live? |
| **Ne zaman geldin?** | When did you come? |
| **Neden/ niye/ niçin bize geldin?** | Why did you come to us? |
| **Kaç gün Türkiye'de kaldı?** | How many days did he stay in Turkey? |

There are only subtle differences between **neden**, **niye** and **niçin** (a shortened form of **ne için**, 'for what'). **Niye**, however, sounds a bit like an accusation, or as asking for justification, so we advise you use one of the other two.

In sentences that contain a form of 'to be', the question word tends to appear at the end. This is not a strict rule, however, hence the third example below:

| Şu armutlar ne kadar? | How much are those pears? |
|---|---|
| O şarkıcı kim? | Who is that singer? |
| Hava nasıl oralarda? | How is the weather over there? |

NB: While **orada** means 'there', **oralarda**, with the plural marker, means 'over there', 'in those parts'.

Note also the personal ending **-siniz** 'you':

| **Nerelisiniz?** | Where are you from? |
|---|---|

## Exercise 1

Match the Turkish questions on the right to the English translations on the left

| | |
|---|---|
| 1 where does she work? | a **ne yapıyor?** |
| 2 when does she work? | b **nerede çalışıyor?** |
| 3 how much does she work? | c **nasıl çalışıyor?** |
| 4 who is working? | d **nerede yapıyor?** |
| 5 why does she work? | e **nasıl yapıyor?** |
| 6 how does it work? | f **ne kadar çalışıyor?** |
| 7 what does he do? | g **ne zaman çalışıyor?** |
| 8 where does he do it? | h **kim çalışıyor?** |
| 9 how does he do it? | i **neden çalışıyor?** |

## Language point

### Yes/no questions

Yes/no questions are so named because they can be answered with 'yes' or 'no'. An example is Cem's last question in the conversation above. The word **mi** (or **mı, mu, mü**) turns any sentence into a yes/no question. You can always recognise whether a Turkish sentence is a question or not: all questions contain an explicit question marker. This can be either a word from the list above (**kim, ne, nerede**, etc.), or the word **mi** in one of its four forms.

## Exercise 2

Say which type of question marker (interrogative pronoun or **mi**) you need in the Turkish translations of the following English sentences. Keep in mind that the purpose of this exercise is to help you sort out the different types of questions, not to give full, accurate translations (which are given in the Key).

1 Did you see that movie?
2 When did we go to the cinema?
3 Who played the main part in this film?
4 Has it been on television?
5 Are you an actor?

NB: Of course, you can also answer with 'I don't know' which is **bilmiyorum**.

## Language point

### The form of mi-questions

The question marker **mi, mı, mü** or **mu** follows **-iyor**, e.g.:

| | |
|---|---|
| **çalışıyor** | she works |
| **çalışıyor mu?** | does she work? |

In **-iyor** sentences, the personal ending comes *after* the question marker. As you remember from Lesson 2, the personal endings express the subject. In **çalışıyor mu?** there is no personal ending because there is no added ending for the third person singular. Some examples with other subjects:

| | | | |
|---|---|---|---|
| **çalışıyorsun** | you work | **oturuyorsunuz** | you sit/live |
| **çalışıyor musun?** | do you work? | **oturuyor musunuz?** | do you sit/ live? |

| | | | |
|---|---|---|---|
| **görüyorum** | I see | **istiyoruz** | we want |
| **görüyor muyum?** | do I see? | **istiyor muyuz?** | do we want? |

An exception to the rule that the personal ending comes *after* the question marker is the third person plural (they): the question marker comes after the personal ending **-lar**, e.g.:

| | |
|---|---|
| **çalışıyorlar** | they work |
| **çalışıyorlar mı?** | do they work? |

Here are all the forms for present tense questions:

| *singular* | 1st person | **çalışıyor muyum?** | do I work? |
|---|---|---|---|
| | 2nd person | **çalışıyor musun?** | do you work? |
| | 3rd person | **çalışıyor mu?** | does he/she/it work? |

| *plural* | 1st person | **çalışıyor muyuz?** | do we work? |
|---|---|---|---|
| | 2nd person | **çalışıyor musunuz?** | do you (*pl.*) work? |
| | 3rd person | **çalışıyorlar mı?** | do they work? |

Note again how vowel harmony works in the following examples. The first four translate with the verb 'to be'. This type of sentence will be dealt with in Lesson 4.

| | |
|---|---|
| **hasta mı?** | is he ill? |
| **güzel mi?** | is it beautiful? |
| **bozuk mu?** | is it broken? |
| **şoför mü?** | is he a driver? |
| **düşünüyor musun?** | do you think? |
| **Türkçe öğreniyorlar mı?** | do they learn Turkish? |
| **anlıyor musunuz?** | do you understand? |

**Exercise 3 (Audio 1: 18)**

Form questions from the following sentences, by using the question marker **mi**. The first item has already been filled in.

| | | |
|---|---|---|
| 1 **Görüyorsun** | **Görüyor musun?** | Do you see? |
| 2 **Çalışıyoruz** | _____ | Are we working? |
| 3 **Gidiyorsunuz** | _____ | Are you going? |
| 4 **Türkçe konuşuyor** | _____ | Does he/she speak Turkish? |
| 5 **Yardım ediyoruz** | _____ | Are we helping? |
| 6 **Ankara'ya geliyorum** | _____ | Am I going to Ankara? |
| 7 **Ailemi biliyorsun** | _____ | Do you know my family? |
| 8 **Anlıyorlar** | _____ | Do they understand? |
| 9 **İngilizce öğreniyor** | _____ | Is he/she learning English? |
| 10 **Türkiye'yi beğeniyorsunuz** | _____ | Do you like Turkey? |

**Dialogue 2** (Audio 1: 19)

## Resepsiyonda

**At reception**

*Fatma is talking to Seyfi, one of the guests in the hotel.
Her husband Cem is trying to fix the phone on the reception desk*

| | |
|---|---|
| FATMA: | Fethiye'ye ne zaman geldiniz? |
| SEYFİ: | Bir hafta önce geldim. |
| FATMA: | Buralar nasıl, güzel mi? |
| SEYFİ: | Evet, çok güzel. |
| FATMA: | Ölüdeniz'e gittiniz mi? |
| CEM: | Ben mi? |
| FATMA: | Hayır, sen değil, konuğumuza sordum tabii ki! |
| SEYFİ: | Dün gittim. Orası Türkiye'nin en şahane yeri. |

*Meanwhile Cem tests the telephone, but in vain.*

| | |
|---|---|
| CEM: | Allah allah! |
| SEYFİ: | (*to Cem*) Çalışmıyor mu? |
| CEM: | Bozuk herhalde. |
| SEYFİ: | Yardım edebilir miyim? Elektrikçiyim. |
| FATMA: | Elektrikçi misiniz? O zaman kocama yardım edin, lütfen. |

| | |
|---|---|
| FATMA: | *When did you come to Fethiye?* |
| SEYFİ: | *I got here a week ago.* |
| FATMA: | *Is it nice around here?* |
| SEYFİ: | *Yes, very nice.* |
| FATMA: | *Have you been to Ölüdeniz?* |
| CEM: | *Me?* |
| FATMA: | *No, not you, I was obviously asking our guest!* |
| SEYFİ: | *I went there yesterday. It's the most beautiful place in Turkey.* |

| | |
|---|---|
| CEM: | *Oh no!* |
| SEYFİ: | (to Cem) *Isn't it working?* |
| CEM: | *It's probably broken.* |
| SEYFİ: | *Shall I help you? I am an electrician.* |
| FATMA: | *You're an electrician! Then please help this husband of mine, would you?* |

## Key vocabulary

| | | | |
|---|---|---|---|
| Fethiye'ye | to Fethiye | önce | earlier |
| buralar | these places | Ölüdeniz'e | to Ölüdeniz |
| | (*i.e.* 'here') | konuğumuza | to our guest |
| değil | not | sormak | to ask |
| konuk | guest | orası | that place |
| tabii ki! | of course! | en | most |
| Türkiye'nin | of Turkey | yer | place[1] |
| şahane | great, fantastic | herhalde | probably |
| bozuk | broken | elektrikçiyim | I'm an |
| yardım edebilir | can I help? | | electrician |
| miyim? | | elektrikçi | are you an |
| elektrikçi | electrician | misiniz? | electrician? |
| o zaman | then | kocama | to my husband |
| koca | husband | yardım edin! | help! |

## Language point

### Past tense questions

In past tense questions, the question marker comes last, so *after* the personal markers:

| *singular* | 1st person | çalıştım mı? | did I work? |
|---|---|---|---|
| | 2nd person | çalıştın mı? | did you work? |
| | 3rd person | çalıştı mı? | did he/she/it work? |

| *plural* | 1st person | çalıştık mı? | did we work? |
|---|---|---|---|
| | 2nd person | çalıştınız mı? | did you (*pl.*) work? |
| | 3rd person | çalıştılar mı? | did they work? |

Compare:

Present tense: **sinemaya gidiyor musun?**
are you going to the cinema?

Past: **sinemaya gittin mi?**
did you go to the cinema?

In the present tense, the order is (1) *verb stem* plus (2) *tense* plus (3) *question marker* plus (4) *personal ending*:

1 The ending -i on **yer** has to do with the -nin in **Türkiye'nin**. It will be explained in Lesson 6.

| gid- | iyor | mu- | sun |
|------|------|-----|-----|
| 1 | 2 | 3 | 4 |

In the past tense, on the other hand, it is (1) *verb stem* plus (2) *tense* plus (3) *personal ending* plus (4) *question marker*:

| git- | ti- | n | mi |
|------|-----|---|-----|
| 1 | 2 | 3 | 4 |

Some further examples:

| *present tense* | *past tense* |
|-----------------|--------------|
| **geliyor musunuz?** | **geldiniz mi?** |
| do you come? | did you come? |
| **yapıyor muyum?** | **yaptım mı?** |
| do I make it? | did I make it? |
| **çalışıyor musun?** | **çalıştın mı?** |
| do you work? | did you work? |
| **Kaş'ta oturuyor mu?** | **Kaş'ta oturdu mu?** |
| does he live in Kaş? | did he live in Kaş? |

Note that the question marker **mi** is always preceded by a space.

More examples of typical past tense questions:

| **oraya gittin mi?** | have you been there? (*literally:* did you go there?) |
|----------------------|-------------------------------------------------------|
| **beğendin mi?** | did you like it? |
| **Türkiye'de mi aldın?** | did you buy that in Turkey? |
| **kaça aldın?** | how much did you pay for it? (*literally:* to how much did you buy?) |

A couple of notes on these examples: (1) the form for 'there' is **oraya**, and not **orada** because the verb **gitmek** involves direction. **Oraya** means 'to that place'. (2) the last three examples illustrate that words such as 'it' and 'that' are often not expressed in Turkish when they are the direct object in the sentence.

 **Exercise 4** (Audio 1: 20)

Below are some answers. You have to supply the questions. Their English versions have been given, but you can make the exercise harder by blocking them off. By way of example, the first item has been done. Three of the words (all direct objects) used in this exercise contain what is called the accusative case suffix. One of those is **Ali'yi** in number 3. When the verb **görmek** 'see', is used, there is also something that is seen, in this case **Ali**. The thing or person that is seen, is the *direct object*. Turkish often adds a suffix to the noun that functions as the direct object in a sentence, something we will explain more fully in Lesson 6. The other accusative-marked direct objects here are **Türkiye'yi** in number 5, and **onu** *him/her* in number 7.

1 **İstanbul'da oturuyorum.**     **Nerede oturuyorsun(uz)?**
            Where do you live?
2 **Hayır, çalışıyorum.**     _____
            Are you a student?
3 **Ali'yi gördüm.**     _____
            Who did you see?
(NB: 'who' is translated here as **kimi**)
4 **Dün akşam gitti.**     _____
            When did he go?
5 **Türkiye'yi çok beğeniyorlar.**     _____
            Do they like Turkey?
6 **Sinemaya gittik.**     _____
            Where did you go?
7 **Onu biliyoruz.**     _____
            Do we know him?
8 **Evet, yardım ettiler.**     _____
            Did they help?

student **öğrenci**

The question form **mi** may be used for emphasis. Whatever is followed by **mi** is what is emphasised.

**Bu kız Eskişehir'de oturuyor mu?**
Does this girl live in Eskişehir? (*no particular emphasis*)

**Bu kız mı Eskişehir'de oturuyor?**
Does this girl live in Eskişehir? (*emphasis on* 'this girl')

**Bu kız Eskişehir'de mi oturuyor?**
Does this girl live in Eskişehir? (*emphasis on the place name* 'Eskişehir')

# Language point

## Location: in, at, on (locative case)

English uses prepositions to express the place where you are, where you are going to or from where you came. You say that you are *in* London, go *to* London, or came *from* London. Turkish does not have prepositions. Instead, it has postpositions and case endings. We will leave the postpositions for later; for the time being the case endings will suffice to express location and direction. The element expressing location is **-de**, and we have encountered it a few times, as in **Nere*de* oturuyorsun?** Where do you live? This ending **-de** is subject to vowel harmony (*see* Reference Grammar) and also to the kind of 'assimilation' earlier seen for the past tense ending **-di** (*see* Lesson 2), and may therefore also appear as **-da**, **-te** or **-ta**.
Examples:

| | |
|---|---|
| **Londra'da** | in London |
| **İstanbul'da** | in İstanbul |
| **Eskişehir'de** | in Eskişehir |
| **İznik'te** | in İznik |
| **Kaş'ta** | in Kaş |
| **hastanede** | in hospital |
| **evde** | at home, in the house |
| **sokakta** | in the street |
| **yürekte** | in the heart |
| **nerede?** | where? |
| **nerelerde?** | where?, in which places? |
| **İngiltere'de oturuyorum** | I live in England |
| **bugün okulda** | he's in school today |
| **şimdi Adana'da oturuyor** | she lives in Adana now |

Note that the ending is preceded by an apostrophe when it is attached to a name. (The same is true for other case markers.)
The ending **-de** is also used to express the *time* when something takes place. Examples are:

| | |
|---|---|
| **saat yedide** | at seven o'clock (**yedi** = 7) |
| **beşte geliyor** | he comes at five (**beş** = 5) |
| **bir Ağustosta** | on the first of August |

More on times and numbers in Lesson 5.

*Exercise 5*

Fill in the correct ending (-de, -da, -te, -ta), to give 'in Bursa', etc.
The words that are not translated are all Turkish place names.

1 **Bursa___**
2 **İzmir___**
3 **kütüphane___**     in the library
4 **kitap___**          in the book
5 **Kars___**
6 **gözlerin___**       in your eyes
7 **okul___**           at school
8 **Antep___**

## Direction: to (dative case)

The case ending **-e** or **-a** is used for expressing direction towards
something or someone. After vowels the form is **-ye** or **-ya**:

| | |
|---|---|
| **Londra'ya** | to London |
| **İstanbul'a** | to İstanbul |
| **Eskişehir'e** | to Eskişehir |
| **Fethiye'ye** | to Fethiye |
| **hastaneye** | to the hospital |
| **eve** | to the house |
| **sokağa** | to the street |
| **yüreğe** | to the heart |

Pay special attention to the last two examples and see what happens
to a **k** between two vowels: it turns into a **ğ**: thus **sokak-a** becomes
**sokağa** and **yürek-e** becomes **yüreğe**. Similarly, a **ç** becomes a **c**,
and a **p** becomes a **b**:

| | |
|---|---|
| **ağaç – ağaca** | tree – to the tree |
| **kitap – kitaba** | book – to the book |

The **-e** or **-a** case ending (to a noun, person's name or a place) is
also used to mark the *indirect* object or the receiver, as in the
following examples:

**Aynur'a bir hediye verdim.** I gave Aynur a present.
    (i.e. I gave a present *to* Aynur.)
**Kediye mamayı verdin mi?** Did you give the cat its food?
    (i.e. Did you give its food *to* the cat?)

## Exercise 6

Fill in the correct ending (-e, -ye, -a, -ya)

| | | |
|---|---|---|
| 1 | kim____? | to whom? |
| 2 | köpek____ | to the dog |
| 3 | oda____ | to the room |
| 4 | aile____ | to the family |
| 5 | at____ | to the horse |
| 6 | kedi____ | to the cat |
| 7 | Ankara____ | to Ankara |
| 8 | sancak____ | to the flag |

## Language point

### Direction: from (ablative case)

The direction *from* which you, someone or something comes, is expressed by the ending **-dan** (or **-den, -tan, -ten**):

| | |
|---|---|
| Londra'dan | from London |
| İstanbul'dan | from İstanbul |
| Eskişehir'den | from Eskişehir |
| İznik'ten | from İznik |
| Kaş'tan | from Kaş |
| hastaneden | from the hospital |
| evden | from home, from the house |
| sokaktan | from the street |
| yürekten | from the heart |

Besides *direction from*, the **-den/-dan** ending may also indicate 'along', 'via', 'through' or 'across', as in:

**Anayoldan geldiniz mi?**
Did you come via the motorway?

**Toros Dağlarından yolculuk ettik.**
We travelled through the Taurus Mountains.

**Köprüden geçtiler.**
They came across the bridge.

Do you remember the word **nerede?** 'where?' Now you have learnt the case endings expressing direction to and from, you can add these two to your list of question words:

| | |
|---|---|
| **nereye?** | where to? |
| **nereden?** | where from? |

### Exercise 7

Fill in the correct ending (**-den**, **-dan**, **-ten**, **-tan**)

1 **Türkiye____**
2 **Erzurum____**
3 **İstanbul____**
4 **İngiltere____**
5 **şehir____**          from the city
6 **Cardiff____**
7 **York____**
8 **Londra____**

## Language point

### Comparison of adjectives

The ablative case (*direction from*) is also used for the comparison of adjectives (i.e. for expressions such as 'bigger'). The case-marker follows the word that in the English construction follows 'than':

**İstanbul Tarsus'dan güzel.**
Istanbul is prettier than Tarsus.

It may be followed by **daha** 'more' or **az** 'less'.

**İstanbul Tarsus'dan daha güzel.**
Istanbul is prettier than Tarsus.

**Tarsus İstanbul'dan az güzel.**
Tarsus is less beautiful than İstanbul.

The superlative contains the word **en** 'most':

| | |
|---|---|
| **güzel** beautiful | **hızlı** fast |
| **daha güzel** more beautiful | **daha hızlı** faster |
| **en güzel** most beautiful | **en hızlı** fastest |

**Sen en iyi arkadaşım.**
You are my best friend.

# Atatürk

During and after the **Birinci Dünya Savaşı** 'First World War', in which the Ottoman Turks had chosen the side of the Germans, foreign powers threatened Turkish sovereignty. Postwar treaties subdivided the land between the various Allies (such as the Greeks, the English and the French). Although officially the sultan was still the head of state, a nationalist Turkish movement took over power. When the Greeks invaded the city of **İzmir** 'Smyrna', the Turks started their fierce **Kurtuluş Savaşı** 'War of Independence' (1920–1922). The Greeks nearly captured Ankara (the seat of the nationalist movement), but in the end the nationalists, under the leadership of **paşa** 'general' Mustafa Kemal, almost literally drove the Greeks into the sea at İzmir. The sultan was deposed, a **cumhuriyet** 'republic' was formed.

Mustafa Kemal became Turkey's national superhero, as he was the Conqueror of the Greeks, the Founder of the new Turkish Republic, and his surname became **Atatürk**, the Father of all Turks. He strongly believed in Turkish identity and self-assurance. His reforms drastically changed the **siyasal** 'political', **dinsel** 'religious', **ekonomik** 'economic' and **eğitimsel** 'educational' aspects of Turkish life. The Arabic script was replaced by the Latin alphabet and efforts were made to clear the language of foreign influence. This meant that all 'loanwords' (Ottoman Turkish had many from **Arapça** Arabic and **Farsça** Persian) should be replaced by an **öztürkçe** 'originally Turkish' word. A **Türk Dil Kurumu** 'Turkish Language Committee' was set up to reform the language.

There were new dress codes: 'old' clothing (such as the oriental **fez** which was seen as a reminder of the old days) was not allowed, at least not in public buildings. Moreover, Atatürk's republic was no longer based on the **şeriat** 'the Sharia', 'Islamic law', but was turned into the **layık** 'laicist', 'secular' nation which it nowadays still is, based on a rather strict separation between state and religion.

# 4 Muhallebicide

## At the cake shop

---

**In this lesson you will learn how to:**

- express the present and past tenses of 'to be' or 'not to be'
- say whether things are around or not
- use the word 'not', i.e. use negatives
- talk and ask about possession
- ask for things
- use demonstratives ('this' and 'that')

---

 **Dialogue 1** (Audio 1: 21)

## Muhallebicidedirler

**They are at the cake shop**

*Demet meets Özlem in a cake shop*

| | |
|---|---|
| DEMET: | Selam, canım. Nasılsın? |
| ÖZLEM: | Bomba gibiyim. Sen nasılsın? |
| DEMET: | Sağ ol. O çanta yeni mi? |
| ÖZLEM: | Evet. Dün aldım. |
| DEMET: | Çok güzel, güle güle kullan! Ne içersin? |
| ÖZLEM: | Çay. Sen ne içmek istiyorsun? |
| DEMET: | Portakal suyu alayım. (*looks around*) Garson nerede? Yok mu? |
| ÖZLEM: | Var! Gözlerin görmüyor mu? (*to the waiter:*) Bakar mısınız? |

| | |
|---|---|
| DEMET: | *Hello, dear. How are you?* |
| ÖZLEM: | *Great. How are you?* |
| DEMET: | *Fine, thanks. Is that bag new?* |

ÖZLEM: *Yes. I bought it yesterday.*
DEMET: *Nice, have fun with it! What are you drinking?*
ÖZLEM: *Tea. What do you want to drink?*
DEMET: *I'll have orange juice.* (looks around) *Where's the waiter. Isn't there one?*
ÖZLEM: *There is a waiter! Are you blind?* (to the waiter:) *Can you help us please?*

NB: **Güle güle kullan!** means literally 'Use it with pleasure!' The literal translation of **Gözlerin görmüyor mu?** is 'Don't your eyes see?' The word 'blind' is **kör** in Turkish (*see* Exercise 1).

## Key vocabulary

| | | | |
|---|---|---|---|
| **selam** | hello | **portakal suyu** | orange juice |
| **canım** | dear, love | **portakal** | orange |
| **bomba gibiyim** | I am doing very well | **su** | water, juice |
| | (*literally:* I am like | **alayım** | let me take |
| | a bomb) | **göz** | eye |
| **bomba** | bomb | **bakar mısınız** | can you help |
| **gibi** | like, as | | us, please? |
| **sağ ol** | thanks | | (*literally:* do |
| **çanta** | handbag | | you look?) |
| **yeni** | new | **bakmak** | to look |
| **ne içersin** | what do you drink? | | |

## Language points

 **'Verbless' sentences** (Audio 1: 22)

In earlier lessons you have seen sentences such as **iyiyim** 'I am fine'. In the dialogue above, similar forms appear, such as **O çanta yeni mi?** 'Is that bag new?' This type of sentence contains a form of the verb 'to be' in the English translation. Remember that Turkish does not have a verb 'to be'. Instead it makes use of personal endings. We will call this type of sentence the 'verbless' sentence.

The personal endings follow a noun or an adjective, not a verb stem. They are, however, the same as on verbs: **-im** ('I am') for first person singular; **-sin** ('you are') for second person singular, no ending at all for third person singular; **-iz** ('we are') for first person plural, **-siniz;** ('you are') for second person plural; and **-ler** ('they are') for third person plural. All endings are subject to vowel harmony, e.g. **-sin** may also become **-sın, -sün** or **-sun**. We will come back to the third person forms in a moment. First, look at the following examples.

**Examples:**

| | |
|---|---|
| **öğretmenim** | I am a teacher |
| **öğretmensin** | you are a teacher |
| **ögretmen** | he/she is a teacher |
| **öğretmeniz** | we are teachers |
| **öğretmensiniz** | you are teachers |
| **öğretmenler** | they are teachers |
| **hastasın** | you are ill |
| **hazırım** | I am ready |
| **öğrencisiniz** | you are students |
| **arkadaşlarımız öğrenci** | our friends are students |
| **elektrikçidir** | he is an electrician |

If the noun or adjective ends in a vowel, the ending for the first person (singular 'I' and plural 'we') has an extra **-y-**, so becomes **-yim** and **-yiz** respectively. Examples:

| | | | |
|---|---|---|---|
| **hastayım** | I am ill | **iyiyim** | I am fine |
| **hastayız** | we are ill | **iyiyiz** | we're fine |

The third person singular normally has no ending at all (**öğretmen** 'he/she is a teacher').

Sometimes, however, the ending **-dir** (**öğretmendir**) is added. The difference between the two is that **-dir** is used more in writing and formal speech. In everyday speech you don't need to use it, except for emphasis. There is a similar difference between **-ler** and **-dirler** as third person plural forms. Vowel harmony may turn the **-dir** form into **-dır, -dür** or **-dur**; after **ç, f, h, k, p, s, ş** or **t** the **-d** becomes a **-t: -tir, -tır, -tür** or **-tur.**

| | |
|---|---|
| **akıllı bir kızdır** | she is a clever girl |
| **yüksek bir binadır** | it is a tall building |

## Saying where someone/something is

The endings are not solely used for sentences of the 'he is an X' or 'she is a Y' types. Phrases expressing location often take them as well. For instance, **evde**, as you already know, means 'in the house' or 'at home'. To say 'I am in the house' or 'I am at home' you use **evdeyim**. 'You (plural) are in the restaurant' is **lokantadasınız**: **lokanta** 'restaurant' + **-da** in + **-sınız** 'you are (plural)'. If you want to express 'they are on holiday', you say **tatildeler**: **tatil** 'holiday/vacation' + **-de** 'on' + **-ler** 'they are'.

The title of the dialogue above consists of **muhallebici** 'cake shop', the ending **-de** 'in' and the third person plural ('they') ending **-dirler** 'they are'.

## Exercise 1

Fill in the right forms of 'to be'.

| | | |
|---|---|---|
| 1 **kör** | *(you sing.)* | **körsün** |
| 2 **parkta** | *(they)* | _____ |
| 3 **şoför** | *(I)* | _____ |
| 4 **memur** | *(we)* | _____ |
| 5 **gelin** | *(you sing.)* | _____ |
| 6 **Türkçe öğretmeni** | *(we)* | _____ |
| 7 **hastanede** | *(he)* | _____ |
| 8 **arkadaş** | *(they)* | _____ |
| 9 **polis** | *(I)* | _____ |
| 10 **öğrenci** | *(you plur.)* | _____ |

| | | | |
|---|---|---|---|
| **kör** | blind | **memur** | officer/civil servant |
| **şoför** | driver | **gelin** | bride |

And do you still remember the following words?

| | | | |
|---|---|---|---|
| **park** | park | **arkadaş** | friend |
| **öğretmen** | teacher | **öğrenci** | student, pupil |
| **hastane** | hospital | | |

## Language point

 **Negation:** değil **(Audio 1: 23)**

Of course, once you know how to say that you are, for instance, a teacher, you may also want to say what you are not. Then you use the word **değil**, meaning 'not'. The personal ending follows **değil**.

*Examples:*

| | |
|---|---|
| öğretmen değilim | I am not a teacher |
| öğretmen değilsin | you are not a teacher |
| öğretmen değil | he/she is not a teacher |
| | (*also:* öğretmen değildir) |
| öğretmen değiliz | we are not teachers |
| öğretmen değilsiniz | you are not teachers |
| öğretmen değiller | they are not teachers |
| | (*also:* öğretmen değildirler) |
| hasta değilsin | you are not ill |
| öğrenci değildirler | they are not students |
| | (*also:* öğrenci değiller) |
| arkadaşlarımız öğrenci değil | our friends are not students |

*Exercise 2*

Fill in the right forms of 'not to be', by using **değil**.

| | | |
|---|---|---|
| 1 **kör** | *(you sing.)* | **kör değilsin** |
| 2 **parkta** | *(they)* | _____ |
| 3 **şoför** | *(I)* | _____ |
| 4 **memur** | *(we)* | _____ |
| 5 **gelin** | *(you sing.)* | _____ |
| 6 **Türkçe öğretmeni** | *(we)* | _____ |
| 7 **hastanede** | *(he)* | _____ |
| 8 **arkadaş** | *(they)* | _____ |
| 9 **polis** | *(I)* | _____ |
| 10 **öğrenci** | *(you plur.)* | _____ |

Until now you have encountered few comments on word order in Turkish. You may have noticed, however, that verbs always seem to be found at the end of a sentence. The same is true for 'verbless sentences' where the personal endings play the role of 'to be'. You may be able now to see the difference between the following pairs:

| | | |
|---|---|---|
| öğretmen hasta | and | hasta öğretmen |
| kız güzel | and | güzel kız |
| bina eski | and | eski bina |

You may have guessed that the left column contains 'verbless' sentences which mean 'the teacher is ill', 'the girl is pretty' and 'the building is old'. The words on the right, on the other hand, mean 'the sick teacher', 'the pretty girl' and 'the old building'. These are not 'verbless' sentences, but are nouns modified by an adjective.

### Exercise 3

Translate into Turkish:

1 The teacher is handsome.
2 She is not the pretty teacher.
3 The museum is old.
4 The old museum is closed.
5 You are in the big building.
6 He is a jobless electrician.
7 The electrician is jobless.
8 The jobless electrician is a handsome man.
9 The building is tall.
10 She is a pretty teacher.

| handsome | **yakışıklı** | building | **bina** |
| closed | **kapalı** | tall | **yüksek** |
| jobless | **işsiz** | | |

## Language points

### Past tense

So far, all examples of 'to be' or 'not to be' have been in the present tense, and a tense marker has not been needed. However, in order to express 'was' and 'were' in Turkish, that is, the past tense of nominal sentences, you do need one. The past tense marker is **-di**, and is combined with personal endings, similar to those on past tense verbs: **-dim** for first person, **-din** for second person singular, **-di** for third person singular, **-dik** for first person plural, **-diniz** for second person plural and **-diler** for third person plural. Be aware, as usual, that vowel harmony gives these endings different shapes, depending on the last vowel of the preceding noun.

### Examples:

| **öğretmendin** | you were a teacher |
| **şofördü** | he was a driver |

If you didn't know any better, these could also have been past tense forms of (non-existent) verbs **öğretmenmek** and **şoförmek**. There is, however, a minor difference with the past tense verb endings. After words that end in a vowel, such as **hasta**, the endings have an additional **y** right before the **-di** marker. The correct form for 'I was ill' is not **hastadım** but **hastaydım**. 'You were at home' is not **evdediniz**, but **evdeydiniz**.

NB: In written texts, the past tense ending of nominal sentences is sometimes written as **idim**, **idin**, **idi**, **idik**, **idiniz** and **idiler** with a space between the past tense marker and the word it belongs to. In daily life, however, you would not say **hasta idim**.

 **Exercise 4** (Audio 1: 24)

The following text is written in the present tense. Change all verb forms and 'verbless' sentences into the past tense. Then translate into English.

Ankara Üniversitesinde okuyorum. Yani bir öğrenciyim. Her gün üniversiteye gidiyorum. Her akşam çok yorgunum. En iyi arkadaşım aynı sokakta oturuyor. Onunla beraber sık sık sinemaya ve tiyatroya gidiyoruz. Arkadaşım öğrenci değil. O bir gazeteci. Gazete için röportaj yapıyor. Bazen de televizyon için röportaj yapıyor. O zaman onu televizyonda görüyorum. Arkadaşım çok ünlü.

| üniversite | university |
|---|---|
| okumak | to read; to study |
| yorgun | tired |
| aynı | same |
| sokak | street |
| onunla | with him/her |
| onunla beraber | together with her, with him |
| tiyatro | theatre |
| gazeteci | journalist |
| gazete | newspaper |
| gazete için | for a newspaper |
| bazen | sometimes |
| röportaj | article, documentary |

## Negation in the past tense

In the previous exercise you tried to find the past tense of **öğrenci**

**değil.** You may have come up with the right answer (**öğrenci değildi**). As you see, in the negative form of past tense 'verbless' sentences, **değil** is used again. The past tense marker (**-di**) comes right after **değil**.

*Examples:*

| | |
|---|---|
| **hasta değildim** | I was not ill |
| **gazeteci değildiniz** | you were not journalists |
| **arkadaşım ünlü değildi** | my friend was not famous |

## Language point

### Questions

This might be a good moment to quickly look again at the section on questions with **-iyor** and **-di** in Lesson 3. In order to turn 'verbless' sentences into questions, you also use the question marker **mi**. In the present tense, the personal endings are added to **mi**, except for, of course, the third person (he/she/it) which has no personal ending for 'to be'. In the past tense, however, the past tense endings (**-ydim**, **-ydin** etc.) come right after **mi**. Watch how this works in the following examples:

| *3rd person singular* | *statements* | *questions* |
|---|---|---|
| *present tense* | **bu patlıcan iyi**<br>this aubergine is good<br>**patlıcan iyi değil**<br>the aubergine is not good | **patlıcan iyi mi?**<br>is the aubergine good?<br>**patlıcan iyi değil mi?**<br>the aubergine is not good? |
| *past tense* | **patlıcan iyiydi**<br>the aubergine was good<br>**patlıcan iyi değildi**<br>the aubergine was not good | **patlıcan iyi miydi?**<br>was the aubergine good?<br>**patlıcan iyi değil miydi?**<br>was the aubergine not good? |

| *2nd person singular* | *statements* | *questions* |
|---|---|---|
| *present tense* | **hastasın**<br>you are ill<br>**hasta değilsin**<br>you are not ill | **hasta mısın?**<br>are you ill?<br>**hasta değil misin?**<br>are you not ill? |

| | | |
|---|---|---|
| *past tense* | **hastaydın** | **hasta mıydın?** |
| | you were ill | were you ill? |
| | **hasta değildin** | **hasta değil mıydın?** |
| | you were not ill | were you not ill? |

**More examples:**

| | |
|---|---|
| **Patlıcan iyi.** | Aubergines are good. |
| **İyi misin?** | Are you okay? |
| **Tehlikeli değil mi?** | Isn't it dangerous? |
| **Tehlikeli, değil mi?** | It is dangerous, isn't it? |
| **Müze güzel değil miydi?** | Wasn't the museum nice? |

The third person plural questions ('are they?') are a bit tricky, since both forms (**-ler** and **-dirler**; *see* earlier in this Lesson) have a different placement of the question word **mi**. The written and slightly more formal variant (**-dirler** 'they are') is added to **mi**, as in **Öğrenci midirler?** 'Are they students?'. In the more colloquial version, however, **-ler** is used instead of **-dirler**, and is added to the noun. The question word **mi** comes last: **Ögrenciler mi?** 'Are they students?'.

**Exercise 5**

Find the right forms, using the information on person, tense and sentence type:

Example:

| | | |
|---|---|---|
| **gazeteci** | *they, present tense, question* | |
| | **Gazeteci midirler?** | 'Are they journalists?' |
| *or:* | **Gazeteciler mi?** | 'Are they journalists?' |

| | | |
|---|---|---|
| **gazeteci** | *I, past tense* | _____ |
| **gazeteci** | *we past tense, negation* | _____ |
| **gazeteci** | *you plur., present tense, question* | _____ |
| **şoför** | *you sing., past tense* | _____ |
| **şoför** | *you sing., present tense, question* | _____ |
| **şoför** | *she, present tense* | _____ |
| **şoför** | *they, past tense* | _____ |

By now you know much of the basics of how to make a sentence in Turkish.

## Exercise 6

Translate the following text into Turkish. You'll have to use both 'verbless' sentences and ones with verbs (with **-iyor** and **-di**).

1 Did you see the accident?
2 Yes, I did see it. Were there injured people?
3 Yes, there were. The drivers are in hospital.
4 How are they?
5 They are doing well now.
6 Are you sure?
7 No, I am not sure.

| the accident | **kazayı** | injured people | **yaralılar** |
| were there | **var mıydı?** | sure | **emin** |

 **Dialogue 2** (Audio 1: 25)

# Maalesef yok

## Unfortunately not

*The waiter arrives at Özlem and Demet's table*

GARSON: Buyurun?
DEMET: Kahve var mı?
GARSON: Maalesef yok.
DEMET: Neyse, bana portakal suyu getirir misiniz?
GARSON: Tabii, getiririm.

*(The waiter returns with a bottle of orange juice)*

ÖZLEM: Tatlı olarak ne var?
GARSON: Çeşitlerimiz çok. Baklava, kadayıf, aşure ve muhallebi var.
DEMET: Bize ne tavsiye edersiniz?
GARSON: Kadayıfımız çok nefis.

GARSON: *Yes please?*
DEMET: *Do you have coffee?*
GARSON: *Unfortunately not.*
DEMET: *Well then, can you bring me an orange juice?*
GARSON: *Of course, I'll bring it.*

(The waiter returns with a bottle of orange juice)

ÖZLEM: *What do you have for dessert?*
GARSON: *We've got various things. Honey-and-almonds-filled pastry, syrup-and-nuts-filled pastry, fruit-and-nut pudding and rice pudding.*
DEMET: *What do you recommend?*
GARSON: *Our **kadayıf** is very tasty.*

## Key vocabulary

| | | | |
|---|---|---|---|
| **kahve** | coffee | **olarak** | as, for |
| **neyse** | well then | **çeşit** | kind, sort, variety |
| **bana** | (to) me | **tavsiye etmek** | to recommend |
| **getirir misiniz?** | do you bring? | **tavsiye edersiniz** | you recommend |
| **tatlı** | dessert, sweet | **nefis** | tasty |

## Language point

### Existential sentences

In order to express whether things are around or not, Turkish has a special type of sentence, called existential sentences. They typically contain either **var** 'there is/are' or **yok** 'there is/are not'. Both words come at the end:

**Kahve var.** There is coffee/They have coffee.
**Çay yok.** There is no tea/They haven't got any tea.

**Londra'da eski binalar var.**
In London there are old buildings.

**Ankara'da ilginç müzeler var mı?**
Are there interesting museums in Ankara?

**Var** and **yok** are also often used where English would use 'to have' e.g. **kardeşim var** 'I have a brother'.

### Exercise 7

Say whether the Turkish translation of the following English sentences is a **var/yok** sentence or a 'verbless' sentence. You will then see whether you've grasped the difference between the two types.

1 He is not very smart, is he?
2 Do you have any money?
3 Is there any hope?
4 The smart students are in my class.
5 There is no smart student in my class.
6 There are many bookshops in this street.

## Language point

### Possession

You have learnt before that Turkish usually does not use pronouns where English does. One case in which Turkish uses pronouns, such as **ben** 'I' and **sen** 'you', is when the English translation is 'to have with me/you/him/her' etc. So, when you want to say you have something with you, the words **var** and **yok** are used, in combination with a pronoun and the ending for place **-de**.

| | |
|---|---|
| **Bende para var.** | I have money (on me). |
| **Sende para yok mu?** | Don't you have money (on you)? |

For an answer you can just say **var** if you have, or **yok** if you haven't got money in your pocket. You don't have to repeat **para** 'money' in the answer.

Maybe you do have money, but you're not carrying it around all the time. If you have it in your bank account, you say:

| | |
|---|---|
| **Param var.** | I've got money. |

The **-m** ending after **para** is the ending signifying possession. The literal meaning of **param var** is 'my money is there' i.e., it exists. The difference between **bende para var** and **param var** is that the first is focused on the fact that you have it 'on you' at the time of speech, whereas the latter means 'I've got money' in a more general sense.

You also use this format with things that you cannot possibly carry with you:

| | |
|---|---|
| **Vaktim var.** | I've got time. |
| **İyi bir fikrimiz var.** | We have a good idea. |
| **İsteğim yok.** | I don't fancy . . . (I don't have the wish to . . .). |
| **Cesareti yok.** | He hasn't got the courage. |

This form also is used with persons other than first singular 'I'. The possessive endings are: **-im** (or after a vowel **-m**) for first person singular; **-in** (or after a vowel **-n**) for second person singular; **-si** (or after a vowel **-i**) for third person singular; **-imiz** (or after a vowel **-miz**) for first person plural; **-iniz** (or after a vowel **-niz**) for second person plural; and **-leri** for third person plural.

**More examples:**

| | |
|---|---|
| **Annesi var.** | He/she/it's got a mother. |
| **Boş odalarınız var mı?** | Have you got vacancies ('empty rooms')? |
| **Maalesef boş odalarımız yok.** | Unfortunately we haven't got vacancies. |
| **Çocukları yok.** | They haven't got children. |
| **Tatlı olarak neleriniz var?** | What have you got for dessert? |

You may already have seen some similarity between the first person possessive marker **-(i)m** 'my' and the first person personal ending **-(y)im** 'I am'. See for yourself in the following examples how the two differ when the word before ends in a vowel:

| | |
|---|---|
| **babam** | my father |
| **babayım** | I am a father |
| **öğretmenim** | my teacher/I am a teacher |

In Lesson 6 we will elaborate on this. For the time being, just take a look at the following examples. The **-un** in **çocuğun** and the **-in** in **evin** are so-called genitive case markers.

| | |
|---|---|
| **Çocuğun annesi var.** | The child has got a mother. |
| **Evin bahçesi yok.** | The house hasn't got a garden. |

## Language points

### Past tense: vardı/yoktu

The past tense forms of **var** and **yok** are **vardı** ('there was/there were') and **yoktu** ('there was not/ there were not').

## Examples:

**Dün dersler yoktu.**
Yesterday there were no lessons.

**Geçen hafta başka bir öğretmen vardı.**
Last week there was another teacher.

**Geçen yıl başka bir arabamız vardı.**
Last year we had a different car.

**Parası yoktu.**
He did not have any money.

**Gücümüz vardı.**
We had the strength.

**Cesaretin yoktu.**
You didn't have the courage.

## Questions

If you want to ask questions about whether something is available, such as specific vegetables at the greengrocer's, use the **mi** question marker. It follows **var** and **yok**, but precedes the past tense marker. In this situation, you don't need to use the possessive ending (which you might think when you look at the English translation).

### Examples:

**Patlıcan var mı?**
Have you got any aubergines?

**Kavun yok mu?**
Haven't you got any honeydew melons?

**Dün tek bir öğrenci yok muydu?**
Wasn't there a single student yesterday?

**Geçen hafta ders var mıydı?**
Were there any lessons last week?

But remember that **mi** comes after the past tense **-di** in normal questions about the past:

**Dün döndün mü?**
Did you return yesterday?

## Exercise 8

You should now be able to make questions from the following sentences. The first one has been done for you. Remember that **mi** may be placed in different positions to stress different elements in a sentence (*see* Lesson 3).

1 O çok yaşlı.                    O çok yaşlı mı? (*or:* **Çok mu yaşlı?** if you want to stress **çok** 'very')
2 Bunlar.
3 Kahve istiyorsun.
4 Bir tane kavun aldık.
5 Hiç çay yoktu.
6 Ankara'daydılar.
7 Ankara'da var.
8 İngiltere'de oturuyoruz.

**yaşlı**          old (used of people)

##  Dialogue 3 (Audio 1: 26)

# Bu ne?

## What's this?

*Eileen joins Demet and Özlem and stares in amazement at a plate filled with sweets and pastries*

EILEEN: Ne kadar güzel görünüyor!
DEMET: Hadi, bir tadına bak!
EILEEN: Tamam. Bu ne?
DEMET: Bu mu?
EILEEN: Hayır, şu pasta.
DEMET: Ha, bu bülbül yuvası. Çok güzel! İstersen, bir tane al.

*(Eileen tastes the 'nightingale's nest')*

EILEEN: Hmm, çok nefis!

EILEEN: *How nice this looks!*
DEMET: *Come on, try something!*
EILEEN: *All right. What's that?*
DEMET: *This one?*
EILEEN: *No, that cake.*

DEMET:   *Oh, that's 'nightingale's nest'. It's very nice! Take a piece,*
         *if you want.*
EILEEN:  *Hmm, very tasty!*

## Key vocabulary

| | | | |
|---|---|---|---|
| **görünmek** | to look, appear | **bir tane** | a piece |
| **bir tadına bak** | try something (*literally:* just look at its taste) | **istersen** | if you want |
| | | **al!** | take! |
| **tat** | taste | **almak** | to take |
| **pasta** | cake | | |

## Language point

### Demonstratives: bu, şu, o

In everyday conversation you often need gestures to accompany your words. Demonstratives often accompany your gestures. Turkish has three of them, and you've encountered them all before:

**bu**   this (close)
**şu**   this or that (used when you want to focus the
         listener's direction)
**o**    that (far away), but also used as personal pronoun
         ('he', 'she' or 'it')

### Examples:

| | |
|---|---|
| **Bu Müjgan.** | This is Müjgan. |
| **Bu ne? Patlıcan.** | What is this? (It's) aubergine. |
| **O Orhan.** | That is Orhan. |
| **Şu armut ne kadar?** | How much are those pears? |

**Bu**, **şu** and **o** can be used both as modifier of a noun and by themselves. Sometimes this may lead to some ambiguity:

| | |
|---|---|
| **Bu Ford.** | 1 This Ford. |
| | 2 This is a Ford. |
| **O kasap.** | 1 That butcher. |
| | 2 He is a butcher. |

You use **şu** whenever you want to direct the attention of the listener towards an object or a person not previously mentioned in the conversation. As soon as the listener notices the object or person referred to, both speakers have to use **bu** when object or person are nearby, or **o** when object or person are further away. For instance, the answer to the question **Şu bina ne?** 'What's that building?' is **O bina bir kütüphane** 'That building is a library' and never *Şu bina bir kütüphane.* **Şu** may have a slightly derogatory meaning, so be careful with this form. Examples are:

**Şu adam kim?**
Who's that (suspicious-looking) man?

**Şunu yapmak istemiyorum.**
I don't want to do that (lousy) job.

Note that in the second example, **şu** carries the accusative case, because it is a direct object. Remember we saw **onu** 'him/her/it/that', the accusative of **o** 'he/she/it/that' in Lesson 3 (*see* the Reference Grammar for the complete list of case markings on **bu/şu/o**). You will learn more about the accusative in Lesson 6.

**Şu** may also refer to something mentioned in the sentence following it, or to things that are handed over to someone else:

**Şunu diyelim: Ali bugün burada yoktu.**
Let me say this: Ali wasn't here today.

**Şunu alır mısın?**
Can you take this?

The word **bu** may have an idiomatic use when it is used after nouns:

**Türk Hava Yolları bu!** That's Turkish Airlines for you! (i.e.: what would you expect!?)

| hava | air (*in addition to* 'weather') |
| yol | way |
| hava yolları | airways, airlines |

These three forms form the basis of a host of other words. You already know **burada** 'here' and **orada** 'there'. Similarly, there is also **şurada** 'there', 'yonder'. The plural forms of **bu**, **şu** and **o** are:

| bunlar | these |
| şunlar | those |
| onlar | those |

These plural forms are often used as the subject of a sentence, meaning 'these/those [are] . . ..'). Note in the following examples that the word after **bunlar** doesn't have to be marked for plural:

| | |
|---|---|
| **Bunlar Alman.** | These are Germans. |
| **Bunlar normal insan.** | These are normal people. |

but:

| | |
|---|---|
| **Bu ağaçlar yüksek.** | These trees are tall. |

In colloquial speech, the plural demonstratives are also used for people:

**Bunlar lokantaya gider sık sık.** They often go to the restaurant.

## Exercise 9

Translate into English:

1 Bu kitap iyi.
2 Bu iyi kitap şimdi kütüphanede.
3 Böyle bir kitap dün kütüphanede yoktu.
4 Onlar kitap.

Translate into Turkish:

5 This is Aylin.
6 That girl is not Aylin.
7 Those aubergines are in the kitchen.
8 Are these in the library?

| | |
|---|---|
| **böyle** | such |
| **kütüphane** | library |
| **mutfak** | kitchen |

## Reading text

The main purpose of the following text is to enlarge your vocabulary, in particular the part devoted to food.

# Türk mutfağının zenginliği

## The richness of Turkish cuisine

When you go to a Turkish **lokanta** 'restaurant', you will certainly have a great time. The **Türk mutfağı** 'Turkish cuisine' is renowned, and combines the best of Central Asian, Oriental and Balkan dishes and ingredients. In many restaurants, although not in the expensive ones, it is common not to have a **yemek listesi** or **menü** 'menu' available. Instead, you will be invited to come and have a look in the **mutfak** 'kitchen' and point at the things you would like to eat. So, what can you expect from eating out in Turkey? You may eat one of several delicious **çorba** 'soups' for starters, for **öğle yemeği** 'lunch', or even for **kahvaltı** 'breakfast', such as **mercimek çorbası** 'lentil soup', or **düğün çorbası** "wedding soup" containing eggs and lemon juice. Another way of starting a meal is to have some **meze** 'hors d'oeuvres', such as **yaprak dolması** 'stuffed vine leaves', **sigara böreği** "cigar pastry" (fried dough filled with white cheese), or **cacık** (diced cucumber with yoghurt and garlic). You may also order a plate of **karışık** 'mixed' **meze** as a full meal.

As a main course, you may have **et** 'meat', **balık** 'fish', **tavuk** 'chicken' or **sebze** 'vegetable' dishes, accompanied by a nice **pilav** 'pilaf rice dish'. **Su** 'water' and **ekmek** 'bread' are always served. Popular meat dishes are given names of cities, such as **Adana kebap**, a spicy variant, **Bursa kebap** (made from **döner kebap**, lamb roasted on a vertical spit, on **pide** 'bread').

Turkey's national drink is **çay** 'tea', which is offered everywhere, whether you are visiting a family, buying a carpet, or taking a rest in a shady park. At dinner, however, you'll find other drinks, such as different kinds of **meyve suyu** 'fruit juice' or **içkiler** 'alcoholic beverages', such as **şarap** 'wine', **bira** 'beer' and **rakı**, a pastis- or ouzo-like drink. Of course, **kola** and **fanta** are popular as well. You can end your meal with a dessert (see the dialogues above for some possibilities). When you order **Türk kahvesi** 'Turkish coffee', you'll have to state whether you want it **sade** 'black, no sugar', **orta** 'with a medium amount of sugar' or **şekerli** which usually is 'very, very, very sweet'. If you want milk in your coffee, specifically state that you want it **sütlü** 'with milk'.

When you're ready to pay the bill, ask the waiter **'Ödeyebilir miyim?'** 'Can I pay?' or **'Hesap, lütfen'** 'The bill, please.' When you read the bill, you will notice that in most cases **servis** 'service' is **dahil** 'included'. If you leave satisfied, you may want to leave a small **bahşiş** 'tip'.

## More useful words:

| | | | |
|---|---|---|---|
| **bulgur** | broken wheat | **işkembe** | tripe |
| **ayran** | salty yoghurt drink | **kaşık** | spoon |
| **lahmacun** | Turkish version of pizza | **bıcak** | knife |
| **beyin** | brain | **çatal** | fork |

| | |
|---|---|
| **aile salonu** | family room (meaning that no single men are allowed there) |
| **aileye mahsustur** | reserved for families (with a similar implication) |

See Lesson 8 for a recipe.

# 5 Kaç yaşındasın?

## How old are you?

In this lesson you will learn how to:

* use numbers
* ask and answer questions
* say how old you are
* use 'negative' expressions
* ask and answer questions in more detail
* use plurals
* say 'first', 'second', etc.

## Dialogue 1 (Audio 1: 27)

## O kadar gençsin!

## You're so young!

*Nursen and Eser have struck up a friendship after both joining an evening class. They are hanging around in the school building after the class*

NURSEN: Sana bir soru sormak istiyorum: kaç yaşındasın?
ESER: Kaç gösteriyorum?
NURSEN: Yirmi beş mi?
ESER: Hayır, o kadar genç değilim.
NURSEN: Ya öyle mi? Peki, kaç doğumlusun?
ESER: Bin dokuz yüz altmış dört.
NURSEN: Aya ilk ayak basan insanı hatırlıyor musun?
ESER: Hatırlıyorum, ama çok iyi değil. Sen kaç yaşındasın?
NURSEN: Ben yirmi üç yaşındayım.

NURSEN: *I want to ask you a question: how old are you?*

ESER:      *How old do I look?*
NURSEN:    *Twenty-five?*
ESER:      *No, I'm not that young.*
NURSEN:    *Oh, really? OK, when were you born?*
ESER:      *In 1961.*
NURSEN:    *Do you remember the first man who walked on the moon?*
ESER:      *I do, but not very well. And how old are you?*
NURSEN:    *I'm twenty-three.*

## Key vocabulary

| | | | |
|---|---|---|---|
| **soru** | question | **ayak** | foot |
| **yaş** | age | **insan** | people, human |
| **göstermek** | to show | **basan** | stepping |
| **o kadar** | that much | **basmak** | to step, to tread |
| **doğumlu** | born | **ilk ayak basan insan** | the first person who |
| **ay** | moon, | | set foot |
| | month | **hatırlamak** | to remember |

## Language points

### Numbers

The word for 'zero' is **sıfır**. Here are the numbers for '1' to '10' and for '20' to '100':

| | | | |
|---|---|---|---|
| **bir** | one | **yirmi** | twenty |
| **iki** | two | **otuz** | thirty |
| **üç** | three | **kırk** | forty |
| **dört** | four | **elli** | fifty |
| **beş** | five | **altmış** | sixty |
| **altı** | six | **yetmiş** | seventy |
| **yedi** | seven | **seksen** | eighty |
| **sekiz** | eight | **doksan** | ninety |
| **dokuz** | nine | **yüz** | hundred |
| **on** | ten | | |

Numbers between 10 and 20, between 20 and 30 etc., are regularly formed by putting **on** before **bir**, **iki** etc. Thus, 'eleven' is **on bir**, and 'seventy six' is **yetmiş altı**. With numbers over a hundred, the pattern is exactly the same. For '523' you say **beş yüz yirmi üç**. The word for 'thousand' is **bin**. An important sequence of numbers to know is **bin dokuz yüz**, for the 1900s. And from now on, the sequence **iki bin** 'two thousand' will be heard more and more.

**Bin dokuz yüz altmış beşte doğdum.**
I was born in 1965.

**Bu fabrikada iki sene çalıştım.**
I worked in this factory for two years.

**Bu üniversite için bin dokuz yüz seksen üçten beri çalışıyorum.**
I've been working for this university since 1983.

The last example shows how to express 'since' in Turkish: you add the ablative case suffix (the one that indicates 'direction away from') to the name of the year, and then add the word **beri**. In the Glossary, you will see this as: **beri (-den)** 'since'. The second example shows how to express 'for X years': you simply say **X sene**. Note that the noun following a number is not in the plural form.

For 'half', there are two words: **yarım** and **buçuk**. The latter means 'and a half', as it is only used after another numeral. Thus, it is also the word used in telling the time (*see* Lesson 7). At all other times, 'half' is translated by **yarım**.

**Yarım kilo peynir aldım.**
I've bought half a kilo of cheese.

**Üç buçuk kilometre yürüdük.**
We walked three and a half kilometers.

**Saat dört buçukta geldi.**
He came at half past four.

Note that for 'a hundred' and 'a thousand', Turkish never uses **bir**. It does do this, however, for the higher numbers. The word for 'a million' (1,000,000) is **bir milyon**.

 *Exercise 1* (Audio 1: 28)

In the following little text, some important dates in the life of an old man are mentioned. First, read the text and then match the dates given with the events listed on the right-hand side. Try to resist the temptation of listing the dates according to the most logical progression in a person's life. In other words, look for the written-out dates in the text and see what is said about them. You'll find a translation in the Key. After you've completed the exercise, go through that translation carefully, making sure you know the meaning of the words underlined there.

Günaydın. Adım Orhan. Bin dokuz yüz onda, Kars'ta doğdum. Bin dokuz yüz on altıda ilk defa okula gittim. Dört sene sonra ailemiz Ankara'ya taşındı. Babam orada iyi bir iş buldu. Ben, bin dokuz yüz yirmi üçten yirmi yediye kadar rüştiyeye gittim. Ondan sonra benim karımla tanıştım. Bin dokuz yüz otuz beşte evlendik. Eser Hanım iyi bir kadındı. İlk çocuğumuz iki sene sonra doğdu. Kızdı, adı Sumru. Daha beş çocuğumuz oldu. En sonuncusu bin dokuz yüz kırk dokuzda doğdu. Bin dokuz yüz altmışa kadar çok mutluydum. O sene karım öldü. Bin dokuz yüz yetmiş üçe kadar çalıştım. Şimdi kızlarımızın birinin yanında oturuyorum. Dediğim gibi, hayatım çok güzeldi. Birde, en büyük başarım bin dokuz yüz otuz birdeydi. Ankara güreş yarışmasına katıldım, yendim ve ödül aldım.

## Key vocabulary

| | | | |
|---|---|---|---|
| **ailemiz** | our family | **mutlu** | happy |
| **bulmak** | to find | **yanında** | at; next to |
| **kadar (-e)** | until | **hayat** | life |
| **Hanım** | Mrs | **birde** | you know, . . . |
| **en sonuncusu** | the very last | **başarı** | success |
| **son** | end | | |

| | |
|---|---|
| 1910 | did a few years of secondary school (**rüştiye** is what it was called at the time, the modern equivalent is a **lise**) |
| 1916 | won wrestling competition |
| 1920 | retired |
| 1920s | had their last child |
| 1931 | got married |
| 1935 | lost his wife |
| 1937 | had their first child |
| 1949 | was born |
| 1960 | went to school |
| 1973 | lives with one of his three daughters |
| now | family moved to Ankara |

## Exercise 2 (Audio 1: 30)

Match the English and Turkish numbers. As numbers are frequently used in daily speech, it is important that you try and master them as soon as possible. It is advisable to repeat this exercise every once in a while, for example at the beginning of every new lesson. While doing that, try and work on your speed by trying to complete the exercise as quickly as possible. You could time yourself each time to monitor your progress. The effects will be even better if you jumble the numbers around a bit (e.g. by writing them out a few times on different pieces of paper in various random orders).

| three | altı | fifty | doksan |
|-------|------|-------|--------|
| five | bir | twenty | seksen |
| eight | dokuz | hundred | otuz |
| two | on | sixty | yirmi |
| nine | yedi | seventy | elli |
| six | iki | ninety | kırk |
| one | dört | thousand | altmış |
| ten | beş | forty | bin |
| seven | sekiz | eighty | yetmiş |
| four | üç | thirty | yüz |

## Saying how old you are

The important word here is **yaş**, 'year'. The phrase **... yaşındayım** means 'I'm ... years old.' Simply insert your age, say **otuz bir**, and you've answered the question **kaç yaşındasın?** An alternative answer would be **yaşım otuz bir.** To talk about your age at some point in the past, use **yaşındaydım.**

**Çocuklarımız iki ve beş yaşında.**
Our children are two and five.

**Bin dokuz yüz yetmişte on bir yaşındaydım.**
In 1970 I was 11 years old.

**Dialogue 2** (Audio 1: 31)

## Dükkanda

### In the shop

*Mehmet has run into the **bakkal** (the grocer's) on the corner to get a few things for tonight's meal. The **bakkal** (grocer) is now ready to take his order*

BAKKAL: Hoş geldiniz, nasılsınız?
MEHMET: Hoş bulduk. Teşekkürler.
BAKKAL: Buyurun!
MEHMET: Biraz peynir istiyorum.
BAKKAL: Ne kadar istiyorsunuz?
MEHMET: Bakayım, bir kilo yeterli.
BAKKAL: Tamam. Başka birşey istiyor musunuz?
MEHMET: Evet, iki tane ekmek de alayım.
BAKKAL: Buyurun.
MEHMET: Birde, dolmalık biber var mı?
BAKKAL: Yok, maalesef bitti.
MEHMET: Peki, o zaman. Hepsi bu kadar. Borcum ne kadar?
BAKKAL: Sekiz yüz bin lira, lütfen.
MEHMET: Buyurun. Hayırlı işler.
BAKKAL: Teşekkür ederim, efendim. İyi günler.

BAKKAL: *Welcome, how are you?*
MEHMET: *The pleasure's mine. Thank you.*
BAKKAL: *What can I do for you?*
MEHMET: *I'd like some cheese please.*
BAKKAL: *How much would you like?*
MEHMET: *Let me see, a kilo would be fine.*
BAKKAL: *OK. Would you like anything else?*
MEHMET: *Yes, I'll have two loaves of bread as well.*
BAKKAL: *There you are.*
MEHMET: *And, er, have you got any peppers for stuffing?*
BAKKAL: *No, we're out, unfortunately.* (literally: it has finished)
MEHMET: *OK, then. That's everything. What do I owe you?*
BAKKAL: *800.000 lira please.*
MEHMET: *There you go. Have a good day.*
BAKKAL: *Thank you, Sir. Goodbye.*

## Key vocabulary

| | | | |
|---|---|---|---|
| **peynir** | cheese | **bakayım** | let me see |
| **yeterli** | enough | **alayım** | let me take |
| **ekmek** | bread | **biber** | pepper; paprika |
| **bitmek** | to finish | **dolmalık biber** | pepper for stuffing |
| **hepsi** | everything | **borç** | debt |
| **iki tane ekmek** | two loaves (*literally:* pieces) of bread | | |

NB: You may remember from Lesson 2 that **buyurun** is used both when giving something to someone and when asking someone what he/she would like.

### Exercise 3

There are of course many other useful phrases for shopping. Some will be said by you as a customer; others will typically be thrown at you by the shop assistant. Here are some; try and figure out on the basis of what you know and the Glossary provided at the end of the exercise, which phrase goes with which English equivalent. Be aware that in some cases the English equivalent is not at all a literal translation (for instance with No. 10 below).

| | |
|---|---|
| 1 ... **niz var mı?** | a could you give me ...? |
| 2 **hepsi ne kadar?** | b your change |
| 3 ... **verir misiniz?** | c in all, that's .... |
| 4 **hepsi ... ediyor.** | d have you got anything smaller? |
| 5 **maalesef bitti.** | e unfortunately, we don't sell that. |
| 6 **bu mevsimde iyi mi?** | f have you got ...? |
| 7 **bu ucuz** | g are they good this time of year? |
| 8 **bir poşet istiyor musunuz?** | h we haven't got any left, unfortunately. |
| 9 **daha küçüğü var mı?** | i how much is that together? |
| 10 **maalesef, üzgünüm** | j do you want a bag? |
| 11 **bozuk paranız** | k oh, that's cheap. |

| | | | |
|---|---|---|---|
| **mevsim** | season | **küçük** | small, little |
| **ucuz** | cheap | **bozuk para** | small change |
| **üzgün** | sad | | (*literally:* broken money) |

# Language point

## Negation

By now you have learned the basic ways of asking things and answering questions, at least when the answer is 'yes'. We will now see how to answer in the negative. After that, all the ground covered so far concerning questions and answers will be reviewed. There are three ways of negating that you will need to know about. Two of them you already know from the previous lesson. Both occur in 'verbless' sentences. Sentences such as 'I'm not', 'he isn't' and 'they aren't' are translated using **değil**, and sentences with 'there isn't' use **yok**.

| | |
|---|---|
| **Türk değilim.** | **Bugün daha Bursa'ya giden tren yok.** |
| I'm not Turkish. | There isn't another train to Bursa today. |
| **Burada değiller.** | **Paramız yoktu.** |
| They're not here. | We didn't have any money. |

What you don't know yet is how to negate sentences with a verb. However, from examples in the dialogues and exercises you may have developed an intuition for how this is done.

**Tanımıyor musunuz?** (Lesson 1: Reading text)
Don't you know (*recognise*) her?

**Sizinle gelmedi mi? Gelmedi.** (Lesson 2: Dialogue 2)
He didn't come with you? He didn't come.

**Ama henüz iyi konuşmuyorum.** (Lesson 2: Exercise 4)
But I don't speak it well yet.

**Şunu yapmak istemiyorum.** (Lesson 4: Demonstratives)
I don't want to do that.

In Turkish, a verb is negated by adding a suffix, **-me** or **-ma**, to the verb stem. That is, this suffix comes before the tense (e.g. **-iyor**) and person markers. The negation of **geldi** is **gelmedi**. The **e** or **a** of the negative suffix is omitted if the following sound is a vowel, so that in **-iyor** forms the negation is solely expressed through an **-m** after the verb stem. The negative of **bakıyor** is **bakmıyor**, and of **gidiyorsun** it is **gitmiyorsun**.

Some more examples:

**Karım şimdi çalışmıyor.**
My wife isn't working at the moment.

**Ergün hiçbir şey fark etmedi.**
Ergün didn't notice a thing.

**Bunun iyi olduğunu sanmıyorum.**
I don't think that's right.

### Exercise 4

Give the dictionary forms of the following finite verbs. Be careful, as they are not all negative. The first one has been done already.

1 Beklemedik.          **Beklemek.**
2 Uğramıyorum.
3 Açmadı.
4 Yaşıyor.
5 Batmıyor.
6 Pişirmedi.
7 Yıkıyorlar.
8 Kazanmadım.
9 Seviyorsunuz.
10 Dinlenmiyor.

## Questions and answers: an overview

Here is a review of asking and answering questions. You will see that both positive and negative answers are given.

*Questions:*

1 Add **mi** (or **mı, mu** or **mü**) to the word that you're questioning.
2 Use one of the question words, such as **ne** or **ne zaman.**

*Answers:*

I If the question was a **mi**-type sentence containing a verb marked with **-iyor** or **-di**, such as **Ankara'ya gidiyor musunuz?** 'Are you going to Ankara?' or **Ankara'ya gittiniz mi?** 'Did you go to Ankara?', then:

(a) if you want to say 'yes':
use the normal type of sentence, as illustrated by most of the examples encountered so far. You can precede it by **evet.** If

there was a verb with for example **-iyor** or **-di** in the question, try and use that verb in your answer too.

Example: **Gidiyorum.**    I'm going.
**Gittim.**    I went.

(b) if you want to say 'no':
repeat the verb that was used in the question, but with the negative marker **-me-** (or **-ma-**). You can always precede your answer with **hayır**, but be warned that this word is not used nearly as often in Turkish as 'no' is in English.

Example: **Gitmiyorum.**    I'm not going.
**Gitmedim.**    I didn't go.

II If the question was a **mi**-type sentence without a verb marked with **-iyor** or **-di**, such as **Hasta mısın?** 'Are you ill?' or **Hasta mıydın?** 'Were you ill?' then:

(a) if you want to say 'yes':
repeat the word that was questioned plus the relevant person marker, possibly preceded by **evet**.

Example: **Evet, hastayım.**    Yes, I'm ill.
**Hastaydım.**    I was ill.

(b) if you want to say 'no':
use **değil** plus the relevant person marker (for 'I'm not' the right form is **değilim**).

Example: **(Hasta) değilim.**    I'm not (ill).
**(Hasta) değildim.**    I wasn't (ill).

III If the question contained **var mı?** or **yok mu?**, as in **Çay var mı?** 'Is there tea?' or **Çay var mıydı?** 'Was there tea?' then:

(a) if you want to say 'yes':
answer with **var**, possibly preceded by **evet** and, also optionally, the word that was questioned.

Example: **(Çay) var.**    There is (tea).
**(Çay) vardı.**    There was (tea).

(b) if you want to say 'no':
answer with **yok**, possibly preceded by **hayır** and/or the word that was questioned.

Example: **Hayır, (çay) yok.**    No, there isn't (any tea).
         **(Çay) yoktu.**    No, there wasn't (any tea).

IV If the question was a sentence without **mi**, but with a question word (often in first position), as in **Nerede oturuyorsunuz?** 'Where do you live?' then:

use a normal type of sentence, providing a relevant answer.

Example: **Londra'da oturuyorum.**    I live in London.

## Exercise 5

Give an appropriate answer to the following questions.

1 Bu akşam evde misin?
2 Nereden geldin?
3 Bize uğramak istiyor musunuz?
4 Bu hafta sonu neler yaptınız?
5 Şu ağacı görüyor musunuz?
6 Lahmacun seviyor musun?
7 Buralarda bakkal var mı?
8 Kaç dil biliyorsunuz?
9 Türkiye'de kilo aldınız mu?
10 Siz nerelisiniz?
11 Vaktiniz yok mu?
12 Kahvaltı dahil mi?

| | | | |
|---|---|---|---|
| **uğramak** | to visit | **dil** | language |
| **ağaç** | tree | **kilo almak** | to put on weight |
| **lahmacun** | Turkish pizza | **dahil** | included |
| **bakkal** | grocery store | | |

## Exercise 6

In the following dialogue, the question words are omitted. Using the list given, supply the correct forms.

**misiniz, var mı, mu, ne kadar, mı, nasıl, mı**

1 Merhaba. Kıymalı et var . . .?
2 Var. Kuzu . . . sığır . . . istiyorsunuz?
3 Sığır istiyorum lütfen. Baklava bugün . . .?
4 Çok iyi. Buyurun, tadına bakın!
5 Oh, çok nefis! Bir kilo verebilir . . .?

6 Tamam. Başka bir isteğiniz ...?
7 Hayır, teşekkürler. Borcum ...?

| | | | |
|---|---|---|---|
| **kıymalı et** | ground meat | **verebilir** | could you give |
| **kuzu** | lamb | **istek** | wish |
| **sığır** | beef | **borcum** | my bill |
| **tadına bakın!** | have a taste! | | |

## Language points

### The use of bir

The word **bir** 'one' also functions as an indefinite article. When a noun combines with an adjective, they are separated by **bir**, as long as the noun is singular:

**Eskişehir güzel bir şehir, değil mi?**
Eskişehir is a nice city, isn't it?

**Türkiye'de güzel yerler gördün mü?**
Did you see any nice places in Turkey?

**Bir** is also part of a great many other words, many of them frequently used. Examples include 'something' **birşey**, 'someone' **birisi** or **biri**, and 'sometimes' **bir zaman** (compare 'one time'). Their negations are handy to know as well. In Turkish, most negation is done through negative verbs, i.e. through verbs with the **-me/-ma** suffix. However, you should also know the word **hiç**, which must be used to negate **bir zaman**, and serves to emphasise the negation of **birşey**. For 'no-one', use the word **kimse**. **Birisi** and **biri** can also be preceded by **hiç** and then mean 'none of them'. From now on, look out for new occurrences of these types of words.

**Birşey anlamadım.**
I didn't understand a thing.

**Hiçbir şey anlamadım.**
I didn't understand a single thing.

**Hiçbir zaman rakı içmem.**
I never drink rakı.

**Biri cevabı bildi.**
Someone knew the answer.

**Kimse cevabı bilmedi.**
No-one knew the answer.

## Use of plural

The plural suffix is **-ler** or **-lar**, depending on vowel harmony. It is one of the few suffixes that are used with both nouns and verbs. Its use is fairly straightforward (that is, similar to English), except for a few details. Importantly, absence of **-ler** does not necessarily mean that the noun in question is singular. The basic principle is that you don't use the plural suffix if you don't have to. Contrary to English, for instance, you don't say 'three ducks' in Turkish, but 'three duck'. Numbers higher than one are assumed to make clear that you're not talking about something in the singular, so the plural marker is considered redundant. This principle extends to uses where it is irrelevant (or you want to make it seem irrelevant) whether you are talking about one or more items. Of the next three examples, the last one is the least specific about the number of CDs bought by the speaker: it may be one or any number of CDs.

| | |
|---|---|
| **Çarşıda iki tane CD aldım.** | I've bought a couple of CDs in town. |
| **Çarşıda CDler aldım.** | I've bought CDs in town. |
| **Çarşıda CD aldım.** | I've bought a CD/CDs in town. |

So, where English forces you to use the plural if you are talking about more than one instance of something, Turkish doesn't, though note that numbers do often co-occur with the word **tane** 'piece'. When you're listening to somebody, that means that without further context (such as being shown five CDs at the same time), you can't be sure whether absence of **-ler** actually means that the speaker is talking about 'one' and not about 'more'. If you want to make sure, ask a question with **kaç**:

| | |
|---|---|
| **Patlıcan aldım.** | I bought aubergines. |
| **Kaç tane?** | How many? |
| **Üç.** | Three. |

### Exercise 7

Go over all the nouns used so far in the dialogues in this lesson. Give their plural forms.

## Exercise 8

Translate English sentences into Turkish and Turkish ones into English:

1 **Bir şey içiyor musun?**
2 **Şimdi hangi romanı okuyorsun?**
3 I was born in the US.
4 **Bu tişörtü bin dokuz yüz doksanda aldım.**
5 No, I don't know anybody in Turkey.
6 **Türk gazetelerini okuyor musunuz?**
7 **Hiçbir şey yapmadım.**
8 What happened here? (*use* **oldu**)
9 We have four dogs at home.
10 **Sokakta bir kaza oldu ve hemen polis geldi.**

## Language point

### Ordinal numbers

The suffix **-inci** (or **-ıncı**, **-uncu** or **-üncü**, of course) turns the numerals into ordinals, i.e. words like 'first', 'second' and 'thirtieth':

| | | | |
|---|---|---|---|
| **birinci** | first | **altıncı** | sixth |
| **ikinci** | second | **yedinci** | seventh |
| **üçüncü** | third | **sekizinci** | eighth |
| **dördüncü** | fourth | **dokuzuncu** | ninth |
| **beşinci** | fifth | **onuncu** | tenth |
| **yirmi beşinci** | twenty-fifth | **yüzüncü** | hundredth |

You may have noted an alternative for **birinci** in the first dialogue of this lesson: **ilk**. This word has overtones of 'the very first', so it is for instance often used in the phrase **ilk defa**, 'the first time'. The two words are not interchangeable. **Birinci** is used in summing-up contexts, where you can clearly paraphrase with 'the first of many', 'few', 'a definite set', etc. **İlk**, on the other hand, is more of an abstract 'first', and is often used in contexts where in English you can paraphrase with 'at first'. Both words only mean 'first' when used as an adjective; in phrases like 'first I did this, then that', 'first' is an adverb and translated with **önce**.

**Bu beşinci ders.**
This is the fifth lesson.

**Bugün Olimpiyat oyunlarının kaçıncı günü?**
The 'how many-eth' day of the Olympics is it today?

**İlk aylar kolay değil.**
The first months aren't easy.

**Birinci gün kahve ücretsiz.**
The first day the coffee is free.

**Önce birşey içmek istiyorum, ondan sonra yemek yiyeceğiz.**
First I want something to drink, then we'll eat.

## Ordering

When you find yourself in a shop or a restaurant, there are a few things you typically need to be able to understand and/or say. The numerals are basic, but there are a few other words without which interaction would not be easy. One such word is **tane**, which roughly means 'piece'. Very easy are the international words **gram**, **kilo**, **metre** and **litre** (their particular form gives away that they were borrowed from French). But other things are different, so that other words may be thrown at you. Some of these are introduced in the following exercise.

### Exercise 9 (Audio 1: 32)

Read through the following text and try to reconstruct Mevlüt's shopping list. Watch out: some of the things she wanted she didn't get. In the process, try and find out what the words printed in bold mean.

*Mevlüt is talking to her friend Hatice on the phone,*
*and is telling her how her trip to the shop was*

Bu akşam dolma yemek istedik, ama **biber** yoktu markette. İki **tane** ekmek aldım ve dükkandan çıktım. Ondan sonra başka bir bakkala gittim. Bibere **baktım**, ama iyi değildi. Yalnız beş **şişe** bira aldım. Sonra pazara gittim. Orada iki tavuk, yarım kilo beyaz peynir, biraz siyah zeytin ve bir buçuk kilo elma aldım ama yine de iyi dolmalık biber bulamadım. Nohut istedim, nohut da yoktu. Her yerde aradım durdum. **Sonunda** patlıcan aldım. Daha sonra Eser'e **rastladım**. O beni bir şey içmeye davet etti. O bir **fincan** kahve içti, ben de bir **kadeh** şarap içtim. Bugünkü alışverişler işte böyle **berbat** geçti.

| | | | |
|---|---|---|---|
| **dolma** | stuffed peppers | **nohut** | chickpeas |
| **dükkan** | store | **aramak** | to search for |
| **pazar** | market | **durmak** | to stand (here: keep) |
| **tavuk** | chicken | **şarap** | wine |
| **beyaz** | white | **alışveriş** | shopping |
| **siyah zeytin** | black olives | **geçmek** | to pass |
| **elma** | apple | | |

## Reading text

*Cengiz is humming a song*

| | |
|---|---|
| ALİ: | Bu melodiyi tanıyorum, ya! Fakat ismini unuttum. Dur, söyleme. Tahmin etmek istiyorum. Şarkıcı kim? |
| CENGİZ: | Edip Akbayram. |
| ALİ: | O mu? Biraz düşünelim. (*hums the melody*) Şarkının konusu ne? |
| CENGİZ: | Aşktır, tabii ki. Ama hava durumundan da söz ediyor. |
| ALİ: | Ha, şimdi hatırladım! 'Hava nasıl oralarda ...' |

*Together they start singing the song*

| | |
|---|---|
| ALİ/CENGİZ: | hava nasıl oralarda<br>üşüyor musun?<br>kar yağıyor saçlarıma<br>bilmiyor musun? |

Ali seems to know the melody, but says **ismini unuttum**. What could that mean? **Dur** 'wait' and **söyleme** 'don't sing' are examples of how you 'give orders'. Ali wants to **tahmin etmek** what he has forgotten, and asks **şarkıcı kim**? Now, once you know that a **şarkı** is 'a song', and the ending **-cı** may denote someone's profession, you can easily derive the meaning of **şarkıcı**. Again, as in previous reading texts, you see a subjunctive ending **-elim** in the word **düşünelim** 'let me think'. Note also the word combination **şarkının konusu**, of which you might gather the meaning. The **konu** of the song which Cengiz hums is **aşk**. The word **tabii** 'of course' indicates that there are many more songs about **aşk**. But the song is also about **hava durumu** 'the weather condition'. Now Ali remembers the title: **hava nasıl oralarda**. Can you find out what it means? The question **üşüyor musun?** relates to the fact that in the next line **kar yağıyor** 'snow falls' or 'it is snowing', and can be taken as a sign that the singer seems rather concerned about the listener's well-being. The **kar yağıyor** not just to the ground, but **saçlarıma** 'on my hair'. Can you figure out what the root word is of **saçlarıma** (i.e. what the Turkish word for 'hair' is), and which suffixes follow it? Note the negative verb **bilmiyor** in the last line.

# 6 Ali'nin yeni evini gördün mü?

## Have you seen Ali's new house?

In this lesson you will learn how to:

- say something is someone's, i.e. use 'possessives', such as 'mine', 'yours', etc.
- use 'to have' in more detail
- use the accusative and genitive cases, when to use them, and how to form them

## ⋒ Dialogue 1 (Audio 1: 33)

## Yeni evin nasıl?

## How's your new house?

*Mehmet runs into İlhan at the train station. He starts telling him about his new apartment.*

İLHAN: Merhaba, acelen ne böyle?
MEHMET: Trenim kalktı mı?
İLHAN: Yoo, kalkmadı henüz, daha beş dakika var. N'haber?
MEHMET: İyilik. Geçen hafta taşındık. Yeni evimiz var.
İLHAN: Öyle mi? Hayırlı olsun. Ev nasıl, güzel mi?
MEHMET: Evet, çok güzel. Hem de çok geniş, bahçemiz bile var.
İLHAN: Kaç odanız var?
MEHMET: Büyük bir salon ve iki yatak odası. Yukarıdaki yatak odalarının birinde balkon var.
İLHAN: Evinizi satın mı aldınız?
MEHMET: Hayır, kirada oturuyoruz. *(A train pulls in at the station.)* Bu benim trenim mi yoksa seninki mi?

İLHAN: Bu benimki. Eviniz tekrar hayırlı olsun. Görüşürüz.
MEHMET: Teşekkür ederim. Görüşürüz.

## Sözcükler *(Vocabulary)*

From now on, the dialogues will not be accompanied any more by full translations. Instead, you'll find word lists like the following, introducing new words. These will usually be in their dictionary forms, so any verb will appear as an infinitive in the list. In general, the word will be given without any suffixes; only words with suffixes you have not heard about yet will be translated fully.

| | | | |
|---|---|---|---|
| **acele** | hurry | **satın almak** | to buy |
| **hayırlı olsun!** | congratulations! | **kira** | rental |
| **geniş** | wide | **yoksa** | or |
| **bile** | even | **seninki** | yours |
| **salon** | living room | **benimki** | mine |
| **yatak** | bed | **tekrar** | again |
| **yukarıda** | upstairs | | |

### Exercise 1

What do the following words mean?

1 acelen          4 odanız
2 kalktı mı?       5 kirada
3 taşındık         6 eviniz

## Language point

### Possession

In English, there are several ways of saying that something is yours. You can use a possessive pronoun, as in 'This one's my car'; you can use a form of the verbs 'have' or 'got', as in 'I had a great time'; or you can use the 'apostrophe s' construction with people's names ('Betty's house').

Turkish has several ways of indicating possession, too. The one most comparable to the English pronoun is the possessive suffix. Similar to the 'apostrophe s' is the Turkish genitive case, which indicates possession as well as a host of other things. For instance,

English 'Aylin's' is **Aylin'in** (the name **Aylin** plus the genitive case -**in**); English 'of the house' (as in 'the roof of the house') is **evin** (**ev** 'house' with the genitive case -**in**). For 'to have', Turkish uses a construction which includes both the possessive suffixes and the verb **var** (or, as the case may be, **yok**). (Turkish has possessive pronouns, too, just like English, but these are of more limited use.) The similarity with English stops here. Although they are used differently, here is how the two systems roughly compare:

| English | Turkish |
|---|---|
| my, your etc. house | **ev** + suffixes (and pronouns) |
| X's house | X-genitive + **ev** + suffixes |
| have a house | **ev** + suffixes + **var/yok** |

As you can see, the suffixes are all-important in Turkish, while the pronouns are optional, just as we saw with the personal pronouns.

## The suffixes

In Lesson 4, you were introduced to the possessive suffixes, when the translation of 'to have' was discussed. Off and on you have come across them in the dialogues and example sentences as well. Here is the schema:

| | |
|---|---|
| -**im** | -**imiz** |
| -**in** | -**iniz** |
| -**i/-si** | -**leri** |

If the noun ends in a vowel, the vowel of the suffix is dropped, so that the suffix for 'my' can be just -**m**, as in **arabam** 'my car'. The third person singular suffix, however, already is just one vowel. Dropping it would leave nothing to indicate possession. Therefore, when it is attached to a word that ends in a vowel, an extra consonant is inserted. In this case, that consonant is an -**s**, yielding the easy to recognise third person possessive suffix -**si** (or, of course, -**sı**, -**su** or -**sü**). Contrary to English, where you choose between 'his', 'her' and 'its', the suffix -**(s)i** means 'his', 'hers' or 'its' – you don't know from the suffix alone. Note, finally, that for the third person plural suffix there are two, not four possible forms. (This is because the suffix begins with the plural suffix, a member of the

two-class vowel harmony group.) The possibilities are therefore
**-leri** and **-ları**. Some examples:

**Evim uzak değil.**
My place is not far.

**Notları çok iyiydi.**
His grades were very good.

**Memleketin nasıl?**
What's your country like?

### Exercise 2

Turn the following nouns into possessed nouns. Who the possessor
is in each case, is indicated between brackets. The first item has
been done already.

1 **Kitap** (*my*)  **kitabım** (Note that the final **-p** of
**kitap** has changed to **-b**)
2 **Ev** (*your*, sing.)
3 **Hediye** (*your*, sing.)
4 **Kedi** (*their*)
5 **Kız kardeş** (*his*)
6 **Oda** (*her*)
7 **İş** (*your*, plural)
8 **Şehir** (*our*)
9 **Yemek** (*your*, singular, polite)
10 **Kahve** (*her*)

## The possessive versus the personal suffix

You may have noticed that these suffixes are largely similar to the
ones learned earlier as expressing 'I am', 'you are' etc. Don't worry,
in practice you won't often confuse them as they tend to appear
in different contexts, much like in English the similar sounding 's's
in 'John's gone home', 'John's working' and 'John's leg' seldom get
in each other's way. Thus, **doktorum** can mean 'my doctor', and it
can mean 'I'm a doctor'. But consider the contexts in which the
two constructions would be typically used and you'll realise they
are not likely to coincide. Nouns with a possessive suffix tend to
be part of a larger sentence, usually as subjects or objects, while
nouns with personal suffixes tend to be an utterance in themselves,
of the type referred to earlier as the 'verbless' sentence.

## 🎧 Exercise 3 (Audio 1: 34)

The following sentences all contain a noun carrying a suffix. Say whether the suffix is a possessive or a personal one. Listen closely to the tape to hear the slight differences in emphasis.

1 Babam yaşlı bir adam.
2 Gazeteciyim.
3 Evi bu sokakta.
4 Ankara'dalar.
5 Ablası seni davet etti, değil mi?
6 Evli bir adamım.
7 Çocuklarımız üç ve sekiz yaşında.
8 Bu senin sigaran mı?
9 Bu yenisi mi?
10 Siz delisiniz.

| abla | older sister | deli | crazy |
|------|--------------|------|-------|
| evli | married | sigara | cigarette |

Note, in 7 above, that the possessive suffix follows the plural ending. 'Our dogs' is **köpeklerimiz**, not **köpeğimizler**. That would mean 'they are our dogs'. Also note, from Examples 9 and 10, that adjectives can take the possessive ending. This is because adjectives can be used as nouns (nominalised) as in most languages (compare the English forms 'my old ones', or 'the good, the bad and the ugly').

With these suffixes you can express every construction of the type 'your country', 'his arm' and 'our kitchen'. However, just as you need a special construction in English when you want to use a person's name instead of just 'his' or 'her' (the 'apostrophe s' construction), something else is needed in Turkish, too. The equivalent of the 's' is the genitive case. (Note, however, that we are not finished yet with the possessive suffixes. One of their main uses, for instance, is in making compound nouns, (see page 151). They also feature prominently in genitive constructions of the type 'the X of the Y' (see below). And much later we will even see that they play an important role in subordinate clauses.)

## Genitive

The genitive case is formed in what by now should be a familiar way: with a suffix. The suffix is **-in** or **-nin** (with the usual alternatives, because of vowel harmony). As indicated above, its basic function is to indicate possession: **Ali'nin** is 'Ali's', **Demet'in** is 'Demet's', **John'un** is 'John's', **Türkiye'nin** is 'Turkey's'. (Actually, the name 'John' is often pronounced 'Jahn' in Turkey, written as **Can**, for example in **Can F. Kenedi caddesi**, 'John F. Kennedy street'. In that case, the genitive suffix is, of course, **-ın**.) No possessive construction is complete without mentioning the thing that is possessed. This noun follows the genitive-marked one, and this is where it starts to get unfamiliar to the English speaker. It is marked itself with the third person possessive suffix. Carefully read the examples:

| | |
|---|---|
| **Müjgan'ın cüzdanı** | Müjgan's purse/wallet |
| **Gül'ün arabası** | Gül's car |
| **Almanya'nın şehirleri** | Germany's cities |

The structure is:

> Possessor + Genitive + Possessed thing + 3rd person possessive suffix

In the examples above the construction is used with names in the role of the possessor, but it is much more widely used than that. As a rule of thumb, you can assume that you always need to use this construction when the construction in English would be 'the/a X of the Y', for example 'the centre of this town' or 'a big part of the day'. The Turkish translations of those are:

**bu şehrin merkezi**         **günün büyük bir bölümü**

One more thing: as with all nouns, compound nouns may be suffixed with case markers. This whole complex may be marked with, say, the *locative* case marker, the little element that indicates place. For instance, the phrase **şehrin merkezi** will often be used as part of the larger phrase 'in the centre of town'. As you know, the preposition is translated by the locative case marker in Turkish. This is added to the complex noun, but we do not get **şehrin merkezide**. When a case marker is added to the possessive suffix, an **-n-** is inserted, so that we get **şehrin merkezinde**.

### Exercise 4

Combine the following word pairs. First figure out what the likely combination is (i.e. which noun will be the possessor and which one is being possessed). Then build up the construction, as has been done for the first item.

1 **Dilek, kitap**   **Dilek'in kitabı** (Note that you don't change the final **-k** before a suffix when names are concerned)
2 anahtar, araba
3 biber, fiyat
4 kitap, isim
5 gün, son

**anahtar**   key          **isim**   title
**fiyat**     price

## 🎧 Dialogue 2 (Audio 1: 35)

## Kimin evinde?

## In whose house?

*A group of friends is waiting at Nursen's house. They got together
to plan a joint weekend in the country. However, one person, Ali,
is missing*

NURSEN:   Ne yapalım şimdi?
ÖMER:     Bence toplantıya Ali'siz başlamalıyız.
NURSEN:   Git ya, Ali'yi bekliyoruz.
ÖMER:     Belki başına birşey geldi. Toplantılarımıza hiç geç
          kalmaz.
NURSEN:   Ali'nin her zaman iyi fikirleri var, değil mi?
ÖMER:     Yenge, hepimizin iyi fikirleri var. Üçümüz de alışveriş
          listesini yazabiliriz.
NURSEN:   Ona telefon edelim mi?

*Ömer calls Ali on his mobile phone*

ÖMER:     Alo. Ali, koçum, neredesin ya?
          Evde misin? Ne oldu?
          Bizi mi bekliyorsun? Biz de seni bekliyoruz.
          Nursen'lerdeyiz.
          Kusuru bakma, ama, 'onun evinde' dedim, 'senin evinde'
          demedim. Evet. (*to the others:*) Jeton yeni düştü.
          Evet, şimdi hemen buraya gel!

# Sözcükler

| | | | |
|---|---|---|---|
| **bence** | according to me | **yazabiliriz** | we can write |
| **toplantı** | meeting | **koçum!** | mate! |
| **başlamalıyız** | we have to start | | (*American:* |
| **git ya!** | come on! | | my man!) |
| **belki** | maybe | **kusura bakma** | I'm sorry |
| **başına gelmek** | to be in trouble | **yeni** | new (*here:* |
| **geç kalmaz** | he doesn't come late | | finally) |
| **yenge** | aunt (*here used as a* | **düşmek** | to fall |
| | *form of address for* | | |
| | *a female peer*) | | |

## Exercise 5

Answer the following questions about the text.

1 What's the initial discussion about?
2 Is Ali usually late?
3 How many people are present at Nürsen's?
4 Does Nürsen live alone?
5 What do you think **jeton düştü** means?

# Language point

## The genitive forms of the personal pronouns

**Dikkat et!**, 'be careful!', there's potential for ambiguity, in spite of the systematic overall appearance that Turkish grammar makes. You know now that whenever a possessive suffix that ends in a vowel (that is: a third person possessive suffix) is followed by a case ending (e.g. locative **-de** for 'place' ('at', 'in'), or dative **-e** for *direction* ('to')), an **-n-** is inserted between the two suffixes. Thus, 'to her house' is **ev-i-n-e** (House-her-**n**-to). All other possessive suffixes end in a consonant, so you won't need to use the **-n-** with anything other than a third person possessive suffix. However, note that the second person singular now causes a new problem, since it happens to end in an **-n**. Thus, **evine** could also mean 'to your house' (**ev-in-e**; House-your-to). It will usually be clear from the context which meaning is intended, but confusion can arise, as in the dialogue above. In that case, extra pronouns come in handy. The pronouns to use are the *genitive* cases of the personal pronouns:

| | | | |
|---|---|---|---|
| **benim** | my, of mine | **bizim** | our, of ours |
| **senin** | your, of yours | **sizin** | your, of yours |
| **onun** | his, of his, her, of hers, its | **onların** | their |

*Exercise 6*

Go back to the dialogue and try to reconstruct the misunderstanding: what do you think Ömer had said to Ali when they were arranging the meeting?

 *Exercise 7* (Audio 1: 36)

Add the right form of the genitive suffixes to the first noun and form compounds with the second nouns.

1 Aylin, para
2 bu bakkal, ekmek
3 üniversite, yabancı öğrenci
4 Türkiye, başkent
5 onun okulu, öğretmen
6 bu banka, memur
7 bizim ev, banyo
8 firma, eski müdür

NB: In 7 above, the form **bizim ev** 'our house' reflects a characteristic of colloquial Turkish. Whereas you would have expected 'our house' to be **bizim evimiz**, the possessive suffix (*in this case* **-imiz**) can sometimes be omitted in everyday speech. This can only happen if there is a genitive pronoun (*here:* **bizim**).

| | | | |
|---|---|---|---|
| **yabancı** | foreign | **firma** | company |
| **başkent** | capital | **müdür** | director |
| **banyo** | bathroom | | |

## Language point

### 'To have' revisited

Recall from Lesson 4 (**Possession**, see page 64) that 'to have' can be translated in two ways, both involving the pair **var** and **yok**.

Either the possessed noun is marked with a possessive suffix, or the possessor is marked with the locative case (**-de**):

**param var**           I have money
**bende para var**      I have money (on me)

Note that these patterns are only good for contexts where the possessor is a pronoun such as 'I', 'you', etc., because then the suffix (**-m** 'my' or **-n** 'your' etc.) is enough to make clear who the possessor is. If the possessor is anybody else, then you have to use a noun plus genitive, though still in a construction with possessive suffix and **var/yok**:

| Noun + Genitive + Thing possessed + **-i/-si/-leri** + **var/yok** |
| --- |

Don't forget the possessive ending on the thing (or person) that is possessed; the other elements are fairly logical if you think about it. An example is 'The bank has a new director', in which 'the bank' is the possessor and therefore gets the genitive case **-nin**. The whole sentence then becomes **Bankanın yeni bir müdürü var**. To take one of the compounds from Exercise 7, if we want to turn **onun okulunun öğretmeni** into a 'to have'-construction, for instance in 'Ali's school has good teachers', it will suffice to simply add **var** (and **iyi**):

**Ali'nin okulunun iyi öğretmenleri var.**

One last thing: now that you know the genitive pronouns, you can add emphasis to constructions like **arabam var**. Adding **benim** does the same thing heavy emphasis does in English 'I have a car':

**Benim arabam var, babamın arabası yok.**
I have a car, my dad doesn't.

## Accusative

You might be familiar with languages that use an accusative case. That is a case used to indicate the direct object in a sentence. Turkish too has such a case. However, not every direct object in Turkish gets an accusative case marker: only direct objects that are definite. What exactly is 'definite'? Well, consider, first of all, possessed nouns: they are definite. The noun refers not to the thing it stands for in general, but to one particular instance of it. A word like **köpek** simply means 'dog', but **köpeğimiz**, 'our dog', refers to one (or more) particular dog(s). The reference is definite, as opposed to indefinite (e.g. **köpek, bir köpek** or **köpekler**). The accusative has occurred a few times already in example sentences, for example in this one from Lesson 5 (Exercise 8):

**Bu tişörtü̱ bin dokuz yüz doksanda aldım.**
I bought this T-shirt in 1990.

New examples are:

**Saat altı sularında eve dönüyor ve yemeği hazırlıyorum.**
I return home around six and prepare dinner.

**Türkiye'de güzel yerleri̱ gördün mü?**
Did you see nice places in Turkey?

As these examples show, the form of the accusative is **-i**. After a vowel, it is **-yi**.

When you add an accusative suffix to a noun, you are making that noun definite, just as you do when you put 'the' before an English noun. Consider the difference between 'a cat' and 'the cat'. This much is easy. What you have to also learn is that there are all kinds of contexts where adding an accusative suffix is simply obligatory. But don't forget: all this is limited to where the noun functions as the direct object of a verb. Thus, **babam** 'my father', though definite, does not get an accusative when it is the subject of a sentence, as in **babam söyledi** 'my father said', it does when it is a direct object: **babamı gördüm** 'I saw my father'. If the possessed noun in a genitive construction is a direct object, the whole construction is followed by the accusative. This yields the very common sequences **-(s)ini**, in which **(s)i** is the possessive, **-n-** is the extra consonant that separates the possessive and case suffixes, and the final **-i** is the accusative, and its plural form **-lerini**. Some examples:

**Erol'un yeni evini gördün mü?**
Have you seen Erol's new house?

**Yeğenimin kutularını yeni dairesine götürüyorum.**
I'm taking my nephew's boxes to his new flat.

Demonstratives have the same effect as possessives. Just like 'your town', 'this town' singles out one particular town, so it is definite. Nouns with **bu**, **şu** or **o** in front of them must be marked with the accusative case if they are used as a direct object:

**Bu kitabı okudun mu?**
Have you read this book?

**O kızı görüyor musunuz? Kız arkadaşım.**
Do you see that girl over there? That's my girlfriend.

Some words are inherently definite even if they are not marked with a possessive suffix. This is so because they refer to one and only one thing. Examples include names of people, countries, institutions etc.; after all, there is only one Turkey or Ali. So these too always get marked with the accusative case when they are direct objects.

**Emel'i tanıyor musun?**
Do you know Emel?

**Cuma günü Pamukkale'yi gördük.**
On Friday we saw Pamukkale.

## Exercise 8

The following English sentences all contain nouns. Say which of those would get accusative case if the sentences were to be translated into Turkish.

1 Did you mail the letter?
2 Are you going to write him a letter?
3 He's walking his dog.
4 Did you see that movie?
5 I'm waiting for a friend.
6 We're watching the match tonight.
7 Cengiz really likes Fatma.
8 Extinguish your cigarette please.
9 Do you want a drink?
10 Little Ahmet wants that car.

## Exercise 9

Give the accusative form of the following:

| | |
|---|---|
| 1 **kedi** | 6 **bu** |
| 2 **adam** | 7 **ev** |
| 3 **kadın** | 8 **pencere** ('*window*') |
| 4 **bisiklet** ('*bicycle*') | 9 **sen** |
| 5 **mektup** | 10 **kitap** |

11 araba                          16 lamba (*'lamp'*)
12 çocuk                          17 otobüs (*'bus'*)
13 ziyaret (*'visit'*)            18 gazete
14 o                              19 ben
15 eskisi                         20 kız arkadaşı

## Exercise 10

Translate the following sentences.

1 **Dün akşam erkek kardeşinize telefon ettim.**
2 **Bu yaz tatil için Azerbaycan'a gidiyoruz.**
3 **Pervin'in çayı en güzeli.**
4 **Filiz'in Amerikalı arkadaşı bugün varıyor.**
5 I can't believe the price of these aubergines.
6 Rahime's friend got married last week.
7 Ahmet's girlfriend works in Istanbul.
8 I'm looking for your brother's address (**adres**).

**inanamamak**       to not be able to believe
**inanmak**          to believe

## Exercise 11

In the dialogues of this lesson, identify all possessive, genitive and accusative suffixes. Keep genitive–possessive combinations together as single units.

# 7 Yedide gideceğiz
## We'll leave at seven

In this lesson you will learn how to:

* express your intentions, wishes and future plans
* say the days of the week
* urge people to do something
* use 'let's' do something
* practise pronunciation
* tell the time
* talk about the future
* say when you did something
* express some useful 'time' words

## 🎧 Dialogue 1 (Audio 2: 1)
## Kamp yapacağız
## We'll go camping

*Nursen calls her friend İpek about holiday plans*

İPEK:      Alo?
NURSEN:    Merhaba. Benim.
İPEK:      Merhaba Nursen! Ne zaman gideceksiniz?
NURSEN:    Otobüs öğleden sonra kalkacak. Bu sabah tatil üzerine
           konuştuk, yani ne yapacağımızı filan. Planlarımızı
           duymak istiyor musun?
İPEK:      Tabii, anlat!
NURSEN:    Oldu. Dinle o zaman. Bu akşam Fethiye'ye vardıktan
           sonra, çadırlarımızı kuracağız, kamp yapacağız. Yarın,
           pazartesi günü, plaja gideceğiz. Tatil köyü denize çok
           yakın. Salı günü bir müzeyi ziyaret edeceğiz. Çarşamba

günü çarşıda alışveriş yapacağız. Perşembe günü bir
tekneyle biraz gezeceğiz. Adaları gezmek istiyoruz. Ne
yazık ki, cuma günü tatilimiz bitecek!

## Sözcükler

| | | | |
|---|---|---|---|
| **kamp yapmak** | to camp | **kurmak** | to prepare, put up |
| **kamp yapacağız** | we'll go camping | **plaj** | beach |
| **alo** | hello | **gideceğiz** | we'll go |
| **gideceksiniz** | you'll go | **köy** | village |
| **kalkacak** | it'll leave | **yakın (-e)** | near, close to |
| **üzerine** | about | **deniz** | sea |
| **ne yapacağımızı** | what we will do | **ziyaret etmek** | to pay a visit |
| **plan** | plan | **ziyaret edeceğiz** | we'll visit |
| **duymak** | to hear | **alışveriş yapacağız** | we'll do shopping |
| **anlat!** | tell! | **tekne** | little boat |
| **oldu** | OK | **gezeceğiz** | we'll sail around |
| **dinle!** | listen! | **ada** | island |
| **dinlemek** | to listen | **yazık** | pity |
| **vardıktan sonra** | after arriving | **ne yazık ki!** | what a pity! |
| **çadır** | tent | **bitecek** | it'll finish |
| **kuracağız** | we'll put up | | |

## Language points

### Future plans and intentions

Until now, we have looked at saying things by using **-iyor** verbs
for the present tense and **-di** for the past tense. But, when you
want to express emotions, attitudes, intentions etc., you will need
different verb forms. These are introduced here and in the next
lesson.

Now, in Dialogue 1, Nursen expresses future plans and intentions.
She uses the suffix **-ecek** or **-acak**, after vowels **-yecek** or **-yacak**.
Although it is tempting to see it as the equivalent of the English
'going to', Turkish **-ecek** indicates a wish, willingness, intention or
commitment (more like English 'shall'/'will'). It does not just state
what is going to happen, but expresses what the speaker *wants* to
happen, or is *planning* to do. Though it is basically true that **-iyor**
refers to things happening *now*, **-di** to things that happened in the

*past*, and -ecek to things that will happen in the *future*, there is more to it than just that: -ecek also expresses the emotion and attitude of the speaker. Examples:

**Buraya gelecek.**
He'll come here.

**Haftaya karar verecek.**
She'll decide in a week.

**Mektubu yazacak, eminim!**
She'll write the letter, I'm sure!

**Başlayanlar için yeni dil kursu yarın başlayacak.**
The new language course for beginners will start tomorrow.

The personal endings (indicating 'I', 'you' etc.) are the same as with -iyor. That means you already know that these are, in singular, -im for the first, and -sin for the second person; in plural -iz for the first, -siniz for the second, and -ler for the third person. Remember that a -k- between two vowels often becomes a -ğ- in Turkish (e.g. konuk 'guest' plus case suffix -a becomes konuğa 'to the guest'). Likewise, the first persons singular and plural of the future tense are not -ecekim and -ecekiz, but -eceğim and -eceğiz. Examples:

**Senin için yapacağım.**
I'll do that for you.

**Garda buluşacağız.**
We'll meet at the station.

**Dış İşleri Bakanları müzeyi yarın sabah ziyaret edecekler.**
The ministers of Foreign Affairs will visit the museum tomorrow morning.

**Hesabı resepsiyonda ödeyeceksiniz.**
You'll pay the bill at reception.

### Exercise 1

Find the right forms, using the future marker -ecek, as has been done for the first item:

| | | | |
|---|---|---|---|
| 1 başlamak | we | başlayacağız | |
| 2 ödemek | I | _____ | ('to pay') |
| 3 girmek | you (*plural*) | _____ | ('to enter') |

| 4 söylemek | they | _____ | |
|---|---|---|---|
| 5 sormak | you (*singular*) | _____ | |
| 6 tanışmak | we | _____ | |
| 7 iyi bir öğrenci olmak | you (*singular*) | _____ | |
| 8 kapatmak | I | _____ | ('to close') |
| 9 tamamlamak | they | _____ | ('to finish something') |
| 10 denemek | you (*plural*) | _____ | ('to try') |
| 11 uymak | it | _____ | ('to satisfy') |
| 12 uyumak | they | _____ | ('to sleep') |

## Exercise 2

Translate the text on the postcard:

Fatih Sultan Mehmet 15.Yüzyıl
Portrait of Mehmet II (the Conqueror) 15th Century

*Fethiye, 28. 07. 1999*

TÜRKİYE CUMHURİYETİ

Merhaba John!

Dalaman'dan sonra Fethiye'ye geldik. Burası çok güzel, sokaklar cıvıl cıvıl. Yarın dünyanın en temiz deniz kıyısı, "Ölüdeniz" e gideceğiz. Biraz güneşleneceğiz, biraz da yüzeceğiz. Öbür gün Saklıkent'i görmeye gideceğiz. Fethiye'den selamlar,

Ertuğrul

Sayın John Adams
11 New Fetter Lane
London EC4P 4EE
İngiltere

TUR-KART
Turistik Yayıncılık Kartpostalcılık
Sanay ve Ticaret A.Ş. Sirkeci İstanbul

HER HAKKI MAHFUZDUR

| burası | this place | deniz kıyısı | coast |
|---|---|---|---|
| cıvıl cıvıl | lively | güneşlenmek | to sunbathe |
| dünya | world | yüzmek | to swim |
| temiz | clean | öbür gün | the day after tomorrow |

# Language points

## Days of the week

Recall that the names of days of the week are

| Sunday | pazar |
| Monday | pazartesi |
| Tuesday | salı |
| Wednesday | çarşamba |
| Thursday | perşembe |
| Friday | cuma |
| Saturday | cumartesi |

If you want to say 'on Sunday', you don't have to express the English 'on':

**Pazar günü çarşıya gittik** (*or:* **pazar çarşıya gittik**).
On Sunday we went to the centre of town.

For regular activities on a certain day of the week, use the plural form:

**Pazar günleri çarşıya giderdik.**
On Sundays we used to go to the centre of town.

**Çarşamba günleri İngilizce dersimiz var.**
On Wednesdays we have English classes.

Instead of **pazar günleri** and **çarşamba günleri**, **pazarları** and **çarşambaları** are also possible.

## Other functions of -ecek

Apart from future plans and intentions, you can also use **-ecek** for what you want to happen, or what you want another person to do (**-eceksin**). The functions range from a kind but strong suggestion to a rather fierce command:

**Ödevini yapacaksın.**
You are going to do your homework.

**Şimdi dinleyeceksin!**
And now you'll listen!

**Çenesini kapatacak!**
He will have to shut up! (*literally:* he'll shut his chin)

## Exercise 3

Translate the following monologue into English.
Gelecek hafta Ankara'ya taşınacağız. Umarım, komşularımız iyi
çıkar. Bir yerde durabilmek için, iyi bir komşu şart. Taşındıktan
sonra, bütün komşularımızı davet edeceğiz. Tatilden sonra,
çocuğum yeni bir okula gidecek, yeni arkadaşları olacak.

| umarım | I hope | çıkar | they turn out |
| komşu | neighbour | bütün | all |

| durabilmek | to be able to stand, to be able to feel at home |
| taşındıktan sonra | after we'll have moved |

How did you figure out what **şart** means? And **-dıktan sonra**? How
do you apparently say 'to make friends'? Do you know the difference between **-dıktan sonra** and **-den/-dan sonra**?

## Other ways of expressing future events

Both **-iyor** verb forms and forms with the future marker **-ecek** can
express future events. There is, however, a difference. Whereas an
**-iyor** verb merely states that a certain event is going to happen, an
**-ecek** verb expresses the speaker's confidence (he or she is *sure*)
that such and such *will* happen.

Compare:

**Yarın geliyorum.**
I am coming tomorrow. (*rather indefinite statement*)
**Yarın geleceğim.**
I will come tomorrow. (*confident assumption: I want to come,
so count on me, I'll be there*)

**Ağustosta İstanbul'dayım.**
In August, I'll be staying in Istanbul. (*neutral statement*)
**Ağustosta İstanbul'da olacağım.**
In August, I'll stay in Istanbul. (*I am planning to do that*)

**Bu akşam annene bir mektup yazıyorsun, değil mi?**
Tonight you'll write a letter to your mother, won't you?
(*neutral statement*)
**Bu akşam annene bir mektup yazacaksın.**
Tonight you'll write a letter to your mother. (*I want you to do
that*)

## Exercise 4

Translate the following sentences into Turkish. More than one translation may be possible. Nevertheless, in choosing the verb tense, keep the differences in context in mind!

1 Tomorrow I'll go to the beach.
2 Next week they'll come to my house.
3 Kutlay is coming tomorrow.
4 I will definitely come to your party.
5 This evening you'll work!

| mutlaka | definitely | parti | party |
| --- | --- | --- | --- |

# Language points

## Negation and questions of -ecek

Negative future forms (meaning 'won't' or 'not going to') contain the negative suffix **-me** or **-ma**, which is placed after the stem, before the future marker **-ecek**. This is the same order as used in **Negation** in Lesson 5 when negating verbs in the **-iyor** tense. You also learned there that the negation of **-iyor** forms is always shortened to a single **-m-** (as in **gel-m-iyorum**). The negation of **-ecek**, on the other hand, requires an additional **-y-** between the final vowel of the negation and the initial vowel of the future marker:

| **gelmeyeceksin** | you will not come |
| --- | --- |
| **kalmayacağım** | I will not stay |
| **başlamayacağız** | we will not begin |

In questions, the form to use is the stem (with or without the negation marker **me/ma**) plus **-ecek**, then the question marker **mi**, and finally a personal ending.

**Gelecek misin?**
Will you come? (= stem **gel-** + future marker **-ecek** + question marker **mi** + personal ending **-sin**)

**Buraya gelmeyecek misiniz?**
Won't you come here?

**Okumaya başlamayacaklar mı?**
Won't they start to read?

As the last example shows, the third person plural is again the exception to the rule. This won't cause too much trouble, though, since it is the same principle (-**lar** attaches to the verb, not to the question marker) as we saw in -**iyor** and -**di** (**gidiyorlar mı?** and **gittiler mi?**).

## Exercise 5

Translate into Turkish:

1 I won't listen to that nonsense.
2 Ülkü is not intending to speak English to our American neighbour.
3 Will you buy milk?
4 We won't give him a present.
5 Won't they pay the bill?

| **laflar, saçmalık** | nonsense | **hesap** | bill |
| **süt** | milk | | |

 **Dialogue 2** (Audio 2: 2)

# Hadi, gidelim

## Come on, let's go

DEMET: Gidelim mi?
ŞENER: Dur be. Kamp malzemelerimizi henüz kontrol etmedik, değil mi? Her şey var mı? Her şey çalışıyor mu? (*checks luggage*) El feneri, çekiç, kibrit, çakı, uyku tulumu, çadır, cibinlik ... Aman, cibinliğimiz yok. Bu mevsimde dağlarda sivrisinek çok. Mutlaka bir cibinlik kullanacağız! Hemen bir tane alayım.

*Şener goes out and after a while returns with a mosquito net*

ŞENER: Buyurun. Güzel bir cibinlik buldum. Şimdi hazırız. Hadi, kalkalım!
DEMET: Otur. Biraz daha bekleyelim. Hasan demin telefon etti. Biraz geç kaldı, fakat mutlaka bizimle birlikte gitmek istiyor. Bu arada bir çay içelim!

# Sözcükler

| | | | |
|---|---|---|---|
| **gidelim** | let's go | **cibinlik** | mosquito net |
| **dur be** | wait! | **dağ** | mountain |
| **kamp malze-** | our camping | **sivrisinek** | mosquito |
| **melerimizi** | equipment | **kullanmak** | to use |
| **şey** | thing | **alayım** | let me take |
| **el** | hand | **kalkalım** | let's leave |
| **el feneri** | torch | **otur!** | sit! |
| **çekiç** | hammer | **bekleyelim** | let's wait |
| **kibrit** | match | **demin** | just now |
| **çakı** | pocket knife | **birlikte (ile)** | together |
| **uyku tulumu** | sleeping bag | **bu arada** | meanwhile |
| **çadır** | tent | **içelim** | let's drink |

## Language points

### Let us . . .

The most common form in 'let's' or 'let me' sentences is the subjunctive **-eyim**. The ending is placed after the verb stem. Depending on vowel harmony the ending may become **-eyim** or **-ayım**; after a stem that ends in a vowel the ending is **-yeyim** or **-yayım**. This is the first person singular form. The first person plural form is frequently used as well. This form is **-elim**, **-alım**, **-yelim** or **-yalım** and means 'let's' . . .

Whereas **-ecek** is used to convey a future plan that with some *certainty* will be carried out, **-eyim** and **-elim** refer to an intended or proposed action. Either you want to perform this action right now, immediately after you say it, or you have the intention to do it later. The first person plural form also conveys meanings such as willingness (compare the English 'we could' . . .), invitation or proposal. When used in a question, the proposal meaning is stronger.

| | |
|---|---|
| **Bak, sana anlatayım.** | Come on, let me explain it to you. |
| **Kalkalım.** | Let's leave, let's go. |
| **Kapıyı kapatayım mı?** | Shall I close the door? |
| **Haftaya hamama gidelim.** | Let's go to the Turkish bath next week. |

Compare the following three examples:

| | |
|---|---|
| **İngiltere'ye dönelim mi?** | Shall we go back to Britain? |
| | (*now, right away, proposal*) |
| **İngiltere'ye dönecek miyiz?** | Will we go back to Britain? |
| | (*some time in future, intention*) |
| **İngiltere'ye dönüyor muyuz?** | Are we going back to Britain? |
| | (*statement about near future*) |

In the **dönelim** case the speaker himself does the proposal. On the other hand, in the second and third sentences, the speaker doesn't know exactly what the plans are. The first and second sentence can be said by a husband to his wife or vice versa, when they are English and have been living in Turkey for quite some time; the third by their child who has overheard them talking about it. In the **dönecek** case the decision has already been made without the speaker's knowledge. The first can also be an ironic statement, said to the travel companion who hasn't stopped moaning since arriving in Turkey.

### Exercise 6

With what you know about **-ecek**, try to explain why you cannot use **-ecek** for 'let's'.

### Exercise 7

Try to propose the following in Turkish:

1 to have a drink (**içmek**), let's say coffee
2 to return (**dönmek**) to the airport (**havaalanı**)
3 to travel around (**gezmek**) Turkey
4 to sit down (**oturmak**)
5 to open (**açmak**) the parcel (**paket**)
6 to try (**denemek**) tripe soup (**işkembe çorbası**)
7 to give (**vermek**) the right (**doğru**) answer (**yanıt** or **cevap**)
8 to go (**gitmek**) to the cinema
9 to go for a walk (**yürüyüş yapmak**)
10 to have dinner (**akşam yemeği yemek**) together (**beraber**)

### Desire

Turkish has another option for expressing a desire, in addition to the subjunctive **-eyim/-elim**. You can also use the verb **istemek** 'to want'. This conveys a more definite, well-considered and sometimes also stronger desire. Examples:

**Baklava almak istiyorum.**
I want to take (*or* buy) baklava.

**Baklava alayım.**
Let me take (*or* buy) baklava.

**Çocuklar patates yemek istiyorlar.**
The children want to eat potatoes.

In the first example, you have already decided to buy baklava. Therefore, you are ready to go to the shop. In the second case, you're in the shop or at the restaurant, where you decide on the spot that you want to have some baklava.

## Exercise 8

By now, your head must be spinning from all the different functions all these forms can have. To bring things into focus, fill in the following items in the tree diagram below, so that it reflects the relation between the Turkish forms at the bottom and the functions above them.

1 desire
2 strong intention
3 **-eyim**
4 **-elim**
5 **istemek**

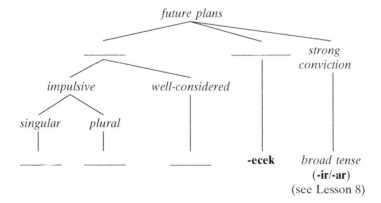

114

 **Colloquial pronunciation** (Audio 2: 3)

Both future and subjunctive endings have some peculiarities in pronunciation, and sometimes in spelling as well. The first peculiarity occurs when the verb stem ends in -e or -a. The -e or -a is pronounced as -i or -ı, e.g. **başlayacaksınız** becomes **başlıyacaksınız** in speech. Other examples:

| | | | |
|---|---|---|---|
| **ödeyeceğim** | I'll pay | *becomes* | **ödiyeceğim** |
| **isteyeceğim** | | *becomes* | **istiyeceğim** |
| **söyleyeyim** | | *becomes* | **söyliyeyim** |

Two frequently used one-syllable verbs are actually written this way:

**yemek** to eat **yiyeceğim** he'll eat (and not *yeyeceğim*)
**demek** to say, speak **diyecek** he'll say (and not *deyeceğim*)

The future and subjunctive forms may be reduced even further in ordinary speech. The first person singular form **-eceğim/-acağım** is often reduced to **-ecem/-acam**; first person plural **-eceğiz/-acağız** to **-ecez/-acaz**. Vowel harmony causes the pronunciation of future and subjunctive forms to be different from the written forms, and finally, dialect differences play a role here. The forms **-ecen/-acan** for second person singular (instead of **-eceksin/-acaksın**) are common in daily speech.

Therefore:

| | | |
|---|---|---|
| **kalacağım** | *can become* | **kalıcam** |
| **ödeyeceğiz** | | **ödüycez** |
| **başlayayım** | | **başlayım** |
| **yapayım** | | **yapim** |
| **söyliyeyim** | | **söyleyim** |
| **içecek misin** | | **içecen mi?** |

Even though you may ask people to slow down (**yavaş!**), you could still hear these forms.

## Telling the time

For telling the time in Turkish, you need to use the locative (place where something is, **-de**, **-da**, **te** or **-ta**; see Lesson 3), dative (place towards which one goes, **-e**, **-a**, **-ye**, **-ya**; see Lesson 3) and accusative (used for direct objects, **-i**, **-ı**, **-u**, **ü**, **-yi**, **-yı**, **-yu**, **-yü**; see Lesson 6) case endings. An important word when telling the time is **saat** (hour), which is used in most time expressions. The question 'What's the time?' is **Saat kaç?** Answering it is easy when it is on the hour, since you use the verbless 'It is ...' pattern:

| | |
|---|---|
| **Saat kaç?** | What's the time? |
| **Saat beş.** | It's five (o'clock). |

For the other times, however, you use full sentences with **-iyor** or **var**. Other important words for telling the time are **çeyrek** ('quarter') and **geçiyor** (from the verb **geçmek**, 'to pass'). They are used in telling the times between the hours. Taking **saat dört**, 'four o'clock', as a starting point, you use **geçiyor** until you reach **saat dört buçuk** ('half past four'), and from then on you use **var** (to indicate how many minutes *there are* left until the next hour). In the first half hour **dört** is your reference point; in the second half hour **beş** is. Of those, the first number is in the accusative case and the other one is in the dative case. This gives us:

| | |
|---|---|
| **dördü beş geçiyor** | it's five past four |
| **dördü on geçiyor** | it's ten past four |
| **dördü çeyrek geçiyor** | it's a quarter past four |
| **dördü yirmi sekiz geçiyor** | it's twenty-eight minutes past four |
| **dört buçuk** | it's half past four |
| **beşe yirmi var** | it's twenty to five |
| **beşe çeyrek var** | it's a quarter to five |
| **beşe beş var** | it's five to five |

An idiosyncrasy is the expression for 12:30 in the afternoon, which is **saat yarım**, using one of the two words for 'half' (although you sometimes hear people say **on iki buçuk**). To express all other half hours use **buçuk**.

Now you should be able to understand the following dialogue.

## 🎧 Dialogue 3 (Audio 2: 4)

## Tam beşte kalkan bir tren var mı?

### Is there a train at exactly five o'clock?

*Mehmet is standing in line in front of the ticket booth at the train station. Lokman is the **gişe memuru**, the ticket salesman*

MEHMET: Affedersiniz, saatiniz var mı?
LOKMAN: Dört buçuk.
MEHMET: Saat beşte kalkan bir tren var mi?
LOKMAN: Evet, var.
MEHMET: Nereye?
LOKMAN: İstanbul'a.
MEHMET: Tam beşte mi kalkıyor?
LOKMAN: Hayır, beşi beş geçe kalkacak.
MEHMET: Maalesef. Bursa'ya giden tren kaçta kalkıyor?
LOKMAN: Bursa treni saat 16.45'te kalkıyor, yani beşe çeyrek kala.
MEHMET: Tam beşte kalkan bir tren yok mu?
LOKMAN: Maalesef yok.
MEHMET: O zaman yarın yine deneyeceğim. İyi günler.
LOKMAN: İyi günler, efendim. *(whispers)* İlginç bir tip!

## Sözcükler

| | | | |
|---|---|---|---|
| **tam** | precisely, exactly | **kala** | at . . . to . . . (*used in* |
| **kalkan** | leaving (*from* **kalkmak**) | | *time-telling*) |
| **geçe** | at . . . past . . . . (*used in* | **yine** | again |
| | *time-telling*) | **ilginç** | interesting |
| **giden** | going (from **gitmek**) | **tip** | character |

## Language point

### Digital time-telling

In these modern times it is also possible to resort to digital time-telling, for which you only need to know the numbers. You often use this at places like airports and train stations.

**Bursa'ya giden tren saat on altı kırk beşte kalkıyor.**
The train to Bursa will leave at 16.45.

 *Exercise 9* (Audio 2: 5)

Write the digital times in full, and convert them into regular Turkish time-telling.

**Saat kaç?**

| | | |
|---|---|---|
| 1 13.26 | on üç yirmi altı | biri yirmi altı geçiyor |
| 2 23.07 | | |
| 3 08.43 | | |
| 4 12.30 | | |
| 5 13.01 | | |
| 6 04.58 | | |
| 7 02.32 | | |
| 8 18.27 | | |
| 9 11.11 | | |
| 10 21.49 | | |

Other useful words:

| | | |
|---|---|---|
| **hemen hemen** | almost | |
| **bir iki geçiyor** | just after | as in **altıyı bir iki geçiyor** |
| | | 'it's just after seven' |
| **sularında** | at about | |
| **yarım saat** | half an hour | |
| **beri** [+ -den/-dan] | since | as in **saat on birden beri** |
| | | 'since 11 o'clock' |

The other question that often comes up when time is concerned, is **(saat) kaçta?**, which asks when something is going to take place. In answering these, the locative case (**-de**, **-da**, **-te** or **-ta**, see Lesson 3) must be used as long as the time is an exact hour or half hour:

**Bu akşam konser kaçta başlıyor?**
When does the concert start tonight?

**Sekiz buçukta başlıyor.**
It's starting at eight thirty.

**Müze saat kaçta kapanıyor?**
At what time does the museum close?

**Saat altıda.**
At six.

Note that you do not always have to use **saat**, though it is never wrong to use it. Some more examples:

| | |
|---|---|
| **Uçak kaçta varıyor?** | When does the plane arrive? |
| **Onda.** | At ten. |

For the other times, things are again a little more complicated. While **geçiyor** and **var** are used in saying what time it is now, two other words, **geçe** ('passed') and **kala** ('remaining') are used in

## ▬▬ sinema ▪ ▪ sinema ▬▬

Cherbourg Şemsiyeleri, Jacques Deny
Bunker Palace Hotel, Enki Bilal
Taş Yıllar, Pantelis Vulgaris
Türk Tutkusu, Vicente Aranda
Tutsaklar, Angela Pope
Ölümü Beklerken, Bertrand Tovernier
Elenya, Steve Gough

**Üç Ustadan Üç Film :**
Kartal Taçlı Yüzük
Yön : Andrej Wojda
Gündüz Güzeli
Yön: Luis Bunuel
Yüzyüze,
Yön : I. Bergman

**19 Mart Türk Dünyası Sineması Günü :**
Yıldızımı Bana Ver, Ferit Devletin, Özbekistan
Sampiyon, Muhammed Soyunhanov, türkmenistan
Ölüm Meleği, Manabayev, Kazakistan
Umutla, Marat Sarulu, Kırgızistan
Kar Leoparının Soyu, Tölömöş Okeyev, Kırgızistan
Kurt Sultanı, Tölömöş Okeyev, Kırgızistan
Evin Nerade Salyangoz, Aktan Abdikalıkov, Kırgızistan
Tahmine, Rasım Ocagev, Azerbaycan
Suyun Öte Yanı, Tomris Gırıtlıoğlu, Türkiye

### FESTİVAL PROGRAMI

**KAVAKLIDERE SİNEMASI**

**15 MART CUMA**
12.30 Xinqua'nın Öyküsü
15.30 Tanık
18.30 Yeniden Tanık
21.30 Sevdiğim Mevsim

**16 MART CUMARTESİ**
12.30 Taş Yıllar
15.30 Yeşil Papayanın Kokusu
18.30 Shangai Triad
21.00 Kartal Taçlı Yüzük, Beyaz Geceler : Tanık, Xinqua'nın Öyküsü, Macon Bebeği, kısa film

**17 MART PAZAR**
12.30 Macon Bebeği
15.30 Sevdiğim Mevsim
18.30 Tanık
21.00 Yeniden Tanık (Yönetmenle söyleşi)

**18 MART PAZARTESİ**

12.30 Xinqua'nın Öyküsü
15.30 Profesör Hannibal
18.30 101 Gece
21.00 Onbin Güneş

**19 MART SALI**
12.30 Şampiyon (yönetmenle söyleşi)
15.30 Kurt Sultanı (yönetmenle söyleşi)
18.30 Kar Leoparın Soyu
21.00 Kar Leoparının Soyu

**20 MART ÇARŞAMBA**
12.30 Profesör Hannibal
15.30 Aşk
18.30 Yeşil Papayanın Kokusu
21.00 Profesör Hannibal

**21 MART PERŞEMBE**
12.30 Yeşil Papayanın Kokusu
15.30 Kimse Beni Sevmiyor
18.30 Sevdiğim Mevsim
21.00 On Bin Güneş

**22 MART CUMA**
12.30 Tanık
15.30 Yeniden Tanık
18.30 Shangai Triad
21.00 Xinqua'nın Öyküsü

**23 MART CUMARTESİ**
12.30 Aşk
15.30 Shangai Triad
18.30 Macon Bebeği
21.00 Xinqua'nın Öyküsü
Beyaz Geceler : Profesör Hannibal, Aşk, Taş Yıllar, kısa film

**24 MART PAZAR**
12.30 Aşk
15.30 Taş Yıllar
18.30 Kimse Beni Sevmiyor
21.00 101 Gece

**MEGAPOL**

*Mavi Salon*

**15 MART CUMA**
12.15 Bunker Palace Hotel
15.15 Ölümü Beklerken
18.15 Türk Tutkusu
21.15 Ölümü Beklerken

**16 MART CUMARTESİ**
12.15 Düş Gerçek Bir De Sinema (Yönetmenle söyleşi)
15.15 Bir Kadının Anatomisi
18.15 Yüzyüze
21.15 İstanbul Kanatlarının Altında

▬▬▬▬▬ 7 ▬ ▪ 8 ▬▬▬▬▬

saying at what time something happened or will happen. Everything else remains the same. The case endings are again accusative with **geçe** and dative with **kala**:

| | |
|---|---|
| **Dokuzu on bir geçe** | at eleven past nine |
| **Saat dokuzu yirmi beş geçe** | at twenty-five past nine |
| **Saat ona çeyrek kala sularında** | at about a quarter to ten |
| **Ona beş kala** | at five to ten |
| **Yarımda** | at twelve thirty p.m. |
| **Yarım saatte** | in half an hour |

### Exercise 10

Look at the timetable above of the International Film Festival in Ankara and compile your own programme of films. You may choose between three locations: **Kavaklıdere**, the **Megapol Mavi Salon** and the **Megapol Kırmızı Salon**. Pretend that you have plenty

sinema ■ ■ sinema

**17 MART PAZAR**
12.15 Özlem... Düne... Bugüne... Yarına (yönetmenle söyleşi)
15.15 Böcek
18.15 Gündüz Güzeli
21.15 Türk Tutkusu

**18 MART PAZARTESİ**
12.15 Kanayan Yara Bosna
15.15 Soğuk Geceler
18.15 Okuyan Kız
21.15 Don Giovanni

**19 MART SALI**
12.15 Sokaktaki Adam
15.15 Gerilla
18.15 Tahmina (yönetmenle söyleşi)
21.15 Suyun Öte Yanı (yönetmenle söyleşi)

**20 MART ÇARŞAMBA**
12.15 Sekizinci Saat
15.15 80. Adım
18.15 Yüzyüze
21.15 Carmen

**21 MART PERŞEMBE**
12.15 Dün Giovanni
15.15 Mezeppa
18.15 Türk Tutkusu
21.15 Carmen

**22 MART CUMA**
12.15 Bunker Palace Hotel
15.15 Mezappa
18.15 Seçiciler kurulu Özel Ödülü
21.15 En İyi Film

**23 MART CUMARTESİ**
12.15 Cherbourg Şemsiyeleri
15.15 Vatanseverler
18.15 Ölümü Beklerken
21.15 Okuyan Kız

**24 MART PAZAR**
12.15 Gündüz Güzeli
15.15 Türk Tutkusu
18.15 Seçiciler Kurulu Özel Ödülü
21.15 En İyi Film

**MEGAPOL**

**Kırmızı Salon**

**15 MART CUMA**
12.00 Vatanseverler
15.00 Cherbourg Şemsiyeleri
18.00 Yüzyüze
21.00 Gündüz Güzeli

**16 MART CUMARTESİ**
12.00 Baba
15.00 Boğmacı
18.00 Elenya
21.00 Captives
Beyaz Geceler : Türk Tutkusu, Boğmaca, Kızıl İlahi, kısa film

**17 MART PAZAR**
12.00 Boğmaca
15.00 Kızıl İlahi
18.00 Umutsuzlar
21.00 Yıldızların Altında

**18 MART PAZARTESİ**
12.00 Umutsuzlar
15.00 Lumiere'in Çocukları
18.00 Düşen Adamlara Bak
21.00 Sevgililer

**19 MART SALI**
12.00 Yıldızımı Bana Geri Ver
Asman (yönetmenle söyleşi)
15.00 Salyangoz Evin Nerede?
18.00 Ölüm Meleği (yönetmenle söyleşi)
21.00 Umutla

**20 MART ÇARŞAMBA**
12.00 Düşen Adamlara Bak
15.00 Normal İnsanların Olağanüstü Hiçbir Şeyi Yoktur
18.00 Kızıl İlahi
21.00 Umutsuzlar

**21 MART PERŞEMBE**
12.00 Elenya
15.00 Yıldızların Altında
18.00 Yüzyüze
21.00 Baba

**22 MART CUMA**
12.00 Normal İnsanların Olağanüstü Hiçbir Şeyi Yoktur
15.00 Yıldızların Altında
18.00 Boğmaca
21.00 Ölümü Beklerken
Beyaz Geceler : Baba, Okuyan Kız, Ulusal Uzun Film Seçiciler Kurulu Özel Ödülü, kısa film

**23 MART CUMARTESİ**
12.00 Boğmaca
15.00 Normal İnsanların Olağanüstü Hiçbir Şeyi Yoktur
18.00 Kızıl İlahi
21.00 Captives
Beyaz Geceler : Ulusal Uzun Film Yarışması En İyi Film, Umutsuzlar, Yüzyüze

**24 MART PAZAR**
12.00 Kızıl İlahi
15.00 Sevgililer
18.00 Baba
21.00 Vatanseverler
• Programda küçük değişiklikler olabilir.

**9 ■ ■ 10**

of time and money to see two films a day, for three days in a row (March 15 through March 17). If you plan carefully enough, you will be able to see two films a day without having to rush to the next movie and miss the ending of the first one.

For the sake of the exercise, try to be as explicit as you can. For instance, on Friday 15 March you want to see the film **Türk Tutkusu** *Turkish Passion* at 18.15 at the Mavi Salon of the Megapol. You may say:

*Friday:*

1 Cuma günü saat altıyı çeyrek geçe Megapol'da Türk Tutkusu filmini seyretmek istiyorum.

2 _____

*Saturday:*

3 _____

4 _____

*Sunday:*

5 _____

6 _____

Let's explore the Turkish time system a little more. You may have to state from when until when you will be or were at a given place. You'll have to use the **-den/-dan** case for 'from' and the dative case **-e/-a** plus **kadar** for 'until'. Examples:

**Saat sekizden dokuza kadar spor salonundaydım.**
From 8 until 9 o'clock I was at the sports centre.

**Ondan on buçuğa kadar alışveriş yaptı.**
From 10 until 10.30 he went shopping.

**On buçuktan on bire kadar kiraathanedeydi.**
From 10.30 until 11 he was at the café.

## Exercise 11

Try to sort out Ali's daily schedule by rearranging times and actions. Use the locative ending **-de/-da** for points in time at which something happens, and use the combination of **-den/-dan** and **-e/-a kadar** for longer periods of time. Make full sentences, for instance:

17.30–18.00    **Saat beş buçuktan (saat) altıya kadar yemek pişirdi.**

Choose from the following actions:

**yemek pişirdi** ('cooked dinner'); **kitap okudu; kalktı; yemeğini yedi; parkta koştu** ('ran'); **çalıştı; arabayla iş yerine gitti; evine döndü; kahvaltı yaptı; televizyon seyretti; yattı; giyindi.**

| | | | | |
|---|---|---|---|---|
| 7.00 | : | | 17.30–18.00 | : |
| 7.00–7.30 | : | | 18.00–18.30 | : |
| 7.30–8.00 | : | | 18.30–19.00 | : |
| 8.00–8.30 | : | | 19.00–22.00 | : |
| 8.30–17.00 | : | | 22.00–23.00 | : |
| 17.00–17.30 | : | | 23.00 | : |

| | | | |
|---|---|---|---|
| **pişirmek** | to cook | **koşmak** | to run |
| **yatmak** | to lie down | **giyinmek** | to get dressed |

# Vocabulary

In this lesson you learned how to express future events, and how to express time in Turkish. Below, you will find a lot of time words (most occur throughout this book).

| | | | |
|---|---|---|---|
| **akşamları/** | in the evenings | **ilk** | first |
| **akşamleyin** | | **ilkbaharda** | in spring |
| **ay** | month | **kışın** | in the wintertime |
| **bazen** | sometimes | **mevsim** | season |
| **bir gün** | one day | **nihayet** | finally, in the end |
| **birazdan** | just before, a | **o zaman** | then |
| | little while ago | **önce** | before |
| **daha** | still, not yet | **saatinde** | on time |
| **demin** | just before | **saatlerce** | for hours |
| **dün sabah** | yesterday | **sabah akşam** | all day long |
| | morning | **sabah sabah** | very early |
| **erken** | early | **sabahları/** | in the mornings |
| **ertesi gün** | the next day | **sabahleyin** | |
| **evvelki gün** | the day before | **saniye** | second |
| | yesterday | **seneye** | in a year, next |
| **gayrı** | at last, | | year |
| | henceforth | **sık sık** | often |
| **geç** | late | **son** | last |
| **gece gündüz** | night and day | **son zamanlarda** | recently (*in past*) |
| **geceleri** | at night | **sonbaharda** | in autumn |
| **haftaya** | in a week, next | **sonuçta** | in the end |
| | week | **şu anda** | right now |
| **hala** | just, yet, not yet | **yakınlarda** | some time soon |
| **henüz** | still, yet, not yet | | (*in future*) |
| **her zaman** | always | **yarın akşam** | tomorrow evening |
| **her yıl** | every year | **yazın** | in the summer- |
| **hiç bir zaman** | never | | time |

# 8 Sizi bekleriz!

## We're expecting you!

---

In this lesson you will learn how to:

- express habits
- ask for permission
- express obligation or need
- influence people by means of commands and requests

---

 **Dialogue 1** (Audio 2: 6)

## Toplantıda

### In the meeting

*Several friends have gathered for a meeting of the 'İngiltere-Türkiye İşbirliği Vakfı', the foundation for economic and cultural cooperation between Britain and Turkey. The meeting is about to begin*

AYHAN:  *(whispers to Betül)* Hasan gelmedi mi?

BETÜL:  Hayır, gelmedi. Devamlı geç kalır, onu benden daha iyi biliyorsun ...

AYHAN:  Geçen sefer tam zamanında geldi, Mehmet'le beraber. Bugün Mehmet de gelmedi.

BETÜL:  Fakat o mutlaka gelecek. Bak, ne dedim? İşte, Mehmet!

*(Mehmet takes his seat and Orhan starts the meeting)*

ORHAN:  Hadi arkadaşlar, başlayalım mı? Funda, lütfen kapıyı kapatır mısın? Sağ ol. Ayhan, sen bugün not alır mısın? Tamam, gündemde ilk konu vakfımızın başkan seçimleri. Betül, sözü sana verebilir miyim?

BETÜL:  Sağ ol. Şimdiye kadar, aday listesinde tek bir isim var:

Hasan. Ben başka bir kişiyi aday göstermek istiyorum. Seçimler üzerine konuşurken hemen aklıma bir isim geldi: Fatma Hanım. Başkan görevine en uygunu odur. Ekonomi öğrencisidir. Yaz aylarında rehberlik yapar. Turistik seyahat dünyasında iyi ilişkileri var. Hem İngilizcesi, hem de Almancası var. Sanırım, Fatma Hanım'dan daha iyi bir aday yok.

*(After this speech, Fatma is elected as the new chairperson of the foundation)*

## Sözcükler

| | | | |
|---|---|---|---|
| **devamlı** | over and over, repeatedly | **aday göstermek** | to propose a candidate |
| **sefer** | time | **konuşurken** | while talking |
| **tam zamanında** | right on time | **aklıma gelmek** | to come to my mind |
| **bak!** | look! | | |
| **kapatır mısın?** | can you close? | **görev** | function |
| **not almak** | to take notes | **uygun** | fit, capable |
| **not alır mısın?** | can you take notes? | **odur** | she is |
| | | **rehberlik** | to work as a guide |
| **gündem** | agenda | **yapmak** | guide |
| **vakıf** | foundation | **rehberlik yapar** | she works as a guide |
| **başkan** | chairperson | | |
| **seçim** | election | **seyahat** | travel |
| **söz vermek** | to give the word to | **ilişki** | contact, relation |
| **söz verebilir miyim?** | can I give the word? | **Almanca** | German (language) |
| **aday** | candidate | **sanırım** | I think, believe |

## Language points

 **Geniş zaman** (Audio 2: 7)

The 'other' present tense we have mentioned a few times is called **geniş zaman** 'broad time' in Turkish. It refers to (static) situations that have a timeless, general character. You cannot really tell exactly when the situation started or when it will end. For example, when in the dialogue above Betül says about Hasan **geç kalır** 'he is late', she doesn't refer to the actual situation of Hasan being late for the present meeting, but rather to Hasan's habit of being constantly late. Compare the use of the **geniş zaman** to the present tense **-iyor**, which describes actual, dynamic events taking place at the time of speech:

| | |
|---|---|
| **Geç kalır.** | He is late. |
| | (implies that he *always* is) |
| **Geç kalıyor.** | He is late. |
| | (is only true for this *one* occasion) |
| **Sizi beklerim.** | I'm expecting you. |
| | (whenever; used as an invitation) |
| **Sizi bekliyorum.** | I'm waiting for you. |
| | (here and now) |
| **Hakan fabrikada çalışıyor.** | Hakan works at a factory. |
| **Türk işçileri fabrikalarda çalışır.** | Turkish workers work in factories. |

Formation of the **geniş zaman** is complicated: it has three different endings (**-r**, **-ir** and **-er**), depending on the form of the stem. (And there are exceptions.) Once you have extended the stem with the **geniş zaman**, you have to add the usual personal endings (and remember that the third person singular of a verb ('he', 'she', 'it') *never* carries a personal ending):

| | singular | plural |
|---|---|---|
| *1st person* | **-im** | **-iz** |
| *2nd person* | **-sin** | **-siniz** |
| *3rd person* | – | **-ler** |

Let's start with the three **geniş zaman** endings:

1 Add **-r-**, when the verb stem ends in a vowel. Examples:

| **Dinle-r.** | He listens. |
|---|---|
| **Sizi bekle-r-iz.** | We wait for you; we're expecting you. |

2 Add **-er-** (or **-ar-**), when the verb stem consists of only one syllable and ends in a consonant. Examples:

**Bak-ar-sın.** You look.
**Bilmezsem sor-arım.** If I don't know, I ask.
**Ulus'a gid-er mi?** Does it (i.e. the bus) go to Ulus?

3 Add **-ir-** (or **-ır-**, **-ur-**, **-ür-**), when the verb stem consists of more than one syllable and ends in a consonant.

Examples:

**Bagajlarınızı bırak-ır-sınız.**
You leave your luggage.

**Aynı iş yerinde çalıştığımız için, akşamları komşumu evine bırak-ır-ım.**
In the evenings I take my neighbour home, because we work at the same place.

**Teyzem Avrupa'dan hediye getir-ir.**
My aunt brings presents from Europe.

*Exercise 1*

Do the following verbs take **-ir**, **-ar** or **-r**? Give the form in full.

1 **oturmak**
2 **çağırmak** ('to call out')
3 **bitmek**
4 **söylemek**
5 **dökmek** ('to pour')
6 **çimdiklemek** ('to pinch')
7 **kaşımak** ('to scratch')
8 **seçmek**

## Language points

### Exceptions

As we said, there are some exceptions. There is a set of frequently used verbs, all consisting of a one-syllable stem, and most of them ending in **-l** or **-r**, that do not take **-er-**, but **-ir-**:

| | | |
|---|---|---|
| **al-** | take, buy | **alır-** |
| **bil-** | know | **bilir-** |
| **bul-** | find | **bulur-** |
| **gel-** | come | **gelir-** |

| kal- | stay | kalır- |
| ol- | be, become | olur- |
| öl- | die | ölür- |
| dur- | stop, stand | durur- |
| var- | arrive | varır- |
| ver- | give | verir- |
| vur- | shoot, strike | vurur- |
| gör- | see | görür- |
| san- | think | sanır- |

Don't worry too much about these exceptions: you will see and hear them often and learn that they take -ir soon enough.

## Exercise 2

Find the right form. The first one has been done for you.

| 1 oturmak | you (*singular*) | oturursun |
| 2 çağırmak | we | |
| 3 bulmak | they | |
| 4 söylemek | you (*singular*) | |
| 5 dökmek | they | |
| 6 vermek | I | |
| 7 kaşımak | he/she/it | |
| 8 sanmak | you (*plural*) | |

## When to use the geniş zaman

The **geniş zaman** describes a situation which is timeless, general. Therefore, you can use it to talk about habits.

**Çaydan çok kahve içerim.**
I drink more coffee than tea.

**Gazete okur musun?**
Do you read a newspaper? (*in the sense of* 'Are you a regular reader?')

**Yazın dedem koyunlarını yaylaya götürür.**
In summer, my grandfather takes his sheep to the meadow.

Here are some more examples of how to use the **geniş zaman**. You may use it in:

## 'Making promises'

**Yarın gelirim.** I'll come tomorrow.
(This statement is almost like a promise, as it means 'I am someone who makes a habit of being on time, so I will definitely be there tomorrow.')

**Avrupa'ya taşındıktan sonra, orada yaşayan vatandaşlarım için yeni bir gazete yayınlarım.**
After I have moved to Europe I will publish a new newspaper for my fellow citizens who live there.

## 'Making general statements or claims'

**Enflasyon işsizliği artırır.**
Inflation causes unemployment to rise.

**Süt insana güç verir.**
Milk gives people strength.

**Ağustos ayında buğday toplarlar.**
In August they harvest the wheat.

## 'Talking about people's abilities, skills etc.'

(1) basic information:

| | |
|---|---|
| **Babam çok okur.** | My daddy reads a lot. |
| **Ahmet saz çalar.** | Ahmet plays the saz. |

(2) qualities/profession:

**Ben Türkçe konuşurum.**
I speak Turkish. (= I know Turkish)

**Yaz aylarında rehberlik yaparız.**
In the summer months we work as guides.

(3) habits:

| | |
|---|---|
| **Hasan çok içki içer.** | Hasan drinks a lot (of alcohol). |
| **Pembe dizileri sever.** | She loves soap operas. |
| **Yalan söylersin.** | You tell lies. (= You're a liar.) |

## 'Making suggestions'

Here you see the **geniş zaman** in combination with a past tense, comparable to English **would**.

| | |
|---|---|
| **Hap içerdim.** | I would take a pill (if I were you). |
| **Bursa kebap alırdım.** | I would take Bursa kebap (suggestion). |
| **Doktora gidersin.** | You should see a doctor. |

## 'Asking questions'

In questions, the question particle **mi/mı/mu/mü** is placed right after the **-er/-ir/-r** suffix, and before the personal marker (except, as usual, in the case of the third person plural **-ler/-lar**, that precedes **mi/mı/mu/mü**, as in **Gelirler mi?** 'Do they come?').

You can use the **geniş zaman** in questions like these:

1 related to qualities, skills etc.:

| | |
|---|---|
| **Türkçe konuşur musun?** | Do you speak Turkish? |

This not only relates to qualities of persons. It is quite common to ask a bus driver about the direction of the bus, as:

| | |
|---|---|
| **İstanbul'a gider mi?** | Does it go to İstanbul? |

2 polite requests:

| | |
|---|---|
| **Tekrarlar mısın?** | Could you repeat that? |
| **Bana anlatır mısın?** | Could you tell me that? |

The effect of politeness is even stronger when the question is negative. (Don't worry yet about the form.)

| | |
|---|---|
| **Oturmaz mısın?** | Won't you sit down? |
| **Buyurmaz mıydınız?** | Won't you please come in? |
| | (*Literally:* 'Didn't you come in?') |

3 some idiomatic questions:

| | |
|---|---|
| **Olur mu?** | Is that okay? |
| **Bakar mısınız?** | (*to a waiter:*) Could you come please? |
| **Olur mu öyle şey?** | Is such a thing possible? |

## Exercise 3 (Audio 2: 8)

Here are some Turkish sentences. Indicate the function of the verbs in **geniş zaman**. Choose from the following: promise, qualities/ profession, habit, request.

1 Haftaya sana uğrarım.
2 Ablası İngilizce dersi verir.
3 Her gün dokuza kadar çalışırsın.
4 Bana bir mektup yazar mısınız?
5 Arabanı tamir eder.
6 Türkçeden Almancaya çeviri yaparım.
7 Araba tamir ederim.
8 Tabii, yarın şu mektubu İngilizceye çeviririm.

| tamir etmek | to repair |
|---|---|
| çeviri yapmak/çevirmek | to translate |

## Language point

### -iyor **versus the** geniş zaman

Using **-iyor** signals that the action is ongoing. It also means that you are able to say when this action started and when it will probably end. On the other hand, when you hear a verb marked with the **geniş zaman**, you only know that the action may take place, because it is something someone would do out of routine. You don't know for *sure* whether it is actually happening. When someone uses both **-iyor** and the **geniş zaman** in turn, verbs marked with **-iyor** describe the main course of events, and those in the **geniş zaman** the setting or background.

Compare:

| | |
|---|---|
| **Hasan geliyor.** | 'Hasan comes/is coming.' This refers to something that is happening now or will surely happen in the near future. Hasan's 'coming' has a clear beginning and end. |
| **Hasan geç gelir.** | 'Hasan comes late.' This, on the other hand, is a general statement about the probability of Hasan's coming late. It is not a statement about an actual action taking place; it is not even clear when (if at all) Hasan will come. |

The **geniş zaman** is never used with expressions that indicate a time span, such as 'from 9 to 5'. English 'From 9 to 5, she works at a bank' is **Dokuzdan beşe kadar bankada çalısıyor.** (Never **çalışır,** which can only be used as a more general remark, without reference to time: **Bankada çalışır** 'She works at a bank.')

## Exercise 4

Read the following text carefully and translate, paying attention to the verb tenses. Try to work out why a certain tense (**geniş zaman**, present tense **-iyor** or past tense **-di)** is used.

Anneannem koskoca beyaz bir yalıda oturuyor. Her yaz olduğu gibi, bu yaz da anneannemin yanında kalıyorum. Bugün onunla beraber kuşlara yardımcı olmaya çalışıyoruz. Geçen hafta, bize çok yakın bir körfezde büyük bir tanker battı. Petrol denizi kirletti. Bu olay kuşları mahvetti. Ne yapacağımızı bilmedik. Onun için bu sabah veterinere telefon ettim. Kendisi dedi ki: 'Bazı kuşlar kirli sulara bulaştıktan sonra, uçamazlar. Kuşları kurtarmak için genelde bir kepçe kullanırız. Kuşlar biraz toparlandıktan sonra, onları yıkayabilirsiniz.'

| | |
|---|---|
| **anneanne** | grandmother (the mother of your mother) |
| **koskoca** | large, enormous |
| **yalı** | (wooden) house, villa |
| **her yaz olduğu gibi** | like every summer |
| **yanında** | at, next to |
| **kuş** | bird |
| **yardımcı olmak** | to be of help |
| **çalışmak (-e)** | to try |
| **körfez** | bay |
| **batmak** | sink |
| **kirletmek** | to make dirty, to pollute |
| **olay** | situation |
| **mahvetmek** | to damage |
| **ne yapacağımızı** | what we should do |
| **veteriner** | vet |
| **kendisi** | himself/herself (*here:* he/she) |
| **kirli** | dirty, polluted |
| **bulaştıktan sonra** | after coming into contact with |
| **uçmak** | to fly |
| **uçamazlar** | they can't fly |
| **kurtarmak** | to save |

| genelde | in general, generally |
|---|---|
| kepçe | scoop |
| kullanmak | to use |
| toparlanmak | to regain strength |
| toparlandıktan sonra | after regaining strength |
| yıkamak | to wash |
| yıkayabilirsiniz | you can wash |

## Negative forms of the geniş zaman

Recall that for **-iyor** (present) and **-di** (past) sentences, the negation marker is **-me**. The **geniş zaman**, however, has a 'deviant' negation marker, **-mez**, for second and third persons singular and plural.

| Negative | Negative questions | |
|---|---|---|
| Gel-mez- | Gelmez mi? | Doesn't he come? |
| Gel-mez-sin | Gelmez misin? | Don't you come? |
| Gel-mez-siniz | Gelmez misiniz? | Don't you come? |
| Gel-mez-ler | Gelmezler mi? | Don't they come? |

The negated first person forms of the **geniş zaman** are also a bit tricky. In negative questions, the negation marker **-mez** is used. In regular negations, however, the marker is not **-mez**, but **-me**:

| Negative | Negative questions |
|---|---|
| Gel-me-m | Gelmez miyim? |
| Gel-me-yiz | Gelmez miyiz? |
| Oku-ma-m | Okumaz mıyım? |
| Oku-ma-yız | Okumaz mıyız? |

Examples:

| Sana hiç yardım etmez. | He'll never help you. |
|---|---|
| Seni hiç unutmam. | I'll never forget you. |
| Türkçede böyle söylemeyiz. | We don't say it like that in Turkish. |
| Et yemez. | She doesn't eat meat. |
| Sigara içilmez. | No smoking. ('cigarettes are not smoked') |

## Exercise 5

Turn the following sentences into negatives. The first one has been done already.

1 **Haftaya sana uğrarım.** ('I'll visit you next week.') >> ('I won't visit you next week.') = **Haftaya sana uğramam.**
2 **Ablası İngilizce dersi verir.** ('Her sister gives English lessons.')
3 **Her gün dokuza kadar çalışırsın.** ('Every day you work until 9.')
4 **Bana bir mektup yazar mısınız?** ('Will you write me a letter?')
5 **Arabanı tamir eder.** ('He repairs your car.')
6 **Türkçeden Almancaya çeviri yaparım.** ('I translate from Turkish into German.')
7 **Araba tamir ederim.** ('I repair cars.')
8 **Şu mektubu İngilizceye çeviririm.** ('I translate that letter into English.')

## Language point

### The geniş zaman in formulas

The **geniş zaman** is often part of well-known phrases and proverbs:

| | |
|---|---|
| **teşekkür ederim** | thank you |
| **rica ederim!** | I beg you! please! you're welcome! not at all! don't mention it! |
| **tebrik ederim!** | congratulations! |
| **gözlerinizden öperiz** | (*literally:* 'I kiss your eyes', used as a concluding greeting in a letter to someone you know very well) kind regards |
| **yine bekleriz!** | we're expecting you again! please come again! |
| **her horoz kendi çöplüğünde öter** | every cock crows at his own garbage heap |
| **köpeğe atsan yemez** | not even a dog would eat it |
| **çocuk düşe kalka büyür** | a child learns by experience ('grows falling and standing up') |

# 🎧 Dialogue 2 (Audio 2: 9)

## Büyük bir ihale

## A big order

*Ali is called into the director's office*

MÜDÜR: Buyurun, ne içersin?

ALİ: Varsa, orta şekerli kahve içeyim.

MÜDÜR: *(through the intercom)* Hülya Hanım, iki tane orta şekerli kahve getirir misin? *(to Ali)* Tamam. Konuya gelelim. Seni önemli bir iş için buraya çağırdım. Durum şöyle. Devletten büyük bir ihaleyi kazandık. Büyük para kazanacağız, milyarlarca lira! Devlet 5000 tane çakmak sipariş etti. Sadece, bir şartı var. Çakmakları bir ay içinde teslim etmek zorundayız. Ürünümüzü vaktinde teslim edebiliriz, sanırım. Yalnız bu demektir ki, senin ekibinin daha hızlı çalışması lazım.

ALİ: Ama, efendim, şimdi çok kaliteli çakmakları üretebiliyoruz. Daha hızlı çalışırsak, kalite kesinlikle kalmaz.

MÜDÜR: Ali Bey, aslında sana bir soru sormadım, emir verdim. Sen istenilen şartlara uymak durumundasın. Yani daha çok çalışılacaktır. O şekilde üretimimiz artacak. Başka seçeneğimiz yok.

ALİ: *(gives in)* Peki, efendim, nasıl isterseniz . . .

## Sözcükler

| | | | |
|---|---|---|---|
| ihale | order | sadece | just, only |
| varsa | if there is | içinde | within |
| orta şekerli | with normal amount of sugar | teslim etmek | to deliver |
| | | -mek zorunda | to be obliged |
| | | teslim edebiliriz | we can deliver |
| konuya gelmek | come to the point | ürün | product |
| | | bu demektir ki | that means that |
| şöyle | such | ki | that |
| devlet | state | ekip | team |
| büyük para | a lot of money | lazım (-ması) | must |
| çakmak | lighter | kaliteli | of high quality |
| sipariş etmek | to order | isterseniz | if you want |

| üretmek | to produce | -a uymak | to satisfy |
|---|---|---|---|
| üretebiliyoruz | we can produce | şekil | shape, form |
| çalışırsak | if we work | o şekilde | that way |
| kesinlikle | surely, for sure | üretim | production |
| Bey | Sir | artmak | to go up |
| emir vermek | to give an order | seçenek | choice, option |
| istenilen | wanted, required | | |

## Permission and obligation

The suffix **-ebil** means 'to be able to'. It is placed right after the verb stem, but before the tense marker (**-iyor/-di/-ecek** etc.) It is useful to learn it now because it very often occurs in combination with the **geniş zaman**. This makes sense when you think about it, because to be *possible*, you cannot be *sure* if or when the action will happen. Remember that the **geniş zaman** typically refers more to habits than to actual situations.

| | |
|---|---|
| **Gelebilirim.** | I am able to come/ I can come/ I may come. |
| **Anlatabilir miyim?** | Did I make myself understood (was I able to tell)? |
| **Telefon numarasını tek tuşla arayabilirsiniz.** | You can choose the telephone number with one single button. |

The negative form of **-ebil** is **-eme** 'not able to':

| | |
|---|---|
| **Şunu bilemem.** | I cannot know that. |
| **Anlayamam.** | I cannot understand that. |
| **Buraya gelemez.** | He cannot come here. |
| **Bana emir veremezler.** | They cannot give orders to me. |
| **Ne yapacağımızı bilemedik.** | We didn't know what to do. |

In first person questions, **-ebil** is typically used for asking permission:

| | |
|---|---|
| **Pencereyi açabilir miyim?** | May I open the window? |
| **Fotoğraf çekebilir misiniz?** | Could you take a picture? |
| **Notlarınızı okuyabilir miyiz?** | May we read your notes? |

NB: Here, **-ebil** resembles the **geniş zaman**, which is more common in the second person. Compare:

| | |
|---|---|
| **Pencereyi açar mısın?** | Can you open the window? |
| **Fotoğraf çeker misin?** | Can you take a picture? |
| **Notlarınızı okuyabilir mi?** | Can he read your notes? |

## Obligation or need

To express things similar to English 'have to' or 'must', Turkish has a number of options. First, as we already saw in Lesson 7, **-ecek** may denote a necessity ('still have to . . .'). The suffix **-meli** on the other hand, indicates a moral necessity ('should', 'have to'). In choosing between these two possibilities, think of the difference in English between 'I should' and 'I was going to'. But be careful – tenses don't tend to be the same across languages, so you should try and get a feel for the Turkish system! Some examples:

**Gelmelisin.**
You must come.

**Geleceksin.**
You'll come/you'll have to come.

**Beni uyku bastırıyor ama direnmeliyim.**
I feel sleepy (*literally:* sleep is pressing me), but I have to resist it.

**Yeni Sezen Aksu'yu almalıyım.**
I have to buy the new Sezen Aksu (*Sezen Aksu is a Turkish popstar*) ('I really must do that').

**Yeni Sezen Aksu'yu alacağım.**
I'll buy the new Sezen Aksu ('I still have to do that').

**İngilizce iyi öğrenmelisin!**
You should learn English well.

**Pencereleri kapatmalı.**
He should shut the windows.

**İki parti bir koalisyona hazır olmalıdırlar.**
The two parties should be prepared for a coalition.

There is a third possibility for expressing what you need to do: the use of the infinitive plus **gerek** or **lazım** 'necessary'. This combination is used for generalised sentences such as:

**Kalkmak gerek.**
One should stand up. (*literally:* standing is necessary)

**Bırakmamak gerek.**
One should not leave. (*literally:* not leaving is necessary)

**Senin ekibinin daha hızlı çalışması lazım.**
Your team has to work faster. (*literally:* the faster working of
your team is necessary)

You will learn more about this in Lesson 9.

## Exercise 6

Fill in the correct translations:

| | |
|---|---|
| 1 _____ | You have to visit your mother. |
| 2 **Beni rahatsız etmemelisiniz.** | _____ |
| 3 _____ | Students have to buy these books. |
| 4 **Radyo dinlemesi gerek.** | _____ |
| 5 _____ | We have to go now! |
| 6 **Daha fazla yemek hazırlamalıyım.** | _____ |
| 7 _____ | You should not accept that. |
| 8 **Onu hiç bırakmaman gerek.** | _____ |

| | |
|---|---|
| **rahatsız etmek** | to disturb |
| **hazırlamak** | to prepare |
| **kabul etmek** | to accept |

# Language point

## Influencing people

When you want someone else to do something, you can use one
of the following ways:

1 Imperatives
The most direct, though somewhat impolite way of giving
commands is to use the imperative. If you say 'Give!' or 'Stop!'
or 'Come!' in English, it sounds impolite. The Turkish counter-
part, however, is far more common and less impolite. The
singular form of the imperative is similar to the stem of the verb:
the imperative of **gelmek** 'to come' is **gel!** 'come!'.

The imperative is often followed by the expression **bakalım**
literally 'let's see', but here used to mean 'come on!'.

**Gel bakalım!**          Come here!

**Anlat bakalım!**     Come on, tell your story!

Another form of the imperative is verb stem followed by **-sene**, used for emphasis, and for expressing impatience. It is usually said with a sigh.

| | |
|---|---|
| **Baksana!** | Look here! |
| **Otursana!** | Now sit down! |

When you are talking to more than one person you use the plural form of the imperative: stem + **-in**:

| | |
|---|---|
| **Buraya gelin!** | Come here! |
| **Beni rahat bırakın!** | Leave me in peace! |
| **Beni dinleyin!** | Listen to me! |

And of course **buyurun** 'please', 'look here' is, in origin, also an imperative.

The 'stem + **-in**' form is also a slightly more polite way to address single persons. In public places, in trains, on planes etc. you may encounter a third form of the imperative, even more polite than **gelin**: stem plus **-iniz**, as in:

| | |
|---|---|
| **Geliniz, lütfen.** | Come, please. |
| **Bakınız.** | Look. |
| **Kemerlerinizi bağlayınız.** | Fasten your seatbelts. |
| **Dokunmayınız.** | Please don't touch. |

2 Politer commands and suggestions
Questions in the **geniş zaman** and suggestions with **-elim** are more polite ways of commanding people. Examples:

| | |
|---|---|
| **Sigaranızı söndürür müsünüz?** | Could you extinguish your cigarette? |
| **Bitirir misin?** | Could you finish? |
| **Şarkı söyleyelim mi?** | Shall we sing a song? |
| **Yüzmeye gidelim mi?** | Shall we go swimming? |

Finally, here is a small but useful list of interjections, intensifiers and exclamations that may come in handy in casual conversations. (Turkish speakers use 'my God' more than English speakers – it is very natural in Turkish.)

| | | | |
|---|---|---|---|
| **öf** | ugh! yuk! | **aferin** | well done! |
| **of** | oof! ouch! | **ah** | oh! o dear! |
| **hadi/haydi** | come on! | **Allah** | O God! Gosh! |

| Tanrım | God! | boş ver/ önemli | never mind |
|---|---|---|---|
| Allahım | my God! | değil/ fark etmez | |
| Allah aşkına | for heaven's sake! | sana ne! | mind your own |
| aman | my goodness! | | business |
| Vallahi | I swear! | | (rather rude) |
| tamam | okay | baksana | now look here! |

## Exercise 7

Ask in polite and less polite ways:

1 whether to go to the lunchroom or not
2 whether your friend wants to join you going to the cinema
3 whether your fellow traveller is inclined to put out his/her cigarette
4 whether someone wants to be silent
5 whether your children want to eat vegetables or not

| lunchroom | pastane |
|---|---|
| be silent | susmak |
| vegetable | sebze |

# Reading text

The imperative is also used in recipes. The form used in the example below is the most polite one of the three forms we gave above, the one with the **-iniz** ending. Just read through the text and try to get a good idea of how the pilav is made.

# Bulgur pilavı

From the book *Türk Mutfak Sanatı (The Art of Turkish Cuisine)*, by Necip Usta.

## Malzeme (5 kişilik)

| | |
|---|---|
| **500 g bulgur** | 500 g bulgur (pounded wheat) |
| **200 g yağ** | 200 g butter (or oil) |
| **1 büyük soğan ince kıyılmış** | one large finely chopped onion |
| **5 adet sivri biber halka halka doğranmış** | 5 pieces of hot pepper, sliced in rings |
| **1 adet iri domates kabukları soyulup ince doğranmış** | 1 large tomato, peeled and diced |

**1 tatlı kaşığı tuz**          1 tablespoon of salt
**4 su bardağı et suyu, yoksa su**   4 cups ('watercups') of meat
                                       broth, or water

Bulguru iyice temizleyip yıkadıktan sonra bir süzgece çıkarıp suyunu tamamen süzdürünüz. Tencereyi ateşe koyup yağ ve soğanı ilâve ediniz. Orta ateşte soğanları sararıncaya kadar karıştırarak kavurup biberleri ve bulguru da ilâve ederek 5 dakika daha karıştırarak kavurunuz.

Sonra domatesi, suyunu, tuzunu, ilâve edip bir kere kuvvetlice kaynatıp karıştırdıktan sonra ağır ateşte 10 dakika pişirip ateşten alınız. 10 dakika demlendirdikten sonra servis ediniz.

**Not:** Domates ve sivri biber bulamadığınız zaman bibersiz ve domatessiz yapınız.

| | | | |
|---|---|---|---|
| **kıyılmak** | finely chopped | **ilâve etmek** | to add |
| **halka halka** | in rings | **sararmak** | to turn yellow |
| **doğranmak** | to be chopped | **kavurmak** | to roast |
| **kabuk** | skin | **kuvvetlice** | vigorously |
| **süzgeç** | colander, filter | **kaynatmak** | to boil |
| **süzdürmek** | to drain | **demlendirmek** | to stew, to brew |

# 9 Dedikodu yapma!

## Don't gossip!

In this lesson you will learn how to:
- combine two verbs
- find the dictionary form of a verb
- express 'have to'
- combine two nouns into a compound noun
- combine an adjective and a noun

Read the following dialogue with the help of the glossary. Then do Exercise 1.

##  Dialogue 1 (Audio 2: 10)

## Ne almak istiyorsun?

### What do you want to buy?

*İlknur and Hülya are waiting for their mother who is meeting them in town to go shopping*

İLKNUR:    Ne almak istiyorsun?

HÜLYA:     Yeni bir etek almam gerek, gelecek hafta eğlence var.
           Fatma için hediyeye bakmak istiyorum. Şu an bir fikrim
           yok. Ya sen?

İLKNUR:    Seyahat acentasına gitmemiz gerek; Atina'ya yolculuk
           için reservasyonumu değiştirmek istiyorum.

*The waiter comes by to clear their table. The girls explain why they are there*

HÜLYA:     Affedersiniz, annemizi bekliyoruz; burada bekleyebilir
           miyiz?

GARSON: Tabii, bu arada birşey içer misiniz?
HÜLYA: Evet, çay lütfen.

*The sisters are looking out the window*

HÜLYA: Şu kıza bak! Ay, şu ayakkabı!
İLKNUR: Sana alacağım şunu. Elbisesini gördün mü?
HÜLYA: Allahım. Acaba, annem şehir merkezine nasıl gelecek?
İLKNUR: Bilmiyorum, önce Ayşe Hanıma uğrayacaktı. O Can F. Kenedi Caddesinde oturuyor.
HÜLYA: Oraya nasıl gider?
İLKNUR: Otobüsle gitmesi gerek herhalde.
HÜLYA: Ben de Ayşe Hanım'a gitmek istiyorum. Yemekleri çok lezzetli oluyor.
İLKNUR: Ben de, yemeğine bayılıyorum. Özellikle onun köftesi nefis.
HÜLYA: Bu akşam ne yapıyorsun?
İLKNUR: Bilmiyorum, galiba kitap okuyacağım. Belki Eser Hanım'a telefon açacağım, biraz dedikodu yapalım.

## Sözcükler

| | | | |
|---|---|---|---|
| etek | skirt | uğrayacaktı | she was going to |
| almam | my buying | | visit |
| almam gerek | I have to buy | Can F. Kenedi | JFK Street |
| eğlence | party | Caddesi | |
| an | moment | cadde | street |
| seyahat acentası | travel agent | gitmesi gerek | she has to go |
| gitmemiz gerek | we have to go | lezzetli | delicious |
| Atina | Athens | bayılmak | to really like |
| yolculuk | journey | özellikle | in particular |
| reservasyon | reservation | köfte | grilled meat dish |
| değiştirmek | to change | galiba | probably |
| ayakkabı | shoes | telefon açmak | to call up |
| elbise | dress | dedikodu | to gossip |
| acaba | I wonder | yapmak | |

### Exercise 1 ⊙⊙

Say in your own words what went on in this dialogue. Try to imagine you overheard the conversation and are now telling a mutual friend about it. You can always refer to the Glossary, if necessary.

# Language point

## Infinitives

You are familiar with verbs that have tense and person endings, such as **-iyorum** or **-dik**. These forms indicate for instance that the action is on-going, or that it took place at a certain time in the past. They also signal who did or is doing the described action (compare **okuyorsun** 'you are reading' and **okuyorlar** 'they are reading').

However, sometimes you just want to name the action, without specifying who did it or when. An example of this is combining **istiyorum** with a verb: 'I want to X'. **İstiyorum** already contains the relevant markers **-iyor** and **-um**. There is no need to repeat them with the other verb. So, just like in English, you use the infinitive of that other verb: **gitmek istiyorum**.

Actually, these kinds of constructions are more common in English than in Turkish, as Turkish doesn't have separate auxiliary verbs like 'can', 'must', 'should' etc. As we saw earlier, Turkish uses **-ebil-**, **-meli** or **gerek** instead. But the infinitive is used where English would use the construction: Possessive + '-ing'. You could paraphrase 'I think he played well' with 'I liked his playing'. This is the normal way of saying these kinds of things in Turkish. To translate 'playing', you use the (short) infinitive on **-me**, **oynama**. Other examples are **gitme** 'going' and **yapma** 'doing'.

There is another reason why you need to know the infinitive: it is the dictionary form of the verb. It is therefore important that, when you encounter an unfamiliar verb, you are able to strip it of its endings and reconstruct its infinitive form.

## The form of the infinitive

Turkish infinitives end in **-mek** or **-mak** (in dictionaries). In actual sentences, they also often end in **-me** or **-ma**. In both, what precedes the **-m-**, is the verb stem. The ending itself is often followed by a possessive ending, for example **git-me-m**: 'my going'. When to use **-mek** and when to use **-me** is explained below.

### Exercise 2

Try to find all infinitives in the dialogue above. Look for the sequences **-ma** and **-mak**.

## Functions of the infinitive ending -mek

1 The most common use for the -mek ending is the 'I want to . . .' type of sentence.

**Biz de Amerika'ya gitmek istiyoruz.**
We want to go to America as well.

**Biber almak istedim.**
I wanted to buy peppers.

2 Another relevant context is 'I'm trying to . . .'. The word for 'try' is the same as for 'work': **çalışmak**. If this follows an infinitive, the meaning becomes 'to try' (compare the English 'to work on'). The infinitive followed by **çalışmak** is marked with the dative case ending **-e**. For pronunciation reasons, the **k** in **-mek** is softened to **ğ**:

**Türkçe öğrenmeğe çalışıyorum.**
I'm trying to learn Turkish.

The **-ğ-** is usually written as **y**: **öğrenmeye**.

3 The -mek infinitive is also often found with **için**, to give 'in order to. . .'. For example:

**Futbol maçını seyretmek için eve gidiyorum.**
I'm going home to see the match.

4 Finally, you also use -mek in sentences of the type 'to . . . is . . .'. For example:

**Yüzmek sıhhatli bir spordur.**
Swimming is a healthy sport.

## The infinitive ending -me

To express 'I have to . . .' Turkish uses the short form of the infinitive, the one with the ending **-me** or **-ma**. There is not really much of a difference in meaning between the two forms of the infinitive; if anything, you could translate the **-me** as an '-ing' form and the **-mek** as an infinitive with 'to':

| | | | |
|---|---|---|---|
| **beklemek** | to wait | **bekleme** | the waiting |
| **konuşmak** | to talk | **konuşma** | the talking |

## To have to

To express 'have to' or 'must' you use **-me** combined with the possessive ending (except if you use the **-meli** forms you learned in Lesson 8). They are followed by the words **lazım** or, preferably, **gerek** 'necessary'. Like **var** and **yok**, these words never change form, that is: they don't take personal or tense endings. The construction is:

> Verb stem + Infinitive ending **-me/-ma** + Possessive ending + **lazım/gerek**

### Exercise 3

Now, see if you can work out the Turkish translations of the following:

1 I have to go.
2 You must read this.
3 She has to do this.
4 We have to write a letter.

There is, however, also a verb **gerekmek** 'to be necessary'. In the present tense, i.e. for 'I have to', it is normally used in the **geniş zaman**. This is logical if you realise that the **-iyor** tense is often translated by English '-ing' forms: you can't say 'I'm having to' either.

> **Türkiye'de biraz daha kalmamız gerekti.**
> We had to stay in Turkey a bit longer.

> **Daha çok meyve yemem gerekir.**
> I have to eat more fruit.

Can you feel the difference with the **-meli** form? Whereas **-meli** expresses an *obligation*, such as in the first example below, the **lazım/gerek/gerekir** form is less compulsory. Here are some more examples:

> **Bana yardım etmelisiniz.**
> You (all) have to help me.

> **Evet demen lazım.**
> You have to say 'yes'.

**Yarın çalışmanız gerek, değil mi?**
You have to work tomorrow, haven't you?

**Biraz beklemen gerekir.**
You have to wait a little.

**Bu pahalı hediyeyi kabul etmen lazım.**
You have to accept the expensive present.

In question forms a funny thing happens: **gerek** now needs to be replaced by **gerekli**. Otherwise, everything is as expected. The most common negated form is not **lazım değil** or **gerek değil**, but **gerek yok** (**gerek yok** with dative **-e/-a**). An alternative, somewhat more formal, is **gerekli değil**.

**Cevap vermeniz gerekli miydi bu soruya?**
Did you have to answer that question?

**Bunu yapman gerek değil.**
It is really not necessary that you do this.

**Bunu yapmaman gerek.**
It is necessary that you don't do this.

**Bunu doldurmağa gerek yok.**
You don't have to fill this out.

Another way of saying this is:

**Bunu doldurmanın gereği yok.**
There's no need to fill this out.

If you used **lazım** or **gerek** every time you needed to express 'have to', nobody would misunderstand what you were trying to say. However, it is more natural to use **gerekli** and **-meli** where needed.

### Exercise 4

Make a list of all the forms you learned to express 'have to', 'must' and 'should' and their negative counterparts (such as 'don't have to'), and put them in order of urgency, using 'I have to return to London' and, for the negative versions, 'You don't have to return.' The verb 'to return' is **dönmek**.

## Exercise 5

Here is a list of verb forms. Some have tense and person endings, some contain 'short' infinitives with **-me** (with or without additional suffixes), and yet others are full infinitives with **-mek**. Work out the dictionary forms for all of them and look up their meaning in the glossary. They are all frequently used and most have not appeared in the dialogues so far.

| | | | |
|---|---|---|---|
| 1 | kaybetmeleri | 6 | unutmadan |
| 2 | çekmesi | 7 | sevmek |
| 3 | uçtu | 8 | göndermeği |
| 4 | attılar | 9 | koyuyorsun |
| 5 | göstermen | 10 | taşımağa |

## Case endings on infinitives

The short forms of the infinitive are widely used, and often as direct objects of other verbs. That means that this infinitive is often marked with a case marker. For example, you know from earlier lessons that 'pleased to meet you' is **memnun oldum**. Well, **memnun olmak** 'to be pleased' requires that the word it co-occurs with is marked with the ablative case **-den**. So if you want to say 'I'm very happy that we met' you take the short infinitive of **görüşmek** (which yields **görüşme-**), add the first person plural **-miz** to convey the 'we' (this yields **görüşmemiz**), and then supply the ablative case marker: **görüşmemizden çok memnun oldum**.

Infinitives are often used in Turkish with case marking. For example, 'I forgot to ...'. The verb **unutmak** combines with a **-me** infinitive that is marked with the accusative case (**-i, -ı, -u, ü, -yi, -yı, -yu, -yü**; see Lesson 6).

**Ödemeyi unuttum.**       I forgot to pay.

In general, it will be a good educated guess that Turkish will use an infinitive construction when English has one. This also works the other way round: English uses subordinate clauses with certain other verbs, for instance in 'I think (that) he's right.' Turkish does this too. (Subordinate clauses are discussed in Lesson 11.)

'I like ...' (**... severim**) also requires the accusative case, so if the direct object is not a normal noun (such as, for instance, **atları**, 'horses') but a verb, that verb (the **-me** infinitive) needs to be marked with the accusative case:

| **Koşmayı severim.** | I like running. |
|---|---|
| **Müzik dinlemeyi severim.** | I like listening to music. |

When a verb ending in **-me** is followed by a possessive marker, a case marker following this has to be preceded by an **-n-**. Do you recall from Lesson 6 that when a possessive **-(s)i** or **-leri** is followed by a case marker, an extra **-n-** is used in between? See how this works in the form **evini** in **evini gördüm** 'I've seen his house':

---

**ev** 'house'
+ Possessive = **evi** 'his house'
+ Accusative = **evi + -n- + -i: evini gördüm** 'I've seen his house'

---

Likewise, in the following example, **sigara içme-** 'smoking' is followed by **-si** 'his' (which refers back to **babasının** 'of her dad'). This form **sigara içmesi** 'his smoking' is the direct object of **istemiyor** 'she doesn't want', so it has to be marked by the accusative case marker. This marker is preceded by the **-n**. Literally, this sentence means 'she doesn't want her father's cigarette-smoking'.

> **Babasının sigara içmesini istemiyor.**
> She doesn't want her dad to smoke.

### Exercise 6

The following sentences all illustrate one context in which Turkish uses an infinitive plus other verb construction. Identify these contexts (look up unfamiliar words in the Glossary). The first one has been done already.

1 Ablam elbise almak için çarşıya gidecek.  'in order to'
2 Tatil resimlerini görmemi istediler.
3 Meseleyi anlamağa başladı.
4 Oraya gitmemi düşünüyorum.
5 Burada beklememi söyledi.
6 Beni mi görmeye geldin?
7 Ayşe bu yıl Karadeniz'e gitmemizi istiyor.
8 Onları beraber görmeğe alışman gerek.

## 'I want to . . .' *versus* 'I want you to . . .'

Above, we have said that the **-mek** infinitive is used with **istemek**. However, this is only so if the sentence concerned is of the type 'I want to . . .', 'he wants to . . .', etc. If you want someone else to do something, you have to use the short infinitive. To take 'I want you to listen to him' as an example, the subject of **istemek** is 'I', giving **istiyorum**. The subject of the infinitive verb, **dinlemek**, is 'you'. This has to be marked on the infinitive with the second person singular 'you' possessive ending **-in**. Since these endings cannot possibly be attached to **-mek** infinitives, the short version must be used: **dinleme + -n** (or **-niz**), yielding **dinlemen** (or **dinlemeniz**). Finally, since the infinitive is the object of **istiyorum**, it has to be marked with the accusative case: **ona dinlemeni istiyorum** (or **dinlemenizi istiyorum**).

By the way, even in the 'I want to . . .' construction, **istemek** may combine with the short infinitive. Do not be surprised when you hear somebody say **Yemeyi istiyor musun?** instead of **Yemek istiyor musun?** On the other hand, this person may as well have said the noun **yemeği** 'the food', which sounds the same!

## ⌒ Confusion between negative verbs and short infinitives (Audio 2: 11)

Seen in isolation, the form **yapma** can mean two things: 'doing' and 'don't do it!' Confusion between the two will not often arise in practice, because of the wildly different contexts in which these two forms are used. Also, in speech they sound very different. The negative suffix always causes the preceding syllable to be heavily stressed, while the short infinitive suffix is stressed itself. Besides, there are never other personal suffixes after the imperative.

**Dörtten sonra gelme!**
Don't come later than four!

**Dörtten sonra gelmem kızdırdı onu.**
My coming after four annoyed him.

**Gelmemem kızdırdı onu.**
It annoyed him that I didn't come.

## 🎧 *Exercise 7* (Audio 2: 12)

Read through Dialogue 2 below, using the following questions and the glossary below as a guide. Provide the actual answers afterwards.

1 İmdat's first two sentences contain three compound nouns, i.e. nouns that are made up out of two parts. Which ones?
2 How was the weather?
3 İmdat's fifth and sixth sentences contain reported speech. Identify the verb with which these sentences end.
4 Does Şükran agree with İmdat's course of action?
5 The suffix **-siz** means 'without', so what's the news about Hasan?
6 How would you characterise İmdat's reaction to the news?
7 There are two more compound nouns in İmdat's third turn. Identify them.
8 Explain why **Adana kebap** and the other food terms are not marked with the accusative case.
9 At some point Şükran tries to change the conversation back to the earlier topic. How does she do that? Do you still remember what **sana ne!** means? It was introduced in Lesson 8 (also be aware that it is not a very polite thing to say).
10 Does İmdat accept that changed topic?
11 What is the final topic Şükran tries to introduce?
12 Now fill in the line at the beginning that describes the setting of the dialogue and what it is about.

## Dialogue 2

## Konuşma

## Conversation

*Şükran and İmdat ...*

İMDAT:  Kötü bir gün idi. Şehir merkezindeki belediye binasına gittim. Yeni bir park müsaadesi için başvurmam gerekti. Kötü hava şartlarında otuz dakika yürüdüm. Oradaki memura bana yardımcı olur musunuz dedim. Gişe şimdi kapanacak dedi. Fakat beşe sekiz kalaydı! Hiç birşey demeden hemen dışarıya çıktım.

ŞÜKRAN: Haklısın, boktan herif o! Neyse, Hasan hakkındaki
haberi duydun mu?
İMDAT: Ne oldu? Hadi, anlat bakalım.
ŞÜKRAN: Hasan artık yemekleri etsiz yiyecek! Et yemeyi bıraktı.
Buna ne dersin?
İMDAT: Sahi mi? Kim anlattı? Sen her zaman herşeyi biliyorsun!
Hayat böyle işte, hiç belli olmuyor! Vejetaryenler için
yemek kitapların var mı? Bari Hasan için yemek tarif-
lerini toplayayım! (*suddenly raises his voice*) Aman,
Adana kebap hiç yemeyecek mi? Yalnız kabak, patates,
lahana, ne bileyim, havuç mavuç filan mı yiyecek? Aklını
kaçırmış galiba! Tavşan gibi!
ŞÜKRAN: Allah bilir! Ama neden öyle kızıyorsun? Boş ver ya!
Sana ne? Hm, demin ne dedin? Yani memur sana bilgi
vermek istemedi mi?
İMDAT: Ya biliyor musun, pazartesi Hasan'la Aylin bize geliyor,
akşam yemeği için. Etli nohut yahnisi pişirecektim.
Fakat içeceğe gelince, henüz kararsızım. Ne düşünüyorsun, hala rakı içiyor mu, acaba, yoksa onu da mı
bıraktı?
ŞÜKRAN: Dur be! Dedikodu yapmayı bırakalım, Allah aşkına.
Sana sormak istedim az önce: deden nasıl?

## Sözcükler

| | | | |
|---|---|---|---|
| kötü | bad | haber | news |
| şehir | the one in the | anlat bakalım | let's hear ('tell, |
| merkezindeki | centre of town | | let's see') |
| belediye | state, city council | artık | from now |
| müsaade | permit | etsiz | meatless |
| park müsaadesi | parking permit | sahi mi? | really? |
| başvurmak | to apply | belli | certain |
| oradaki | the one there | vejetaryen | vegetarian |
| memur | civil servant | bari | at least |
| gişe | counter, booth | tarif | recipe |
| demeden | without saying | toplamak | to collect |
| dışarıya | outside | kabak | courgette |
| haklı | right | lahana | cabbage |
| boktan herif | fool | havuç | carrot |
| hakkında | about | havuç mavuç | carrots and |
| hakkındaki | the one about | | stuff |

| aklını kaçırmış | he must've lost | kızmak | to get angry |
|---|---|---|---|
| | his mind | bilgi | information |
| aklını kaçırmak | to lose one's | yahni | stew, sauce |
| | mind | gelince | when it comes |
| tavşan | rabbit | kararsız | undecided |
| Allah bilir! | Lord knows! | | |

## Language points

### Compound nouns

As in English, two nouns can be combined to form a compound noun. The two nouns are put next to each other and the last one is followed by the possessive ending of the third person (**-i, -si** or **-leri**).

It's best to learn these compounds as one word. Just as you don't think of 'bedroom' any more as consisting of two words, you may not do that with **yatak odası** 'bedroom' either. Or else maybe with **pazar günü** 'Sunday' or **havaalanı** 'airport'. In order to remind yourself of the possessive marker, it might be helpful to think of Turkish compounds as literally saying: 'the air, its field', or 'the bed, its room'. There is one more thing you should be aware of: as the Turkish compound noun ends in a possessive suffix (the **-ü** in **pazar günü** and the **-ı** in **havaalanı**), an extra **-n-** must be inserted before any case marker:

| pazar gününden | from Sunday on |
|---|---|
| havaalanına | to the airport |

NB: The word **havaalanı** is the exception to the rule that compounds are written as two words.

As you see illustrated overleaf, you can encounter compounds everywhere:

**Türkiye Cumhuriyeti** 'Turkish Republic' on the stamp, and a whole lot of them on the bus ticket: **EGO Müdürlüğü** 'the EGO office', **EGO Müdürlüğü Denetiminde** 'under the auspices of the EGO office', **halk otobüsü** 'public bus', **yolcu bileti** 'traveller ticket', and **yolculuk sırası** 'the duration of the journey'.

If a compound noun is followed by a possessive marker that is not the third person marker, i.e. if you want to say 'my/your/our X', then the third person possessive marker that is found at the

end of compounds is replaced by the appropriate one. For instance, the combination of 'picture' **fotoğraf** and 'machine' **makine** yields the word for 'photo camera': **fotoğraf makinesi**. Now, if you want to say 'my photo camera' you don't just add **-m** for 'my'. Instead, you replace the **-si** with the **-m**, so that you don't get **fotoğraf makinesim**, but **fotoğraf makinem**.

## Country names as adjectives: Turkish, British, American etc.

Often the compound option will come naturally to you, as with **park müsaadesi** 'parking permit' and **yemek kitabı** 'cookery-book' in Dialogue 2. Even if you have never used or heard the word before, you may be able to construct the compound on the spot. Things are a little harder with certain categories of compounds where, approaching things from English, you wouldn't expect them. One of those categories is when names of countries are used as adjectives. English would use the combination Adjective + Noun here, but Turkish forms compound nouns with many of these. 'Turkish coffee', for instance, is the compound **Türk kahvesi**, and not the Adjective + Noun combination **Türk kahve**.

Perhaps the hardest habit to break will be to use Adjective + Noun combinations in these contexts. Not all names of countries behave this way; the short list does, however, include some of the most frequent ones: **Türk**, **İngiliz**, **Fransız**, **Alman**, **İtalyan**, **Rus** and **Yunan** (the latter means 'Greek'). NB: Speakers increasingly leave out the possessive ending.

**Rus firması yeni sahip oldu.**
A Russian firm has become the new owner.

**Fransız köylerini beğeniyorum.**
I like French villages.

Most other country names are formed with the suffix **-li**, with which you can form adjectives. The possessive marker does not occur with these so, as in English, you simply put the noun after the adjective. Actually, for 'American', both **Amerikalı** and **Amerikan** are in use; for 'Greek' both **Yunan** and **Yunanlı**:

**Amerikalı bir kadınla evlendim.**
**Amerikan kadınıyla evlendim.**
I'm married to an American woman.

**Her yaz çok sayıda İsveçli ve Hollandalı turistler Türk plajlarına geliyor.**
Every year many Swedish and Dutch tourists come to the Turkish beaches.

As **-li** is used to say 'someone from . . .', you will probably hear this suffix more often with names of cities and regions than with names of countries when you are in Turkey:

**Kocam Karslı, ben ise Yozgatlıyım.**
My husband is from Kars, but I'm from Yozgat.

Many adjectives end in **-li**; consider the following words that contain this suffix:

| | | | |
|---|---|---|---|
| **pahalı** | expensive | **köylü** | peasant |
| **bulutlu** | cloudy | **gerekli** | necessary (see |
| **yaşlı** | aged | | earlier this lesson) |

Names of languages end in the suffix **-çe/-ce/-ça/-ca**: **Türkçe**, **Hollandaca**, **İngilizce**, **Yunanca**, **Almanca**, etc.
Sometimes names of languages can combine with a noun that is not marked with the possessive marker. The result has a different meaning. Take the following pair:

**İngilizce kitap**          **İngilizce kitabı**

Both combine the meanings 'English' and 'book'. Both denote a book, but they differ in meaning. The first combination is a regular Adjective + Noun combination, and refers to a book in English. The second combination, on the other hand, is a compound, as can be seen from the possessive ending on **kitap**. It refers to a textbook for learning English. English only uses intonation to distinguish between the two, with accent on 'book' in the first one, and on 'English' in the second. For further illustration: the book that you are holding in your hands right now is a **Türkçe kitabı**, but it is an **İngilizce kitap**.

## The place of adjectives

Adjectives can be used before a noun or with the verb 'to be'. For example, 'the red coat' gives more specific information than 'the coat'. With 'to be', the adjective tells you something new about something or someone. In 'the coat is red', for instance, something is said about the coat you didn't know, namely that it is red. Turkish is a lot like English, in that the two uses are likewise distinguished by different word orders. **Yeşil araba** means 'green car', while **araba yeşil** means 'the car is green'.

When adjectives combine with the indefinite article, the word order is as follows:

```
          Adjective  +  bir  +  Noun
```

So, 'a green car' is **yeşil bir araba**.

### Exercise 8

Just a little question to keep you on guard: how come, in **araba yeşil**, **araba** is translated as 'the car', even though there is no accusative case marker?

### Exercise 9

Here are nine combinations of noun and adjective. Combine the first three to give 'A Adjective Noun', the next three to give 'The Noun is Adjective' and the last three to give 'Adjective Nouns'. The first one has been done already.

| 1 genç, adam | genç bir adam | 6 yeni, lokanta |
| 2 havaalanı, eski | | 7 bardak, boş |
| 3 elbise, beyaz | | 8 tavuk, ucuz |
| 4 tarif, kolay | | 9 yüksek, fiyat |
| 5 inek, deli | | |

**inek** cow
**bardak** glass

## Language points

### Other compound nouns

For good idiomatic usage of Turkish, it is important that you develop a 'feel' for when to form a compound noun. The following are typical examples; probably only the last three look 'natural' to you if you look at things from an English perspective.

| **on beş treni** | the 10.05 train (*or:* the 15.00 train!) |
| **Ankara uçağı** | the plane to Ankara |
| **Boğazıçı Üniversitesi** | Boğazıçı University |
| **Van gölü** | Lake Van |
| **futbol maçı** | football match |
| **taksi şoförü** | taxi driver |
| **çoban salatası** | shepherd's salad |

For identifying a particular train, plane, bus, boat etc., you use constructions as English does in 'the six o'clock train' or 'the Bursa train', *not* 'the train to Bursa' (i.e. you *don't* say **Bursa'ya tren**). **Tren** is marked with the possessive suffix. In the third and fourth examples, a certain university and a certain lake are identified through the first word, which combines with the second word in a compound noun. Note that in Turkish you don't write words like **göl** or **deniz** with capitals. The other three are more straightforward for English speakers: two nouns combine to yield a new noun, often one that depicts a fairly easy concept, as in **futbol maçı** and **taksi şoförü**.

Remember that case endings that attach to a possessive ending must be preceded by **-n-**. If **İngilizce kitabı** functions as a direct object of, say, **bulamadım**, 'I couldn't find', then it must be marked with the accusative case suffix **-ı**, to yield: **İngilizce kitabını bulamadım**. Some more examples:

**Taksi şoförüne para ödemeyi az kaldı unuttum.**
I almost forgot to pay the taxi driver.

**Van gölünü görmedin mi?**
You haven't seen Lake Van?

**Bu korku filmini hatırlıyor musun? Çocuk eti yiyen ağaç üzerine olan mı?**
Do you remember this horror movie? The one about the child-eating tree?

**Üç on treni henüz varmadı.**
The 3:10 train has not arrived yet.

## Material adjectives

One class of adjectives that never occurs with possessive suffixes is *material* adjectives. So a 'leather suitcase' is a **deri bavul**, not a **deri bavulu**.

### Exercise 10

Look at the following English words and combinations, and try to predict which ones will not be compound nouns in Turkish.

1 evening dinner
2 mad cow disease
3 fatigue syndrome
4 gold watch
5 homework
6 Persian rug
7 Turkish government
8 plastic bag
9 Dutch football player

# 10 Tekrarlama

## Review

---

**Lesson 10 contains:**

- a revision of topics dealt with so far

---

In the previous lessons you have learned about case endings on nouns, how to mark a verb for present, past and future tenses and how to form simple sentences. What you have not heard anything about yet is how to combine sentences into more complex sentences. This seems a good place to revise the major points covered so far, and hopefully to clarify a few things. You can use this lesson to review what you have learnt – a chance to catch up so to speak – before moving ahead again.

## Turkish-isms

Going through the lessons of this book, you will have noticed that some constructions were really easy to master, while others left you bewildered, perhaps crying out 'Why does it have to be so complex?' (meaning: 'different'). We will now go over a few of these different structures, and point out some consistencies and principles that should make it easier for you to grasp them if you haven't succeeded in doing so already.

### Suffixes

In English, there are a few suffixes. The plural, for instance, is formed by adding -s to the noun, as in 'house-s'. Adding something to another word is called suffixation. Turkish uses suffixation much more than English. We hope that, now that you've got this far into this book, you have learned to think in a 'suffix' kind of way when you are constructing Turkish phrases. First the stem, then one or more suffixes: that's how Turkish works. One area where you can get away with using an English-style construction once in a while is possession. The normal way of saying 'my husband' is **koca-m**, but **benim koca** is not impossible in colloquial Turkish.

## Exercise 1

Identify the various suffixes in the following sequences. Try to put yourself under time pressure: in real-life situations, you'll have to be able to spot suffixes quite quickly. The up side of suffixation, especially in Turkish, is that the order in which they come is quite regular, almost without exceptions. The down side is that suffixes are short, so that you don't have much time to focus your attention on them.

1 arabamla
2 tatilinizde
3 yürüdük
4 yeşili
5 konuğumuzun arabasında
6 alıyor musunuz?
7 annenden
8 duydun

## Plural

You may remember that the plural suffix in Turkish is not always used where you would in English. First and foremost, you don't use **-lar** if you have used a numeral or words like **kaç** 'how much'/'how many' or **az** 'few' to go with it. You don't use the plural if the noun represents a *group*, rather than separate individual entities. (Often, using the plural ending is not exactly 'wrong', but you will sound more natural if you manage to gradually adopt the principle 'when in doubt, don't use it'.) Compare:

**Rosy adlı Amerikan arkadaşımız bugün dokuz elma yedi!**
**Elma severim dedi.**
Our American friend Rosy has eaten nine apples today! She said she likes apples.

**Benim arkadaşlarım bu haberi bekledi. Onun için çok mutlular.**
My friends have been waiting for this news, so they're very
    happy.

**Köpekleri terbiyeli değil.**
Her dogs are not well-behaved.

**Eski bina öyle temiz değil.**
Old buildings are not that clean.

The last three sentences have no numeral to make clear we're
talking about more than one friend, dog, or building, respectively.
You have the choice then either to mark the plural on the noun,
as in the second and third sentences, or not at all. If the subject is
not a human being, the sentence is more likely to be without **-lar**,
which is why the fourth example doesn't need it.

NB: All this is only relevant for the third person plural 'they';
first and second person plural forms of the verb ('we' and 'you')
have their own unique endings:

**Üçümüz çok mutluyuz.**
The three of us are very happy.

## Adjective + bir + noun

In Lesson 9 you learned about adjectives. As in English, the adjective comes before the noun, but unlike in English, the indefinite
article **bir** follows the adjective, as in **akıllı bir kız**, 'a smart girl'.

When **bir** is really meant to mean *one*, it precedes the adjective,
as do all numerals.

**Sınıfımızda yalnız bir akıllı kız var. Diğerleri çok aptal.**
In our class, there's just one smart girl. The others are very
    stupid.

**Türkiye'deki yolculuğumuz esnasında on iki tane güzel şehri
    gördük.**
During our travels in Turkey, we saw twelve beautiful cities.

### Exercise 2

Translate

1  I just saw two huge birds.
2  Is that white car yours?

3 She was wearing a green skirt at the party.
4 They are very normal people.
5 Galatasaray wants a new good player. (Galatasary is a football team)

| | | | |
|---|---|---|---|
| **kocaman** | huge | **seninki** | yours |
| **üstünde … var** | to wear | **futbolcu** | player |

## To have

Two things are important here:

1 you need to use **var** or **yok**, which you will know mainly as meaning 'there is' and 'there is not' and
2 you need to indicate with a suffix which person has something on the thing that is 'being had'.

So when you want to say 'we don't have a ticket', you need to remember that the 'we' is a suffix on 'ticket': **bilet-imiz**. The negation is expressed with **yok**.

Note that you only use **var** or **yok** for literal 'have'. The numerous other uses 'to have' has in English, such as in 'I haven't done anything', do not have parallels in Turkish **var/yok**, so do not be tempted to experiment with **var/yok** when constructing a past tense verb form. **-Di** and **-miş** are all you need for that (see Lesson 11). **Var/yok** are mostly used for 'there is …' constructions and for *possession* (e.g., **arabam var** 'I have a car', or **bahçeniz yok** 'you don't have a garden').

Similarly, the use of have in 'they have lots of water there' (or 'they've got …') is not paralleled in Turkish **var**. Nobody really 'has' this water; 'they have' just stands for 'in that place'. For 'in', the locative (**-de, -da, -te, -ta**) is used. 'That place' is **ora**, and since the exact spot is not defined, you add a plural suffix (**-ler** or **-lar**) here, which expresses the notion of 'around', 'thereabout', etc. Thus, Turkish uses **oralarda** 'here' rather than just **orada**:

**Oralarda su çok/Oralarda su bol.**
There is much water there.

(*an alternative:*) **Oranın suyu çok/Oranın suyu bol.**
There is much water there.

**Ora** 'that place' has the genitive suffix **-nın**.

NB: Note the irregular possessive ending on **su**: not **susu**, but **suyu**. No other word shows this irregularity.

## Exercise 3

Translate

1 I have no money.
2 She has two dogs.
3 What a beautiful house you (*plural*) have!
4 I have really enjoyed my stay here.
5 In Greece, there's good food.

| **Yunanistan** | Greece | **gerçekten** | really |
|---|---|---|---|
| **kalma** | stay | | |

## Accusative case

It cannot be emphasised enough that the Turkish accusative case and the English definite article are only partially equivalent. The accusative case is only used when a noun functions as the direct object of a verb. Subject nouns can be definite, as in 'the man saw me', but they cannot get accusative case. In **adam beni gördü** 'the man saw me' and **adamı gördüm** 'I saw the man', **adam** and **adamı** both mean 'the man'. In the next example, **çiçekleri** has the accusative marker, because it is a direct object and it is definite, due to the preceding demonstrative pronoun **bu**.

**Konuğumuz bize bu çiçekleri getirdi.**
Our guest has brought us these flowers.

After words denoting quantities, such as **çok** 'much', 'many' **az** 'little', 'few' and **hiç** 'no', you cannot use the accusative case.

## Exercise 4

Look at the direct objects and say whether they need accusative case or not.

1 **Kahvenize süt koyuyor musunuz?**
Do you take cream in your coffee?
2 **Uzun zaman konuştuktan sonra bir sonuca vardık.**
After talking for a long time we reached a conclusion.
3 **Tatildeyken her arkadaşıma kartpostal gönderirim.**
When I'm on holiday, I send postcards to all my friends.
4 **Kapak aç lütfen!** Please open the lid!
5 **Tabağın bana verin!** Give me your plate!

6 **Tabii ki, para kazanmamız lazım!**
Of course, we have to earn money!
7 **Fransa'da işçiler sık sık grev yapar.**
In France, workers strike often.
8 **Dün çok zaman kaybettim.**    Yesterday, I lost a lot of time.
9 **Annenin çöplüğe attığı mektup okudun mu?**
Did you read the letter your mother threw into the rubbish bin?
10 **Onların oğlanları gördün mü?**   Did you see their sons?
11 **Onların bana bir iş teklif edecekleri bekliyorum.**
I expect them to offer me a job.
12 **Bu sözcük anlıyor musunuz?**   Do you understand this word?

| | | | |
|---|---|---|---|
| **uzun** | long, tall | **grev** | strike |
| **sonuca** | conclusion | **çöplük** | dustbin |
| **kartpostal** | postcard | **teklif etmek** | to offer |
| **kapak** | lid | **sözcük** | word |
| **tabak** | plate | | |

## Compound nouns

Another thing you probably had to get used to is having to stick a possessive marker on to the second noun in a compound, the **-sı** in **yatak odası**. You think of possessives as indicating, well, possession, as in **babam**, '*my* father'. But nobody's owning the **oda** in **yatak odası**. And then, once you have mastered that, you will probably go on having some trouble deciding when *NOT* to add the possessive marker. The basic rule is that if you really feel that the two form a unit together, then it is a compound and you use the possessive marker. If the first word feels more like an adjective to you, then you don't use the possessive. Most of the time that will get you the correct result. The most tricky type of combination is when you have a word denoting the name of a country as the first word. Those words feel like adjectives to English speakers, since that is what they are in English; in Turkish they form compound nouns, except when ending in the suffix **-li**.

### *Exercise 5*

Here are some more English combinations; we dare you to guess whether they are compound nouns in Turkish or not, and to give the Turkish translation if you can.

1 housekeys
2 motorway
3 old man
4 gaol
5 employer ('work giver')
6 summermonths
7 the five o' clock train
8 weak tea
9 dish of the day
10 menu (eating list)
11 vegetarian food
12 lentil soup
13 Finnish skier
14 Turkish coffee

| | |
|---|---|
| **açık** | weak (at least in the context of drinks) |
| **mercimek** | lentil |
| **Finli** | Finnish |
| **kayakçı** | skier |

## Exercise 6

Translate the following compounds into English:

1 otel odası
2 Türk kahvesi
3 Almanca öğretmeni
4 Marmara denizi
5 Türk-Yunan dostluğu
6 kız okulu
7 mutfak dolabı
8 otobüs bileti
9 Japon arabası
10 korku filmi
11 Hemingway'in romanları
12 kuzu eti/kuzunun eti
13 Mayıs ayı
14 çocuk odası/çocuğun odası
15 balkon kapısı/balkonun kapısı
16 inek sütü
17 İkinci Dünya Savaşı
18 roman yazarı/romanın yazarı

| dolap | cupboard |
| savaş | war |

## Genitive-possessive constructions

In Lesson 6, you saw another type of construction in which two nouns combine with each other: the genitive-possessive construction, of the type **Hasan'ın koltuğu** 'Hasan's chair'. Again, as these combinations end in a possessive suffix, they always get accusative case if they function as direct object: **benim bavulumu bulamadım** 'I couldn't find my suitcase' (**bavul** 'suitcase' + **-um** 'my' + **-u** accusative). This is logical: the genitive serves to pinpoint exactly one specific thing, namely, the suitcase that belongs to me (**benim**). Definite direct objects must be marked with accusative. Note that the thing that goes with **var** in the 'I have ...' construction is not marked with accusative.

> **Aytekin'lerin güzel banyosu var.** ('to have' construction)
> Aytekin's family has a beautiful bathroom.

> **Bu sene Bahar'ın notları berbattı.** (subject)
> This year Bahar's grades were atrocious.

Accusative marking is seen in the following examples:

> **Hiç kimse memurun yanlışlığını fark etmedi.**
> Nobody noticed the civil servant's mistake.

> **Aman allahım, onun durumunu düşün!**
> Oh my God, think of his/her situation!

> **Funda'nın yemeğini her zaman bitiriyor mu?**
> Does he always finish Funda's dinner?

## Overview of combinations

You have now seen three ways of combining two nouns. The first one, Adjective/Noun + Noun is included here because the names of countries are nouns in Turkish. The difference between 2 and 3 can be illustrated neatly with the pair **hafta sonu** and **haftanın sonu**: the first one means 'weekend' and is a word no Turkish speaker ever has to actively put together out of **hafta**, **son** and the possessive ending. The second one means 'the end of the week', something you are more likely to build up when you need it.

| 1 Adjective/Noun + Noun | **yeşil ağaç** |
| | the green tree |
| 2 Noun + Noun + Possessive | **ev kapısı** |
| | the house door |
| 3 Noun + Genitive + Noun + Possessive | **çocukların oyuncakları** |
| | the toys of the children |

## Exercise 7

Fill in the dialogue below, between a landlady and her tenant, with the most appropriate of the options that are listed at the bottom. Watch out: you may need to add something (e.g. an adjective or a personal ending) to the compounds or change their form!

Ne yapıyorsunuz, Funda Hanım?
Ben (*housewife*). İşte, kahve hazır. İçer misiniz?
Efendim, sizin (*orange juice*) var mı?
Var, tabii. Meyvemizi kendi (*orchard*)'de topladık.
A, harika! Şifalıdır, umarım. Bol vitaminli. Çünkü, soğuk almışım. Hem de (*headache*) var.
Geçmiş olsun. Gerekli olursa, bu sokakta (*excellent doctor*) var. (*Woman doctor*).
Teşekkür ederim ama, galiba doktora gitmeye gerek yok. Kocanız ne yapıyor?
O (*computer programmer*). (*American firm*) için çalışıyor. Akşamlarda (*my poor dad*)'ı yardım ediyor. Babam (*owner of that store*). Geçen ay bir bilgisayar aldı, ama (*aged storeowners*) için çok zor dedi. Sanıyorum, kocam şimdi (*the train from Ankara*)'de.
Ne yiyeceğiz bu akşam?
(*Rice pilav*) ve (*chickpea and meat stew*). Bugün (*Turkish cuisine*), yarın (*Chinese cuisine*) olacak. Onu beğeniyor musunuz?
O, (*Turkish cuisine*)'dan çok farklı.

Choose from these options:

| meyve bahçe | Amerikan firma |
| zavallı baba | kadın doktor |
| etli nohut | ev kadın |
| pirinç pilav | Türk mutfak |

| dükkanın sahip | dükkan sahip |
| uzman doktor | bilgisayar programcı |
| portakal su | baş ağır |
| Ankara'dan tren | Çin mutfak |
| yaşlı dükkan sahip | Türk mutfak |

| harika! | great! | zor | difficult |
| şifalı | healthy | farklı | different |
| bol | full of | zavallı | poor |
| çünkü | because | ağır | pain |

## The sequence -ları/-leri-

An interesting problem arises when you want to say 'their children', i.e. when both the possessive ending and the noun have to be plural. You could expect two '-*lar*'s there: **çocuklar + ları >> çocuklarları**. These double forms do not occur, however: only one plural marker is used. The consequence is that a sequence such as **çocukları** may mean 'their child' (**çocuk + -ları**), 'their children' (**çocuklar + -ları**, with one **-lar** dropped), as well as 'her/his children' (**çocuklar + -ı**). The sequences **-ları** and **-leri** are very common.

Forms with **-leri** or **-ları** will probably cause you some problems in your first months of learning Turkish because they can mean several things. It can be any of the following:

1  possessive ending 'their'

   Example: **ev-leri** ('house – their' >> 'their house')

2  possessive ending 'his' or 'her' on something that is plural

   Example: **evler-i** ('houses – his/her' >> 'his/her houses')

3  possessive ending 'their' on something that is plural

   Example: **evler-i** ('houses – their' >> 'their houses')

4  'they have' (if followed by **var** or **yok**)

   Example: **güzel bir ev-leri var** ('house – their' >> 'they have a nice house')

5  plural plus accusative

   Example: **ev-ler-i aldılar** ('house – -s – the' >> 'They bought the houses')

6  plural of a compound noun

Example: **devlet hastane-leri** (state – hospital – -s >> 'public hospitals')

Note that in No. 3, there is no double plural. As explained above, a form *evlerleri* is *not* possible. The obvious question is: 'How can I know with which one of these senses I'm confronted with when someone says something containing **-leri**?' The just-as-obvious answer is: 'context'. Focus on what the person talking to you is talking about: more often than not only one interpretation will make sense. For instance, if someone is talking to you about her parents' house, it's not very likely that you will interpret **evlerini temizledik** as 'we cleaned their houses', let alone as 'we cleaned his houses'. As there is no **var** or **yok**, the 'they have' interpretation never even comes up; nor does the 'plural plus accusative' interpretation, since presumably they have just one house. The sequence **-lerini** has alerted you immediately to the fact that the final **-i** is the accusative, because it follows the **-n** that typically comes between a possessive suffix and a case suffix. So the only plausible interpretation that is likely to force itself upon you is 'we cleaned their house'. The only problem for the English-speaker, and perhaps speakers of many other languages, is that the **-ler-** element immediately puts 'plural' into your mind, so that you may instantly think 'houses' when you hear **evler**, even though in **evlerini temizledik** ('we cleaned their house') it really doesn't mean that. The form consists of **ev** 'house' and **-leri** 'their'. Don't worry – this is something you will need time to get used to, that's all.

Sometimes, speakers use genitive pronouns in a helpful way, usually to avoid ambiguity. **Onun** for 'his' or 'her' and **onların** for 'their' can give the understanding process just the boost it needs.

**Sevgi, onların bardakları boş!**
Sevgi, their glasses are empty!

**Onun cevapları yeterliydi.**
Her answers were satisfactory.

Because of the need for case markers in practically every sentence, the following sequences are also common:

| | | |
|---|---|---|
| **-lerine** | e.g. **evlerine** | to their house, to their houses, to his/her houses |
| **-lerinden** | e.g. **evlerinden** | from their house, from their houses, from his/her houses |

| | | |
|---|---|---|
| **-larında** | e.g. **arabalarında** | in their car, in their cars, in his/her cars |
| **-larını** | e.g. **arabalarını** | their car, their cars, his/her cars (*all direct objects!*) |
| **-lerinin** | e.g. **evlerinin** | of their house, of their houses, of his/her houses |

This section only concentrated on third person possessives, as that is the only context where this sort of confusion can arise. With the other persons, the possessive ending makes only one interpretation possible. For instance, if you try to think of a different meaning for each of the following examples, you won't succeed. **Arkadaşlarım** can only mean 'my friends'.

**Arkadaşlarımı davet etmedi.**
She didn't invite my friends.

**Akşam yemeklerinizi bitirebilecek miyiz?**
Shall we finish your food?

But, just like **evine** can mean 'to your house' and 'to his house' (*see* Lesson 6, page 97), so **mektuplarını** can mean 'your letters' as well as 'his letters', 'their letters' or even 'their letter'. Again, the context will usually make only one interpretation leap to mind. If the person who says the following sentence is talking to you directly, it is likely that he means 'your letters' (unless you have never sent him any!).

**Mektuplarını severim.**
I love your letters.

Presumably, if he didn't mean 'your letters', he would have said:

**Onun/Onların mektuplarını severim.**
I love his/their letters.

The interpretation 'their letter' is likely to appear only when you already strongly expect it because of the context, for instance when you know that the speaker has received a letter from a company.

Finally, here is an example with an accusative-marked plural compound noun: **sigorta formlarını: sigorta** 'insurance' plus **form** 'form' plus possessive suffix plural **-ları** = **sigorta formları**. When adding the accusative **-ı**, don't forget the extra **-n-**: **sigorta formlarını**:

**Sigorta formlarını doldurdun mu?**
Did you fill in the insurance forms?

## Exercise 8

Among the following twelve sentences, there are two **-leri** combinations of each of the six types mentioned above:

- 'their' + singular
- 'his'/ or 'her' + plural
- 'their' + plural
- 'they have'
- plural plus accusative
- plural compound noun plus accusative

Identify which sentence is of what type.

1 Bu şehirde trafik ışıkları her zaman kırmızı yanıyor.
2 Ahmet ile Hasan odalarında. Yukarıda, sol tarafta birinci odadır.
3 Bu kızlar annelerini çok seviyorlar.
4 Onların çocuklarını tanıyor musun?
5 Önce kızların odalarını boyadık.
6 Bazı çocukların ayaklarında ayakkabı yoktu.
7 Ondan sonra öğretmenlerin çok iyi bir önerileri vardı.
8 Ali komik hikayeleri anlattı.
9 Onun için bana giyeceklerini verdi.
10 Bana göre onun düşünceleri tehlikeli.
11 Çocukluğumda piyano derslerini hiç sevmezdim.
12 Camileri gördünüz mü?

| ışık | light | hikaye | story |
|------|-------|--------|-------|
| yanmak | to burn | giyecek | clothes |
| kırmızı | red | göre (-e) | according to |
| ... ile | with ... | çocukluk | childhood |
| boyamak | to paint | cami | mosque |
| öneri | proposal | | |

## Pronouns

In English, you are used to to the existence of personal and possessive pronouns. You can't express things like 'I'm sick', 'they're coming' or 'my car' without them. In Turkish, these pronouns are usually not necessary. Their basic equivalents are the suffixes: **hastayım** 'I am ill', **geliyorlar** 'they come' and **arabam** 'my car'. Nevertheless, pronouns exist, so you can use them. Just be aware that they usually add emphasis. The basic personal pronouns are the subject pronouns. Object pronouns are marked with the accusative case (**ben** 'I' plus accusative **-i** makes **beni**) and possessive pronouns with the genitive (**sen** 'you' plus genitive **-in** makes **senin** 'of you', 'your'). In addition, the other cases can be added to pronouns to express meanings like 'on', 'near', 'with me', 'to you' and 'from them'. Most of these forms you have already encountered; here they all are:

**Singular:**

|  | **ben** '*I*' | **sen** '*you*' | **o** '*he/she/it*' |
|---|---|---|---|
| *genitive* '*of*' | **benim** 'of me, mine' | **senin** 'of you, your' | **onun** 'his/her/its' |
| *dative* '*to*' | **bana** 'to me' | **sana** 'to you' | **ona** 'to him/her/it' |
| *accusative direct object* | **beni** 'me' | **seni** 'you' | **onu** 'him/her/it' |
| *locative* '*at*', '*in*', '*on*' | **bende** 'in/on/at me' | **sende** 'in/on/at you' | **onda** 'in/on/at him/her/it' |
| *ablative* '*from*' | **benden** 'from me' | **senden** 'from you' | **ondan** 'from him/her/it' |

**Plural:**

|  | **biz** '*we*' | **siz** '*you*' | **onlar** '*they*' |
|---|---|---|---|
| *genitive* '*of*' | **bizim** 'of us' | **sizin** 'of you, your' | **onların** 'of them, their' |
| *dative* '*to*' | **bize** 'to us' | **size** 'to you' | **onlara** 'to them' |
| *accusative direct object* | **bizi** 'us' | **sizi** 'you' | **onları** 'them' |
| *locative* '*at*', '*in*', '*on*' | **bizde** 'in/on/at us' | **sizde** 'in/on/at you' | **onlarda** 'in/on/at them' |
| *ablative* '*from*' | **bizden** 'from us' | **sizden** 'from you' | **onlardan** 'from them' |

## Non-use of pronouns

Especially in the beginning, you probably had the tendency to start out many sentences with **ben**, **sen**, **o** etc. If yours is a language which uses pronouns a lot, such as English, it is hard to break the habit when learning a language that doesn't normally use them, such as Turkish. Pronouns basically only come in for emphasis and to take care of possible ambiguities.

**Biz burada misafiriz, siz değilsiniz.**
We are guests here, you are not.

**Burada misafiriz.**
We're guests here.

**Ya sen, ne düşünüyorsun?**
And you, what do you think?

**Onlar çok tatlı.**
They are very sweet.

**Çok tatlı.**
He/She is very sweet.

 **Exercise 9 (Audio 2: 13)**

Insert pronouns in the spaces only where you think they are needed. This is not an exercise in which you can really make any mistakes. First, you should try the exercise, then listen to the cassette, and finally, compare your answers with the transcript in the Key.

| | |
|---|---|
| BAHAR: | Sabahat, ... Kayseri'den geleli kaç sene oldu? ... Bursa'ya geleli üç yıl oldu. |
| SABAHAT: | ... üç yıl oldu. |
| BAHAR: | ... yedi, sekiz ay sonra yine bir kursa başladım, ... da Kuzey Bursa'daydı. ... oraya altı ay, yok, sekiz ay devam ettim. ... bitti, bu yıl ... yine başlamıştım oraya. Ama ... diğer öğrencileri beğenmedim. Bir tek ... konuşuyorum, ... susuyor. |
| SABAHAT: | Bursa'yı ... sevemiyorum. ... seviyor musunuz? |
| AYHAN: | ... önceleri sevmiyordum, ama. ... nasıl buluyorsun Bursa'yı, Bursa'lıyı? |
| BAHAR: | Mesela Ayhan dönüş yapmak isterse ... hemen dönerim. ... buranın havasından çalışamıyorum. |
| AYHAN: | ... eğer burdan gitsem ... oraya ayak uyduramamki. |
| SABAHAT: | ... hiç uyduramazsın. |
| AYHAN: | ... hiç uyduramam artık. |
| BAHAR: | Çünkü ... Almanya'da büyüdün; ondan sonra da ... tekrar buraya geldi. Ondan sonra da ... buranın hayatına alışmaya çalışıyorsun. |

| | | | |
|---|---|---|---|
| **geleli** | when you came | **devam etmek** | to continue |
| **Kuzey** | North | **başlamıştım** | I had started |

| | | | |
|---|---|---|---|
| **dönüş yapmak** | if he wants to | **gitsem** | if I go |
| **isterse** | return | **ayak uydurmak** | to adapt |
| **eğer** | if | **alışmak** | to get used to |

## Some vocabulary exercises

You have learned many words in the preceding nine lessons, but many of them have only occurred once, so that you have probably forgotten quite a few. The following exercises are meant to help you remember.

## Exercise 10

Connect the words on the left with those on the right that mean something similar:

| | | | |
|---|---|---|---|
| 1 | ad | a | kız kardeş |
| 2 | fakat | b | arkadaş |
| 3 | gibi | c | isim |
| 4 | bırakmak | d | öğrenmek |
| 5 | merhaba | e | da/de |
| 6 | dinlemek | f | tekrar |
| 7 | dost | g | olarak |
| 8 | gelmek | h | bitirmek |
| 9 | ve | i | günaydın |
| 10 | abla | j | duymak |
| 11 | okumak | k | varmak |
| 12 | yine | l | ama |

## Exercise 11

Find the words on the right that mean the *opposite* of the words on the left.

| | | | |
|---|---|---|---|
| 1 | **bozuk** | a | **soru sormak** ('to ask') |
| 2 | **yeni** | b | **güzel** ('beautiful, nice') |
| 3 | **kapalı** | c | **hasta** ('ill') |
| 4 | **almak** | d | **fena** ('bad') |
| 5 | **girmek** | e | **siyah** ('black') |
| 6 | **başlamak** | f | **açık** ('clear') |
| 7 | **cevap vermek** | g | **vermek** ('to give') |
| 8 | **beyaz** | h | **son** ('end') |
| 9 | **berbat** | i | **çalışıyor** ('it works') |

10 **iyi**                 j **bırakmak** ('to leave')
11 **ilk**                 k **çıkmak** ('to come out')
12 **sıhhatli**        l **eski** ('old')

*Exercise 12*

Change the following sentences by replacing the word in parentheses with a (near) synonym, chosen from the list at the bottom. Be sure any endings take their right form. If you feel adventurous and/or self-confident, try doing the exercise without looking at the list of options.

1 Bu şarkıcıyı çok (seviyorum).
2 Cuma günü Fadime bana (söyledi) ki cumartesi günü eğlence var.
3 (Harika!) Gitar çalabiliyorsun!
4 Belediyeye başvurmalı mısın (belki)?
5 Şimdi baş rol oyuncusu (hakkında) konuşacağız.
6 (Doğru), ona iyi cevabı verdin!
7 (Bizim hanım) bana telefon etti, misafir geldi.
8 Ne zaman Güney Türkiye'ye (kalkıyorsunuz)?
9 Ama bu evin iki banyosu yok, biri (hata) yapmış.
10 Affedersiniz, efendim, (neden) dün akşam bana söylemediniz?
11 Nasıl mı buldum? Merak etme, bu pilav çok (iyi).
12 Raporu (tamamlayabildiniz mi)?
13 Geçen (yıl) buraları daha ucuzdu, değil mi?

**yanlışlık** 'mistake'; **gitmek** 'to go'; **karım** 'my wife'; **niçin** 'why'; **bitirmek** 'to finish'; **haklı** 'right'; **üzerine** 'about'; **acaba** 'I wonder . . .'; **şahane** 'great'; **beğenmek** 'to like'; **demek** 'to say'; **nefis** 'tasty'; **sene** 'year'.

| | | | |
|---|---|---|---|
| **baş rol oyuncusu** | starring actor | **merak etmek** | to worry |
| **misafir** | guest, visitor | **rapor** | report |
| **Güney** | South | | |

# 11 Çok değişmiş
## She has changed a lot

In this lesson you will learn how to:

- combine two clauses into a complex sentence
- form relative clauses
- form a second past tense
- decide which of the past tenses to use

If you listen to two people talking to each other, in any language, you will notice that in many of their sentences two or more simple sentences are combined into more complex ones. In Turkish, too, sentences can be combined in this way. This lesson will introduce the first relevant forms. To avoid confusion, we will use the term 'clause' to refer to the parts that constitute a complex sentence in this way. A sentence can consist of a main clause and any number of subordinated clauses, or of two or more coordinated clauses.

## Language point

### 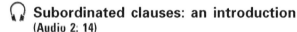 Subordinated clauses: an introduction
(Audio 2: 14)

When you think of subordinated clauses, you are most likely to think of clauses that start with 'that' or 'which' in English. Often these go with verbs such as 'think' or 'say', as in:

I don't think (that) *I'm going tonight.*
What's the title of the book *that you bought?*
Did he say *that he had seen your parents?*

The second sentence contains what is called a 'relative clause': a subordinate clause that goes with a noun (in this case with 'the book'). You use these if you want to say something about the book in order to make it clearer for the listener which book exactly you're talking about. Other common types of subordinated clauses are 'if' and 'when' clauses. For now, you should focus on trying to get a basic grasp of how Turkish handles clause-combining. It is essential that you realise that these clauses are not simply a 'more complex' option, to be used if you don't want to come across as a beginner too much. In many cases, they really are the normal way of saying things. With the types of sentences you have learned to produce so far, you can go a long way in conversation, but you'll soon notice that it would be handy, and that you would sound more eloquent, if you could form slightly more complex sentences. You are most likely to get this feeling in the following two contexts: with verbs like 'say' and 'think' (as in 'do you think that was a good idea?'), and with relative clauses, i.e. constructions such as 'the man I was talking about and the people we met'.

NB: If you want to, you can manage without them by using two sentences, such as:

**Ne düşünüyorsun? Bu iyi bir fikir mi?**
What do you think? Is this a good idea?

**Adam hakkında konuştum. Bu adam benim iş yerimde çalışıyor.**
I talked about the man. This man works at my workplace.

**Bu insanlarla buluştuk. Bunlarla geçen hafta tanıştık.**
We met these people. We got to know them last week.

However, if you want to sound more proficient, try using subordinated clauses:

**Bunun iyi bir fikir olduğunu düşünüyor musun?**
Do you think this is a good idea?

**Benim iş yerimde çalışan adam hakkında konuştum.**
I talked about a man who works at my workplace.

**Geçen hafta tanıştığımız insanlarla buluştuk.**
We met the people we got to know last week.

**Dialogue 1** (Audio 2: 15)

# Funda ve Mustafa

## Funda and Mustafa

The following dialogue contains a few complex clauses. For now, just focus on the general meaning. To check your understanding, answer the questions below and look at the Key.

*Funda and Mustafa are sitting around in their living room at the end of the day. She has just switched off the TV, but they're not quite ready yet to go to bed*

MUSTAFA:  Başka ne var, ne yok?
FUNDA:  Bugün bizim bankada çalışan Meral adlı arkadaşımla bir konu hakkında konuştum. O dedi ki biz, Türkler, kendi kendimizi yönetmiyoruz. Biz daha sert olmalıyız dedi.
MUSTAFA:  Bence zor.
FUNDA:  Tamam. Ali de aynısını dedi.
MUSTAFA:  Belki daha sert olmamız gerekiyor ama, nasıl olur? Ticaret yaptığımız ülkelerle düşman olmak istemiyoruz. Öte yandan, diğer ülkeler bize bunu yap, şunu yapma demesini istemiyoruz.
FUNDA:  Doğru! Ama gel sen, bunu Meral'a anlat! O bana inanmıyor. Ali'yle evlendiğinden beri çok değişmiş.
MUSTAFA:  Merak etme! O onun meselesi, seninki değil.

*(after a period of silence)*

MUSTAFA:  Pf, yoruldum. Yatacağım. Yarınki hava raporunu duydun mu?
FUNDA:  Duydum, rapora göre hava sıcak olacak.
MUSTAFA:  Harika. İyi geceler.
FUNDA:  İyi geceler, Mustafa. Ben biraz daha okuyacağım.

## Sözcükler

| | | | |
|---|---|---|---|
| **ne var, ne yok** | what's new? | **öte yandan** | on the other hand |
| **çalışan** | who is working | **diğer** | other |
| **adlı** | named | **evlendiğinden beri** | since she got married |
| **kendi kendimizi** | ourself | **değişmek** | to change |

| | | | |
|---|---|---|---|
| **yönetmek** | to govern | **değişmiş** | she has changed |
| **sert** | strong | **seninki** | yours |
| **ticaret** | trade | **yorulmak** | to get tired |
| **yaptığımız** | that we do | **yarınki** | tomorrow's |
| **ülke** | country | **sıcak** | warm |
| **düşman** | enemy | **iyi geceler** | goodnight |

## Exercise 1

Answer the following questions:

1 Where does Meral work?
2 What had Meral said that morning?
3 What kind of countries should not be made enemies?
4 What don't they want these countries to say to them, according to Mustafa?
5 When did Meral change?
6 What does Mustafa think is Meral's problem?
7 What strikes you about the way Mustafa says he's tired, compared to the English way of saying it?
8 Now underline the subordinate clauses in the dialogue.

## The basic subordinate clause

You will soon realise that the basic structure of all subordinate clauses is always the same. That structure, in a nutshell, is:

> 1 Subordinated clause
> 2 Suffix indicating subordination, attached to the verb
> 3 Main clause

As you probably realise by now, the main thing talked about usually comes last (a noun comes after its adjective, a **yatak odası** is a room and not a bed, and the verb comes last in the sentence). This order is the mirror image of that in English, where the main clause comes first, then the subordination marker and finally the subordinated clause. In English you say:

> I went to Amsterdam because I like it there.
> (main clause + subordinating conjunction ('because')
>    + subordinate clause)

More similar to the Turkish structure would be:

Because I like it there, I went to Amsterdam.

Given that 'because' is expressed by the suffix **-diği için**, this sentence becomes:

**Oraları sevdiğim için, Amsterdam'a gittim.**

This consists of the subordinated clause **oraları sev-** 'like it there', the suffix **-diğim için** 'because I' (suffixed to the verb), and the main clause **Amsterdam'a gittim** 'I went to Amsterdam'. The complete subordinated clause is **oraları sevdiğim için** 'because I like it there'.

NB: The first person ending **-m**, needed to express the 'I' in 'because I like it there', is added to **-diği** (person marking will be discussed further below).

Here are some more examples you can study in order to get a general feel for the structure. Again, don't spend too much time trying to work them out. Just look at every word in the sentences and try to get an idea of why they are there, why in the position they are in, and why in the form they occur in.

**Gazetecilerin onun üzerine yazdığı biçimi sevmiyorum.**
I don't like the way in which the journalists write about him.

**İstanbul'da oda bulmak istediğim için erken gittim.**
Because I wanted to find a room in Istanbul, I went early.

**Çalan kasetteki şarkıcıyı biliyorum.**
I know that singer on the tape that's playing.

# Language point

## Relative clauses

A relative clause enables you to say something extra about a noun. It can, for instance, be more informative to say 'the cousin who works at the airport' than just 'my cousin', as the former more clearly identifies who you are talking about. The part 'who works at the airport' is an example of a relative clause. This section is about such clauses.

## The form of the relative clause

Just as you had to get used to putting the verb last in a Turkish sentence, so you must try to familiarise yourself with the principle that the noun follows the relative clause. In English it comes first, followed by 'that', 'which' or 'who', but in Turkish the order is just the other way round. So: 'the book that you're reading' becomes 'you're reading that the book' (or, rather, 'the your-reading book'). Further, there is no separate word for 'that'; instead, Turkish uses a suffix. For this suffix you have the choice of two: **-diği** or **-en/ -an**. For deciding which one to use, use the following principles:

1. Possibility 1: the noun is the object of the verb in the relative clause
   In 'the book that you're reading' the noun 'the book' is the object of the verb 'read' in the relative clause 'that you're reading'. So you use **-diği**, stuck on to the verb stem (in the case of 'to read', that stem is **oku-**): **okuduğu** (notice the vowel harmony here) 'that one reads' (how to express 'you' will come later on).
2. Possibility 2: the noun is the subject of the relative clause
   In 'the woman who knows English', the noun 'the woman' is the subject of the relative clause 'who knows English'. In these cases, you use **-en/-an**: **İngilizce bilen** 'who/that knows English'.

## Exercise 2

Read this English text. You will notice that it doesn't read very easily, as it seems to lack a certain fluency. That's because relative clauses have been avoided. Your first task is to rewrite it using such relative clauses, of which you'll need six. As a guide, rewrite it avoiding the underlined words. For example, to avoid the first <u>it</u>, you need to pull the first two sentences together: 'When I went out last night to see the house that Jerry and Jill bought, it was raining pretty hard'. Check the Key after you've finished. Then say whether you would need **-diği** or **-en** in the Turkish translations of these relative clauses, i.e., decide whether the clause makes use of *Possibility 1* or *Possibility 2* above.

Jerry and Jill have bought a new house. When I went out last night to see <u>it</u>, it was raining pretty hard. I once had an umbrella. <u>That</u> umbrella was not to be found, so I had to depend on my raincoat. The streets are usually deserted at this time of night. <u>They</u> were completely devoid of human life. A cat was sheltering under a car. It was the only living creature I saw. All those people stayed in. They turned out to be quite right, because when I got to the house, I was completely soaked. I had intended a surprise for my friends. In addition, that backfired, as neither Jeremy nor Jill turned out to be home.

It is time now to discuss how to build up these structures. The two forms **-diği** and **-en** get attached to the verb stem. In the Turkish translations of 'the book you're reading' and 'the woman who knows English', the forms **-diği** and **-en** are attached to **oku-** and **bil-**, respectively, to give **okuduğu** and **bilen**. Because of the division in subject and object forms (*Possibilities 1* and *2*), you should be able to read these forms immediately as 'that is read' and 'who knows'. As already indicated, the noun that the relative clauses belong to follows:

| | |
|---|---|
| **okuduğu kitap** | the book that he/she is reading |
| **bilen kadın** | the woman who knows |

Compare these closely with their English translations. You still have to derive from **okuduğu kitap** what the Turkish equivalent is of 'he/she' in the English sentence. As you know, subjects are usually expressed through personal suffixes in Turkish. The third person suffix in **okuduğu kitap** is the last **-u** in **-duğu**. This is actually the possessive marker, the same as the **-i** in **evi** 'his/her house', so that **okuduğu** literally means 'his/her reading'. When you want to say 'the book you're reading', you need to express 'you' somehow. To do this, you replace the third person singular ending **-u** in **-duğu** with the second person singular suffix **-un**: **okuduğun kitap**. The full translations of the examples we started out with are:

| | |
|---|---|
| **okuduğun kitap** | the book you're reading |
| **ingilizce bilen kadın** | the woman who knows English |

To summarise, the structure of the relative clause looks like this:

---

1 X + Verb + **-diğ-** + -Personal ending + Noun

Example: **bugün** + **oku-** + **duğ-** + **-um** + **kitap** giving:
**bugün okuduğum kitap** 'The book that I read today'.

2 X + Verb + **-en** + Noun

Example: **İngilizce** + **bil-** + **-en** + **kadın** giving:
**İngilizce bilen kadın** 'The woman who knows English'.

---

The initial 'd' in **-diği** changes to a 't' if it follows one of the consonants that trigger the same change in the **-di**-suffix (*see* Lesson 2). With the personal endings, the forms are:

| | | | |
|---|---|---|---|
| **-diğim** | that I | **-diğimiz** | that we |
| **-diğin** | that you | **-diğiniz** | that you (*plural*) |
| **-diği** | that he/she/it | **-dikleri** | that they |

The 'X' can of course be anything that the sentence calls for. In the first example below, the verb is **göstermek** 'to show'. It is then natural that the 'X' is filled with the words for, e.g., 'to me' **bana** and 'picture' **resim**. Read through the following examples to see more relative clauses in actual sentences.

**Bana dün gösterdiğiniz resim çok güzel.**
The picture you showed me yesterday was very nice.

**Dün gece burada oturan insanlar bu sabah Bitlis'e gitti.**
The people who were sitting here last night have gone to Bitlis this morning.

**Bu gülümseyen kadın bizim hanımdır.**
That smiling woman is my wife. (or '*the woman who is smiling*')

**Dün akşam seyrettiğimiz programı sevdin mi?**
Did you like that programme we watched last night?

**Amsterdam'dan gelen uçak büyük bir rötar yaptı.**
The plane coming from Amsterdam is delayed a lot.

**Yediğin şey işkembeydi.**
The thing you ate was tripe soup.

**Aya ilk ayak basan insan.** (*see* Dialogue on page 73)
The first man who set foot on the moon.

The **-diği**-clause, but not the **-en**-clause, may have a separate subject. This is obvious if you take a closer look again at the two English examples we have been using. In 'the woman who knows', it is impossible to have somebody other than the woman do the 'knowing'. But in 'the book that was read', anybody can have done the 'reading'. That is why **-diğ** is followed by a possessive marker indicating the subject, such as second person **-in** in **okuduğun kitap** 'the book you have read', or first person plural in **okuduğumuz kitap** 'the book we have read'.

If the subject is not a pronoun such as 'I', 'you', 'we', etc., it comes first in the clause and is marked with the genitive case marker: **Meral'ın okuduğu kitap** for 'the book that Meral read'. Here, the name **Meral** is followed by the genitive case marker **-in** (*see* Lesson 6, page 94 for this case marker). If the subject is a pronoun, there is no need for anything but the person marker in **-diğim**, **-diğin**, etc. However, if you want to emphasise the 'you' in 'the book *you* read', you can add the personal pronoun in the genitive form and say **senin okuduğun kitap** (so not **sen okuduğun kitap**; the pronoun has to have the genitive form).

Some more examples:

**John'un sana anlattığı hikaye gerçek değil.**
The story that John told you isn't true.

**Sizin çektiğiniz fotoğrafları çok seviyorum.**
I like the pictures *you* took very much.

Don't overuse the genitive pronouns though. They are often superfluous, and, remember, they add emphasis. (You already know this principle, as we mentioned it several times when cautioning against using subject pronouns, such as **ben**, **sen**, etc., in general.) The following pair of sentences therefore do not mean exactly the same thing: the first one has emphasis on 'he' or 'she' in the English translation.

**Onun verdiği yanıtı beğenmedim.**
**Verdiği yanıtı beğenmedim.**
I didn't like the answer he/she gave.

The **-diği** sequence here indicates that the action indicated by **ver-**, was done by somebody we refer to with the third person singular, that is: a 'he' or a 'she'. Who exactly that 'he' or 'she' is, must of course be known from the context; if not, we would have said something like:

**Politikacının verdiği yanıtı beğenmedim.**
I didn't like the answer the politician gave.

## Exercise 3

Translate into English. Pay particular attention to subjects and objects, that is: check carefully who does what in every sentence.

1 Allahım, çalıştığım yer pistir!
2 O hiç giyinmediğim paltoyu Melike'ye vereceğim.
3 Oturduğun evi çok beğenirim.
4 Çalan kaset Beatles'e benzer.
5 Bana verdiğin kitaba henüz başlayamadım.
6 Durakta bekleyen diğer insanlar da yakındılar.
7 Kızın bulduğu işi sever mi?
8 Dedikodu yapmadığımız tek kişi sensin!
9 Eser ile evlendiği adamı tanıyor musun?
10 Konuşan kadın kim?

| | | | |
|---|---|---|---|
| **pis** | dirty | **-e benzemek** | to be like some- |
| **palto** | coat | | thing, resemble |
| **çalmak** | to play (e.g. tape | **durak** | (bus) stop |
| | recorder) | **yakınmak** | to complain |
| **kaset** | tape | | |

## Exercise 4

Provide the necessary case forms. The first item has been filled in already. Remember that the subject of a relative clause has the genitive case marker, the one used for possession (**-(n)in**, see Lesson 6, page 95). Apart from that, you might need the dative (direction towards, **-(y)e**), locative (place where, **-de**), ablative (direction from, **-den**) or accusative (direct object, **-(y)i**) cases for other nouns in the sentence. (For dative, locative and ablative, see Lesson 3; for the accusative case, see Lesson 6.)

1 Sen onlar yazdığın mektup hiç ellerine geçmedi. Senin, onlara
2 Anneanne yaptığı yaprak dolmasını çok severim.
3 Bu zeytin aldığınız dükkan hangisi?
4 Ahmet söylediği şarkı biliyor musun?
5 Sokak karşı oturan kadın ben güldürücü bir şaka anlattı.
6 Maradona attığı gol bütün zamanın en iyisiydi.
7 Yediğin ekmek beğendin mi?
8 Bütün ay aradığım hediye dün buldum.

| | | | |
|---|---|---|---|
| **el** | hand | **karşı** | across |
| **yaprak dolması** | stuffed vine leaves | **güldürücü** | funny |
| **şaka** | joke | **gol** | goal |

## Exercise 5

Now translate into Turkish. If the first sentence looks familiar, but you don't remember what from, look at the section on time-telling in Lesson 7 again, page 116.

1 The train that goes to Bursa.
2 The bicycle that you got for your birthday.
3 What's that noise you're making?
4 The student who lives across the street is very attractive.
5 Our friends who live in Britain have bought a beautiful new house.
6 I was six the year that you were born.

Now try and guess what the following would be. Translate 'to buy' with **satın almak**, not with **almak**.

7 The house we are going to buy.

| **doğum günü** | birthday | **sokağın karşısı** | across the street |
| **gürültü** | noise | **sevimli** | cute |

 **Dialogue 2** (Audio 2: 16)

# Çok üzüldüm

## I'm very sorry

*The next day Mustafa runs into his old friends Melike and Servet on the bus. Last time he saw them, Melike was looking for a job*

MUSTAFA: Senin iş durumun nasıl şimdi?
MELİKE: İşsizim.
MUSTAFA: Öyle mi? Hala bir şey bulamadın mı? Çok üzüldüm.
MELİKE: Gazetede ilanlara bakıyorum ama, zaten iş bulmak zor bu zamanlarda. Bıktım aramaktan.
MUSTAFA: Haklısın.
SERVET: Demin aklıma geldi: kız kardeşimin çalıştığı büro şey arayordu, sekreter. İstersen, ona telefon edebilirsin.
MELİKE: Benim için yepyeni bir yol olacak. Belki telefon ederim. Belki de okula dönebilirim. Ama o çok pahalı.
SERVET: Belki seninle ilgilenebilirler ... İyi bir sekreter olacaksın.

| | |
|---|---|
| MUSTAFA: | Bilgisayar hakkında birşey biliyor musun? |
| MELİKE: | Sen deli misin? Yirmi birinci yüzyıldayız. Tabii ki biliyorum, bilmeyen var mı? Senden başka yani? |
| MUSTAFA: | Biliyorum vallahi! Birazcık. Ama, haklısın, bilgisayar bilmeyen kalmadı neredeyse. Keşke şirketimizde boş yer olsaydı. Ha, bu konuyu tekrar açmayalım ... Ne yapacaksınız? Çarşıya çıkıyor musunuz? |
| SERVET: | Çıkmıyoruz, diş hekimine gidiyoruz, Kızılay'da. |
| MUSTAFA: | Kentin orasını iyi bilmiyorum. Maalesef, burada inmem gerek. İyi günler ve başarılar, Melike! |
| MELİKE: | Sağ ol. Funda'ya bizden selam söyle! |
| MUSTAFA: | Söylerim. Görüşürüz! |

## Sözcükler

| | | | |
|---|---|---|---|
| üzülmek | to be disappointed | yüzyıl | century |
| ilan | ad | birazcık | just a little bit |
| zaten | anyway | neredeyse | almost |
| bıktım (-den) | I'm fed up with ... | şirket | company |
| büro | office | keşke | if only |
| aranıyordu | they were looking for | diş hekimi | dentist |
| sekreter | secretary | diş | tooth |
| istersen | if you want | hekim | doctor |
| yepyeni | brand new | kent | town |
| ilgilenmek | to be interested in | inmek | to get off (a bus, |
| bilgisayar | computer | | etc.) |

### Exercise 6

Go through Dialogue 2 once more, paying particular attention to the tense endings. List every sentence or phrase under one of the following categories. Try to understand why the tense endings were chosen in each particular sentence. Ignore the endings that don't fit any category, that's those in **Kız kardeşimin bürosunda şey aranıyordu, sekreter olacaksın,** and **İlginç olmuş.**

a Nominal sentences, present tense
b Present tense on **-iyor**
c **Geniş zaman**
d Past tense
e Future tense

**Exercise 7** (Audio 2: 17)

Go through all dialogues you've read so far in this book, and make a list of greetings and formulas you say when starting a conversation, finishing one, responding to someone's polite or informal greeting, etc. Then suggest an appropriate greeting for the following situations:

1 You run into an old friend on the street.
2 Someone says **ne haber** to you.
3 You want to end a conversation.
4 You want to tell someone you're pleased to meet her.
5 You want to wish your friend good luck with his exams.
6 Somebody wishes you a nice holiday (you're by yourself).
7 Somebody wishes you and your partner a nice trip.
8 You run into a colleague you don't know very well for the first time today.

## Language point

### The past tense in -miş

You're very familiar by now with **-di**, the basic past tense. But there is another past tense: **-miş**.

The most important thing about this tense is that it is used to report on things that have already happened (it is, after all, a past tense), but that you *didn't see* happen. English doesn't have a separate tense for this; you simply add things like 'I heard that' or 'apparently'. Turkish adds **-miş** to the verb stem. This tense is often called the 'inferential', because when you use it you are reporting on an action or event you have inferred, as opposed to one you have seen or experienced. Somebody may have told you about it, for instance, or you can see that it has taken place without actually having witnessed it.

Dialogue 1 in this lesson contained the following sentence:

**Meral Ali'yle evlendiğinden beri çok değişmiş.**
Meral has changed a lot since she married Ali.

Funda used **-miş** here because she infers from Meral's behaviour that she has changed; obviously, she hasn't actually observed her friend changing. Just as you can use **-di** after nouns and adjectives as well, to express 'was'/'were', you can add **-miş** to nouns and adjectives. However, when you're doing this, you're not necessarily implying past tense. The sentence **çok ucuzmuş** can both mean 'it was cheap' and 'it is cheap'; the important thing is that in both cases it conveys the 'apparently' sense. The **-miş** form is usually more polite: **elbisen çok güzelmiş** means 'your dress is beautiful', and is used when you want to avoid sounding jealous.

### The forms

There are no surprises here:

| | |
|---|---|
| -mişim | -mişiz |
| -mişsin | -mişsiniz |
| -miş | mişler/-lermiş |

NB: The form **-lermiş** does not occur often.

 **Use** (Audio 2: 18)

It is difficult to give exact rules for when to use **-miş** and when to use **-di**, since often both are possible depending on what exactly you want to say. There are certain things in English which can make you think **-miş** in Turkish. They include the following (again, we do not recommend that you set out now to learn this list by heart; it is more important that you start to get an idea of what is common to all of them. Once you're comfortable with the basic senses of **-miş**, you will find it easier to interpret it when you encounter it, and to use it when it's called for):

1. 'According to . . .'
   **Hükümete göre bu sene iyi olmuş.**
   According to the government, this year turned out well.

2. 'I've heard that . . .'
   **Duyduğuma göre Saliha'ya yeni bir iş teklif etmişler.**
   I've heard they offered Saliha a new job.

3. '... must have ...'

**Bu saatte İngiltere'den ayrılmıştı.**
He must have left Britain by now.

4. 'Apparently ...'

**Bunu yapmayı beğenmiş.**
Apparently, he liked to do this.

**Bebek bugün çok yorulmuş. Hemen uykuya daldı.**
Apparently, the baby was very tired today. She immediately fell asleep.

5. 'I'm afraid that ...'

**Korkarım ki Ülke ona inanmıştir.**
I'm afraid that Ülke believed him.

**Dün akşam fazla içmişim. Bütün gün başım çok fena ağrıdı.**
I'm afraid I drank too much yesterday evening. I have had a terrible headache all day.

6. 'I guess ...'

**Ahmet'gil gelmemiş.**
I guess Ahmet and his family didn't come.

7. 'Well, well, ...'

**Oraya yalnız başına gitmişsin.**
Well, well, you went there by yourself!

8. 'You won't believe ...!'

**Bana ne demiş!**
You won't believe what he said to me!

NB: This shade of meaning highlights one very expressive use of **-miş**: surprise. Note that in this example there's no question of hearsay: the speaker heard exactly what 'he' said: **-miş** just adds the meaning that he can't quite believe what he heard. The speaker uses **-miş** because, in a way, he takes the perspective of the hearer, whom he expects to be surprised.

9. 'It looks as if ...' (**miş gibi**)

**Yağmur yağmış gibi.**
It looks as if it has rained.

10. 'I understand that . . .'

**Almanya tekrar futbol kupasını kazanmış.**
I understand that Germany won the football cup again.

11. 'They say . . .'

**Amerika'da çok zengin olmuş.**
They say he got very rich in America.

All this may look like a dazzling collection of uses at first sight, but it's really quite convenient to have a tense ending taking care of all these nuances, rather than all the separate words and expressions the learner of English has to learn. If you can get into the habit of associating **-miş** with things like uncertainty and surprise, you might just start seeing it as a very convenient aspect of Turkish.

## Exercise 8

Guess whether the verb in the Turkish equivalents of the following sentences will be marked with **-miş** or with **-di**. Then give the translations. (Sometimes, both are possible.)

1 He must have told them.
2 It has rained here (said upon arrival).
3 And then the dog bit her.
4 Fenerbahçe easily won the match we went to see.
5 I *said* to her I didn't do it.
6 She gave a nice concert, according to the papers.
7 I guess I forgot.
8 Did he call the insurance company?
9 Do you think he called?
10 Which number did you dial?

| | | | |
|---|---|---|---|
| **ısırmak** | to bite | **çevirmek** | to dial |
| **kolayca** | easily | **unutmak** | to forget |
| **konser** | concert | **sigorta** | insurance |

## 'Was', 'is' and 'apparently is': -miş versus -di

Above, you saw **-miş** used with verb stems to give an alternative past tense to the one with **-di**. We have seen that **-di** can be used with nouns and adjectives too, as in **doktordu** and **hastaydım**. The same can be done with **-miş** – no surprises there. However, while **-di** means the same thing whether it's stuck on to a verb stem or on to a noun, **-miş** doesn't. First the easy part: on a noun or an adjective **-miş** still means 'apparently'. The confusing bit is that on nouns and adjectives **-miş** is not a past tense marker. Consider the following versions of 'Hatice is a nice person.'

| | |
|---|---|
| **Hatice iyi bir insan.** | (She's nice, period) |
| **Hatice iyi bir insandı.** | (She was nice, back when, when she was alive, etc.) |
| **Hatice iyi bir insanmış.** | (They say she's a nice person) |

So this use of **-miş** has more in common with the normal present tense (**Hatice iyi bir insan**) than with the past tense. You say **Hatice iyi bir insan** when you know her yourself and you know (or you want to let people know that you know) that she's a nice person. But if you have never met her, you can only have it from hearsay that Hatice is nice, so you say **Hatice iyi bir insanmış**: 'they say she's nice'; 'she's supposed to be nice'; 'she appears to be nice'; 'I hear she's nice', etc.

However, the past tense meaning of **-miş** we encountered above with verb stems is possible, as long as some indicator of past tense, words such as **geçen yıl**, **eskiden** ('in the old days'), are used alongside it. For example:

**Eskiden Hatice iyi bir insanmış.**
They say Hatice used to be a nice person.

Like **-di**, **-miş** can also be detached from the noun or adjective, which is then followed by **imiş**, plus any endings of course. There is no vowel harmony in this case:

**Siz Nursen'in arkadaşı imişsiniz.**
You must be Nursen's friend.

### Exercise 9

Fill in the right endings before and after **-miş**, by paying attention to the relevant portion of the translation, given in parentheses

1 **Yap-......, maşallah!** ('Oh, my God, he's done it!')
2 **Yeterli tuz kullan-......** ('They can't have used enough salt.')
3 **Uyu-......** ('I must have fallen asleep.')
4 **O yabancı değil-...... burada.** ('She is apparently not a guest here.')
5 **Ondan memnun ol-......** ('They were probably not pleased with that.')

6 **O zaman evde** ...... ('Was he at home at the time, as far as you know?')

7 **Bu ne-** ...... ('What is this supposed to be?')

8 **Yorul-** ...... ('You must be tired.')

9 **Duyduğuma göre sen dün fazla güneşlen-** ...... ('I heard you were in the sun too much yesterday.')

10 **O maç Kayseri'de-** ...... ('That match was apparently in Kayseri.')

| | | | |
|---|---|---|---|
| **tuz** | salt | **fazla** | too much, excessive |
| **uyumak** | to sleep | | |

## Language point

### The past participle in -miş

When you encounter a form that ends in **-miş**, you have to be aware of one use in which it is not a tense marker. It also may be a past participle. You may have noticed that we haven't talked about the verb system in terms of three forms, like we do in English with 'go', 'went', 'gone'. This is so for two reasons. First, because Turkish is much more regular. If you just learn the right markers for present tense, past tense and future tense, you can conjugate any verb you want. Second, most of the uses of the English participle ('gone' in the list above) are expressed by the **-di** and **-miş** past tenses in Turkish. However, Turkish does have participles, and they are used as adjectives: 'a missed chance', 'the bought tickets', 'chopped tomatoes'. They are third person singular forms on **-miş**.

**Kaçırılmış bir şanstı bizim için.**
It was a missed chance for us.

**Yeni toplanmış elmayı daha çok severim.**
I prefer freshly harvested apples.

### Exercise 10

Read the following little text and then indicate whether the actions 1–13 definitely happened or whether you can only *infer* that.

1 that the narrator ran into Emel.
2 that Emel's sister went to last week's concert.

3 that Ahmet was at the concert, too.
4 that Ahmet lives in Germany.
5 that the narrator has forgotten the place name.
6 that the narrator (and someone else) went for a walk in the park with his dog.
7 that the dog wanted to go home.
8 that the narrator and Emel talked for a long time.
9 that it was wet in the park.
10 that Ahmet's wife is working in a shop in Germany.
11 that at some point it suddenly started raining again.
12 that Emel's sister and Ahmet had talked for a long time.
13 that time went by quickly last night.

Bu akşam parkta köpeği gezdirdik. Her taraf çok ıslaktı. Emel'e rast geldik. Kız kardeşi geçen haftaki konsere gitmiş. Ahmet de oradaymıştı. Almanya'da oturuyormuş. Kentin adını unuttum. Onlar uzun uzun beraber sohbet etmişler. Ahmet'in karısı da Almanya'da çalışıyormuş, bir dükkanda. Birden tekrar yağmur yağmaya başladı. Biz de uzun konuştuk. Zaman ne çabuk geçmişti. Emel trene yetişmek durumundaydı, dokuzda ayrıldı.

| | | | |
|---|---|---|---|
| **köpek gezdirmek** | to take the dog out for a walk | **sohbet etmek** | to chat |
| | | **birden** | suddenly |
| **taraf** | side | **çabuk** | fast |
| **ıslak** | wet | **yetişmek** | to catch (a train, etc.) |
| **uzun uzun** | for a long time | | |
| **uzun** | long, tall | | |
| **-a rast gelmek** | to run into (*alternative to* **rastlamak**) | | |

# 12 Zengin olsam . . .

## If I were rich . . .

In this lesson you will learn how to:

- say something would happen, if . . .
- say that you would do something, if . . .
- use temporal clauses ('when', 'while')
- use signals to structure what you want to say

## *If:* conditional clauses

In the previous lesson, we introduced subordinated clauses. Now we will look at several other types of clause combination. First, you will learn how to express *if*-sentences (also called conditional clauses, since 'if' expresses a condition). You will find some in the following dialogue. Try to see what these have in common, i.e., work out what the conditional suffix looks like.

## 🎧 Dialogue 1 (Audio 2: 19)

## Zengin olsam . . .

## If I were rich . . .

*In this dialogue, Zeynep and her husband Yusuf have a quarrel about the state of their house. Zeynep thinks their house desperately needs repair*

YUSUF:    Sevgilim, çok sağlam bir evimiz var. İstersek, burada yüz yıl daha oturabiliriz.
ZEYNEP:   Bak hele! Yatak odasının duvarlarında çatlaklar var! Aman, böyle çürük bir evde nasıl yaşayabilirim?

YUSUF: Peki, milli piyangoyu vurursam, sana sıfır, yepyeni bir ev alacağım, güzelim.

ZEYNEP: Yalnız küçük bir sorun var, değil mi? Bir bilet almak için paramız kalmadı. Sen işini kaybetmeseydin, bir, iki, üç ev bile alabilirdin ...

YUSUF: Haklısın. Ne diyeceğim?

ZEYNEP: Şunu diyeceksin: gelecekte bir işim olursa, bu işi korumaya çalışacağım ...

## Sözcükler

| | | | |
|---|---|---|---|
| **sevgilim** | my darling | **vurmak** | to shoot; to strike, (*in* |
| **sağlam** | solid | | *this context:*) to win |
| **duvar** | wall | | (the lottery) |
| **çatlak** | crack | **sıfır** | zero (*here: very new*) |
| **çürük** | rotten | **sorun** | problem |
| **yaşamak** | to live | **korumak** | retain |
| **milli piyango** | national lottery | | |

Conditional clauses discuss the consequence of some event. This event may be hypothetical (*if* this happens, then ...), or it may not have happened at all (if this *had* happened, then ...). In English, the word 'if' is used to convey both meanings. Compare:

1 I'll give him some aspirin, if he feels ill.
2 I would have given him some aspirin, if he had felt ill.

In 1, we don't know whether he feels ill or not. We just speculate about what could happen in the hypothetical case that he does, and if he is indeed ill, he will get his aspirin. This type of condition is called an *open condition*: the possibility remains 'open' whether or not some event may happen. The implication in 2 is that he did not feel ill at all, so there was no reason to give him aspirin. This is called a *closed condition*. The reason we mention this difference is that it matters in Turkish.

### Exercise 1

1 Find the four conditional verb forms ('if' phrases) in the dialogue. They all have the suffix **-se** (or **-sa**) in common.
2 Which tense endings do the personal endings of the conditional remind you of?

# Language point

## 'Open conditions'

The concept expressed by English 'if', is expressed by the suffix **-sa** (or **-se**) in Turkish. Although Turkish treats open and closed conditions differently, both share the **-se** suffix. For open conditions, it is added to **-iyor**, **-di**, **-ar** and **-ecek**. The endings are the same as you use for the formation of the past tense on **-di**:

| | | | |
|-----|----------|---------|--------|
| -sam | if I | -sak | if we |
| -san | if you | -sanız | if you |
| -sa | if he/she/it | -larsa | if they |

The suffix can be used in 'verbless' sentences, where there is no verb stem to add it to. You can just add it to the adjective or noun. English 'if he is ready' becomes **hazır-sa**. In negations, you add the suffix to the negation **değil**: 'if he isn't sick' becomes 'sick not if': **hasta değil-se**. Or take the formulaic expression **vaktin var**, 'you have time'. You can also add the **-se/-sa** suffix here: **vaktin varsa** 'if you have time'. If you study this example closely, you'll see why the **-sa** part is constant: the person marking is done on the noun **vakit**. Thus, 'if we have time' is **vaktimiz varsa**, 'if I don't have time' is **vaktim yoksa**, and 'if Fadime has time' is **Fadime'nin vakti varsa**. For this type of construction expressing possession, reread the part about the **param var** type sentences in Lesson 4, page 64. Examples:

**Hasta değilse, niye toplantıya gelmedi?**
If he isn't sick, why didn't he come to the meeting?

**Bilgisayarı yoksa, ona benimkini ödünç veririm.**
If he hasn't got a computer, I'll lend him mine.

The suffix starts with **-y-** if the word before it ends in a vowel. This applies to nouns and adjectives, and to the past tense **-di**, as none of the other verb tenses end in a vowel.

**İyiyse, alayım.**
If it's good, I'll take it.

**Evdeysen bana bir mektup yaz!**
If you are at home, write me a letter!

The suffix has to follow a tense ending, so that common sequences are **-iyorsa**, **-ırsa** and **-ecekse**. The most common tense in conditional clauses is the **geniş zaman**.

**Acele edersem, trene yetişeceğim.**
If I hurry, I'll catch my train.

**Bu dükkanda yeni deri bir çanta alırsanız, cüzdan bedava verilir!**
If you buy a new leather bag at this shop, they give a wallet for free!

**Uçağıma yetişemezsem, otobüs şirketini mahkemeye vereceğim!**
If I don't catch my plane, I will sue the bus company!

**Kendini iyi hissetmezse, aspirin vereyim.**
If he doesn't feel well, I will give him an aspirin.

An example with past tense **-di** plus **-sa**:

**Yoruldularsa, bizim yatağımızda yatabilirler.**
If they are tired, they can sleep in our bed.

Note especially that the first person plural form is **-sak**, *not* **-samız**.

**İngiltere'ye gidersek, Cornwall'a uğrarız.**
If we go to Britain, we'll visit Cornwall.

**Koşmazsak, yetişemeyiz!**
If we don't run, we won't make it!

Sometimes, mostly in written texts, the **-se** part appears as **ise**, as a word on its own. If it does, vowel harmony does not apply (that is, **ise** is always **ise** and never *ısa*). The word **ise** also means 'on the other hand', as in:

**Fatma Ankara'da çalışıyor, kocası ise Erzurum'da.**
Fatma works in Ankara, her husband, on the other hand, in Erzurum.

**Rehberimiz Mustafa ise, bu sandal gezisi tehlikeli olmaz.**
If Mustafa is our guide, this canoe trip is not dangerous.

You may start your conditional sentence with or without the word **eğer** 'if'. There are two reasons for using **eğer**:

1 highlighting the hypothetical nature of the event;
2 announcing that a conditional form will appear later on in the sentence, in case the conditional sentence is a very long one.

Examples:

**Eğer gelirse, görüşeceğiz.**
*If* he comes, we can meet.

**Eğer yarın Sevil sizi istasyondan almayı unutursa, lütfen bana telefon edin!**
If Sevil forgets to pick you up from the station tomorrow, please call me!

## Exercise 2

Turn these sentences into conditional 'if' clauses, including verb tense, as has been done for the first item. Don't worry about the main clause.

1 Büyük bir şehirde yaşıyorsun. Büyük bir şehirde yaşıyorsan, . . .
2 Bu akşam Fatma'nın partisine gideceğim.
3 Her yaz trenle seyahat eder.
4 Otogarda seni beklerim.
5 Akşamları annem bana bir hikaye anlatır.
6 Kar yağıyor.
7 Abim mühendis olmak istiyor.
8 Sorunuz var.

| parti | party | kar yağmak | to snow |
|---|---|---|---|
| seyahat etmek | to travel | mühendis | engineer |
| otogar | bus station | | |

# Language point

## 'Closed conditions'

After closed conditions you can almost hear the word **ama** or **fakat** 'but' (it didn't happen). Turkish again makes use of the suffix **-se** here, but without tense marking prior to this suffix. You can, however, indicate whether the closed condition itself refers to either the present or the past. If the past, you put the past tense marker **-di** after the conditional suffix. This means that the present tense form consists of the verb stem plus **-se** plus person marker, as in:

**Marmaris'e gitseler, bu küçük balıkçı köyünün monden bir sahil kentine değiştiğini kendi gözleriyle görebilirler.**
If they would go to Marmaris (but they won't), they would be able to see with their own eyes that this small fishing village has changed into a worldly seaside resort.

The past tense form is verb stem plus **-se** plus **-di** plus person, as in:

**Telefon etseydiniz, yardım ederdik.**
If you had called (but you didn't), we would have helped.

As you can see in the previous examples and in the ones below, the usual verb tense in the main clause is the **geniş zaman**, occasionally combined with past tense. More examples:

**Sen olsan ne yaparsın?**
What would you have done, if it had been you?

**Annesinin çok hasta olduğunu bilseydim, yanına giderdim, ama ...**
If I had known her mother was very ill, I would have gone there, but ...

**Hasta hissetse, aspirin veririm.**
If he had felt ill, I'd have given him some aspirin.

There is a small exception to the rule that the stem plus **-se** type of clauses are always closed conditions. If the main clause is, for instance, **iyi olur** 'it would be better', the conditional part more or less expresses a proposal, of the type **şimdi ne yapsak** 'what shall we do now?'

**Evde kalsan daha iyi olur.**
It would be better, if you'd stay at home.

**Daha sonra gelseniz iyi olur.**
It would be fine if you came along later.

In the examples of sentences with open conditions, we saw the conditional suffix being used in existential sentences (such as **vaktim varsa**) and 'verbless' sentences (such as **iyiyse**). If you want to express the equivalent closed conditions, meaning 'if I had the time' etc., you have to use the verb **olmak**.

**Vaktim olsa seyahat ederdim.**
If I had the time, I would travel.

**İyi olsaydı alırdım.**
If it had been good, I would have bought it.

You can also use this form (stem plus **-se**) for conveying a wish, or rather something you long for. What you do then is simply formulate the *if*-part without expressing the main clause.

**Çocuklar yemeklerini bir bitirseler!**
If only the children would finish their meal!

If you want to put extra emphasis on your lamentation, you may use **keşke** or **bari**, both meaning 'if only'. In writing, both usually appear at the beginning of a sentence, although they can also appear at the end.

| | |
|---|---|
| **Zengin olsam keşke!** | If only I were rich! |
| **Bari telefon etseydiniz!** | If only you had called! |

Don't confuse the endings **-seydi** (which is the past tense of closed conditions) and **-diyse** (the past tense of open conditions). There is a difference in meaning between **gelseydim** ('if I had come ...') and **geldiysem** ('if I came ...').

Likewise, compare **bilseydim** and **anladıysan** in the following examples:

**Bilseydim buraya gelmezdim!**
If I had known I wouldn't have come here!

**Bilseydim!** or **Keşke bilseydim!**
If only I had known!

**Dersi anladıysan, sorulara cevap verebilirsin.**
If you have understood the lesson, you can give the answers.

*Exercise 3*

Now turn the sentences in Exercise 2 into conditional sentences, using the form expressing closed conditions.

## Brand new!

We saw in Dialogue 1 that Yusuf wanted to buy a **yepyeni** 'brand new' house for Zeynep and himself. Adjectives and adverbs, such as **yeni** 'new', **başka** 'other', 'different', **temiz** 'clean' and **mavi** 'blue', can be made stronger in meaning by doubling the first syllable and adding an extra **-m**, **-p**, **-r** or **-s**.

**yepyeni**   brand new          **tertemiz**   immaculately
                                                clean
**bambaşka**  completely different **masmavi**    deep blue

*Exercise 4*

What do you think the following adjectives mean?

**kıpkırmızı, dosdoğru, büsbütün, bomboş, taptaze**

**taze**       fresh

# Reading text

The following text about the telephone shop **Faks Maks** ('Faxes and stuff') contains verb suffixes you have not seen before. Try to grasp the meaning of the text and then answer the questions.

# Reklam

Son yıllarda Türkiye'de bir sürü telekomünikasyon cihazları piyasaya getiriliyor. Telefon dükkanlarının sayısı artarken, Türkiye'de ilk olarak cep telefonu, modem ve de çağrı aletleri satan Faks Maks, müşteri çekmek için çeşitli yöntemler denemeye başladı. Milyar liralık bir reklam kampanyası açan Faks Maks, kendi dükkan zincirinde en gelişmiş, en hızlı cihazların Türkiye'de en düşük fiyatlara satacağını bildirdi. Faks Maks'ın genel müdürü Ali Bakırcıoğlu 'Rekabetçilerimiz hala Taş Devrinde yaşarken, biz en yeni cihazları satıyoruz. Fiyatlarımız çok düşük. Ama, sayın müşterilerimiz çabuk davranmalarını tavsiye ediyoruz. Rekabetçiler uyanınca, tabii ki biz de fiyatlarımızı ona göre değiştirmek zorunda kalacağız,' diye söyledi.

| | | | |
|---|---|---|---|
| **bir sürü** | a number of | **artmak** | to grow, to rise |
| **cihaz** | machine | **cep** | pocket |
| **piyasaya** | to be introduced | **çağrı aleti** | buzzer |
| **getirilmek** | on to the | **müşteri** | customers |
| | market | **yöntem** | strategy |
| **sayı** | number | **denemek** | to try |

| milyar liralık | of one billion liras | rekabetçi | competitor |
| zincir | chain | taş | stone |
| gelişmiş | developed, | devir | period, age |
| | advanced | sayın | honourable |
| düşük | lower | davranma | to act, to behave |
| bildirmek | to announce | zorunda kalmak | to have to, to be |
| genel | general | | forced to |
| genel müdürü | general manager | | |

## Exercise 5

1 There are several new verb suffixes in the text. You should already know the meaning of **getirmek**. Here in the first sentence, it carries the suffix **-il**. Can you guess what that means?

2 The second newcomer is **-ken** in **artarken** and **yaşarken**. What might **-ken** express?

3 Finally, you may have found **-ince** in **uyanınca**. What does it mean?

## Language point

### The 'converbs' -ince 'when', 'as soon as' and -ken 'while'

Turkish does not have conjunctions of the type exemplified by 'while', 'after', 'before' or 'when'. Instead, verb endings are used to express whether something happened before, after or at the same time as another event. By attaching these endings to a verb stem, a so-called 'converb' is formed. 'Converbs' carry no tense markers (so, no **-iyor**, **-di** etc.) or person markers (such as **-im**), the exception being **-ken**. In this lesson we'll look at two converb endings: **-ince** and **-ken**.

The form **-ince** means 'when', 'as soon as', and **-ken** means 'while'. These meanings are not entirely temporal: **-ince** very often has a causal implication, **-ken** may express a contrast (as does English 'while').

**Oğlan oyuncakları görünce yüzü gülmeye başladı.**
As soon as the boy saw the toys, a smile appeared on his face (his face started laughing).

**Çoban uyurken koyunları kaçmış.**
While the shepherd was asleep, his sheep escaped.

**Kız okula gelince, arkadaşlarıyla oynamaya başlar.**
When the girl arrives at school, she starts to play with her
friends.

**Kızlar oynarken, öğretmen dışarıya çıktı.**
While the girls were playing, the teacher came outside.

The suffix **-ince** follows the rules of vowel harmony; **-ken**, however,
remains unchanged. When you use **-ken** with a verb, you have to
add a tense, generally the **geniş zaman**. Therefore, it is **uyurken**
and not something like **uyuken**.
Both **-ince** and **-ken** may or may not have different subjects. If
the subjects are different, they should be mentioned explicitly.
More examples, first without a different subject in the subordinated
clause:

**Gazetede bu makale okuyunca çok sevindim.** (subject = I)
When I read this article in the paper, I was glad.

**Çalıştıktan sonra eve gelince duş aldı.** (subject = he)
When he came home after work, he took a shower.

**Televizyonu seyrederken, kitap okurum.** (subject = I)
While I watch television, I read a book.

**Kendisini zorla kaldırıma atan yaya elini havada sallarken
arabanın ardından 'Hayvan herif!' diye bağırıyordu.** (*subject*
= the pedestrian = he)
While the pedestrian who threw himself with difficulty on to
the pavement waved his hands in the air, he shouted after
the car: 'Idiot!'.

And with two separate subjects:

**Kardeşim gelmeyince polisi çağırdım.** (subjects: my brother, I)
When my brother did not show up, I called the police.

**Kız kardeşim televizyon seyrederken, ben kitap okurum.**
(subjects: my sister, I)
While my sister watches television, I read a book.

In an article about Tina Turner there is this sentence containing
two **-ken**'s:

**Sahne o kadar yüksekti ki, basın mensupları fotoğraf çekerken bu hatunun bacaklarına 3 metre aşağıdan bakarken, hayranlıklarını gizleyemediler.**

The stage was so high that, while the reporters took pictures and while they looked from 3 metres below at the legs of this woman, they could not hide their admiration.

| | |
|---|---|
| **basın mensupları** | reporters, members of the press |
| **hatun** | woman |
| **hayranlık** | admiration |

By using **-ken**, you can express a contrast, corresponding to a similar, specific use of English 'while':

**Komşumuz arabayla tatile giderken, kardeşi genellikle uçakla seyahat ediyor.**
While our neighbour goes on holiday by car, his brother usually travels by plane.

**Bütün ailemin buraya geleceğini zannederken havaalanında sadece babamı gördüm.**
While I thought my entire family would come here, I only saw my father at the airport.

## Exercise 6

Consider whether **-ince** or **-ken** is the most appropriate in the following:

1 Üsküdar'a giderken/gidince, yağmur yağdı.
2 Üsküdar'a gelirken/gelince, yağmur yağmaya başladı.
3 Saz çalarken/çalınca, bütün sorunlarım eriyip gider.
4 Öğretmen sınıfa girerken/girince, öğrenciler hemen sustu.
5 Tren istasyona varırken/varınca, tuvalete koşacağım.
6 Müzik dinlerken/dinleyince, televizyonu seyredemem.
7 Polis sahneye çıkarken/çıkınca, kavgayı seyredenler çabuk dağıldı.
8 Annem halk müziği severken/sevince, babam en çok arabesk sever.

| | | | |
|---|---|---|---|
| **sorun** | problem | **kavga** | fight |
| **eriyip gitmek** | to melt away, to disappear | **dağilmak** | to disperse |
| | | **halk müziği** | folk music |
| **sınıf** | class, classroom | **arabesk** | 'Arab-styled' |
| **tuvalet** | toilet | | popular songs |

It is also possible to use **-ken** in 'verbless' and existential sentences. Note that the suffix starts with **-y** if it follows a noun that ends in a vowel.

**Trafik lambası yeşil değilken, karşıya geçemezsin!**
As long as the traffic light isn't green, you cannot cross the street!

**Daha gencecik bir tiyatro yazarıyken bana da usta yardım etti.**
While I was still a young playwright, the master helped me.

**Paran varken, neden yeni bir ev satın almıyorsun?**
Why don't you buy a new house, now that you have money?

**Öğretmen okulda yokken, ders başlayamaz.**
As long as the teacher is not at school, the lessons cannot begin.

## Language points

The following sections will briefly discuss how to say 'when', 'without' and 'before'.

### When

First, two ways of saying 'when'. Both make use of the **-diği** suffix. You may need to review Lesson 11, to see how this suffix is used in building relative clauses. For expressing 'when', you use this format:

stem + **-diği** + person + **-de**
*or:*
stem + **-diği** + person + **zaman**

For instance, **devam ettiğimde** means the same as **devam ettiğim zaman**: 'when I continued . . .'. More examples:

**Seksen yaşına geldiğinde, yüzme dersi almaya başladı.**
When he reached the age of eighty, he started taking swimming lessons.

**Sebze haline girdiğimde sergilenmiş pırıl pırıl meyve ve sebzeler gözlerimi kamaştırdı.**
When I came to the vegetable market, the sparkling fruit and vegetables that were on display made my eyes dazzle.

**Türkiye'ye döndükleri zaman bütün komşularının başka yerlere taşındıklarını öğrendiler.**
When they returned to Turkey, they found out that all their neighbours had moved to other places.

## Without

When you add **-meden** to a verb stem, you have the Turkish version of a subordinate clause which expresses 'without. . .-ing'.

**Hiç bir şey yemeden işe gitti.**
He went to work without eating.

**Çalışmadan sınavı hiç geçemezsin.**
You'll never pass the exam without working.

**Para ödemeden sinemaya girmeyi başardı.**
He managed to sneak into the cinema without paying.

## Before

We already saw **-dikten sonra** 'after' in one of the examples above (**Çalıştıktan sonra eve gelince duş aldı** 'When he came home after work, he took a shower' on page 202). The opposite is **-meden** (or **-meden önce**) 'before', which is placed after the stem. Since there are no personal or temporal markers, the context must provide you with clues about who and when.

**Yatmadan önce, ılık bir duş yapabilirsiniz veya eksersiz yapabilirsiniz.**
Before you go to sleep, you can take a lukewarm shower or you can do exercises.

**Hamlet İstanbul'da yeniden sahneye konmadan önce, yirmi yıllık bir süre geçmiş.**
Before *Hamlet* was put on stage again in Istanbul, a period of twenty years had passed.

**Trene binmeden önce, bir bilet almalısınız.**
Before boarding the train, you have to buy a ticket.

### Exercise 7

Complete the following subordinate clauses by filling in the proper ending (**-ken/-ince/-meden/-se/-diği zaman**). Add personal or tense

markers, if necessary. In some of the items, more than one ending
may be possible.

1  Bin _____ tren kalktı.
2  Dur _____ ilerliyorduk.
3  Sizinle konuş _____ içeri girdi.
4  Okulda _____ evi yandı.
5  Öl _____ oğlu yeni müdür olacak.
6  Hoşça kal de _____ ayrıldı.
7  Doğru cevabı bil _____ hemen söyleyin!
8  Sıkıl _____ bize söylersin.

| ilerlemek | to proceed | yanmak | to burn |
| içeri | in, inside | | |

## Exercise 8

Translate:

1  the hand that rocks the cradle
2  the spy who came in from the cold
3  if looks could kill
4  if you leave me now, you take away the better part of me
5  wake me up before you go
6  without leaving a trace

| sallandırmak | to rock | terketmek | to leave someone |
| beşik | cradle | benim en iyi parçamı | the better part of me |
| casus | spy | uyanmak | to wake up |
| bakışlar | looks | iz | trace |

## Conversation aids

Every language has certain words or idioms by means of which
you can structure your speech. These words focus the attention of
the listener on what you are saying. What you in fact do is help
the listener understand how one idea leads to another. For instance,
you may want to point out that the things you are talking about
happen one after the other, that is, in chronological order (English,
'and then', for instance). Or you may want to say that something
happened *before* or *at the same time*. By using these conversation
aids, you lead the listener to a better understanding. They don't fit
into a single grammatical category. Important functions of conversation aids are the following:

1. Making a new start in the conversation (or changing the subject):

| | | | |
|---|---|---|---|
| **peki/pekala** | OK, well | **işte** | you see. ... |
| **hadi/haydi** | well, come on | **neyse** | OK, well then |
| | | | (suggests resignation) |

| | |
|---|---|
| **Peki ne yapacağız?** | OK, what shall we do? |
| **Hadi gidelim.** | Come one, let's go. |
| **Neyse, eve dönelim.** | Well then, let's head back home. |

2. Saying more about or organising the speech in time (e.g., by specifying the order of events):

| | | | |
|---|---|---|---|
| **ondan sonra** | and then | **kaldı ki** | moreover |
| **önce** | before | **hele** | but first |
| **ilk önce** | first and foremost | **şu anda** | at that moment |
| **ilk olarak** | first, in the first place | **şimdi** | now |
| **üstelik** | moreover | **de/da** | on the other hand |

Various kinds of verbal forms we've seen so far (**-meden önce** 'before', **-diği zaman** 'when', **-dikten sonra** 'after') also belong to this category.

**Oğlan ağaçtan düştü. Ondan sonra ambülans geldi. Ondan sonra oğlan hastaneye götürüldü.**
The boy fell from the tree. And then came the ambulance.
And then the boy was taken to the hospital.

**Hele bavullarımızı açalım.**
Let's first unpack our cases.

3. Adding a 'mood' to what you say (e.g. reinforcement, confirmation, surprise, frustration, doubt):

| | |
|---|---|
| **artık** | finally, (with negation: 'not any longer') |
| **ama ...** | but ... (at the end of a sentence) |
| **ki ...** | so (frustration/ anxiety/ doubt) |
| **ya** | come on (expresses emphasis, reinforcement) |
| **değil mi?** | isn't it? |
| **acaba** | I wonder? |

**Artık uyuyamıyorum.**
I cannot sleep any longer.

**Sana zahmet olur, ama ...**
It's a lot of trouble for you, but ...

208

**Bana inanmadı ki!**
God, he didn't believe me!

**O kadar mutluydum ki ...!**
I was so happy ...!

**O kadar çabuk koştum ki!**
I ran so fast!

**Gelseydin ya!**
If only you'd come!

**Güzel, değil mi?**
Nice, isn't it?

**Giriş nerede acaba?**
I wonder where the entrance is?

4. Summarising, generalising:

| | |
|---|---|
| **kısaca, kısacası** | in short |
| **yani** | so, that is to say ... |
| **ancak** | but still |
| **yine de** | still, nevertheless |
| **nasıl olsa ...** | still, in spite of all |

**Oraya girmek yasaktır. Yine de girdi.**
It's forbidden to enter that place. Still, he did.

**Nasıl olsa, iş işten geçti.**
Still, it was too late to do anything about it. (*literally:* 'the work passed the work')

5. Providing an explanation:

| | |
|---|---|
| **bu yüzden** | therefore, for that reason |
| **bunun için** | therefore, for that reason |
| **dolayısıyla** | because, consequently |

6. Reformulating:

| | |
|---|---|
| **daha doğrusu** | in other words, better |
| **şey** | what-do-you-call-it |

*Exercise 9*

Read the dialogues from Lesson 6 to Lesson 12 and search for conversation aids. Try to understand why speakers use these forms in particular situations.

# 13 Geçmiş olsun!

## Get well soon!

In this lesson you will learn how to:

- use the verb 'to be'
- translate 'and'
- express 'because'
- string together coordinated and subordinated clauses

 **Dialogue 1** (Audio 2: 20)

## Güzel çiçekler

### Nice flowers

*Melike and Hasan, who own a small hotel, are at the reception desk. She is finishing a phone conversation, and he is talking to a guest who has just given them a nice bunch of flowers in appreciation of the good service*

HASAN: Bakın, Melike Hanım, sevgili konuğumuz bize bu çiçekleri getirdi.

MELİKE: Allahım, ne güzel! Niçin zahmet ettiniz? Hasan Bey, lütfen masanın üstüne koyar mısınız? Sanırım ki bu günlerde eskisine oranla sayıca daha az terbiyeli insanlar var.

HASAN: Affedersiniz, herhalde önemli birşey yapmanız gerek. Çarşıya çıkıyor musunuz?

ARİF BEY: Hayır, çarşıya gitmeyecektim, sadece yürüyüşe çıkmak istiyorum şimdi, birde parkta gezeceğim. Ama, daha sonra hediyeler için alışverişe çıkmalıyım, yani bu akşam çarşıya gideceğim.

HASAN: Peki, beklemeni istemiyoruz, güzel çiçekler için tekrar çok teşekkür ederiz.

| | |
|---|---|
| ARİF BEY: | Bir şey değil. |
| MELİKE: | Kendinize iyi bakın. Hoşça kalın! |
| ARİF BEY: | Görüşürüz! |

*After he's gone, the couple remain at the desk*

| | |
|---|---|
| HASAN: | Melike, telefonda kim vardı? |
| MELİKE: | Kız kardeşimdi. Bana bir kitabı geri vermek için öğleden sonra buraya uğrayacak. |
| HASAN: | Kız kardeşin nasıl? |
| MELİKE: | Oh, her zamanki gibi, kocasıyla kavga etti, parası da bitti ... Niçin gülüyorsun? Durumunu düşün! *(laughter)* Çiçekler çok güzel ama, değil mi? Şuna ne dersin? |
| HASAN: | Arif Bey'in iyi bir insan olduğunu sana dedim ya dün akşam. |
| MELİKE: | Doğru, bana söyleyeceğin her şeye inanıyorum artık. |

## Sözcükler

| | | | |
|---|---|---|---|
| **sevgili** | sweet, dear | **bekletmek** | to make someone wait |
| **zahmet etmek** | to go to the trouble | **geri** | back |
| **masa** | table | **kavga etmek (ile)** | to quarrel with |
| **üstü** | top | **her zamanki gibi** | as always |
| **masanın üstüne** | on the table | **durumunu düşün!** | think of her situation! |
| **oranla (-e)** | compared to ... | | |
| **sayıca az** | fewer | **dün akşam** | last night |
| **gitmeyecektim** | I wasn't going to go | | |

## Exercise 1

1 Give a brief account of what transpires in this conversation. Answer at least the following questions:
   a. Did the guest give the flowers to Hasan, to Melike, or to both?
   b. Melike asks Hasan at some point why he's laughing. What, do you think, is the answer? And what is Melike's reaction?
   c. What was Melike's phone call about?
   d. Is the guest going out to the shopping mall?
   e. What is Hasan's opinion about the guest?

2 Here are some additional questions, meant to point out some useful vocabulary:
  a How does Melike ask Hasan to put the flowers on the table? Can you think of other ways of asking the question?
  b Which expression did you find for 'I think'?
  c What do you think is the difference between **alışveriş yapmak** and **alışverişe çıkmak**?
  d How does one say 'I'm broke' in Turkish?
  e If you have trouble working out what **şuna ne dersin?** means, be aware that the verb is the **geniş zaman** form of **demek**.
  f How is 'right', 'exactly' expressed in the dialogue?
  g Which new formula for leave-taking did you find? Add it to the list you established in Exercise 7 of Lesson 11.

*Exercise 2*

There is one occurrence of the particle **de/da** in this conversation. What does it tell you about its meaning?

# Language point

## And

The particle **de/da** has been present in examples throughout the earlier lessons, starting with this sentence in Lesson 2:

**Hem de Buckingham Sarayı.**
And [I] even [saw] Buckingham Palace.

In the Key to Exercise 2, you have seen **de/da** (the form, of course, depends on vowel harmony) translated as either 'and' or 'too', 'as well, also'. It is not really a separate word: it is pronounced as part of the word that precedes it, so it's almost like a suffix (that's why it's sensitive to vowel harmony).

The fact that Turkish has different forms for expressing 'and' may be confusing. The most English-like is **ve**, but this option is not used very much. A typical context in which it is used is when you're joining two or more nouns or adjectives:

**Güzel ve temiz.**
It's nice and clean.

Another word that is often used for 'and' is **ile**, often in its suffixed form **-(y)le/-(y)la**. Its uses are similar to **ve**, except that **ile** tends to be used more when the two things it joins form a unit. In the example above, for instance, **güzel** and **temiz** describe two separate qualities of whatever the sentence is about, let's say a hotel room. It is nice and it is *also* clean. Now take cases like 'Ali and Funda' (assuming they are a couple), 'bread and butter', or 'salt and pepper':

**Ali'yle Funda'yı gördün mü, çarşıda?**
Did you see Ali and Funda, in the centre of town?

**Bakkaldan ekmekle tereyağ aldım.**
I bought bread and butter at the grocer's.

**Tuzla biber uzatabilir misiniz bir zahmet?**
Could you please pass the salt and pepper?

The third major option is **de/da**. It is often used when there is no clear joining of things. It is equivalent to the English use of 'And' to start a sentence. You can always use **de/da** to express English 'too'. If you hear someone use it at the end of the sentence and you wonder how it could possibly mean 'too', it is probably used as an emphasiser, the other major function of **de/da**. Examples of each meaning:

**Bana da söylemedi!**     *And* he didn't tell me either!
**Biz de onu gördük.**     We have seen it too.
**Ne güzel filmdi de!**     It was such a beautiful film!

Sometimes, **de/da** is a synonym of **ama**:

**Bu otel güzel ve temiz de, fiyatlar felaket!**
This hotel is nice and clean, but the prices are disastrous!

## Indefinite pronouns

1 Someone
Which word is used to express 'someone' depends on whether the verb is affirmative or negative. If affirmative, you use **biri** or **birisi**; if negative, you use **bir kimse**. 'Someone I know' is **tanıdığım biri**; 'someone I didn't know' is **tanımadığım bir kimse**. The two other words you need here are **herkes**, 'everyone' and **kimse**, 'nobody'. With **kimse** the verb has to be negative, too. Alternatives are **hiçbiri** and **hiç kimse**:

**Kimse/hiçbiri/hiç kimse gelmedi.**
No-one came.

There is a subtle difference between **kimse** and **hiçbiri** in that **hiçbiri** presupposes a bigger group, from which nobody came ('none of them came' would be the most accurate translation of **hiçbiri gelmedi**).

2 Other

The basic word for 'another' is **başka** (which also means 'different'). However, when you want to say 'the other one(s)' instead of 'another', Turkish instead uses two different words: **diğer(ler)i**, 'the other ones', and **öbürü**, 'the other one'. As a way of remembering which is which, **öbür** (historically) comes from **o bir**, 'that one', so it normally refers to *one* thing. A couple of examples:

**Ayşe ile Arzu konsere gitti, diğerleri ise evde kaldılar.**
Ayşe and Arzu went to the concert; the others stayed at home.

**Başka bir telefon var mı burada?**
Is there another phone here?

 **Dialogue 2** (Audio 2: 21)

Sen olmasaydın!

**If it weren't for you!**

*Serkan and Erol are discussing the day ahead; their conversation soon drifts off into other topics*

EROL: Oh, şimdi aklıma geldi: akşama kadar gözlükçüye gidip yeni gözlüğümü almam gerekiyor ama bir işimin olması nedeniyle gidemeyeceğim.
SERKAN: Merak etme, ben yaparım.
EROL: Serkan, sen olmasaydın! Geçen hafta güzel bir gözlük buldum, tam aradığım modeli. Sürekli arıyordum, bulamıyordum. Çok sağ ol. Parasını ödedim. Belki formu doldurman gerekecek.
SERKAN: Birşey değil. Biliyor musun kime rastladım bu sabah? Necat! Ben merdiveni çıkarken o indi, Yıldız Merkezinde.

| EROL: | Hala Beşiktaş'ta oynuyor mu? |
|---|---|
| SERKAN: | Oynuyor, ama oranın en eski futbolcusu bu günlerde. Çocukken ben de sporcu olmak istiyordum ama, ... Uzun yıllar antremanalara gittim, evde de az kalsın her gün çalıştım, ve fena bir futbolcu değildim, ama eksikti. Devam etmek istemedim, bıraktım, onun için şimdi Fransızca öğretmenim. İşte, hayat böyle derler ya. |
| EROL: | Ne yazık ki! Böyle şeyler olur. Çok dil biliyorsun, bu da güzel. Hangilerini biliyorsun? |
| SERKAN: | Türkçe'yi ve diğer Türk dillerini, Fransızca'yı, İngilizce'yi ve İspanyolca'yı biliyorum. Yalnız, Almancam çok kötü. Bir sayfayı yirmi dakikada ancak okuyorum. |
| EROL: | İzmir'de bir tanıdığım altı dil biliyor: Türkçe'yi, İngilizce'yi, İtalyanca'yı, Fransızca'yı, Özbekçe'yi ve Çerkezce'yi. |
| SERKAN: | İnanmıyorum. Vallahi, son zamanlarda Özbekçe'yi bilen çok buralarda, yani Türkiye'de, ama gerçekten biliyor mu? Hadi be, bu kadar olmaz. |
| EROL: | Nurettin'le Türkmenistan'daydım. Bu trenden indiğimiz andan itibaren herkesle konuştu ve millet onu anlıyordu, vallahi. Bir kere yaşlı bir amca bizimle konuşuyordu sonra çok kızdı, ben korktum, Nurettin'e ne oluyor diye sordum, o da bilmiyorum, ama yanlış bir şey demişim herhalde diye cevap verdi. Koştuk. Ne olduğunu hala bilmiyoruz. Aslında şahane bir ülkedir, Türkmenistan. |
| SERKAN: | Öyle mi? |
| EROL: | Gerçekten, çok güzel. Neyse, başka zaman sana anlatırım, şimdi gitmem gerek. Gözlüğü alıp getireceğin için çok teşekkürler. |
| SERKAN: | Bir şey değil canım. Öyleyse, üçte gözlükçüye gideceğim. |
| EROL: | Çok iyi. Allahaısmarladık. |
| SERKAN: | Güle güle. |

## Sözcükler

| | | | |
|---|---|---|---|
| **gözlük** | glasses | **neden** | reason |
| **gözlükçü** | optician | **sürekli** | for a long time |
| **gidip** | go and | **bulamıyordum** | I wasn't able to find |
| **nedeniyle** | because, for the reason that | **merdiven** | stairs |
| | | **inmek** | (*here:*) to go down |

| | | | |
|---|---|---|---|
| yıldız | star | itibaren (-den) | from . . . on |
| Yıldız Merkezi | Star Centre | herkes | everyone |
| Beşiktaş | (a football team) | millet | people |
| antrenman | practice | anlıyordu | they were under- |
| sporcu | athlete | | standing |
| eksik | not enough | bir kere | one time |
| ne yazık ki! | what a pity! | yanlış | wrong |
| İspanyolca | Spanish (the | amca | (*here:*) old man |
| | language) | konuşuyordu | he was talking |
| sayfa | page | diye sordum | I asked |
| ancak | (*here:*) really | diye cevap verdi | he answered |
| tanıdık | acquaintance | alıp getireceğin | you'll take and |
| İtalyanca | Italian (the | | bring |
| | language) | öyleyse | OK then |
| Özbekçe | Uzbek (the | Allahaısmarladık | Goodbye |
| | language) | güle güle | goodbye (answer |
| Çerkezce | Circassian (the | | to **Allahaıs-** |
| | language) | | **marladık**) |

NB: Where names of languages are followed by an accusative case marker in the above text, they are separated from that marker by an apostrophe. Sometimes we have written this without an apostrophe. Some writers use the apostrophe in this case (with proper names it is *always* used) and some don't. It is never *wrong* to use it after language names.

## Exercise 3

Are the following statements true or not?

1 Erol has ordered new glasses from a store.
2 He is going to pick them up himself.
3 They have already been paid for.
4 Erol knows Necat.
5 Necat is a football player.
6 Serkan was a really good player once, he thinks.
7 Erol teases him about his football career.
8 Serkan speaks many languages, but his German isn't very good.
9 Serkan doubts that many people in Turkey actually speak Uzbek.
10 The friend in Izmir is called Nurettin.
11 Nurettin hesitated speaking Turkmenian.
12 Nurettin and Erol had a pleasant conversation with an old man in Turkmenistan.

13 Erol has no idea what caused the confusion.
14 Serkan is going to pick up the glasses at noon.

## Quantifiers: words like 'all', 'some' and 'every'

Life would be easy if there were a clear one-to-one relationship between one word in one language and one other word in another language. It is relatively easy to give the translations for concrete nouns and verbs, but grammatical words, such as prepositions or articles, sometimes have to be translated using various words. It is often better to understand the Turkish equivalents relative to each other, rather than to pinpoint the most exact English equivalent. The words listed in the heading above, generally referred to as 'quantifiers', are typical examples. Some of these words have a pretty clear meaning; others need some illustration:

| | | | |
|---|---|---|---|
| **bir** | one | **bütün** | all |
| **çok** | many, much | **tüm** | all |
| **az** | few | **her** | every |
| **bazı** | some | **hepsi** | all, everything |
| **herkes** | everyone | **her şey** | everything |
| **hep** | always | **birşey** | something |
| **biraz** | some, a little (bit) | **birkaç** | some |
| **birçok** | a lot | **bir sürü** | a lot |

The problem is, that for some of these concepts, there are alternative ways of saying it, and sometimes the context calls for one of the alternatives: only one is right, using the other(s) would be incorrect. This is what this section is about.

### *All*

The difference between English 'all' and 'every' has its uses in coming to grips with the Turkish system. If you are not aware of the difference, pause for a minute to consider the sentences 'He ate all the food' and 'He ate every bar of chocolate'. With 'all', you focus on the total mass of whatever noun follows it (e.g. 'food'); with 'every' you focus on the individual elements (e.g. 'bars of chocolate'). 'Foods' is not 'countable', i.e. you cannot have 'one food' or 'three foods'. But bars of chocolate *are* countable. This difference is relevant for understanding the difference between **bütün** and **tüm** (both mean 'all') on the one hand, and **her** 'every' on the other:

**Şimdi ben bütün Türkiye'yi davet edemem ki!**
I can't very well invite all of Turkey now, can I?

**Şimdi ben her Türk davet edemem ki!**
I can't very well invite every Turk now, can I?

On the basis of phrases like **her gün** 'every day', you may have already guessed that **her**, just like English 'every', is followed by a singular, not a plural noun. Between **bütün** and **tüm** there is not much difference. We suggest you treat them as exactly the same, so you can use either one.

**Tüm akşamı düşündük.**
We were thinking of the whole evening.

**Bütün gün yattım.**
I spent all day in bed (*literally*: I laid down all day).

Then there's **hepsi**, which also means 'all'. Compare the following sentences; you might be able to work out when to use **hepsi**.

**Bunun dışında bütün yemeği yedi.**
Apart from that, he ate all the food.

**Çocukların hepsi gülüyordular.**
All of the children were laughing.

**Hepsini yedi.**
He ate it all.

**Her şeyi yedi.**
He ate everything (there was).

**Hepsi** and **her şey** 'everything' mean pretty much the same thing; the difference is that with **hepsi** you know exactly what 'all' refers to, while with **her şey** you don't have that kind of knowledge; the difference, that is, between 'all of it' and 'everything (there is)'. **Hepsi**, by the way, is derived from **hep**, which means 'always':

**Seni hep hatırlayacağım.**
I will always remember you.

Note that you can't use **hepsi** or **her şey** when you want to use the word in combination with the thing it goes with. For example, if you want to say 'he ate all the food', that is, if you want to specify that it's *food* you're talking about, then you have to use **bütün**. The difference between **bütün** and **hepsi** is similar to that between 'all' and 'all of it'. The first is used as an adjective, that is, with a following noun; the second is just used by itself (so, for 'he ate all the food', you can't say **bütünü yedi**, nor **hepsi yemeği yedi**).

Choosing the right form for 'nothing' is easier, since there is just one form (really): **birşey** (possibly intensified as **hiç birşey**) plus negated verb:

**Ona (hiç) birşey anlatmadım.**
I didn't tell her anything.

## Some

You have learned two words that express this: **bazı** and **birkaç**. We recommend you learn **bazı** as **bazı . . . -lar**, as it virtually always co-occurs with the plural ending on the noun. This is not so with **birkaç**. But there is more. Consider the following sentence and try to think of the most natural word to fill in the dots with:

**Yalnız . . . et yedim.**
I just ate a little meat.

You may have guessed that neither **bazı** nor **birkaç** would fit here, but that **biraz**, 'a little', is the better choice. You'd be right. You use **bazı** with things you can count, such as, for example, shoes or days, and **biraz** with things you cannot count, such as meat or snow. Remember how this difference between countable and uncountable things was also important for the choice between **bütün** and **her**. The construction 'some of the . . .' is expressed by putting **bazıları** after a noun and adding the genitive case (the one used to indicate possession and which is formed with **-in** or **nin**, *see* Lesson 6) to the noun. In the following example **öğrencilerin** consists of the noun **öğrenciler** 'students' and the genitive ending **-in**.

**Öğrencilerin bazıları yüksek bir not aldılar.**
Some students got a high mark.

### Much, many

So far, we have consistently used **çok** for saying 'many' or 'much'. You can also use **bir sürü**, which means 'a range', 'a great many', or 'lots of', or **birçok** 'a lot'.

**Bir sürü dili biliyorken, hiç bir zaman bir yere gitmez.**
Although he knows a lot of languages, he never goes anywhere.

You can intensify this by adding the plural marker to **dil**, to give **bir sürü dilleri biliyorken**, 'although he knows lots and lots of languages . . .'

### Exercise 4

Fill in the blanks with one of the following alternatives. For a more challenging version of the same exercise, cover the alternatives and try to fill in the blanks without looking. Remember to add any necessary case markers.

**çok, diğer, herşey, birisi, bir, az, bazı, hepsi, kimse, birşey, her, bütün, herkes, hiçbir, biraz**

1 **Dikkat et! Ayhancık** ('little Ayhan') **. . . duyur.**
2 **Bence Türkçe . . . zor.**
3 **Buraya geldiğim zaman hiç . . . yok.**
4 **Hiç . . . anlamadım.**
5 **Merak etme, . . . için aynı.**
6 **Şimdiye kadar Türkiye'de . . . şey görmedim.**
7 **. . . dünya futbolu sevdiğini pek iyi biliyorsun.**
8 **. . . sınavı bitirdikten sonra parti var.**
9 **Arkadaşım . . . sonra bana telefon edecek.**
10 **Ben ile Ahmet trenle gittik; . . . arabayla gittiler.**
11 **Yaşlı insan bizlerden, gençlerden . . . bekliyorlar.**
12 **Ondan sonra bu kız da . . . aşık oluyor** ('fell in love with').
13 **Sorunların . . . için bir çözüm** ('solution') **bulduk.**
14 **Ali'nin onu yaptığına . . . kızdım.**
15 **Şehrimizde yeni . . . tiyatro yapacaklar.**

## Olmak

You have seen the verb **olmak** 'to be', 'to become', many times before in this book. It is time we tell you something about this versatile word. First, consider the following sentences, three of which are taken from previous lessons, and try to get a feeling for what the verb **olmak** means.

1 **Amerika'da çok zengin olmuş.**
They say he got very rich in America.
2 **Hasta olursan, hap alırsın.**
If you're ill, you take a pill.
3 **Az kalsın trafik kazası oluyordu!**
There was almost a traffic accident!

4  **Saat kaçta orada olacaksın?**
   At what time will you be there?
5  **Rapora göre hava sıcak olacak.**
   According to the weather report, it will be warm.

## Exercise 5

**Olmak** cannot be left out of any of these sentences. In 2, 4 and 5, the resulting sentence would be ungrammatical; in 1 and 3, the meaning would be different. Construct 1 and 3 without **olmak**, and think about the possible meaning differences. Also note the following: in sentences 4 and 5 **olmak** expresses the future tense. Compare these future tense examples with their present tense equivalents:

| | |
|---|---|
| **Saat kaçta oradasın?** | When are you there? |
| **Hava sıcak.** | The weather is nice. |

In the future tense, **olmak** is needed because there are no 'verbless' sentences in that tense.

## Exercise 6

Here are ten more sentences from previous lessons, but with the form of **olmak** blanked out. Provide the right form.

1  **Geçmiş** ... (Lesson 1)
2  **Sağ** ... (Lesson 1)
3  **Sokakta bir kaza** ... **ve hemen polis geldi.** (Lesson 5)
4  **Memnun** ... (Lesson 1)
5  **Hiç belli** ... (Lesson 9)
6  **Biz daha sert** ... **dedi.** (Lesson 11)
7  **Ne** ...? **Hadi, anlat bakalım.** (Lesson 9)
8  **Bunun iyi** ... **sanmıyorum.** (Lesson 5)
9  **Yemekleri çok lezzetli** ... (Lesson 9)

**Olmak** is often used where you would expect a 'verbless' sentence. This is because such sentences are only possible in the present tense and in the past with **-di** or **-miş**. So you can say **Erol hasta** 'Erol is ill', **Erol hastaydı** 'Erol was ill' and **Erol hastaymış** 'Erol must have been ill'. But you cannot say **Erol hastayacak.** Instead you use **olmak**: **Erol hasta olacak** 'Erol is going to be ill'.

The suffix **-sa**, which means 'if', can also be added without **olmak**: **Erol hastaysa** 'if Erol is ill'. But in virtually every other context in which you may be tempted to use a verbless sentence, it is likely that you need to use **olmak**. Here are some more examples:

**Bunu yapmış olana ceza verilecek.**
The one(s) who did this will be punished.

**Bunun iyi bir fikir olduğunu düşünüyor musun?**
Do you think this is a good idea?

In the first example, **bunu yapmış olan** means 'the ones who did this', using the relative clause construction (*see* Lesson 11, in case you forgot). The final **-a** in **olana** is a dative case marker (*see* Lesson 3), which is needed because the verb **ceza vermek** 'to punish' requires it. The person who is punished is indicated with this dative ending. The second example consists of **bunun iyi bir fikir olduğu** 'that this is a good idea' (using the subordinated clause construction, *see*, again, Lesson 11) and the verb form **düşünüyor musun?** 'do you think?' The final **-nu** in **olduğunu** is the accusative case ending (*see* Lesson 6), needed because the subordinated clause **Bunun iyi bir fikir olduğu** is the direct object of the verb form **düşünüyor musun?**

### Exercise 7

Translate

1 As it always happens. (use a subordinate clause with **-diği gibi**, 'as')
2 How much should it be? (use the word **olsun** 'should be' here)
3 In order to be a good student.
4 An American firm has become the new owner.
5 You will be a very good employee.
6 That must have been interesting. (add **-dir** to the form of **olmak** here)
7 Don't be like that!
8 That can't be.
9 The man whose hair is wet.
10 If it's necessary.

## Exercise 8

Read this e-mail, and answer the questions about it. There is a translation in the key.

Sevgili Funda,

Umarım iyisindir. Londra'da hava nasıl diye sormayacağım. Kesin iyi bir zamanın vardır. Bugün burada hava çok güzel, fakat tadını çıkaramayacağım, işimi bitmem gerek. Sana birşey sormak istiyorum. Eğer günün birinde kitabevine uğrarsan, bazı kitaplara bakar mısın? Geçen e-mailimde gördüğün gibi, İngiliz tarihi beni çok ilgilendiriyor bugünlerde. İstediğim kitapları milli kütüphanede bulamadım. Fakat bir kitabevine uğrama fırsatın olmazsa merak etme, o kadar önemli değil. Bundan sonraki gelecek mesajımda adını vereceğim. Bütün hafta sonu dinlenmek istiyorum. Yarın Kanadalı arkadaşıma, Dave'e, gideceğim. Onu iyi tanıyorsun, değil mi? Maalesef, şehrin dışında oturuyor. Sen ne yapacaksın? Hafta sonu için planın var mı? Umarım müzikallerin birine gitmemelisin! Öpüyorum.

Kamile

## Sözcükler

| kesin | surely | dinlenmek | to rest |
|-------|--------|-----------|---------|
| tadını çıkarmak | to enjoy | fırsat | possibility |
| kitabevi | bookstore | dışında | outside |
| gördüğün gibi | as you saw | öpmek | to kiss |
| tarih | history | | |

1 Which fixed expressions are used for addressing, greeting and leave-taking?
2 Is Kamile having a good day?
3 How does Kamile ask Funda to do something for her?
4 Is her request a forceful one?
5 In which library has she looked for the books?
6 Why is she asking Funda, do you think?
7 Does Funda know Dave, as far as Kamile knows?
8 What's the Turkish for 'outside of town'?
9 What is Kamile talking about in her last sentence (before **Öpüyorum**)?
10 Are Funda and Kamile good friends, do you think?

# 14 Sayın öğrencilerimizin dikkat edeceği hususlar

## Matters to which our respected students should pay attention

---

**In this lesson you will learn how to:**

- say when something will happen in the future
- express the way in which things are done
- link two events that happen at the same time, or one after the other

---

## Dialogue 1

### İnşaat

## Construction

*In the following dialogue, the **müdür** (director) of a large **şirket** (company) is talking to the **mimar** (architect). The director is anxious to know when the building of a new office will commence*

MÜDÜR: Mimar Bey, şirketimizin yeni binasının inşaatına ne zaman başlayacaksınız?

MİMAR: Çerçeveler teslim edildiği gibi başlayabiliriz.

MÜDÜR: İnşallah kıştan önce olacak. Kar yağarsa ne yapacaksınız?

MİMAR: Kar yağdığı takdirde, yapım ertelenecek. Ertelendiği zaman, büyük bir sorunumuz var. Endişelenirim ki, o halde altı aydan önce başlayamayız.

| | |
|---|---|
| MÜDÜR: | Felaket olacak! Her gecikme işlerimizi çok kötü etkiler! Bu çerçeveleri ne zaman ısmarlattınız? |
| MİMAR: | Ismarlatamadım. |
| MÜDÜR: | *(looks puzzled)* Neden ısmarlatamadınız? |
| MİMAR: | Siz bütün zorunlu formları doldurmadığınız için. |
| MÜDÜR: | O zaman hepsini hemen doldurayım! |
| MİMAR: | Nihayet! Hiç soracağınızı zannetmedim. *(immediately hands over the paperwork)* |
| MÜDÜR: | *(fills out the forms and signs)* Şimdi daha ne kadar sürecek? Çerçeveler ne zaman teslim edilecek? |
| MİMAR: | İmzalı kağıtları bugün aldığımız için, yarın mutlaka teslim edilecekler ... |

## Sözcükler

| | | | |
|---|---|---|---|
| mimar | architect | o halde | in that case |
| inşaat | building, construction | etkilemek | to influence |
| | | gecikme | delay |
| çerçeve | window frame | ısmarlatmak | to have some- |
| teslim edildiği | as soon as they | | thing ordered |
| gibi | are delivered | zorunlu | necessary |
| inşallah | hopefully | soracağınızı | that you would |
| takdirde | in the event of | | ask |
| yapım | making, building | sürmek | to last |
| ertelenmek | to be postponed | imzalı | signed |
| ertelendiğ zaman | when it will be postponed | kağıt | paper |
| endişelenmek | to be anxious about | | |

### Exercise 1

Look at these extracts from Dialogue 1 and answer the questions:

1 **şirketimizin yeni binasının inşaatına** – Work out what the suffixes are and what they mean.

2 **başlayamayız** – What is the suffix immediately after the verb stem?

3 **imzalı kağıtları bugün aldığımız için, yarın mutlaka teslim edilecekler** – What do you notice about the position of the words **bugün** 'today' and **yarın** 'tomorrow'?

## Exercise 2

See if you understood the dialogue by answering these questions:

1 What effect will the winter season have on the building process?
2 Why haven't the window frames arrived yet?
3 What was the **mimar** waiting for?
4 How long does it take to deliver the window frames?

# Language point

## 'When' in the future

You've learnt how to express English 'when' in Turkish by using **-diği zaman** or **-diğinde**, which refer either to things that happened in the past or to something which is happening now. For future events, however, you use **-eceği zaman**, in which you probably recognise the future marker **-ecek**. The **-i** is the third person singular possessive suffix. So, literally, it says 'its', 'his', or 'hers', but you translate it with 'it', 'he' or 'she'. For other persons (I, you, we), use the appropriate first or second person markers. Here's a list of all markers:

| 1ˢᵗ singular | -eceğim zaman | when I ... |
|---|---|---|
| 2ⁿᵈ singular | -eceğin zaman | when you ... |
| 3ʳᵈ singular | -eceği zaman | when he/she/it ... |
| 1ˢᵗ plural | -eceğimiz zaman | when we ... |
| 2ⁿᵈ plural | -eceğiniz zaman | when you ... |
| 3ʳᵈ plural | -ecekleri zaman | when they ... |

Examples:

**İngiltere'ye gideceğiniz zaman, sözlüğünüzü unutmayın!**
When you go to England, don't forget your dictionary!

**Türkiye'de tatil yapacağımız zaman, size geleceğiz.**
When we're in Turkey for our holiday, we're going to visit you.

The form **-eceği** (without **zaman**) is also used as the future equivalent of **-diği** in basic subordinate clauses:

**Sayın yolcularımızın dikkat edeceği hususlar.** (text on a bus ticket)
Matters to which our respected travellers should pay attention.

**Bineceğim tren hangisi?**
Which is the train I am to take?

**Bekleyecekleri para henüz gelmedi.**
The money they are expecting hasn't arrived yet.

## -diği zaman's little cousins

By changing the word **zaman** in the **-diği zaman** or **-eceği zaman** (both meaning 'when') constructions into a number of other words (such as **kadar** 'as', **gibi** 'like' or **için** 'for') you can express other notions for which English uses separate words. Don't forget that the final **-i** in **-diği** 'that' or **-eceği** 'that' changes with person. The following list gives a basic idea of the kind of forms we are talking about:

**-diği kadar** as much as    **-diği için** *or* -**diğinden** because
**-diği halde** although        **-diği takdirde**       in the event of
**-diği gibi**    as, as soon as

### Examples

**Tren geç kaldığı için/ kaldığından İngiltere vapuruna yetişemedik.**
Because the train had been delayed, we could not catch the ferry to England.

**Sana yazmadığımız için bize kızıyor musun?**
Are you angry with us because we didn't write to you?

**Bana hiç bir şey söylemedikleri için hiç bilgim yok.**
Because they didn't tell me anything, I know nothing.

**İstediği kadar tatlı yiyebilir.**
He can eat sweets as much as he likes.

**Çerçeveler teslim edildiği gibi başladık.**
We started as soon as the window frames were delivered.

**Siz bütün zorunlu formları doldurmadığınız için.**
Because you did not fill out all necessary forms.

**Doktor yapabildiği gibi yaptı, fakat yaralı kamyoncuyu kurtaramadı.**
The doctor did what he could do, but he couldn't save the injured lorry driver.

**Yağmur yağdığı takdirde, yüzme yarışması yarına kadar ertelenecek.**
In the event of rain, the swimming contest will be postponed.

**Giriş sinavını geçmediği halde, üniversiteye girebilirdi.**
Although he didn't pass the entry exam, he was able to go to college.

## Exercise 3

Translate into Turkish:

1 Although the film star was offered a contract worth one million, she declined the offer.
2 Because the conference fee was too high, the students had to stay in an inexpensive hotel (use **zorunda** for 'had to'; *see* for other constructions for 'to have to' Lesson 8, p. 135).
3 Please, take as much as you need.
4 Although Ahmet likes to complain, I haven't heard anything from him.
5 Could you give me a call as soon as you arrive at the airport?
6 Because the train was late, I had to run to the theatre.
7 Should the train be late, don't wait for me.
8 Although the train was late, I made it in time to the theatre.
9 As soon as the train arrived, I ran to the theatre.
10 Although I eat fresh fruit and vegetables every day, I caught a cold.
11 As soon as we stopped eating fresh fruit and vegetables, we caught a cold.
12 'Because you haven't done your homework, I cannot continue with the class', the angry teacher shouted.

## Word list

| | | | |
|---|---|---|---|
| **sinema yıldızı** | movie star | **reddetmek** | to decline |
| **bir milyonluk** | a contract worth | **konferans ücreti** | conference fee |
| **sözleşme** | one million | **çok** | too |

| şikayet etmek | to complain | üşütmek | to catch a cold |
| aramak | to give a call | ev ödevi | homework |
| tatlı diye | pester for sweets | kızgın | angry |
| tutturmak | | diye bağırmak | to shout |
| taze | fresh | | |

## Language point

### -ki

Adjectives and adverbs don't take suffixes, unless they're used 'as a noun'. For instance, in the case of **zengin adamlar** 'the rich men' the plural suffix comes after the noun **adam** 'man', not after the adjective **zengin** 'rich'. But just as easily, you might say **zenginler** 'the rich', when you'll find **-ler** after **zengin**. In this example, **zengin** is used as a noun.

You can also turn an adverb into an adjective: suppose you have an adverb **bugün** 'today' which you want to use as an adjective, meaning 'today's' as in 'today's newspaper'. For this, you use the suffix **-ki**. Contrary to most suffixes in Turkish, vowel harmony does not affect **-ki**, except after the words **bugün** 'day' and **dün** 'yesterday':

| bugünkü | today's |
| bugünkü toplantı | today's meeting |
| dünkü | yesterday's |
| dünkü Şov TV yayımı | yesterday's Show TV broadcast |

Other examples with adverbs of time and place (such as 'tomorrow', 'here' etc.):

| yarınki radyo yayımı | tomorrow's radio broadcast |
| bugünkü gazete | today's newspaper |
| dünkü gösteri | yesterday's performance |
| şimdiki halde | in the present state |
| buradaki kitaplar | the books that are here ('the here books') |

Like all adjectives, these forms can be used in 'verbless' sentences, too. However, they never occur in Adjective + **bir** + Noun constructions. Compare the forms on the right and left sides:

| eski kitap | the old book |
| dünkü gösteri | yesterday's performance |
| eski bir kitap | an old book | never: *dünkü bir gösteri* |
| kitap eski | the book is old |

**bilet aldığımız gösteri dünküydü**
the performance for which we bought tickets was yesterday's

Analogous to **zenginler**, you can also use **-ki** type adjectives as nouns:

**bugünküler**          people nowadays

The suffix **-ki** also forms adjectives from other bases:

- after a noun carrying the locative case marker **-de** (e.g. **Türkiye'de** 'in Turkey')
- after a noun or pronoun carrying the genitive case marker **-(n)in** (e.g. **senin** 'your')

Before we give any examples, try to work out what the forms in Exercise 4 mean.

## Exercise 4

What do the following mean:

1 **seninki**
2 **Mustafa'nınki**
3 **kalem** ('pen') **sizinki mi?**
4 **onlarınki**
5 **Türkiye Cümhuriyeti'ninki**

The difference between these nouns or pronouns marking possession (i.e. the ones that end in **-(n)inki**) and words such as **günkü** 'today's', is that the latter behave as ordinary adjectives, such as **güzel** 'nice' or **büyük** 'big', and possessive pronouns such as **seninki** 'yours' don't. They cannot appear before a noun (as in 'the big house'), but only after a noun (as in 'the house is big').

| güzel bisiklet | the nice bike | never: *benimki bisiklet* |
| | | (*always* **benim bisikletim**) |
| güzel bir bisiklet | a nice bike | never: *benimki bir bisiklet* |
| bisiklet güzel | the bike is nice | **bu bisiklet benimki** |
| | | the bike is mine |
| güzel(dir) | it's nice | **benimki(dir)** it's mine |

| | | |
|---|---|---|
| **büyük bina** | the large building | never: ***hükümetinki bina*** |
| **büyük bir bina** | a large building | never: ***hükümetinki bir bina*** |
| **bina büyük** | the building is large | **bu bina hükümetinki** the building is the government's |
| **büyük(tür)** | it's big | **hükümetinki(dir)** it's the government's |

As the final examples show, these nouns or pronouns can be complete 'verbless' sentences by themselves (for **-dir**, *see* Lesson 4). Further examples:

**Öğretmeninki** (*or:* **öğretmeninkidir**)
(it's) the one of the teacher/ the teacher's

**Benimki** (or: **benimkidir**)
(it's) mine

**Orhan'ınki** (*or:* **Orhan'ınkidir**)
(it's) Orhan's

**Seninkiyim**
I'm yours

**Ali'ninkiler**
they're Ali's

In order to understand in what way **-ki** differs from simple genitive constructions, look at the following examples:

**Bu bisiklet Bülent'in değil.**
It's not Bülent's bike (simply expresses who owns the bike, or, in this particular sentence, who doesn't own it).

**Bu bisiklet Bülent'inki değil.**
This is not Bülent's (bike)! (implies that Bülent has a bicycle, but this is not it).

**-ki** is often used in combination with a noun carrying a possessive marker (which, as you know, varies with person) and a genitive ('of'):

| | |
|---|---|
| **komşumuzunki** | our neighbour's, of our neighbour |
| **komşularımızınki** | our neighbours', of our neighbours |

The first example consists of the noun **komşu**, the possessive marker **-muz**, the genitive **-un** and **-ki**. The other example looks, at first sight, a bit more complicated. As soon as you notice the plural marker **-lar**, however, things start to unravel: **-lar** is followed by the possessive marker **-ımız**, the genitive **-ın** and **-ki**. And to prove Turkish is an agglutinative language (the property of adding bits to words to add shades of meaning), case markers can be added as well:

**Arabamız eskidir. Komşumuzunkinde ise hava yastığı var.**
Our car is old. In my neighbour's (car), however, there are airbags.

**Evlerimiz komşularımızınkilerden daha küçük.**
Our houses are smaller than those of our neighbours.

The latter example contains the plural marker **-ler/lar** twice, which is rare in Turkish. In fact, this type of construction with **-ki** is the only possible time where you can have two similar suffixes in one word. The first one in **komşularımızınkilerden** refers to 'more than one neighbour', whereas the second one expresses that we are talking about 'more than one house'.

Finally, words with **-de/-da** 'in', 'at', 'on' can be followed by the **-ki** suffix. Again, the result of the combination is an adjective.

**evdeki hesap çarşıya uymuyor**
the bill you draw up at home doesn't apply at the market
(Turkish proverb, meaning 'things never go the way you expect them to be'.)

**hapishanedekiler**
those that are in jail, people in jail

**üstümdeki yorgan** (**üstümde** on top of me)
the duvet on top of me

### Exercise 5

Translate:

1 people in the street
2 yesterday's child is tomorrow's grown-up
3 don't take my uncle's, take mine
4 doctors in hospitals are better

5 **lokantadaki yemekleri sevmiyor**
6 **büyükanneminkilerden daha pahalı**
7 **istasyondaki tarife başka bir hareket saati yazıyordu**

**8 şarap tadındaki üzüm suyu**

| | | | |
|---|---|---|---|
| **yetişkin** | grown-up | **büyükanne** | grandmother |
| **hekim** | doctor | **tarife** | timetable |
| **amca** *or* **dayı** | uncle | **hareket** | departure |

## Reading text

Read through the following text in its entirety. Do not translate it word for word, but try to get the gist of the story.

## Sabahleyin erken

## Early in the morning

Evde, annem bütün gün didinip dururdu. Sabahları ilk olarak kalkıp kahvaltı hazırlamaya başlardı. Sonra da, tam zamanında okula gideceğimize bakardı. Ben bir gün çok erken kalkmalıydım. Annem, kardeşlerimi uyandırmamaya özen göstererek 'Hadi, kalk, oğlum' dedi. Sırtımı dönerek 'Ama uyuyorum, anne!' dedim. Fakat, çaresizce üstelemeden üstümdeki yorganı sıyırıp attım. 'Tamam, olur, anne!' dedim, gözkapaklarımı kırparak. Annem gülümseyen yüzüyle bana dönerek 'Aferin!' dedi.

| | | | |
|---|---|---|---|
| **didinmek** | to work hard | **çaresizce** | inevitable |
| **özen göstermek** | to make sure that, be careful that | **üstelemek** | to repeat, insist |
| | | **sıyırmak** | to take off, to shove away |
| **uyanmak** | to wake up | **gözkapağı** | eyelid |
| **sırt** | back | **kırpmak** | to blink |

### Exercise 6

Answer the following questions:

1 Consider **dururdu**, **başlardı** and **bakardı** in the little story above. These seem to have a double verb marking. Which two suffixes can you distinguish?

2 Why does the first-person narrator use these forms?

3 And why does he change into using simple past tense forms, such as **dedi**, **dedim** and **attım**?

# Language point

## Expressing two simultaneous or consecutive actions

In Lesson 12, you were introduced to two 'converbs': **-ince** 'as soon as' and **-(y)ken** 'while', as in **gidince** 'as soon as he went' and **giderken** 'while he is going'. For combining two clauses with 'and', Turkish uses a similar construction. Don't be tempted to use **ve** or **ile**, which are used to combine two nouns (*see* Lesson 13):

**Ahmet ve Zeynep**          Ahmet and Zeynep

Although it is not wrong to use **ve**, a 'converb' is the normal form to use. In the story **sabahleyin erken** above, this new converb, formed with the suffix **-ip**, is used a few times. It does not have a tense, nor a person marker. You have to mark the tense and person endings on the verb next in line. If you have two verbs in a row, of which the first one ends in **-ip**, the tense and person markings of the second verb also apply to the **-ip** verb. This **-ip** is the normal way of combining and expressing two actions that happen at the same time, or right after one another.

If this sounds a little abstract, look again at these examples taken from the story above:

**Sabahları ilk olarak kalkıp kahvaltı hazırlamaya başlardı.**
In the mornings she was the first to get up (*literally:* she stood up as the first) and started preparing breakfast.

    **kalkıp** stands for **kalkardı**

**Üstümdeki yorganı sıyırıp attım.**
I pushed the duvet on top of me off and threw it away.

    **sıyırıp** stands for **sıyırdım**

Most of the time both verbs (the one with **-ip** and the main verb) form a kind of conceptual unit, or they are two phases of one action. Common pairs are for instance:

| | |
|---|---|
| **kalkıp gitti** | he got up and left |
| **bakıp gördü** | he looked and saw |
| **kafadan silip attı** | he put it out of his mind (*literally:* to erase from his head and throw away) |
| **kapıyı çekip gitti** | he shut the door and went |
| **kayıp düştü** | he slipped and fell |

## Exercise 7

Read the following verb sequences and find out for which suffixes the **-ip** part is the replacement.

1 Çocuk kalkıp kurbağayı aramaya başladı.
2 Kuşlar gelip bahçemizdeki ağaca konunca iyiydi.
3 Gidip dans oynayalım.
4 Gidip benim annem ve onunki görüşeceğiz.
5 Koşup onları yakalarsam . . .!

| | | | |
|---|---|---|---|
| **kurbağa** | frog | **yakalamak** | to catch |
| **dans oynamak** | to dance (Turkish-style) | | |

## Exercise 8

Translate the sentences from Exercise 7.

Expressions such as 'it's not clear if . . .', 'I wonder whether . . .', etc., are often followed by a choice between a 'positive' and a 'negative' action ('I wonder whether he went or not'). This sort of thing is most commonly expressed by means of the combination of an **-ip** verb with the same verb ending in **-mediği** or **-meyeceği** (that is, the negative forms of **-diği** or **-eceği**). Examples are:

**Gelip gelmeyeceği emin değilim.**
I'm not sure if he'll come (or not).

**Ayhan'ın bunu söyleyip söylemediğini bilmiyorum.**
I don't know whether Ayhan said this or not.

**-ip** followed by the the verb **durmak** 'to stand' has a less literal, more idiomatic meaning. It means something like 'continue to do something' or 'constantly doing something'.

**Annem bütün gün didinip dururdu.**
My mother kept working hard all day.

**Söylenip duruyorsun.**
You just keep on yacking.

## Manner of actions

There is one more converb you should know about. This one, **-erek** '(by) doing', denotes the way or the manner in which something was done. Examples:

**Kardeşlerimi uyandırmamaya özen göstererek 'Hadi kalk oğlum,' dedi.**
Taking care not to wake my brothers and sisters, she said 'Come on, get up, my son.'

**Çalışarak Türkçe öğrendim.**
I learned Turkish by working.

**Geçen yaz tatilini Fransa'da üzüm toplayarak geçirdim.**
I spent the last summer holiday in France, picking grapes.

**Yürüyerek buraya geldi.**
He came here on foot (by walking).

Sometimes the **-erek** part contains a reason.

**Para dökerek iflas etti.**
By wasting his money he went bankrupt.

**iflas etmek**     to go bankrupt

The **-erek** form of the verb **olmak** 'to be', 'to become' is a fossilised form, usually translated as 'as':

**İlk olarak kalktı.**
She stood up (as) first (*literally:* being the first).

**Garson olarak çalışıyor.**
He works as a waiter.

**Öğretmen olarak Doğu Türkiye'ye gönderildi.**
He was sent to East Turkey as a teacher.

### Exercise 9

Translate these sentences. (In the next exercise you will be asked to choose either the **-ip** or the **-erek** form of the verb underlined.)

1 İki kovboy atlarından indikten sonra silahlarını <u>çekip/ çekerek</u> birbirlerini delik deşik ettiler.
2 Yarışmacı <u>gülümseyip/ gülümseyerek</u> sunucunun sorduğu soruya cevap verdi.
3 Hasta sınıf arkadaşımıza <u>uğrayıp/ uğrayarak</u> sağlık durumunu sorduk.
4 Önemsiz ayrıntıları <u>araştırıp/ araştırarak</u> değerli zamanını kaybetti.
5 Dalgın komşumuz bugün bayram olduğunu <u>unutup/ unutarak</u> iş yerine gitti.

6 Korkan çocuk ödevini bahane <u>edip/ ederek</u> dişçiyle randevusunu ertelemeye çalıştı.

## Sözcükler

(Not all of these appear in the Glossary at the end of the book, as they are not all equally useful)

| | | | |
|---|---|---|---|
| **silah** | gun, weapon | **araştırmak** | to investigate |
| **delik deşik etmek** | to fill with holes | **değerli** | valuable |
| **yarışmacı** | contestant | **dalgın** | absent-minded |
| **sunucu** | quiz master | **bayram** | feast |
| **sağlık durumu** | health condition | **bahane etmek** | to use as a pretext |
| **önemsiz** | unimportant | **randevu** | meeting, appointment |
| **ayrıntı** | detail | | |

### Exercise 10

Choose whether **-ip** or **-erek** is the most logical suffix in the sentences above. Make sure you've checked the translation in the Key to Exercise 9 before you do this.

## Language point

### Converbs

By now, you have seen four different converbs, each with its own characteristics. Two final remarks:

1 When you use **-ip** 'and' **-erek** 'by doing' or **-ince** 'when', 'as soon as', you never add a present or past tense suffix, whereas when you use -**ken** 'while', you always have to add one (mostly the **geniş zaman**).

2 **-ip** and **-erek** always have the same subject as the main verb (and so are not unlike English '-ing' forms), whereas **-ince** and **-ken** may have a subject which is different from the one in the main clause (and are thus more like English subordinate clauses).

## Exercise 11

Translate these sentences. (In Exercise 12 you will be asked to choose whether to use -**ip**, -**erek**, -**ince** or -**ken**.)

1 Ben bunları düşünüp/ düşünerek/ düşününce/ düşünürken zil çaldı.
2 Sınava geç kaldığını anlayıp/ anlayarak/ anlayınca / anlarken montunu giyip/ giyerek/ giyince/ giyerken sokağa fırladı.
3 Ocağin önünde durup/ dururken/ durarak/ durunca, ısındı.
4 Daktilosuna kağıdı takıp/ takarak/ takınca/ takarken bir şiir yazmaya başladı.
5 Şişman adam tüm tatlıları yemeyi kesip/ keserek/ kesince/ keserken kilo vermeye çalıştı.
6 Yemekten sonra bulaşıkları yapıp/ yaparak/ yapınca/ yaparken yardım etti.
7 Amerika'ya varıp/ vararak/ varınca/ varırken bana bir e-posta gönderecek.
8 Anneler niye çocuklarını hep balkondan seslenip/ seslenerek/ seslenince/ seslenirken sofraya çağırırlar?

## Sözcükler

| | | | |
|---|---|---|---|
| düşünmek | to think, to contemplate | şişman | fat |
| mont | jacket | kesmek | to stop, to refrain from (*literally:* to cut) |
| fırlamak | to rush | kilo vermek | to lose weight |
| ocak | fireplace | bulaşıkları yapmak | to wash the dishes |
| ısınmak | to warm oneself | e-posta | e-mail |
| daktilo | typewriter | seslenmek | to call out, to address |
| şiir | poem | sofra | dinner table |
| takmak | insert in | | |

## Exercise 12

Choose whether -**ip**, -**erek**, -**ince** or -**ken** is the most logical suffix to use. Make sure you've checked the translation in the Key to Exercise 11 before you do this.

## Exercise 13

Read through the following text, taken from a bus ticket from a bus company called **Kasırga** 'Hurricane'. Use the word list below the text; again, there are quite a few words here that are relatively unimportant, so you won't find them in the Glossary. Besides the odd word you don't know, there will also be some forms and suffixes that you have not yet seen. Make a list of things you don't understand. Read the translation in the Key, if you need. Then, answer the questions below.

---

### Sayın yolcularımızın dikkat edeceği hususlar:

1. Satılan bilet geri alınmaz.
2. Bilet verildiği gün ve saat için geçerlidir.
3. Bilet alırken yanınızda bulunan bavul, valiz ve kutu gibi eşyalarınızı göstereceksiniz. Eşyalarınız teslim edilip ve teslim fişine yazılacaktır.
4. Teslim edilmeyen ve teslim fişine yazılmayan eşya, bavul, valiz, kutu, çanta gibi şeylerin kaybolmasından dolayı Otobüs Firması sorumlu değildir.
5. Her hukuk sorumluluk otobüs sahibi aittir.
6. Teslim fişinde vasfı ve değeri belirtilmeyen eşyalar kaybolursa, eşya sahibine bilet değerinin iki katı otobüs sahibi ve şoförü tarafından ödenir.
7. Otobüsün herhangi bir kazasından doğacak sorumluluk KASIRGA firmasına ait olmayıp, her türlü sorumluluk kazaya karışan otobüs sahibine aittir.

---

| | | | |
|---|---|---|---|
| **verildiği gün** | day of issue | **hukuk** | justicial |
| **geçerli** | valid | **sorumluluk** | responsibility |
| **bavul** | suitcase, trunk | **vasıf** | characteristics, nature |
| **valiz** | suitcase | **değer** | value |
| **kutu** | parcel | **iki kat** | double amount |
| **teslim edilmek** | to be handed over | **tarafından** | by |
| **kaybolmak** | to get lost | **karışmak** | to be involved |

Turkey has a well-organised system of public transport: you can travel almost anywhere by bus. In order to understand this text, you should know that most bus companies do not own buses. Instead, they hire them from bus owners, who, in return for using the company name, pay a commission fee.

1 Compare **husus** 4 and 5. Who is responsible for lost luggage?
2 Who is responsible in case of an accident (**husus** 7)?
3 Throughout this text, you see some examples of clause combining. In **husus** 3, what does the **-ip** in **teslim edilip** stand for?
4 Several passives (to be taken, to be bought) occur in this text. For instance, **satılan**, **alınmaz**, **edildiği** (in **husus** 1 and 2). So, which two suffixes are used for the passive?
5 What would **dolayı** in the sequence **-masından dolayı** (see **husus** 3) mean?
6 In **husus** 7 you see **olmayıp**. Which function has **-ip** here? What does it stand for?

## Vocabulary lists

In order to cool down from the difficult exercise above, here are some easy and handy word lists. Add these items to your vocabulary and then proceed to Exercise 14!

| ocak | January | mayıs | May | eylül | September |
|------|---------|-------|-----|-------|-----------|
| şubat | February | hazıran | June | ekim | October |
| mart | March | temmuz | July | kasım | November |
| nisan | April | ağustos | August | aralık | December |

| kırmızı | red | sarı | yellow | kahverengi | brown |
|---------|-----|------|--------|------------|-------|
| yeşil | green | turunç | orange | gri | grey |
| mavi | blue | portakal rengi | orange | boz | grey |
| pembe | pink | mor | purple | beyaz | white |
| siyah | black | lacivert | deep, dark blue | türküaz/ firuze | turquoise |

### Exercise 14

Translate:

1 I think every month has its own colour (NB: use **ait** 'belonging to' with dative case).
2 January is white.
3 February, as well as October and November, are usually grey months.

4 March, on the other hand, is green.
5 Flowers turn April, May and June into pink and blue.
6 July and August are yellow because of the sun.
7 September is orange and brown and December is either grey or white.

| | | | |
|---|---|---|---|
| **bence** | according to me, I think | **-a değiştirmek** | turn into |
| **renk** | colour | **güneş** | sun |
| **-e ait** | belonging to | **hem ... hem** | either. . . or |
| **ise** | on the other hand | **de ...** | |
| | | **dolayı (-den)** | because of |

## Exercise 15

Below, a number of items are listed. Try to make sets of four 'related' items. One set is formed by **sabun, diş macunu, tıraş bıçağı** and **güneşyağı**, the last three of which contain at least one part (they are compound nouns) that you know. Can you now guess what they are and what makes them a related set?

| | | | |
|---|---|---|---|
| etek | sabun | batı | çaydanlık |
| kol | güneşyağı | güney | tencere |
| diş macunu | bacak | elbise | tişört |
| bıçak | doğu | gömlek | ayak |
| tıraş bıçağı | göz | kuzey | tabak |

| | |
|---|---|
| **kol** | arm |
| **batı** | West |

# 15 Size öğretip öğretemedik- lerimiz

## The things we could and couldn't teach you

In this lesson we will:

- show you some other features of Turkish you haven't yet seen
- give you an update of some of the trickier elements of the language
- provide you with a number of written texts to improve your reading skills

## What else is in store?

After 14 lessons, you may ask yourself how much more there is to know about Turkish. You can manage quite a bit of conversation now, and read the odd newspaper item. But there is more to Turkish than we can show you in this book. This lesson is a final attempt to show you a few of those things.

## Language points

### Causative

The causative suffix is used to express English 'to let (someone) do (something)':

**yapmak**  to do, to make  **yaptırmak**  to let someone do/ make something

**ölmek** to die     **öldürmek** to kill

As you see, this is expressed by the suffix **-tır** (and **-tir, -tur, -tür,
-dır, -dir, -dur** and **-dür**). However, some of the more common
verbs have a different suffix, so they are best learned as separate
words. Examples:

| | |
|---|---|
| **anla-** | **anlat-** |
| to understand | to make understand, to explain, to tell |
| **gez-** | **gezdir-** |
| to walk around | to show around (*also used in* 'to walk a dog') |
| **bit-** | **bitir-** |
| to finish | to finish something |
| **piş-** | **pişir-** |
| to boil | to cook something |
| **kork-** | **korkut-** |
| to fear | to frighten |

In the following examples, you see that the person who is made to
do something is marked with the dative ending (**-e**, *see* Lesson 3):

**Kraliçe aşçıya akşam yemeğini hazırlattı.**
The queen had the cook prepare the dinner.

**Arabasını yaşlı tamirciye tamir ettiriyor.**
He has the old mechanic repair his car.

**Exercise 1**

Other suffixes which are used to extend the verb stem are **-iş-/-ş-**,
expressing 'each other' and **-in/-n-**, expressing 'oneself'. Read these
example sentences and determine the basic form of the verbs:

**Görüşmemizden sonra anlaştık.**
After our discussion we understood each other.

**Kerim yıkanıp giyindi.**
Kerim washed himself and got dressed.

**Erkek kardeşlerim hep dövüşürlarmış.**
My brothers always seem to be hitting one another.

## Colloquial matters

We would like to draw your attention to a number of features of
the language which you do not always find in textbooks. There are

some characteristics of colloquial, spoken Turkish that are reflected in spelling. For instance, the tense endings are usually pronounced rather fast, and may not sound like you would expect on the basis of the written forms. An example is the the **-r-** in the **iyor** suffix, which is normally not pronounced. Instead of **korkuyor**, you will probably hear 'korkuyo'. Sometimes you see this written as well.

## Exercise 2

Give the 'full versions' of these verb forms.

1  gidecem          gideceğim
2  gidiyon
3  öğrenicez
4  yazcam
5  korkuyodum
6  geliyo
7  diyo

Similarly, the **r** is sometimes dropped in the word **bir**, and the plural marker can be pronounced as **-ner**:

**bi gün** *for* **bir gün**          one day
**bugünnerde** *for* **bugünlerde**   these days

Instead of **ile**, the form **-nen** is often used:

**babasıynan** *for* **babasıyla**    with her/his dad

## Double tenses

Throughout this book you may have spotted 'double tenses', such as the **-mişti** pluperfect in **yazmıştı** 'he had written'. This tense indicates that something happened earlier than another event. There are more of these double-marked tenses, such as the 'progressive past' **-iyordu** in **gidiyorduk** 'we were going' and the future past **-ecekti** in **hepsini anlatacaktım** 'I would tell everything'. We will not devote much time and space to them, as they are pretty straightforward in form and meaning. Other examples:

**Ne demiştim sana?**
What had I told you?

**Bütün gece çalışıyordu.**
He was working all night.

**Neredeyse aynı ayakkabıları alacaktık.**
We would almost have bought the same shoes.

## Reading text 1

Read the following excerpt and try to understand the author's line of reasoning. Then answer the questions below.

Birçok kişi herhangi bir Avrupa ülkesinde konuşulan dili is mini düşünmeksizin doğrudan doğruya ülkenin ismine bağlar: İngilizce, İngiltere'nin dilidir; Fransizca ve Almanca aynı şekilde Fransa ve Almanya'nin dilidir. Bu kadar basit. Fakat, bu varsayımdan yola çıkarsak hata yapmış oluruz; diğer ülkeleri ve dillerini gözden geçirdiğimiz zaman birçok devletin ve dilinin bir olmadığını hemen idrak edebiliriz. Belçikaca, Avusturyaca veya İsviçrece gibi dillerin varolmadığını örnek olarak gösterebiliriz.

## Sözcükler

| düşünmeksizin | without thinking | gözden geçirmek | to scrutinise |
|---|---|---|---|
| doğrudan doğruya | directly | idrak etmek | to understand |
| basit | simple | varolmak | to exist |
| varsayım | assumption | | |

1 What does the author say about names of countries and languages?
2 Which alternative do you know for the **-meksizin** suffix in **düşünmeksizin**?
3 Can you detect the typo in this text?

## Reading text 2

Read this weather forecast, taken from the internet version of the newspaper *Hürriyet* (*www.hurriyet.com.tr*).

İstanbul'da yağmursuz 45 gün    (45 days without rain in Istanbul)

Yağışsız geçen 43 günden sonra, önceki gün Meteoroloji tarafından verilen rapordan 'sağanak yağıp beklendiği' bildirmesine rağmen, İstanbul'da yine güneşli bir hafta sonu yaşandı. Böylece İstanbul'da son kez yağmur yağan 10 Temmuz'dan sonra, yağışsız 45 gün geçti.

Meteoroloji, bugün İstanbul'da havanın parçalı bulutlu olacağını, sıcaklığın da 30 derece civarında bulunacağını bildirdi.

(*Hürriyet*, 24 Ağustos 1998, Pazartesi)

## Sözcükler

| | |
|---|---|
| **sağanak** | cloudburst |
| **rağmen** | in spite of |
| **civar** | surrounding |

## Postpositions

In the last text several postpositions occurred (**sonra, tarafından, rağmen, civarında**). Turkish does not have prepositions. The equivalents of English prepositions are often case endings (**lokantada** 'in the restaurant', **lokantaya** 'to the restaurant', **lokantadan** 'from the restaurant'), or postpositions. Two types can be distinguished: simple postpositions and more complex constructions. Most of the simple postpositions have been with us throughout this book.

Some of the simple postpositions require a case marker on the word before it; others do not:

| no case marking | no case marking or genitive (after personal pronouns and **bu, şu** and **o**) | dative (**-e**) | | ablative (**-den**) | |
|---|---|---|---|---|---|
| **üzere** on | **gibi** like | **-e doğru** | towards | **-den önce** | before |
| | **ile** with | **-e göre** | according to | **-den sonra** | after |
| | **için** for | **-e rağmen** | in spite of | **-den beri** | since |
| | | | | **-den dolayı** | because of |

NB: **üzere** also means 'in order to'

The complex postpositional constructions are based on words that mean 'the inside', 'the outside', 'the down side', etcetera. The most important ones are the following:

| | | | |
|---|---|---|---|
| **ara** | space between | **iç** | interior |
| **alt** | underside | **ön** | front |
| **arka** | back | **peş** | space behind |
| **baş** | close surroundings | **üst** | top |
| **dış** | exterior | **yan** | space beside |

These are followed by a possessive suffix and a case marker. For instance, the word **üst** 'top', followed by the third person singular possessive and the locative case (place where something is; indicated by **-de**), becomes **üstünde**. This means 'on top of'. Now, if you want to say 'on top of the table', you need to put this postposition after the word for 'table', which is **masa**. This word must be suffixed with the genitive case (because of the possessive **-ü-** in **üstünde**, this form literally means 'on its top'): **masanın üstünde** 'on top of the table'. Here are the same words again, but now as complete postpositions; the case used is the locative, the one meaning 'in', 'at' or 'on', as this is the one you will encounter most often in these postpositions. However, other case markers may sometimes have to be used instead (see **peşinden** and **üstüne** in the examples below).

| **ara** | space between | **arasında** | between |
|---------|---------------|--------------|---------|
| **alt** | underside | **altında** | under |
| **arka** | back | **arkasında** | behind |
| **baş** | close surroundings | **başında** | near |
| **dış** | exterior | **dışında** | outside |
| **iç** | interior | **içinde** | in |
| **ön** | front | **önünde** | in front of |
| **peş** | space behind | **peşinde** | after |
| **üst** | top | **üstünde** | above, on |
| **yan** | space beside | **yanında** | next to |

More examples:

| **Onun peşinden koştum.** | I ran after him. |
|---------------------------|------------------|
| **Arkamızda.** | Behind us. |
| **Benim yanımda durdu.** | He stood next to me. |
| **Evinin önündeler.** | They are in front of the house. |
| **Masanın üstüne koy!** | Put it on the table. |

### Exercise 3

Translate:

1 She's in the house.
2 I went into the house.
3 What's behind this wall?
4 The film starts after the news.
5 Your pen has fallen under the table.
6 There's a garden between the houses.

7 Your brother is a good man just like you.
8 Like my older brother, I don't drink beer.
9 The car is in front of the house.
10 This car is too (**fazla**) big for our family.

## Vocabulary

One of the things we will be doing in this final lesson is provide
vocabulary exercises with which you can practise your command
of all the words you have learned throughout the earlier lessons.
You'll have forgotten many of these words; the exercises will help
your memory.

### Exercise 4

Connect the opposites.

| | |
|---|---|
| 1 **doğmak** | a **gelecek** |
| 2 **pahalı** | b **yok** |
| 3 **geçen** | c **tembel** ('lazy') |
| 4 **gelmek** | d **kapatmak** |
| 5 **soru** | e **ucuz** |
| 6 **uzak** | f **ileri** |
| 7 **var** | g **cevap** |
| 8 **geri** | h **gitmek** |
| 9 **çalışkan** ('hard-working') | i **ölmek** |
| 10 **açmak** | j **yakın** |

### Exercise 5

Connect the verbs on the right with the direct objects on the left.
Note that some of the nouns are case-marked.

| | |
|---|---|
| 1 ders | a yıkamak |
| 2 film | b çalmak |
| 3 indirim | c bulunmak |
| 4 bulaşık | d pişirmek |
| 5 lambayı | e gitmek |
| 6 çözüm | f göndermek |
| 7 kart | g yetişmek |
| 8 yer | h söndürmek |
| 9 uykuya | i seyretmek |

| | |
|---|---|
| 10 gitar | j vermek |
| 11 çarşıya | k yapmak |
| 12 alışverişe | l dalmak |
| 13 trene | m çalışmak |
| 14 söz | n çıkmak |
| 15 yemekleri | o bulmak |

| | |
|---|---|
| **indirim** | discount |
| **bulaşık** | dirty dishes |

## Exercise 6

Fill in one of the nouns given at the bottom in the following sentences.

1 Çocuklar iyice . . . söylüyor.
2 Ayşe . . . yapmak için çıktı.
3 . . . çıktıktan sonra çok yorgundum.
4 . . . silmem gerek ama istemiyorum.
5 Oğlunuz o önemli . . . geçti mi?
6 Türkiye'deki tatil zarfında beş . . . aldım.
7 Yeni bir araba için . . . biriktiriyoruz.
8 Sordum, fakat . . . vermedi.
9 Önce lokantada yedik, ondan sonra kulübe gidip . . . ettik
10 Acele et, . . . kaybetmek istemiyoruz.
11 İstanbul'da bir . . . bulmak zor değil.
12 Abim Türkçe ve iki başka . . . biliyor.
13 Şimdiye kadar bütün . . . doldurdunuz mu?
14 Affedersiniz, belki siz bana biraz . . . verebilir misiniz?
15 Annem her gün . . . alması lazım.

| | | | |
|---|---|---|---|
| **silmek** | to wipe | **cam** | window |
| **biriktirmek** | to gather | **sınav** | exam |
| **şimdiye kadar** | already | **ilaç** | medication |
| **merdiven** | stairs | **zarfında** | during |

a kilo; b formleri; c şarkı; d dans; e merdivene; f dili; g camları;
h vakit; i sınavı; j ilaçları; k taksi; l para; m alışveriş; n bilgi;
o cevap

## Verbs that require a subordinate clause

Now that you know how subordinate clauses are formed (*see* Lesson 11), you are ready to learn how to say things like 'I think that . . .' or 'he knows that . . .'. A moment's reflection on the way in which these types of verbs are used in English will show that they are all used in combination with subordinate clauses. In 'I think that he knows by now', 'he knows by now' is a subordinate clause. Turkish too combines these verbs with subordinate clauses. Subordinate clauses come before the main clause and the verb often has the suffix **-diği**, the Turkish equivalent of English 'that'.

The verbs we are concerned with here refer to mental activities, such as saying, hearing, wishing, knowing, believing, thinking, telling, etc. They all tend to co-occur with subordinate clauses with **-diği**. The following sequences are therefore very common (the **-ni** part in the first two examples is the accusative case suffix and **-ne** in the last one is the dative case suffix; they will be explained below):

... **X-diğini** ... **söyle-** ...   say that
... **X-diğini** ... **düşün-** ...   think that
... **X-diğine** ... **inanma-** ...   not believe that

Below are some examples of these patterns. Note that the **-diği-** forms are normally marked with case endings. This is logical if you consider the structure of these sentences. Take, for instance, a simple verb, such as **almak** 'to buy'. This can have a direct object: the thing you buy. That thing, let's say a book, is marked with accusative case, as in **kitabı aldım** 'I bought the book'. A verb such as **düşünmek** 'to think' can have a direct object too. The only difference is that **almak** normally has a simple noun for its direct object, because one buys a concrete thing, but that **düşünmek** typically has a whole clause for its direct object. This becomes obvious if you compare typical English examples of these two verbs: 'I bought a book' and 'I thought that you weren't going to come anymore'.

However, Turkish sees both 'the book' and 'that you weren't going to come anymore' as the direct objects of 'bought' and 'thought', respectively. That means they both need to be marked with the accusative case suffix, the case marker that is used for direct objects (*see* Lesson 6). To build up the sentence 'I think that he has done it', you go through the following steps:

---

*Step 1:* first form the clause 'he has done it': **o yaptı**
*Step 2:* turn it into a subordinate clause (adding **-diği** to the verb stem and the genitive case suffix to the subject; *see* Lesson 11): **onun yaptığı**
*Step 3:* add 'I think': **onun yaptığı düşünüyorum**
*Step 4:* add the accusative case suffix: **onun yaptığını düşünüyorum**

---

Everything said here about adding the accusative case suffix (Step 4) applies in exactly the same way when a particular verb requires a dative case suffix. The verb **inanmak** 'to believe', for instance, requires 'me' in 'Believe me' to be in the dative form: **bana inan!** So, in building up the Turkish for 'I don't believe that he has done it', the same steps are followed:

---

*Step 1:* first form the clause 'he has done it': **o yaptı**
*Step 2:* turn it into a subordinate clause (adding **-diği** to the verb stem and the genitive case suffix to the subject; *see* Lesson 11): **onun yaptığı**
*Step 3:* add 'I don't believe': **onun yaptığı inanmıyorum**
*Step 4:* add the dative case suffix: **onun yaptığına inanmıyorum**

---

In the examples above, **-diği** forms were not followed by a noun. Consider again the following pair:

**Geçen akşam televizyonda seyrettiğimiz programı çok beğendim.**
I loved that programme we saw on TV last night.

**Senin biraz deli olduğunu herkes bilir.**
Everybody knows that you're a bit crazy. ('That you are crazy, everybody knows')

In the first sentence the clause with **-diği** is a relative clause that goes with the noun **program**; in the second sentence it is a subordinate clause that goes with the verb **bilir**. This second structure is also used when the main clause is a 'verbless' sentence, i.e. where the English equivalent would have a form of 'to be':

**Onların gelecekleri kesin.**    It's certain that they will come.
                                  ('That they will come, is certain')
**Yaptığın çok güzeldi.**    What you did was very nice.

*Exercise 7*

Translate:

1 Did you know that I like pop music?
2 I told her that I did it.
3 Is this what you want?
4 I couldn't understand what the politician was saying.
5 He doesn't believe that I love him.
6 Congratulations, I have heard that you have found a new job!
7 You should thank them for coming.
8 He told me that he graduated.
9 What the museum showed in their Van Gogh exhibition was very interesting.
10 I'm fed up with his behaviour!

| | | | |
|---|---|---|---|
| **pop müziği** | pop music | **sergi** | exhibition |
| **politikacı** | politician | **davranış** | behaviour |
| **mezun olmak (-den)** | to graduate | **bıktım (-den)** | I'm fed up with |
| **tebrikler!, tebrik ederim!** | congratulations! | | |

## Diye

This is a very common word in Turkish, literally meaning 'saying', but often meaning 'because'. It is useful for you as a learner, because you can use it once in a while instead of a more complex subordinated clause.

When building a sentence with **diye**, you start with the clause that would follow 'because' in the English equivalent, so you use the familiar order of things in Turkish. This first clause is a normal sentence, that is, complete with verb tense and person endings. Follow this with **diye** and then add the main clause (the part you would start out with in English).

Let's say you want to explain why your friend, who is a big Galatasaray fan, a so-called 'Cimbomlu', seems so happy. What you want to do is build up the sentence according to the above plan:

'Galatasaray beat Beşiktaş' becomes **Galatasaray Beşiktaşı yendi** . . .
Add **diye**: **Galatasaray Beşiktaşı yendi diye** . . .
And then 'he's laughing': **Galatasaray Beşiktaşı yendi diye gülüyor.**

Some more examples:

**Karım tekrar arkadaşlarını ziyaret etmek istiyor diye kavga ediyoruz.**
We're arguing because my wife wanted to go and visit her friends again.

**Yakında savaş çıkacak diye o ülkeye gerçekten gitmek istemiyor.**
Because there's a war in the area, he really doesn't want to go to that place.

Literally, **diye** means 'saying', so it's a form of **demek**. The origin of its use lies in constructions of the sort 'he goes there often, he says (saying) he likes that kind of music'. This way of expressing 'because' may sound a little weird for English-speakers but is really fairly common among the world's languages.

The word **diye** combines with other words that refer to some way of saying something (though not with **demek** itself) to yield the Turkish equivalents of words like 'answered', 'shouted', 'asked' etc. The word with the more specific meaning follows **diye** and it contains the tense and person endings. So let's say you want to say 'I answered "that would be better"', then you start out with the quote (Step 1), then you add **diye** (Step 2), and then you add the word for 'I answered' (Step 3).

---

*Step 1:* **'O daha iyi olur'**
*Step 2:* **'O daha iyi olur' diye**
*Step 3:* **'O daha iyi olur' diye cevap verdim.**

---

Similarly, for 'I complained that I was broke':

---

*Step 1:* **Param bitti**
*Step 2:* **Param bitti diye**
*Step 3:* **Param bitti diye yakındım.**

---

You can then follow this with a new clause, if you wish, such as in:

**Param bitti diye yakındım, 'önemli değil, biletini ben öderim' dedi.**
I complained that I was broke, so he said 'don't worry, I'll pay for your ticket'.

Though **diye** cannot combine with **dedi** and other forms of **demek**, it does combine with its near synonym **söylemek**, for instance in **delisin diye söyledi** 'he said "you're crazy"'. Without it, **söylemek** combines with subordinated clauses, as in the first example below. The 'verbs of saying' that combine with **diye** include a few that you maybe didn't expect, like **yazmak** and **merak etmek**, 'to wonder about something':

**Burada çok sevdiğini bana söyledi.**
He told me he really enjoyed it here.

**Eğitimini gelecek sene bitirecek diye yazdı.**
She wrote that she would finish her studies next year.

**O soruya ne cevap verecek diye merak ediyorum.**
I wonder what he will answer to that question.

**Diye** and several other words can be used for short answers of the type 'because I don't want to':

**Niye Türkçe öğreniyorsunuz?**
Why are you learning Turkish?

**Sizlerle konuşabilmek istiyorum diye.**
Because I want to be able to speak with you.

Other useful words are **için** 'in order to' and **onun için** 'that's why'. The answer to the above question could also have been:

**Sizlerle konuşabilmek için.**
In order to be able to speak with you.

**Sizlerle konuşabilmek istiyorum. Onun için Türkçe öğreniyorum.**
I want to be able to speak with you. That's why I'm learning Turkish.

Other examples:

**Bugünkü gazeteyi okudum. Onun için artık biliyorum.**
I read today's paper. That's why I know already.

**Niye iyi değilsin?**        Why aren't things going so well?
**İşsizim diye.**             Because I'm unemployed.

# Two words, one meaning

For 75 years there has been a kind of language battle going on about Turkish vocabulary, set in motion after Atatürk started his language reform in order to 'purify' or to 'turkify' the Turkish language (*see* the Reading text in Lesson 3). His purpose was to get rid of most Arabic and Persian 'loans' and constructions by replacing them with **öz Türkçe** 'real' Turkish words. These real Turkish words were words with a Turkish root or stem, as found in many of the Central Asian Turkic languages, such as Uzbek or Uyghur, as well as in already dead languages. Unfortunately, these Central Asian languages were not always all that 'pure': they contain lots of borrowings from Russian and Chinese. In addition, the other Turkic languages are not intelligible to Turkish speakers, making borrowings from those languages not much easier than the Arabic and Persian words they had to replace.

Turkey has been divided into two camps: some prefer language reform and turkification of the language, and others stick to the long-established loan words from Arabic or Persian. As a result, many concepts are expressed by two words.

## Examples

| | | |
|---|---|---|
| **kent** | **şehir** | both mean 'city' |
| **sözcük** | **kelime** | both mean 'word' |
| **öneri** | **teklif** | both mean 'proposal', 'offer' |
| **yanıt** | **cevap** | both mean 'answer' |

Using words from either the left column (**öz Türkçe**) or the right one (loan words) was and sometimes still is a political statement, though they are also often purely stylistic variants.

Maybe it is a fitting conclusion to this book to end with some examples of modern-day loan words. Even nowadays, there is a strong tendency to 'turkify' loan words from other languages (mainly English), for instance in the field of computers. Of the pairs below, **bilgisayar/kompüter** favours the Turkish variant; in the other two, the borrowed words are much more common.

| | |
|---|---|
| **bilgisayar** | **kompüter** |
| **uzyazım** | **teleks** |
| **uzyazar** | **faks** |

For other computer terms, Turkish equivalents are available. To name but a few:

| | | | |
|---|---|---|---|
| **kaydetmek** | save | **veri** | data |
| **yazılım** | software | **güncellemek** | update |
| **fare** | mouse | **yüklemek** | download |
| **imleç** | cursor | **C sürücüsü** | C-drive |
| **silmek** | delete | **sanal alem** | virtual |
| **sunucu** | server | | market-place |
| **program** | to run a | **e-post** | e-mail |
| **çalıştırmak** | program | | |

# Ready-reference grammar

Most of what you read in this ready-reference grammar, has been dealt with in one of the lessons. Some (and certainly not all) important aspects of Turkish grammar are brought together here, which makes it a lot easier to look up particular parts of the grammar for reference.

## Agglutination

Turkish is an agglutinative language. Whereas English uses separate words to express meanings, Turkish has a rich system of *suffixes*, small 'endings' which are stuck to the 'root' of a word. This process of glueing meaningful parts to other meaningful parts is called agglutination.

There are verbal and nominal roots. A verbal root, or stem, can be followed by suffixes expressing, for instance, tense (past, present, future), person, negation, passive, reflexivity (oneself), reciprocity (each other). An example is **gelemediniz** 'you couldn't come' consisting of the verb stem **gel-** 'come', plus **-eme** 'not being able to', **-di** 'past tense' and **-niz** 'second person plural'.

A noun can be followed by such suffixes as the plural marker **-ler,** a case marker (see below), diminutive, or productive suffixes, e.g. those which turn the word into 'the person working with X' (**-çi**) or into an abstract noun (**-lik**):

| | | | |
|---|---|---|---|
| **iş** | work | **bakan** | minister |
| **işçi** | worker, workman | **bakanlık** | ministry |
| **kitap** | book | **çocuk** | child |
| **kitapçi** | bookseller | **çocukluk** | childhood |

# Vowel Harmony

So, Turkish is a language in which a lot of meaning is expressed by word endings (suffixes). It would have been convenient for you as a learner, if one particular meaning (e.g., 'you' or 'they' or 'with') was expressed by one single word ending. Unfortunately, it is a bit more complicated than that. Turkish has a feature which is called vowel harmony. The vowels of these endings may change, depending on the last syllable of the preceding noun or verb stem. There are two types of vowel harmony. The first one has two forms, and you will have to choose between **e**- or **a**- in the stem. The second one can have four different vowels: either **i**, **ı**, **u** or **ü**. It all has to do with place of articulation in the mouth.

Two-fold (**e** or **a**)　　after **e, i, ü, ö**　　>　　**e**
　　　　　　　　　　　　after **a, ı, u, o**　　>　　**a**

This means that English 'to' can be expressed either by **-e** or **-a** depending on the final vowel in the word: 'to school' is **okul-a** and 'to the hotel' is **otel-e**.

Four-fold (**i, ı, ü, ü**)　after **e, i**　　　　>　　**i**
　　　　　　　　　　　　after **a, ı**　　　　>　　**ı**
　　　　　　　　　　　　after **ü, ö**　　　　>　　**ü**
　　　　　　　　　　　　after **u, o**　　　　>　　**u**

English 'my' can be expressed by either **-im, -ım, -üm** or **-um**: 'my bike' is **bisiklet-im**, 'my name' is **ad-ım**, 'my rose' is **gül-üm** and 'my shower' is **duş-um**.

*Examples:*　　the suffix **-im** 'my' is four-fold, so it can appear as **-im, -ım, -üm** or **-um**.
　　　　　　　the suffix **-le** 'with' is two-fold, so it can appear as **-le** or **-la**
　　　　　　　the suffix **-ler** (plural) is two-fold, so it can appear as **-ler** or **-lar**.

**kardeş-im-le**　　　　　　with my brother
**arkadaş-ım-la**　　　　　　with my friend
**kardeş-ler-im-le**　　　　　with my brothers

# Word order

The order of the main parts of a normal sentence in Turkish is:

*subject* first, then
*object* of the sentence, and
the *verb* in final position

Word order is, nevertheless, relatively free. Other arrangements than subject-object-verb occur as well, but affect emphasis: the emphasised or focused element is always in the position *before* the verb. All three sentences **hediyeyi Ali'ye verdim**, **Ali'ye hediyeyi verdim** and **Ali'ye verdim hediyeyi** mean 'I gave Ali the present'. The difference is that in the first sentence emphasis is on *Ali*, and in the second on *the present*. In the third sentence, the emphasis is again on *Ali*, but here the word after the verb, i.e. **hediyeyi**, conveys already given or known information: speaker and hearer know which particular **hediye** is referred to.

# Cases

Turkish has six grammatical cases in the form of suffixes which are attached to nouns and pronouns. The nominative case is the unmarked one (that is, it's just the word without an extra suffix) and is used for subjects and indefinite objects of sentences. The genitive denotes *possession*, the dative the indirect object or goal, the accusative the definite direct object, the locative the *place at which* and the ablative *place from which*, or *cause*:

| | | | |
|---|---|---|---|
| nominative | no marking | **ev** | house (*subject or indefinite direct object*) |
| genitive | **-in** or **-nin** | **evin** | of the house |
| dative | **-e** or **-ye** | **eve** | to the house |
| accusative | **-i** or **-yi** | **evi** | the house (*definite object of the sentence*) |
| locative | **-de** | **evde** | in the house |
| ablative | **-den** | **evden** | from the house |

# Adjectives

Adjectives always come before the noun. When used in combination with the indefinite article **bir**, the adjective comes first, then **bir** and finally the noun, as in **eski bir kitap** 'an old book'. Some suffixes can turn nouns into adjectives (e.g. **-li, -sel**):

| | | | |
|---|---|---|---|
| **yaş** | age | **din** | religion |
| **yaşlı** | aged | **dinsel** | religious |
| **Amerika** | America | **tarih** | history |
| **Amerikalı** | American | **tarihsel** | historical |

Comparison of adjectives is expressed by the ablative case **-den** sometimes followed by **daha** 'more' or **az** 'less'. The superlative contains the word **en** 'most':

| | | | |
|---|---|---|---|
| **güzel** | beautiful | **hızlı** | fast |
| **daha güzel** | more beautiful | **daha hızlı** | faster |
| **en güzel** | most beautiful | **en hızlı** | fastest |

**Tarsus İstanbul'dan az güzel.**
Tarsus is less beautiful than İstanbul.

**yıldırımdan (daha) hızlı**
faster than lightning

## Pronouns

The information conveyed by pronouns in English is in the form of person markers attached to the verb in Turkish. Pronouns are mainly used for emphasis and contrast. In **gidiyorum** 'I am going', the **-um** part already tells you that the subject is 'I'. The pronoun **ben** in **ben gidiyorum** 'I am going', however, tells you the same, but with a lot of stress: 'not YOU, but I am going'.

Pronouns get case marking:

| | | nom. | gen. | dat. | acc. | loc. | abl. |
|---|---|---|---|---|---|---|---|
| *sing.* | *1* | **ben** | **benim** | **bana** | **beni** | **bende** | **benden** |
| | | I | of me/my | to me | me | on me | from me |
| | *2* | **sen** | **senin** | **sana** | **seni** | **sende** | **senden** |
| | | you | of you/your | to you | you | on you | from you |

| | | nom. | gen. | dat. | acc. | loc. | abl. |
|---|---|---|---|---|---|---|---|
| | 3 | o | onun | ona | onu | onda | ondan |
| | | he/she/it | of him/ her/it, his/her/its | to him/ her/it | him/ her/it | on him/ her/it | from him/her/it |
| plur. | 1 | biz | bizim | bize | bizi | bizde | bizden |
| | | we | of us/our | to us | us | on us | from us |
| | 2 | siz | sizin | size | sizi | sizde | sizden |
| | | you | of you/your | to you | you | on you | from you |
| | 3 | onlar | onların | onlara | onları | onlarda | onlardan |
| | | they | of them/ their | to them | them | on them | from them |

The third person singular **o** 'she', 'he', 'it' also means 'that' (both by itself and before nouns). Besides **o** there are two other demonstrative pronouns: **bu** 'this' and **şu** 'this', 'that' (used when you want to focus the listener's attention). You use **şu** whenever you want to direct the attention of the listener towards an object or a person not previously mentioned in the conversation. As soon as the listener notices the object or person referred to, both speakers have to use **bu** when object or person are nearby, or **o** when object or person are further away. For instance, the answer to the question **şu bina ne?** 'what's that building?' is **o bina bir kütüphane** 'that building is a library' and never **şu bina bir kütüphane.**

# Verbs

Turkish has three types of sentences: verbal, existential and nominal sentences. The first type contains ordinary verbs, the second the 'existential' word **var** 'there is' (or **yok** 'there isn't'), and the third type contains a form of 'to be'.

There are two forms of the present, the first one (indicated by the suffix **-iyor-**) being the default present tense, and the second one, called the **geniş zaman** (broad tense), carrying the connotation of habitual actions ('I always . . .') or future plans. There are two distinct pasts as well. The first one, **-di**, is the simple past tense, the second one, **-miş-** carries an inferential meaning ('it seems that. . . .'). The **-ecek** suffix stands for the future tense.

| | | present I | present II | past I | past II | future |
|---|---|---|---|---|---|---|
| *sing.* | *1* | geliyorum | gelirim | geldim | gelmişim | geleceğim |
| | | I come | I come | I came | I came | I'll come |
| | *2* | geliyorsun | gelirsin | geldin | gelmişsin | geleceksin |
| | *3* | geliyor | gelir | geldi | gelmiş | gelecek |
| *plur.* | *1* | geliyoruz | geliriz | geldik | gelmişiz | geleceğiz |
| | *2* | geliyorsunuz | gelirsiniz | geldiniz | gelmişsiniz | geleceksiniz |
| | *3* | geliyorlar | gelirler | geldiler | gelmişler | gelecekler |

| | | conditional I | conditional II | pluperfect | subjunctive/ optative | imperative |
|---|---|---|---|---|---|---|
| *sing.* | *1* | gelsem | gelirsem | gelmiştim | geleyim | |
| | | If I were to come | If I come | I had come | let me come | come! |
| | *2* | gelsen | gelirsen | gelmiştin | | gel |
| | *3* | gelse | gelirse | gelmişti | | gelsin |
| *plur.* | *1* | gelsek | gelirsek | gelmiştik | gelelim | |
| | *2* | gelseniz | gelirseniz | gelmiştiniz | | gelin/geliniz |
| | *3* | gelseler | gelirseler | gelmiştiler | | gelsinler |

Other verb moods and tenses are the conditional **-se** (used with tense marker when the condition is closed, used without a tense marker when the condition is open; see Lesson 12), the subjunctive ('let me ...') and the imperative. There are separate suffixes denoting, for instance, 'ability' (**-ebil**) and 'necessity' (**-meli-**). There are also various combinations of moods, tenses and verb suffixes possible. For instance, you will frequently encounter the pluperfect **-mişti**.

Negation is done by means of the suffix **-me** (**gelmiyorum**) and question by means of the question particle **mi** (**gelmiyor muyum?**).

Existential sentences contain either the word **var** 'there is' or **yok** 'there is not'. If the word in front has a possessive marker, the sentence is equivalent to an English 'to have', 'to possess' sentence. **Arabam var** 'I have a car' is literally 'my car is there'.

Verbless sentences are formed with the help of the Turkish equivalent of 'to be', which is expressed by means of a suffix:

| | | | |
|---|---|---|---|
| **güzelim** | I am pretty | **güzeliz** | we are pretty |
| **güzelsin** | you are pretty | **güzelsiniz** | you are pretty |
| **güzel(dir)** | he is pretty | **güzeller(dir)** | they are pretty |

The word **değil** 'not' is used for negation of these sentences (**güzel değilim** 'I'm not pretty').

# Postpositions

Turkish does not have prepositions. Some case endings are used for the equivalents of English prepositions (**lokantada** 'at the restaurant', **lokantaya** 'to the restaurant', **lokantadan** 'from the restaurant'). Turkish does, however, have two types of postpositions: simple postpositions and postpositional constructions. Some of the simple postpositions require a case marker on the word before; others do not:

| no case marking | *no case marking after nouns or genitive (-in or -nin) after pronouns and bu, şu and o* | *dative marking (-e/-a)* | *ablative marking (-den/-dan)* |
|---|---|---|---|
| **üzere** 'on' | **gibi** 'like' | **-e doğru** 'towards' | **-den önce** 'before' |
| | **ile** 'with' | **-e göre** 'according to' | **-den sonra** 'after' |
| | **için** 'for' | **-e rağmen** 'in spite of' | **-den beri** 'since' |
| | | | **-den dolayı** 'because of' |

Postpositional constructions are based on spatial nouns with a possessive pronoun plus a case marker. For instance, the word **üst** 'top', followed by the third person singular possessive and the locative case, becomes **üstünde**, as in **masanın üstünde** 'on top of the table'.

Other examples are **onun peşinden koştum** 'I ran after him', **arkamızda** 'behind us', **hastanenin yanına taşındık** 'we moved next to the hospital'. Similar constructions can be made with the words: **ara** 'space between', **alt** 'underside', **baş** 'close surroundings', **dış** 'exterior', **iç** 'interior', **ön** 'front', **bitişik** 'next to', **dip** 'underside', and **karşı** 'other side', 'opposite' (see Lesson 15).

# Key to exercises

## Lesson 1

### Exercise 1

thanks – **teşekkürler**; hello – **merhaba**; yes – **evet**; goodbye – **iyi günler**; what's up? – **ne haber?**; how are you? – **nasılsın?**; see you – **görüşürüz**; OK – **tamam**; pleased to meet you – **memnun oldum**; I'm fine – **iyiyim**

### Exercise 2

**dostum** 'my friend' (**-um** means 'my'); **nasılsın** 'how are you?' (**-sın** means 'you are'); **ailene** 'to your family' (**-n** means your; **-e** means to); **babam** 'my father' (**-m** means 'my'); **geldiniz** 'you came' (**-d(i)** expresses past tense; **-iniz** means 'you' (plural)); **bulduk** 'we found' (**-d(i)** expresses past tense; **-k** means 'we'); **annem** 'my mother' (**-m** means 'my'); **kardeşlerim** 'my younger brother and sister' (**-ler** expresses plural; **-im** means 'my')

### Exercise 3

You may say things such as: **Bu kocam, Jim. Bu eşim, Carol.** Etc.

### Exercise 4

2 kadınlar 3 arkadaşla 4 kişiler 5 dostumla 6 evim 7 adamlarla 8 Türkler 9 adım 10 öğretmenlerimle

### Exercise 5

Nasılsın; teşekkür; nasılsın; iyiyim; görüşürüz

## Exercise 6

1 **Öğretmenim** 2 **Dostum** 3 **Biliyoruz** 4 **Tanıştırıyor** (no visible ending for third person singular!) 5 **Ailem** 6 **Konuşuyorsunuz** 7 **Öğreniyorlar** 8 **Yardım ediyorum**

## Reading text

HALİL: What a coincidence! (*literally:* Look at the coincidence)
CENGİZ: Hello, Uncle Halil, how are you?
HALİL: I'm fine, I swear, thank you. How are you?
CENGİZ: Not bad, uncle, thank you.
HALİL: And your mum and dad, how are they?
CENGİZ: My mother is fine. My dad is a bit ill.
HALİL: Good recovery! (*literally:* may it be past). Are your brothers fine?
CİNGİZ: They are. In fact we are waiting for Ali. He'll come in a moment.
HALİL: Is that so? Let's wait together then. I haven't seen him for a year or so. So, who's this beautiful girl?
CENGİZ: Don't you recognise her? This is Müjgan, my sister!
HALİL: Is that so? She has grown a lot!

**tesadüf** 'coincidence'; **fena değil** 'not bad'; **biraz rahatsız** 'a little ill'; **birazdan gelecek** 'in a while he'll come here'; **büyümüş** 'has grown'

# Lesson 2

## Exercise 1

1 suffix 2 **-di** 3 **-iyor** 4 suffix 5 **-di** 6 **-di** 7 **-iyor** 8 **-iyor** 9 suffix 10 suffix

The rule of thumb is that you don't need a 'real' verb, i.e. one that is suffixed with **-iyor** or **-di**, if in English the only verb is 'to be'.

## Exercise 2

2 **gelmek** 'to come', **geliyorsun** 'you come' 3 **kalmak** 'to stay', **kaldık** 'we stayed' 4 **seçmek** 'to choose', **seçiyorsunuz** 'you choose' 5 **gitmek** 'to go', **gitti** 'he/she/it went' 6 **vermek** 'to give', **veriyorlar**

'they give' 7 **satmak** 'to sell', **satıyoruz** 'we buy' 8 **çıkmak** 'to go out, emerge', **çıktın** 'you went out' 9 **varmak** 'to arrive at, reach', **vardınız** 'you arrived' 10 **yardım etmek** 'to help', **yardım ediyoruz** 'we are helping'

## Exercise 3

1 **yazdım** ('I wrote her a letter') 2 **başlıyor** ('Which day does autumn start this year?') 3 **seviyor** ('Ali really likes cloudy and cold weather') 4 **kalkıyor** ('What time does your train leave?') 5 **yürüdün** ('Did you walk?') 6 **ettik** ('Yesterday we danced all evening') 7 **söyledim** ('I told you so') 8 **aldınız** ('What did you buy in the shopping mall?') 9 **buluşuyoruz** ('We're meeting at ten') 10 **yedik** ('We ate in a crowded restaurant')

## Exercise 4

Where do you live? I live in New York; When did you come? I came this morning; Do you like Turkey? I like it a lot; Did you come here on holiday? Yes, on holiday; You speak Turkish well. Thanks, but I can't speak it well yet.

## Exercise 5

1 yazıyor 2 geldin 3 kalıyoruz 4 seçtiniz 5 gidiyor 6 verdiler 7 sattık 8 çıkıyorsun 9 varıyorsunuz 10 yardım ettik

## Exercise 6

2 yaptım 3 gidiyorlar 4 geldi 5 çalıştın 6 gördüm 7 istiyorum 8 veriyor 9 yapıyoruz 10 yaptın

## Exercise 7

1 Eve erken gittim. 2 Türkçeyi iyi konuşuyorsunuz. 3 Bana hediye verdi. 4 Akşamları okula gidiyor. 5 Newcastle'da oturuyoruz. 6 Dün yaptım. 7 Bankada çalışıyorum. 8 Dün akşam geç geldiler.

## Exercise 8

**sergi** 'exhibition'; **söyleşi** 'talks'; **gezi** 'trips'; **kitap** 'books'

## Reading text

**abi** 'older brother'; **İngiltere'ye geldiğimde** 'when I came to England'; **-ya** 'to'; **arabalar hep sol taraftan gider** 'cars always (**hep**) drive on the left (**sol**) side (**taraf**)'; **kazasız belasız** 'safe and sound' (*literally:* without (**-sız**) accident (**kaza**) or harm (**bela**)); **kraliçe** 'queen'

## Lesson 3

### Exercise 1

1b 2g 3f 4h 5i 6c 7a 8d 9e

### Exercise 2

1 **mi** (**O filmi gördün mü?**) 2 **kim**-type (**Sinemaya ne zaman gittik?**) 3 **kim**-type (**Bu filmde baş rolü kim oynadı?**) 4 **mi** (**Televizyonda mıydı?**) 5 **mi** (**Aktör müsünüz?**)

### Exercise 3

2 çalışıyor muyuz? 3 gidiyor musunuz? 4 Türkçe konuşuyor mu? 5 yardım ediyor muyuz? 6 Ankara'ya geliyor muyum? 7 ailemi biliyor musun? 8 anlıyorlar mı? 9 İngilizce öğreniyor mu? 10 Türkiye'yi beğeniyor musunuz?

### Exercise 4

2 Öğrenci misiniz? 3 Kimi gördün? 4 Ne zaman gitti? 5 Türkiye'yi beğeniyorlar mı? 6 Nereye gittiniz? 7 Onu biliyor muyuz? 8 Yardım ettiler mi?

### Exercise 5

1 'da 2 'de 3 de 4 ta 5 'ta 6 de 7 da 8 'te

### Exercise 6

1 e 2 köpeğe 3 ya 4 ye 5 a 6 ye 7 'ya 8 sancağa

## Exercise 7

1 'den 2 'dan 3 'dan 4 'den 5 den 6 'ten 7 'tan 8 'dan

# Lesson 4

## Exercise 1

2 parktalar 3 şoförüm 4 memuruz 5 gelinsin 6 Türkçe öğret-
meniyiz 7 hastanede 8 arkadaşlardır 9 polisim 10 öğrencisiniz

## Exercise 2

2 parkta değiller 3 şoför değilim 4 memur değiliz 5 gelin değilsin
6 Türkçe öğretmeni değiliz 7 hastanede değil 8 arkadaş değiller
9 polis değilim 10 öğrenci değilsiniz

## Exercise 3

1 **öğretmen yakışıklı** ('man')/**güzel** ('woman'; i.e. pretty) 2 **güzel
öğretmen o değil** 3 **müze eski** 4 **eski müze kapalı** 5 **yüksek
binadasınız** 6 **o, işsiz elektrikçi** 7 **elektrikçi işsiz** 8 **işsiz elektrikçi
yakışıklı bir adam** (Note that the order of words differs from
English. 'A handsome man' becomes 'Handsome a man'. See also
10 of this exercise and the example **önemli bir kişi** 'an important
person' in Lesson 1. In Lesson 9, the construction
Adjective + **bir** + Noun is explained.) 9 **bina yüksek** 10 **o, güzel bir
öğretmen**

## Exercise 4

Ankara Üniversitesinde okudum. Yani bir öğrenciydim. Her gün
üniversiteye gittim. Her akşam çok yorgundum. En iyi arkadaşım
aynı sokakta oturdu. Onunla beraber sık sık sinemaya tiyatroya
gittik. Arkadaşım öğrenci değildi. O bir gazeteciydi. Gazete için
röportaj yazdı. Bazen televizyon için bir röportaj yaptı. O zaman
onu televizyonda gördüm. Arkadaşım çok ünlüydü.

I studied at Ankara University. So I was a student. Every day I
went to the university. Every evening I was tired. My best friend
lived in the same street. With him/her, I often went to the theatre

or the cinema. My friend was not a student. He/she was a journalist. He/she wrote articles for the newspaper. Often, he/she made reports for television. Then I saw him/her on TV. My friend was very famous.

### Exercise 5

gazeteciydim; gazeteci değildik; gazeteci misiniz?; şofördün; şoför müsün?; şoför; şofördüler

### Exercise 6

1 **Kazayı gördun mü?** 2 **Evet, gördüm. Yaralılar var mıydı?** 3 **Evet, vardı. Şoförler hastanedeler** (*or:* **hastanededirler**). 4 **Nasıllar?** 5 **Şimdi iyiler.** 6 **Emin misin?** 7 **Hayır, emin değilim.**

### Exercise 7

1 verbless (to be) 2 existential (**var/yok**) 3 existential (**var/yok**) 4 verbless (to be) 5 existential (**var/yok**) 6 existential (**var/yok**)

### Exercise 8

2 **Bunlar mı?** 3 **Kahve istiyor musun?** *or:* **Kahve mi istiyorsun?** 4 **Bir tane kavun aldık mı?** (*or:* **Bir tane kavun mu aldık?**) 5 **Hiç mi çay yoktu?** (*or:* **Hiç çay yok muydu?**) 6 **Ankara'da mıydılar?** 7 **Ankara'da var mı?** 8 **İngiltere'de mi oturuyoruz?** (*or:* **İngiltere'de oturuyor muyuz?**)

### Exercise 9

1 This book is good. 2 This good book is now in the library. 3 Yesterday, there wasn't such a book in the library. 4 Those are books.

5 **Bu Aylin.** 6 **O kız Aylin değildir.** 7 **O patlıcan mutfakta.** 8 **Bunlar kütüphanede mi?**

# Lesson 5

### Exercise 1

Hello. My name is Orhan. I was born in Kars in 1910. In 1916, I went to school for the first time. Four years later <u>our family</u> <u>moved</u> to Ankara. My dad found a good job there. From 1923 <u>till</u> 1927 I went to the *rüştiye* school. After that I met my wife. We got <u>married</u> in 1935. Eser was a good woman. Our first child was born two years later. It was a girl, her name was Sumru. We had five more children. <u>The last one</u> was born in 1949. I was very <u>happy</u> until 1960. That year my wife <u>died</u>. I worked until 1973. Now I live <u>with</u> one of our daughters. As I said, my <u>life</u> was good. <u>And</u> my biggest <u>success</u> was in 1931. I entered the Ankara wrestling <u>competition</u>, <u>won</u> it, and got an award.

### Exercise 2

three **üç**; five **beş**; eight **sekiz**; two **iki**; nine **dokuz**; six **altı**; one **bir**; ten **on**; seven **yedi**; four **dört**; fifty **elli**; twenty **yirmi**; hundred **yüz**; sixty **altmış**; seventy **yetmiş**; ninety **doksan**; thousand **bin**; forty **kırk**; eighty **seksen**; thirty **otuz**.

### Exercise 3

1f 2i 3a 4c 5h 6g 7k 8j 9d 10e 11b

NB: though **üzgünüm** literally stands for 'I'm sad', here it means 'too bad'.

### Exercise 4

2 Uğramak 3 Açmak 4 Yaşamak 5 Batmak 6 Pişirmek 7 Yıkamak 8 Kazanmak 9 Sevmek 10 Dinlenmek

### Exercise 5

Some sample answers:
1 **Evet, evdeyim.** 2 **Avustralya'dan geldim.** 3 **Evet.** 4 **Futbol oynadık, dans ettik, dinlendik.** 5 **Görüyorum.** 6 **Evet, çok seviyorum.** 7 **Evet, var.** *or* **Hayır, yok.** 8 **Üç dil biliyorum.** 9 **Aldım.** 10 **Hollandalıyım.** 11 **Kusura bakmayın, vaktim yok.** 12 **Dahil.**

## Exercise 6

1 mı 2 mu; mı 3 nasıl 5 misiniz 6 var mı 7 ne kadar

## Exercise 7

sorular; aylar; ayaklar; insanlar; peynirler; kilolar; ekmekler; dolmalık biberler; borçlar

## Exercise 8

1 Would you like to drink something? 2 Which novel are you reading now? 3 **Amerika'da doğdum.** 4 I bought this T-shirt in 1990. 5 **Hayır, Türkiye'de kimseyi tanımıyorum.** (also: **tanıdığım yok**, using the word **tanıdık** 'acquaintance'.) 6 Do you read Turkish newspapers? 7 I didn't do anything. 8 **Burada ne oldu?** 9 **Evde dört köpeğimiz var.** 10 There was an accident on the street and the police came immediately.

## Exercise 9

peppers; bread; beer; chicken; cottage cheese; black olives; apples; chickpeas. The aubergines she finally bought probably were not on her list, but she bought them instead of the peppers.
**biber** 'pepper'; **tane** 'loaf, piece'; **baktım** 'I looked'; **şişe** 'bottle'; **sonunda** 'in the end'; **rastladım** 'ran into'; **fincan** 'cup'; **kadeh** 'glass'; **berbat** 'terrible'

## Reading text

**ismini unuttum** 'I forgot its name'; **şarkıcı** 'singer'; **şarkının konusu** 'the topic of the song'; **aşk** 'love'; **hava nasıl oralarda** 'how's the weather over there?'; **üşüyor musun?** 'are you freezing?'; **saç** 'hair'

# Lesson 6

## Exercise 1

1 The ending **-n** indicates 'your'. So **acelen** means 'your hurry'.
2 **mı** indicates a question, **-tı** indicates past tense and the absence of a further suffix indicates 3rd person. The verb stem **kalk-**, finally,

means 'leave', so **kalktı mı?** means 'has it left?' 3 Again, combine the verb stem **taşın-**, 'to move', with **-dık**, 'we', plus past tense, so that we end up with 'we moved'. 4 **-nız** is the form of 'your' (plural or singular-polite) that comes after a word that ends in a vowel (otherwise it would be **-ınız**). **Odanız** means 'your room'. 5 In the Glossary you can read that a **kira** is 'a rental'. The suffix **-da** is the locative case. 6 See 4; **eviniz** is 'your house', with 'your' referring to more than one person (here the couple that got the new house), or to one person who is addressed politely (as with French *vous*).

## Exercise 2

2 **Evin.** 3 **Hediyen.** A vowel is dropped from the suffix, leaving only **-n.** 4 **Kedileri.** 5 **Kız kardeşi.** 6 **Odası.** The suffix in both 5 and 6 can mean 'his' as well as 'her'. 7 **İşiniz.** 8 **Şehrimiz.** Şehir is shortened to **şehr-** when a suffix is added. This only happens if the suffix starts with a vowel. 9 **Yemeğiniz.** The final **-k** is changed to **-ğ.** 10 **Kahvesi.**

## Exercise 3

1 Possessive  2 Personal  3 Possessive  4 Personal  5 Possessive
6 Personal 7 Possessive 8 Possessive 9 Possessive 10 Personal
Note that there could only be potential confusion in 6 and 7, and there only if the rest of the sentence is ignored.

## Exercise 4

2 **Arabanın anahtarı** 3 **Biberin fiyatı** 4 **Kitabın ismi**. Note the changed form of **isim**. 5 **Günün sonu**

## Exercise 5

1  A sure sign of a discussion is the exclamation – **git!** – in Nursen's first line. From her answer to Ömer's preceding line, you can gather that the discussion is about whether to start without Ali or not.
2  No, Ömer offers the information that Ali is never (**hiç**) late for **toplantımız**, 'our meetings'. He even thinks that something may have happened to him. Note that there is no **-lar** in **toplantımız**. If plural meaning is obvious from the context (you can't say 'he's never late for our meeting'), you don't need **-lar**.

3 Three. You could have found this where Ömer says **Üçümüz**: 'the three of us'. Try and remember that this is how you say this kind of thing; you could have expected that maybe Turkish would use the same construction as for 'the centre of the city' and say someting like **bizim üçü**. It doesn't.

4 No, she doesn't live by herself. This was a tricky question as it involves a characteristic of Turkish we haven't dealt with yet, but you may have guessed it from the plural **-ler** after the name **Nursen**. When you want to say 'at Nursen's place' you have to say **Nursen'lerde**, 'at the Nürsens' if she lives with people, for example with her family. If she were living by herself, Ömer would have said **Nursen'in evinde** or **Nursen'de**.

5 From the way the conversation went, you may have gathered that there was a misunderstanding and that Ali thought that the meeting was going to be at his place. When he finally realises that, Ömer whispers to the others that the **jeton düştü**: 'the penny has dropped'.

### Exercise 6

Probably they had been talking about Nursen and so Ömer thought it would be enough to just say **evinde** 'at her house'. However, Ali clearly understood it as 'at your house'.

### Exercise 7

1 **Aylin'in parası** ('Aylin's money') 2 **Bu bakkalın ekmeği** ('this baker's bread') 3 **Üniversitenin yabancı öğrencileri** ('the university's foreign students') 4 **Türkiye'nin başkenti** ('Turkey's capital') 5 **Onun okulunun öğretmeni** ('his school's teachers'). Note the double genitive 'in *his* school's teachers'. 6 **Bu bankanın memuru** ('the employee of this bank') 7 **Bizim evin banyosu** ('the bathroom of our house') 8 **Firmanın eski müdürü** ('the firm's old director').

### Exercise 8

The words indicated force the use of the accusative case:
1 the 3 his 4 that 6 the 7 Fatma 8 your 10 that
What you couldn't really know is that 5 also gets an accusative case marker. This is because **beklemek** requires one: one is always waiting for a specific (definite) person.

273

## Exercise 9

1 **kediyi** 2 **adamı** 3 **kadını** 4 **bisikleti** 5 **mektubu** 6 **bunu** 7 **evi**
8 **pencereyi** 9 **seni** 10 **kitabı** 11 **arabayı** 12 **çocuğu** 13 **ziyareti**
14 **onu** 15 **eskisini** (after a possessive ending the case ending is
preceded by **-n-**) 16 **lambayı** 17 **otobüsü** 18 **gazeteyi** 19 **beni**
20 **kız arkadaşını** (see 15)

## Exercise 10

1 I called your brother last night. 2 We're going to Azerbaijan for
our holiday this year. 3 Pervin's tea is the best. 4 Filiz's American
friend is arriving today. 5 **Bu patlıcanın fiyatına inanamıyorum**
(**inanmak** is 'to believe', and it requires dative, rather than
accusative, case on its object. The specific form – **amıyorum** will
be dealt with later and means 'I can't'). 6 **Geçen hafta Rahime'nin
arkadaşı evlendi.** 7 **Ahmet'in kız arkadaşı İstanbul'da çalışıyor.**
8 **(Senin) Abinin adresini arıyorum** (an **abi** is an older brother).

## Exercise 11

Dialogue 1.
Possessives: **acele-n, tren-im, ev-imiz, bahçe-miz, oda-nız, ev-iniz,
benim tren-im**; In compound nouns: **yatak oda-sı**; Genitive-
Possessive: **yatak oda-ları-nın bir-i**

Dialogue 2.
Possessives: **baş-ı(na geldi), toplantılar-ımız, üç-ümüz, koçu-m**; In
compound nouns: **alışveriş liste-si**; Accusatives: **Ali'yi, alışveriş
listesini, biz-i, sen-i**; Genitive-Possessive: **Ali'nin fikir-leri, hepimizin fikir-leri, Nursen'ler-in ev-i, o-nun ev-i, sen-in ev-in**

# Lesson 7

## Exercise 1

2 ödeyeceğim  3 gireceksiniz  4 söyleyecekler  5 soracaksın
6 tanışacağız 7 iyi bir öğrenci olacaksın 8 kapatacağım 9 tamam-
layacaklar 10 deneyeceksiniz 11 uyacak 12 uyuyacaklar

### Exercise 2

Hello John,

After Dalaman we came to Fethiye. It's very nice here and the streets are lively. Tomorrow we'll go to the world's cleanest coast, we'll go to 'Ölüdeniz'. We'll do some sunbathing, and some swimming. The day after, we'll go see Saklıkent. Greetings from Fethiye, Ertuğrul

### Exercise 3

Next week we'll move to Ankara. I hope that our neighbours will turn out to be nice. To be able to feel at home in a place, a good neighbour is important. After we have moved, we'll invite all our neighbours. After the holiday, our child will go to a new school, and make new friends. That **şart** means something like 'important' should be clear from the context. However, literally **şart** means 'condition', so the Turkish says something like 'good neighbours are a condition (for a pleasant life)'. If **taşındıktan sonra** means 'after we have moved', the **-dıktan sonra** part must mean 'after we. . . .' From **tatilden sonra** and its translation, it should be obvious that **sonra (-den)**, that is: **sonra** preceded by the ablative case ('away from', see Unit 3), means 'after'. 'To make friends' is **olmak** 'to become', combined with **arkadaş** and the third person possessive marker **-ı**.

### Exercise 4

1 Yarın plaja gidiyorum/gideceğim. 2 Gelecek hafta benim evime gelecekler/geliyorlar. 3 Kutlay yarın gelecek/geliyor. 4 Mutlaka partine geleceğim. 5 Bu akşam çalışacaksın.

### Exercise 5

1 Bu lafları/saçmalığı dinlemeyeceğim. 2 Ülkü Amerikalı komşumuzla İngilizce konuşmayacak. 3 Süt alacak mısın(ız)? 4 Ona hediye vermeyeceğiz. 5 Hesabı ödemeyecekler mi?

### Exercise 6

You cannot use **-ecek** in such a context, since it is used for future plans or intentions and not for proposals. It does not refer to a common action, that in the mind of the speaker should take place immediately afterwards. **-elim**, on the other hand, does. Compare: **Kütüphaneye gidelim mi?** 'Let's go to the library' (meaning: 'now!' with **Kütüphaneye gidecek miyiz?** 'Shall we go to the library?' (meaning: 'do we have the intention to go there one day?')

### Exercise 7

1 kahve içelim mi? 2 havaalanına dönelim mi? 3 Türkiye'yi gezelim mi? 4 oturalım mı? 5 paketi açalım mı? 6 işkembe çorbası deneyelim mi? 7 doğru cevabı verelim mi? / doğru yanıtı verelim mi? 8 sinemaya gidelim mi? 9 yürüyüş yapalım mı? 10 akşam yemeğini beraber yiyelim mi?

### Exercise 8

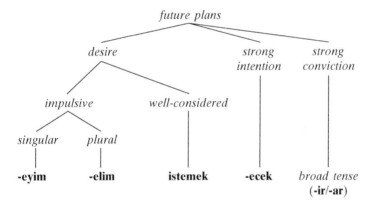

### Exercise 9

1 on üç yirmi altı, biri yirmi altı geçiyor. 2 yirmi üç yedi, on biri yedi geçiyor. 3 sekiz kırk üç, dokuza on yedi var. 4 on iki otuz, saat yarım. 5 on üç bir, biri bir geçiyor. 6 dört elli sekiz, beşe iki var. 7 iki otuz iki, üçe yirmi sekiz var. 8 on sekiz yirmi yedi, altıyı yirmi yedi geçiyor. 9 on bir on bir, on biri on bir geçiyor. 10 yirmi bir kırk dokuz, ona on bir var.

## Exercise 10

*Friday:* 1 **Cuma günü saat altıyı çeyrek geçe Megapol'da Türk Tutkusu filmini seyretmek istiyorum.** 2 **Cuma günü saat dokuz buçukta Kavaklıdere'de Sevdiğim Mevsim filmini seyretmek istiyorum.**
*Saturday:* 3 **Cumartesi günü saat yarımda Kavaklıdere'de Taş Yıllar filmini seyretmek istiyorum.** 4 **Ondan sonra saat üçte Megapol'un Kırmızı Salonunda Boğmacı filmini seyretmek istiyorum.**
*Sunday:* 5 **Pazar günü Megapol'un Mavi Salonunda saat üçe çeyrek geçe Böcek filmini seyretmek istiyorum.** 6 **Ondan sonra, saat dokuzda Kavaklıdere'de Yeniden Tanık filmini seyretmek istiyorum.**

## Exercise 11

Ali's daily schedule may look like this (but other arrangements are OK as well):

7.00          : **saat yedide kalktı** 'he got up at seven'
7.00–7.30     : **saat yediden yedi buçuğa kadar giyindi** 'between seven and seven thirty he got dressed'
7.30–8.00     : **saat yedi buçuktan sekize kadar kahvaltı yaptı** 'between seven thirty and eight he had breakfast'
8.00–8.30     : **saat sekizden sekiz buçuğa kadar arabayla iş yerine gitti** 'between eight and eight thirty he went to his work by car'
8.30–17.00    : **saat sekiz buçuktan beşe kadar çalıştı** 'between eight thirty and five p.m. he worked'
17.00–17.30   : **saat beşten beş buçuğa kadar evine döndü** 'between five and five thirty he returned home'
17.30–18.00   : **saat beş buçuktan altıya kadar parkta koştu** 'between five thirty and six he ran in the park'
18.00–18.30   : **saat altıdan altı buçuğa kadar yemek hazırladı** 'between six and six thirty he prepared dinner'
18.30–19.00   : **saat altı buçuktan yediye kadar yemeğini yedi** 'between six thirty and seven he had dinner'
19.00–22.00   : **saat yediden ona kadar televizyon seyretti** 'from seven to ten p.m. he watched TV'
22.00–23.00   : **saat ondan on bire kadar kitap okudu** 'from ten to eleven p.m. he read a book'
23.00         : **saat on birde yattı** 'at eleven o'clock he went to sleep'

# Lesson 8

## Exercise 1

1 oturur 2 çağırır 3 biter 4 söyler 5 döker 6 çimdikler 7 kaşır
8 seçer

## Exercise 2

2 çağırırız 3 bulurlar 4 söylersin 5 dökerler 6 veririm 7 kaşır
8 sanırsınız

## Exercise 3

1 promise 2 qualities/profession 3 habit 4 request 5 promise
6 qualities/profession 7 qualities/profession 8 promise
By the way, **araba tamir ederim**, as mentioned in 7, has a more
usual variant: **araba tamircisiyim**.

## Exercise 4

My grandmother lives in an enormous white villa. As every summer, I am staying this summer at my grandmother's. Today she and
I are trying ('together with her we are trying') to be of help to the
birds. Last week, in a bay very close to us, a large tanker sank. The
oil polluted the sea. This situation harmed the birds. We didn't know
what we should do. Therefore, I rang the vet this morning. He said:
'Some birds cannot fly after coming into contact with polluted water.
In order to rescue the birds we generally use a scoop. After the
birds regain some strength, you're able to wash them.'

After a couple of present tense sentences, the expression **geçen
hafta** triggers the use of past tense. When the vet is speaking about
birds, he gives them some background information about birds in
general, and therefore uses the **geniş zaman**.

## Exercise 5

2 Ablası İngilizce dersi vermez. 3 Her gün dokuza kadar çalış-
mazsın. 4 Bana bir mektup yazmaz mısınız? 5 Arabanı tamir
etmez. 6 Türkçeden Almancaya çeviri yapmam. 7 Araba tamir
etmem. 8 Şu mektubu İngilizceye çevirmem.

## Exercise 6

1 **Anneni ziyaret etmelisiniz.** 2 You must not disturb me. 3 **Öğrenciler bu kitapları almalılar.** 4 He needs to listen to the radio. 5 **Şimdi gitmeliyiz!** 6 I have to prepare more food. 7 **Bunu kabul etmemelisiniz/ bunu kabul etmemeniz gerek.** 8 You should never leave him.

## Exercise 7

You could have said the following (ranging from impolite to more polite ways):

1 Benimle pastaneye git! Pastaneye gidelim mi? Benimle pastaneye gider misin? 2 Benimle sinemaya git! Sinemaya gidelim mi? Benimle sinemaya gider misin? 3 Sigaranızı söndürün! Lütfen, sigaranızı söndürür müsünüz? 4 Sus! Susun! Susar mısınız? 5 Sebzeleri yiyin! Sebzeleri yer misiniz?

**Bulgur pilavı**

Clean and rinse the bulgur thoroughly, then drain well in a colander. Put the pan on the heat and add the butter and onion. Sauté onions on medium heat, stirring, until yellow. Add the peppers and bulgur and sauté for another 5 minutes, stirring.

Then add the tomatoes, broth and salt, bring to the boil, stirring vigorously and let it boil for 10 minutes on high heat. Take off the heat and let stand for 10 minutes before serving.

**Note**: If you cannot find tomatoes or peppers, prepare it without pepper and tomato.

# Lesson 9

## Exercise 1

The two sisters are going shopping and discuss what they want to buy. Hülya needs a new skirt and also has to look for a present for her friend, Fatma, who is giving a party next week. İlknur has to go to the travel agency to change a reservation for her trip to Athens. When the waiter comes, they order tea, after explaining they are waiting for their mother. They comment on the clothes people outside are wearing, and Hülya is wondering how their mother is coming to town. Since she is visiting her friend Ayşe, who is, apparently, a very good cook, especially of *köfte*, she'll be coming by bus. Finally, when Hülya asks her sister about her plans for that evening, she answers that she doesn't know yet. Maybe she'll read a book, maybe she'll give her friend Eser a call, so they can gossip a bit.

### Exercise 2

You may have found the following: **almak**; **almam**; **bakmak**; **gitmemiz**; **değiştirmek**; **gitmesi**; **gitmek**; **yemekleri**; **yemeğine**; **dedikodu yapmak**

Well, both **yemekleri** and **yemeğine** look like infinitives, but the word **yemek** is also a noun, meaning 'food'. In **yemeğine**, the dative is used because the verb **bayılmak** takes this case. Note that **almam**, **gitmemiz** and **gitmesi** contain a short infinitive on **-me** plus possessive suffix. **Almam**, for instance, means 'my buying'.

### Exercise 3

1 First, you take the infinitive: **gitme**; then you add the possessive: **-m**, which results in **gitmem**. Finally, you add **gerek**, so that you end up with **gitmem gerek**. Similarly with the others: 2 Infinitive **okuma** plus possessive **-n** ('your') plus **gerek** results in **bunu okuman gerek**. 3 **Yapma + -sı + gerek** results in **bunu yapması gerek**. 4 **Yazma + -mız + gerek** results in **bir mektup yazmamız gerek**.

### Exercise 4

All sentences on the left mean 'I have to return to London', and those on the right 'I don't have to go to London'. The further down in the list they are, the more urgent going to London (on the left) or the fact that the speaker shouldn't go to London (on the right) becomes.

| | |
|---|---|
| Londra'ya dönmeliyim. | Londra'ya dönmemelisin. |
| Londra'ya dönmem lazım. | Londra'ya dönmen lazım değil. |
| Londra'ya dönmem gerek. | Londra'ya dönmene gerek yok. |
| Londra'ya dönmem gerekiyor. | Londra'ya dönmen gerekmez. |
| Londra'ya dönmek gerekli. | Londra'ya dönmen gereksiz. |
| | Londra'ya dönmen gerekli değil. |

## Exercise 5

1 kaybetmek 2 çekmek 3 uçmak 4 atmak 5 göstermek 6 unutmak 7 sevmek 8 göndermek 9 koymak 10 taşımak

## Exercise 6

1 My sister is going to town (in order) to buy a dress. 2 They wanted me to look at their holiday pictures. 3 He's beginning to understand the problem. 4 I'm thinking of going there. 5 He told me to wait here. 6 Did you come to see me? 7 Ayşe wants us to go to the Black Sea this year. NB: This is the most common way of expressing 'want to' or 'she's hoping that. . . '. In the first person, however, the idiomatic phrases **umarım** and **umarız** are used. These are straightforward **geniş zaman** forms of the verb **ummak** 'to hope', but it's more common to use **istemek** with third person subjects. 8 You will have to get used to seeing them together.

## Exercise 7

1 **Şehir merkezi, belediye binası, park müsaadesi.**
2 It was very bad (**kötü**).
3 The verb you should have found is **demek** 'to say', which appears here in the forms **dedim** 'I said' and **dedi** 'he said'. Literally, the first quote is: 'To the employee "Can you help me" I said', and the second one ' "The counter will now close" he said'.
4 Yes, she says **Haklısın**, 'you're right', and calls the employee a fool.
5 He won't eat meat anymore: **etsiz yiyecek!**
6 He's quite upset, to the point of obsession, one might say.
7 **yemek kitapları** and **yemek tarifleri**
8 They are used 'in the abstract', as things Hasan will or will not eat. They do not refer to particular ('definite') kebabs, carrots, courgettes, etc.
9 She first says **Allah bilir! Ama neden öyle kızıyorsun? Boş ver!**, asking him why he's so angry and suggesting he let it drop. Which culminates in **sana ne?**, 'what's it to you?'. Then she asks him what he was saying earlier (**demin**).
10 No, he is still wondering what to serve Hasan and Aylin when they come over for dinner next Saturday.
11 Right at the end of the conversation she is wondering how Imdat's grandfather is doing.

12 Hard to do, isn't it, since there is no clear topic? How about: 'Sükran and İmdat argue about the wisdom of a decision a friend of theirs has made'.

## Exercise 8

**Araba** is the subject in this sentence, and subjects never get accusative case, which is reserved for direct objects.

## Exercise 9

2 eski bir havaalanı 3 beyaz bir elbise 4 tarif kolay 5 inek deli 6 lokanta yeni 7 boş bardaklar 8 ucuz tavuklar 9 yüksek fiyatlar

## Exercise 10

The following are compounds:
1 evening dinner (**akşam yemeği**) 2 mad cow disease (**deli dana hastalığı**) (**dana** means 'calf') 3 fatigue syndrome (**yorgunluk sendromu**) 5 homework (**ev ödevi**) 6 Persian rug (**Fars halısı**) (**Fars** forms compounds; of course there was no way you could actually know that **Fars** belongs to this select group of country names) 7 Turkish government (**Türk hükümeti**) (**Türk** forms compounds)

Adjective + Noun combinations:
4 gold watch (**altın saat**) (**altın** is a material adjective) 9 Dutch football player (**Hollandalı futbolcu**) (**Hollandalı** ends in **-li**, meaning it's a normal adjective)

And one was a trick question, as Turkish for 'plastic bag' is **poşet**, borrowed from French. However, it could have been **naylon çanta**.

# Lesson 10

## Exercise 1

1 **-m** ('my'), **-la** ('with') 2 **-iniz** ('your'), **-de** ('in') 3 **-dü** (Past), **-k** ('we') 4 **-i** ('its') 5 **-umuz** ('our'), **-un** ('of'), **-sı** ('his/her'), **-nda** ('in') 6 **-ıyor** (Present), **mu** (Question), **-sunuz** ('you') 7 **-n** ('your'), **-den** ('from') 8 **-du** (Past), **-n** ('you')

### Exercise 2

1 Demin iki tane kocaman kuşu gördüm. 2 Bu beyaz araba seninki mi? 3 Eğlencede üstünde yeşil bir etek vardı. 4 Onlar çok normal insan. 5 Galatasaray yeni iyi bir futbolcu istiyor.

### Exercise 3

1 Param yok. 2 İki köpeği var. 3 Sizin ne güzel eviniz var! 4 Burada kalmayı gerçekten çok beğendim. 5 Yunanistan'da yemek iyi.

### Exercise 4

1 No, is about 'milk' in general. 2 No, indefinite (reach **a** conclusion). 3 No, it's not a particular postcard. 4 Yes, this sentence can only really mean 'Open *the* lid' → **kapağı aç!** 5 Yes, the possessive suffix **-in** makes the plate definite → **tabağını.** 6 No, is about 'money' in general. 7 No, 'often' cannot refer to one particular (definite) strike. 8 No, is about 'time' in general. 9 Yes, which letter is specified by **annenin çöplüğe attığı** ('the one your mother threw away'), so it is definite → **mektubu.** 10 Yes, the possessive makes the boys definite → **oğlanlarını.** 11 No, indefinite (offer *a* job); Yes, the offering is specified ('by them') → **teklif edeceklerini** 12 Yes, is about *this* word → **sözcüğü.**

### Exercise 5

1 Compound: **ev anahtarı** 2 Compound: **karayolu** 3 Adjective: **yaşlı adam** 4 Simple noun: **hapishane** 5 Not a compound: **işveren** ('who gives work') 6 Compound: **yaz ayları** 7 Compound: **saat beş treni** 8 Adjective: **açık çay** 9 Genitive construction: **günün yemeği** 10 Compound: **yemek listesi** 11 Adjective: **etsiz yemek** 12 Compound: **mercimek çorbası** 13 Adjective: **Finli kayakçı** 14 Compound: **Türk kahvesi**

### Exercise 6

1 hotel room 2 Turkish coffee 3 teacher of German (as opposed to **Alman öğretmen** 'German teacher') 4 Sea of Marmara 5 Turkish–Greek friendship 6 girls' school 7 kitchen cupboard 8 bus ticket 9 Japanese car (literally 'Japan car') 10 thriller 11 Hemingway's novels 12 lamb meat/meat of lambs 13 the month of

May 14 children's room/the room of the child 15 balcony door/the door of the balcony 16 cow's milk 17 Second World War 18 novel writer/writer of novels

## Exercise 7

ev kadınıyım; portakal suyunuz; meyva bahçemiz; baş ağrım; uzman doktor; kadın doktoru; bilgisayar programcısı; Amerikan firması; zavallı babam; o dükkanın sahibi; yaşlı dükkan sahipleri; Ankara treninde; pirinç pilavı; etli nohut; Türk mutfağı; Çin mutfağı; Türk mutfağından

## Exercise 8

'their' + singular: 2 Ahmed and Hassan are in their room. It's upstairs, the first one on the left. 3 These girls love their mother(s) very much.
'his'/ or 'her' + plural: 9 So she gave me her clothes. 10 I think his thoughts are dangerous.
'their' + plural: 4 Do you know their children? (can also be 'their child') 5 We first painted the girls' rooms.
'they have': 6 Some children didn't have shoes on their feet. 7 And then the teachers had an excellent proposal.
plural plus accusative: 8 Ali told funny stories. 12 Have you seen the mosques?
plural compound noun plus accusative: 1 In this town, the traffic lights are always red. 11 When I was a kid, I hated the piano lessons.

## Exercise 9

The text is an almost literal rendition of a conversation one of the authors has on tape. The speakers used a lot of pronouns, more than would normally be expected. Here is the transcript. Compare the used pronouns with your expectations. The fact that there were three people present increased the use of pronouns, because often it was necessary to specify who exactly the speaker was talking to.

BAHAR: Sabahat, sen Kayseri'den geleli kaç sene oldu? Ben Bursa'ya geleli üç yıl oldu.
SABAHAT: Üç yıl oldu.
BAHAR: Ben yedi, sekiz ay sonra yine bir kursa başladım, o da

Kuzey Bursa'daydı. Oraya altı ay, yok, sekiz ay devam ettim. Bitti, bu yıl yine başlamıştım oraya. Ama diğer öğrencileri beğenmedim. Bir tek ben konuşuyorum, onlar susuyor.

SABAHAT: Bursa'yı ben sevemiyorum. Siz seviyor musunuz?

AYHAN: Ben önceleri sevmiyordum, ama, sen nasıl buluyorsun Bursa'yı, Bursa'lıyı?

BAHAR: Mesela Ayhan dönüş yapmak isterse ben hemen dönerim. Buranın havasından çalışamıyorum.

AYHAN: Ben eğer burdan gitsem ben oraya ayak uyduramamki.

SABAHAT: Sen hiç uyduramazsın.

AYHAN: Ben hiç uyduramam artık.

BAHAR: Çünkü sen Almanya'da büyüdün; ondan sonra da tekrar buraya geldin. Ondan sonra da buranın hayatına alışmaya çalışıyorsun.

## Exercise 10

1c 2l 3g 4h 5i 6j 7b 8k 9e 10a 11d 12f

Not all of these pairs involve exact synonyms! Most of the time, they share a lot of meaning, but they also imply slight differences. For instance, **bırakmak** means 'to stop doing something', while **bitirmek** means 'to finish'. In **bitirmek**, the job is actually done, while in **bırakmak**, you just stop doing it. With others, there's a difference in style: **merhaba** is more informal than **günaydın**. **Dinlemek** and **duymak** bear the same relationship to each other that 'listen' and 'hear' do in English. A **dost** is a closer friend than an **arkadaş**. Note that **okumak** can mean 'to study', extended from its basic meaning in the same way as English 'to read' in 'I'm reading English literature'. Finally, **de/da** and **ve** both mean 'and', but **de/da** is perhaps translated more precisely with 'and . . . too'.

## Exercise 11

1i 2l 3f 4g 5k 6j 7a 8e 9b 10d 11h 12c

## Exercise 12

1 **beğeniyorum** 2 **dedi** 3 **Şahane!** 4 **Acaba** 5 **üzerine** 6 **Haklısın** 7 **Karım** 8 **gideceksiniz** 9 **yanlışlık oldu** (also cross out **biri** and **yapmış**) 10 **niçin** 11 **nefis** 12 **bitirebildiniz mi?** 13 **sene**

# Lesson 11

## Exercise 1

1 She works **bankada**: in a bank.
2 She had asserted that Turks don't govern themselves, and that, therefore, they had to be **daha sert**: tougher.
3 The countries that shouldn't be made a **düşman** are the **ticaret yaptığımız memleketler**: countries one trades with. The grammar of this sentence will be the focus of much of this lesson.
4 'We', that is, the Turks, don't want other countries to tell them **bunu yap, şunu yapma** ('do this, do that'). Note that literally the idiom says: 'do this, don't do that'.
5 After she married Ali. The form **-diğinden beri** means 'since'. You know the combination **-den beri** 'since' (for example **yazdan beri** 'since summer'). The combination **-diğinden beri** is the same one, except that now 'since' combines with a whole clause, not with a simple noun such as 'summer'. The sequence **Ali'yle evlendiğinden beri** means 'since she got married to Ali'.
6 **Onun meselesi**, 'her problem', is preceded by **O**. He says: 'don't worry, that's her problem, not yours'. The 'that' in the translation is what is expressed by **o** in the Turkish sentence. It refers to something like 'that she has become so different after her marriage' as in 'That she has become so different is her problem, not yours'.
7 Compare the two: the verb **yoruldum** and the 'to be' + adjective-construction 'I am tired'. The English construction focuses on the present state of tiredness, while the Turkish construction profiles the process of becoming tired. That obviously happened in the past, because the result is that one is tired now, hence the past tense ending. It is easiest to just learn the whole phrase **yoruldum** as equivalent of 'I'm tired'.
8 The following clauses were used. Although some are subordinate in the English equivalents, these are not regarded as such in Turkish (that is, they contain 'ordinary' verbs).
-**bankada çalışan**, who works in a bank; -**ki biz, Türkler, kendi kendimizi yönetmiyoruz** 'that we Turks do not govern ourselves' (not subordinate in Turkish); -**biz daha sert olmalıyız** 'we must be tougher' (not subordinate in Turkish); -**ticaret yaptığımız** 'that we trade with'; -**bunu yap, şunu yapma demek** 'to say do this, do that' (not subordinate in Turkish); -**Ali'yle evlendiğinden beri**, 'since she married Ali'

## Exercise 2

When I went out last night to see the house that Jerry and Jill bought, it was raining pretty hard. The umbrella I once had was not to be found, so I had to depend on my raincoat. The streets, that are usually deserted at this time of night, were completely devoid of human life. A cat that was sheltering under a car was the only living creature I saw. All those people who were staying in turned out to be quite right, because when I got to the house, I was completely soaked. In addition, the surprise I had intended for my friends backfired, as neither Jerry nor Jill turned out to be home.

The choices for **-diği** and **-en** are as follows (don't worry about unfamiliar Turkish here; this is an exercise about the structure of relative clauses, not about useful vocabulary. You may want to note down the word for 'umbrella' though: **şemsiye**):

1 In 'the new house that Jerry and Jill have bought', 'the house' is the object of 'bought', so you need to use **-diği: yeni aldığı ev**. 2 In 'the umbrella that I once had', 'the umbrella' is the object of 'had', so you need to use **-diği: benim olan şemsiye**, or **benim sahip olduğum şemsiye**. 3 In 'the streets, that are usually deserted at this time of night', 'the streets' is the subject of 'are deserted', so you need to use **-en: boş olan sokaklar**. 4 In 'a cat that was sheltering under a car', 'a cat' is the subject of 'was sheltering', so you need to use **-en: sığınan kedi**. 5 In 'all those people who were staying in', 'people' is the subject of 'are staying in', so you need to use **-en: içeride bulunan insanlar**. 6 In 'the surprise I had intended', 'the surprise' is the object of 'intended', so you need to use **-diği: niyet ettiğim sürpriz**.

## Exercise 3

1 My God, the place where I'm working is filthy! 2 I'll give that coat I never wear to Melike. 3 I really like the house you're living in. 4 The tape that's playing sounds like the Beatles. 5 I haven't yet started the book you gave me ('have not been able to start'). 6 The other people who were waiting at the bus stop complained too. 7 Does your daughter like the job she found? 8 The only person we didn't gossip about is you! 9 Do you know the guy that's married to Eser? 10 Who is the woman who's talking?

## Exercise 4

The most important thing about this exercise is to make sure you put the subject of the relative clause in the genitive case. Apart from that, some other case forms were needed, such as the dative on **onlar** in 1, forced by the verb **yazmak**. That is: you write *to* someone; this 'to' is expressed by the dative case ending **-a** in **onlara**.

2 **Anneannenin** 3 **zeytini** 4 **Ahmet'in, şarkıyı** 5 **Sokağın karşısında, bana** (no ACC on **şaka** because it's indefinite, indicated by **bir**) 6 **Maradona'nın** 7 **ekmeği** 8 **hediyeyi**

## Exercise 5

1 **Bursa'ya giden tren.** 2 **Doğum günün için aldığın bisiklet.** NB: **için** does not require a case marker on the preceding noun, so **doğum günün** is not marked. 3 **Yaptığın iğrenç gürültü nedir?** 4 **Sokağın karşısında oturan öğrenci çok sevimli.** NB: **karşı** requires the preceding word to have genitive case. 5 **Britanya'da oturan arkadaşlarımız güzel, yeni bir ev satın aldı.** NB: when two adjectives precede one noun, **bir** comes after the last adjective. 6 **Senin doğduğun senede ben altı yaşındaydım.** 7 You probably first tried **satın aldığımız ev**, but that may have already made you uneasy, because by now you should know enough to translate that as 'the house we bought'. For future versions of the relative clause, you use **-eceği** instead of **-diği**, with the future tense form **-ecek** contained in it. This form will be discussed in the next lesson. The right translation is: **satın alacağımız ev.**

## Exercise 6

a. Nominal sentences, present tense. Note that all of the following sentences have 'is' in their English translation.
**Senin iş durumun nasıl şimdi? İşsizim. Öyle mi? Zaten iş bulmak zor bu zamanlarda. Haklısın. Ama o çok pahalı. Sen deli misin? Yirmi birinci yüzyıldayız.**
b. Present tense on **-iyor.** Note that not all of these are necessarily translated by an '-ing' form in English.
**Gazetede ilanlara bakıyorum ama** ('I'm looking' (these days, not right now), i.e.: 'I've looked'). **Bilgisayar hakkında birşey biliyor musun? Tabii ki biliyorum, bilmeyen var mı? Biliyorum vallahi!**

Çarşıya çıkıyor musunuz? Çıkmıyoruz, diş hekimine gidiyoruz,
Kızılay'da. Kentin orasını iyi bilmiyorum.
c. Geniş zaman
Ona telefon edebilirsin galiba. Belki telefon ederim. Belki de okula
dönebilirim. Belki seninle ilgilenebilirler ... Söylerim. Görüşürüz!
d. Past tense
Hala birşey bulamadın mı? Çok üzüldüm. Bıktım aramaktan (this
is a fixed expression and it happens to be past tense). Demin aklıma
geldi (another fixed idiom). Bilgisayar bilmeyen kalmadı neredeyse
('There's almost no-one left who doesn't know computers'). Keşke
şirketimizde boş yer olsaydı ('if only there was').
e. Future tense
Benim için yepyeni yol olacak. İyi bir sekreter olacaksın. Ne
yapacaksınız?

### Exercise 7

The following pairs have all been in the dialogues somewhere.
There aren't many options for 'thank you', so **teşekkür ederim** and
**sağ ol** occur frequently.
**merhaba – merhaba; nasılsın?** – **iyiyim, teşekkür ederim/sağ ol, sen
nasılsın?**; **görüşürüz – görüşürüz; ne haber?** – **iyilik; günaydın
– günaydın; memnun oldum – ben de memnun oldum; iyi günler
– iyi günler; hoş geldiniz – hoş bulduk; buyurun – teşekkür ederiz;
teşekkür ederim – bir şey değil; iyi gezmeler – sağ ol; buyurun?** –
**...** (e.g. **kahve) lütfen; başarılar – teşekkür ederim; alo –
alo/merhaba; oturun – teşekkür ederim; ...** (any request) – **tamam**

1 **merhaba** 2 **iyilik** 3 **görüşürüz** (NB: you may have to precede it
with something explaining why you're ending the conversation, e.g.
**gitmem gerekiyor**) 4 **memnun oldum** 5 **başarılar!** 6 **sağ olun/
teşekkür ederim** 7 **sağ olun/teşekkür ederiz** 8 **günaydın**

### Exercise 8

1 **-miş** 2 **-miş** 3 either one 4 **-di** 5 **-di** 6 **-miş** 7 **-miş** 8 either one
9 **-miş** 10 **-di**

1 **Onlara anlatmış olmalı.** 2 **Burada yağmur yağmış.** 3 **Ondan sonra köpek onu ısırdı** ('you saw it happening') or **ısırmış** ('so you were told'). 4 **Seyretmeye gittiğimiz maçı Fenerbahçe kolayca kazandı.** 5 **Yapmadığımı ona söyledim.** 6 **Gazeteye göre güzel bir konser vermiş.** 7 **Unutmuşum.** 8 **Sigorta şirketine telefon etti mi?** ('did you see him do it?') or **etmiş mi?** ('as far as you know, did he call?') 9 **Telefon etmiş mi sence?** (or: **aramış mı sence?**) 10 **Hangi numarayı çevirdin?**

### Exercise 9

1 **Yapmış, maşallah!** 2 **kullanmamışlardır** 3 **Uyumuşum.** 4 **Yabancı değilmiş.** 5 **Memnun olmamışlar.** 6 **evde miymiş?** 7 **neymiş?** 8 **Yorulmuşsun** (recall that 'tired' is expressed through a verb, **yorulmak**, not through an adjective). 9 **güneşlenmişsin** 10 **Kayseri'deymiş.**

### Exercise 10

1 sure 2 inferred 3 inferred 4 inferred 5 sure 6 sure 7 inferred 8 sure 9 sure 10 inferred 11 sure 12 inferred 13 sure

# Lesson 12

### Exercise 1

1 The text contains the following conditional verb forms: **istersek** 'if we want'; **vurursam** 'if I win'; **kaybetmeseydin** 'if you hadn't lost'; **bir işim olursa** 'if I have a job'. 2 The endings are the same as used for the past tense **-di** (compare, for instance, the **k** in **istersek** and **istedik**)

### Exercise 2

2 Bu akşam Fatma'nın partisine gideceksem, . . . 3 Her yaz trenle seyahat ederse, . . . 4 Otogarda seni beklersem, . . . 5 Akşamları annem bana bir hikaye anlatırsa, . . . 6 Kar yağıyorsa, . . . 7 Abim mühendis olmak istiyorsa, . . . 8 Sorunuz varsa, . . .

## Exercise 3

1 Büyük bir şehirde yaşasan, ... 2 Bu akşam Fatma'nın partisine gitsem, ... 3 Her yaz trenle seyahat etse, ... 4 Otogarda seni beklesem, ... 5 Akşamları annem bana bir hikaye anlatsa, ... 6 Kar yağsa, ... 7 Abim mühendis olmak istese, ... 8 Sorunuz olsa, ...

## Exercise 4

very red; straight ahead; altogether; totally empty; very fresh

## Exercise 5

1 The **-il-** suffix is used to indicate the passive. **Getirmek** means 'to bring', so **getirilmek** means 'to be taken'. 2 **-ken** expresses 'while'. It is one of the so-called 'converbs' – the equivalents of English subordinated clauses. In the remainder of Lesson 12 converbs will be dealt with. 3 **-ince** means 'as soon as' and is also a converb.

## Exercise 6

1 **giderken** (indicating that during the period the first person narrator was on his way to Üsküdar, it was raining all the time) 2 **gelince** (as soon as I came there) 3 both are possible, with a difference in meaning: **çalarken** 'the period during which I play the saz, ...' and **çalınca** 'as soon as I play the saz, ...' 4 **girince** 5 **varınca** 6 **dinlerken** 7 **çıkınca** 8 **severken** (notice, by the way, that in the final sentence of this exercise the subject of the converb ('annem') is different from the subject of the main clause ('babam'))

## Exercise 7

1 **binince** 2 **durmadan** 3 **konuşurken** or **konuşmadan** (depending on whether he talked to you (**-ken**) or not (**-madan**)). 4 **okuldayken** 5 **ölünce** 6 **demeden** 7 **bilirseniz** 8 **sıkılırsan**

## Exercise 8

1 **beşiği sallandıran el.** 2 **soğuktan içeri gelen casus** (although this also can mean 'the spy who came in because of the cold').

3 **bakışlar öldürebilse, ...** 4 **beni şimdi terkedersen, benim en iyi parçamı götürürsün.** 5 **gitmeden önce, beni uyandır!** 6 **bir iz bırakmadan.**

# Lesson 13

## Exercise 1

Below, you will first find a translation of the dialogue. The specific questions in 1 and 2 will be dealt with subsequently.

HASAN:     Look, Melike, our dear guest has brought us these flowers.

MELİKE:    Oh dear, how nice! Why did you go to all that trouble? Hasan could you put them on the table, please? I think that these days there are fewer well-educated people than there used to be.

HASAN:     Excuse us, you probably have something important to do. Are you going out to the centre of town?

ARİF BEY:  No, I'm not going to the centre of town, right now, I only want to go out for a walk, just walk around in the park. But later I must go out to do some shopping for presents, so this evening I will go to the centre.

HASAN:     All right, we don't want to keep you waiting, thank you again for the beautiful flowers.

ARİF BEY:  No problem.

MELİKE:    Take care. Goodbye.

ARİF BEY:  See you.

HASAN:     Melike, who was that on the phone?

MELİKE:    That was my sister. She'll come by this afternoon to return a book to me.

HASAN:     How is your sister?

MELİKE:    Oh, the same as always, she quarrelled with her husband, she's broke ... Why are you laughing? Think of her situation! But those flowers are beautiful, aren't they? What do you say about that?

HASAN:     I told you last night that Arif is a good human being.

MELİKE:    You're right, from now on I will believe everything you tell me.

1:

a. He has given the flowers to both Melike and Hasan. Hasan says **bize** 'to us' in his first line. b. He is laughing because Melike's

sister apparently always (**her zaman gibi** 'as always') has the same problems: quarrel with her husband, and lack of money. Melike jokingly (as it is followed by laughter) begs him to be more considerate (**durumunu düşün!** 'think of her situation'). c. Her sister called to say she was going to bring back a book that afternoon. d. No, he's going out for a walk in the park. e. He thinks Arif is a good person, as he had told his wife the night before (**dün akşam** 'yesterday evening').
2:
a. She uses the polite question form of the **geniş zaman** of **koymak** 'to put', **koyar mısınız** 'do you put?'. Alternatives you have learned before in this book are the more informal question form **koyar mısın?** 'do you put?' or the polite imperative **koyun lütfen!** 'put!'. The short imperative **koy!** 'put!' is quite unacceptable in this situation. A literal translation of the English polite request, **koyabilir misiniz?** 'can you put?' is possible, but perhaps a bit too formal in this congenial setting. b. **sanırım**. c. **yapmak** means 'do'; **çıkmak** means 'go out'. Combined with **alışveriş** 'shopping', the former is the normal word for 'to do shopping'; the latter is said when you want to focus on the act of going out of the house in order to do the shopping (note the dative ending **-e**, indicating motion towards somewhere, in **alışverişe**). In the dialogue it is appropriate because the guest is poised to go out of the hotel right that minute. d. The Turkish way of saying this is 'my money is finished': **param bitti**. In the dialogue, the phrase is 'she's broke': **parası bitti**. The construction, therefore, is **para** plus Possessive ending plus **bitti**. e. **şuna ne dersin?** means 'what' (**bu**) 'do you think/say' (**der-**) 'about' (the dative case ending **-na**) 'that' (**şu**)? f. **Doğru**. g. **Kendinize iyi bakın. Hoşça kalın!**

### Exercise 2

The particle is used in **parası da bitti**. Melike could just as well have said **parası bitti**; the addition of **da** adds the idea of a list: the sister is mad at her husband *and* she's out of money. The basic translation of **de/da** seems to be 'and', 'too', 'as well', 'also'.

### Exercise 3

1 true. He needs to go and pick them up. 2 false. He has something to do (**bir iş** 'a job'). That this creates a problem for picking up the glasses is clear from the context and from the fact that he

starts his sentence with **ama** 'but'. 3 true. (**ödedim** 'I paid'). 4 true. Serkan doesn't need to say anything about who Necat is. 5 true. Erol asks whether Necat is still playing for Beşiktaş and Serkan says that indeed he is (**oynuyor** 'he is playing'). 6 false. He knows he wasn't good enough: **ama eksikti** 'but it wasn't enough'). 7 false. He is compassionate (**ne yazık ki** 'what a pity'). 8 true. (**çok kötü** 'very bad'). 9 true. (**olmaz** 'can't be'). 10 false. Nurettin comes up later as speaking Turkmenian, which is not listed among the languages the friend from Izmir speaks. 11 false. As soon as he (**bu**) got off the train (**trenden indiğimiz andan itibaren**), he started to speak Turkmenian to people. 12 false. The man got mad (**kızdı**). 13 true. He still (**hala**) doesn't know what happened (**ne olduğunu**). 14 false. He will pick them up at 3 (**üçte**).

### Exercise 4

1 **herşeyi** 2 **biraz** 3 **birşeyim** 4 **kimse** 5 **herkes** 6 **hiçbir** 7 **Bütün** 8 **Her** 9 **az** 10 **diğerleri** 11 **hepsini** 12 **birisine** (**aşık olmak** requires the dative ending **-e**); 13 **bazıları** 14 **çok** 15 **bir**

The translations of the sentences are:
1 Watch out! Little Ayhan hears everything. 2 I think Turkish is a bit difficult. 3 When I came here, I had nothing. 4 I didn't understand anybody. 5 Don't worry, it's the same for everybody. 6 Until now I haven't seen a thing in Turkey. 7 You know very well that the whole world loves football. 8 After all classes have finished, there will be a party. 9 My friend will call me in a little bit. 10 Ahmet and I went by train; the others went by car. 11 The old people expect everything from us young people. 12 And then this girl fell in love with someone. 13 We found a solution for some of the problems. 14 I got very angry that Ali had done that. 15 They are going to build a new theatre in our town.

### Exercise 5

Sentence 1 becomes **Amerika'da çok zenginmiş**, which means 'In America, he must have been very rich'. The meaning of 'become' in the original is contributed by **olmak**. In Sentence 3, which becomes **Az kalsın bir trafik kazasıydı**, the meaning difference is much more subtle. This one means 'There was almost a traffic accident', while the one with **olmak** has more of an 'immediate experience' feel to it, as in 'Boy, that was a narrow escape!'

## Exercise 6

The forms in 1, 2, 4 and 7 are fixed expressions. In 3, **oldu** is more likely than **olmuş** because of the following **geldi** (makes it sound as if the speaker saw the accident). In 6, you have to build the familiar structure with **-malı**. In 8, **sanmak** calls for a **-diği** form.

1 olsun  2 ol  3 oldu  4 oldum  5 olmuyor  6 olmalıyız  7 oldu
8 olduğunu  9 oluyor

The translations are: 1 Get well! 2 Thank you! 3 On the street an accident happened and the police came right away. 4 Pleased to meet you. 5 Nothing is certain. 6 She said we have to be stronger. 7 What happened? Come on, tell us! 8 I don't think this is good. 9 Her dishes are very tasty.

## Exercise 7

1 **Her zaman olduğu gibi.** 2 **Ne kadar olsun?** 3 **İyi bir öğrenci olmak için.** 4 **Amerikan firması yeni sahibi oldu.** 5 **İyi bir işçi** (or better: **eleman**) **olacaksın.** 6 **İlginç olmuştur.** 7 **Böyle olma!** 8 **Olmaz.** 9 **Saçı ıslak olan adam.** 10 **Gerekli olursa.**

## Exercise 8

1 'Dear', **Sevgili**; 'I hope you're well', **Umarım iyisindir**; 'Greetings', **Öpüyorum.** 2 No, not really. The weather is nice, but (**fakat**), she has too much work. 3 **Sana birşey sormak istiyorum.** 4 No, she tells Funda not to worry, that it's not important, just to do it if she happens to plan a visit to a bookshop. 5 The **milli kütüphane**, 'public library' (literally 'national library'). 6 It's English history that Kamile is interested in, and Funda is in London at the moment. 7 Yes, she thinks Funda knows him quite well. 8 **şehrin dışında.** 9 Kamile knows London is famous for its musicals and she apparently hates musicals. She says she hopes Funda doesn't have to go to one of those musicals. 10 Yes, the e-mail message is informal: there are no **-siniz** forms, for instance.

Here is a translation of the text:

Dear Funda,

I hope you're well. I won't ask how the weather is in London. I'm sure (*literally:* 'it's sure') you're having a good time. Today the weather is very nice here, but I can't enjoy it, I have to finish my work.

I want to ask you something. If you visit a bookshop one of these days, could you look for some books? As you saw in my last e-mail, I am quite interested in English history these days. I can't find the books I want in the public library. But if there is no opportunity to go to a bookshop, don't worry, it's not that important. I'll give the names in my next message.

I want to rest the whole weekend. Tomorrow I'll visit my Canadian friend, Dave. You know him well, don't you? Unfortunately, he lives outside of town. What are you going to do? Do you have plans for the weekend? I hope you don't have to go to one of those musicals!

Love,

Kamile.

# Lesson 14

### Exercise 1

1 **şirketimizin yeni binasının inşaatına**; **-imiz** possessive suffix 1st person plural 'our'; **-in** genitive case 'of'; **-sı** possessive 3rd person singular 'its'; **-nın** genitive case 'of'; **-ı** possessive suffix 3rd person singular 'its'; **-na** dative case, because of the verb **başlamak** 'to begin with'. The thing you begin with (in this example **inşaat** 'building') always has the **-e/-a** ending.

The whole stretch means 'with the building of a new office of our firm'.

2 **başlayamayız**: the suffix immediately after the verb stem is **-yama-** which is the negative form of **-(y)ebil** and which means 'not be able to' (see Lesson 8, the section on Permission and Obligation).

3 **Bugün** 'today' appears right before the verb, which means that it is emphasised. In fact, in the second sentence, **yarın** 'tomorrow' is followed by **mutlaka** 'surely', which takes the emphasis.

## Exercise 2

1 The winter season might cause a delay of six months, in case there's snow. 2 Because they're not ordered yet. And that is because the director hasn't signed the right papers yet. 3 The **mimar** was waiting for the director to sign. 4 It takes only one day to get the window frames delivered.

## Exercise 3

1 Sinema yıldızı, kendisine bir milyonluk sözleşme teklif edildiği halde, teklifi reddetti. 2 Konferans ücreti çok yüksek olduğu için (olduğundan), öğrenciler ucuz bir otelde kalmak zorundaydılar. 3 Lütfen, istediğiniz kadar alın. 4 Ahmet şikayet etmeyi sevdiği halde, ondan hiç bir şey duymadım. 5 Havaalanına vardığın gibi beni arar mısın? 6 Tren geç kaldığı için (kaldığından) tiyatroya koşmam gerekti. 7 Tren geç kaldığı takdirde, beni beklemeyiniz! 8 Tren geç kaldığı halde, tiyatroya tam zamanında vardım. 9 Tren vardığı gibi tiyatroya koştum. 10 Her gün taze meyve ve sebze yediğim halde, üşüttüm. 11 Taze meyve ve sebze yemeyi bıraktığımız gibi, üşüttük. 12 Kızgın öğretmen 'Ev ödevinizi yapmadığınız için, derse devam edemem' diye bağırdı.

## Exercise 4

1 (It's) yours 2 (It's) Mustafa's 3 Is the pen yours? 4 (It's) theirs 5 (It's) the Turkish Republic's

## Exercise 5

1 **sokaktakiler.** 2 **dünkü çocuk yarınki yetişkin.** 3 **amcamınkini alma, benimkini al** (when the uncle is your father's brother). or: **dayımınkini alma, benimkini al** (when the uncle is your mother's brother). 4 **hastanedeki doktorlar daha iyi.** 5 he doesn't like food from restaurants. 6 they are more expensive than my grandmother's. 7 the station's timetable gave a different departure time. 8 grape juice tasting of wine ('in wine taste').

## Exercise 6

1 The verb foms **dururdu**, **başlardı** and **bakardı** have both a **geniş zaman** (the 'broad tense', see Lesson 8) suffix and a past tense

suffix **-di**. 2 The first part of the story contains general remarks of the narrator about his mother: what she used to do. The appropriate form to use for this kind of habitual behaviour is the **geniş zaman**. Since he also refers to things that happened in the past (things his mother used to do when he was small), the past tense suffix has been added. 3 He changes into using simple past tense forms, such as **dedi**, **dedim** and **attım**, because at that point in the story he switches from general remarks to a specific episode in the past. At that point the main story line starts.

## *Exercise 7*

The items in this exercise show you that **-ip** can replace more verb tenses and verb forms than just a simple past or present tense suffix:
1 **kalkıp** stands for **kalktı** 'he got up', 2 **gelip** stands for **gelince** (that is, at the same level as **konunca**) 'as soon as they came', 3 **gidip** stands for **gidelim** 'let's go', 4 **gidip** stands for **gideceğiz** 'we'll go', 5 **koşup** stands for **koşsam** 'If I run'.

## *Exercise 8*

1 The boy got up and started looking for the frog. 2 As soon as the birds came and landed on the tree in our garden, it was all right. 3 Let's go and dance. (see Lesson 7 for 'let's') 4 We'll go and meet my mother and hers. 5 If I run and catch them . . .!

## *Exercise 9*

1 After the two cowboys got off their horses, they drew their guns and filled each other with holes. 2 The contestant, smiling, answered the question the quizmaster asked. (Well, that's a rather literal translation. A better one would be 'the contestant smiled and answered the question asked by the quizmaster'). 3 We went to see our ill class mate and asked about his condition. 4 By investigating unimportant details, she lost valuable time. 5 Forgetting that it was a holiday today, our absent-minded neighbour went to work. 6 The scared child tried to postpone his visit to the dentist by using the excuse of homework.

---

### Exercise 10

1 çekip  2 gülümseyerek  3 uğrayıp  4 araştırarak  5 unutarak
6 bahane ederek

### Exercise 11

1 While I was contemplating these things, the bell rang. 2 When she understood that she was late for her exam, she put on her jacket and rushed out into the street. 3 By standing in front of the fire, she got warm. 4 He inserted paper into his typewriter and began to write a poem. 5 The fat man tried to loose weight by refraining from eating sweets. 6 After dinner, he helped by washing up. 7 As soon as he arrives in America, he'll send me an e-mail. 8 Why do mothers always call their children for dinner ('to the table') by shouting to them from the balcony?

### Exercise 12

1 düşünürken  2 anlayınca; giyip  3 durarak  4 takıp  5 keserek
6 yaparak  7 varınca  8 seslenerek

### Exercise 13

1 According to **husus** 4, the bus company is not responsible for lost luggage which was not handed in and for which no receipt was given. But, according to **husus** 5, all justicial responsibility lies with the bus owner (not the bus 'company', by the way . . .). 2 Responsibility lies with the bus owner (and again not with the KASIRGA bus company). 3 **Teslim edilip** derives its endings from **yazılacaktır** 'they will be registered/written' and therefore stands for **teslim edilecektir** 'they will be handed over'. 4 The passive suffix is either **-in** or **-il**. 5 **Dolayı** means 'due to', 'on account of'. 6 **-ip** stands at the same level as **aittir** 'belonging to'. Remember from Lesson 13 that **olmak** is used in cases where you would expect a verbless sentence. You need **olmak** because such sentences are only possible in the present tense and in the past with **-di** or **-miş**. **Ait olmayıp** 'not belonging to' is the negative form of **ait**.

Translation:

> **Matters to which our respected travellers should pay attention:**
> 1. Sold tickets are not taken back.
> 2. Tickets are valid on day and time of issue.
> 3. When you purchase the ticket, you show your goods such as trunks, suitcases and parcels which you carry with you. Your goods are to be handed over and registered on a receipt.
> 4. For the loss of things such as trunks, suitcases, parcels or bags that were not handed over, the bus company is not responsible.
> 5. All justicial responsibility lies with the owner of the bus.
> 6. When goods of which the nature and value are not stated on the receipt are lost, the double value of the bus ticket is paid to the owner of these goods by the bus owner and driver.
> 7. The responsibility arising from any accident of the bus does not lie with the KASIRGA company, and all responsibility lies with the bus owner involved in the accident.

### Exercise 14

1 Bence her ayın kendine ait bir rengi var. 2 Ocak beyaz. 3 Hem şubat, hem de ekimle kasım genellikle boz rengi aylar. 4 Mart ise yeşil. 5 Çiçekler nisan, mayıs ve haziran pembe ve maviye değistiriyorlar. 6 Temmuz ve ağustos güneşten dolayı sarıdır. 7 Eylül portakal ve kahverengi; aralık ise hem boz rengi hem de beyaz.

### Exercise 15

**sabun, diş macunu, tıraş bıçağı, güneşyağı** (are all things you buy at the chemist's); **etek, elbise, tişört, gömlek** (are all articles of clothing); **çaydanlık, tencere, bıçak, tabak** (all belong to household equipment); **batı, doğu, kuzey, güney** (are all directions); **bacak, göz, ayak, kol** (are all body parts).

# Lesson 15

### Exercise 1

**anlamak** 'to understand'; **yıkamak** 'to wash'; **giymek** 'to wear'; **dövmek** 'to hit'

### Exercise 2

2 gidiyorsun 3 öğreneceğiz 4 yazacağım 5 korkuyordum 6 geliyor 7 diyor

### Reading text 1

1 The author says that people often tend to think that in one country there's one language, and that if you know the name of the country, you can derive the name of the language. 2 **-meden** as in **düşünmeden**. 3 It says **varolmadığnı** instead of **varolmadığını**.

### Exercise 3

1 Evin içinde. 2 Evin içine gittim. 3 Bu duvarın arkasında ne var? 4 Haberden sonra film başlıyor. 5 Kalemin masanın altına düştü. 6 Evlerin arasında bir bahçe var. 7 Erkek kardeşin senin gibi iyi bir adam. 8 Abim gibi bira içmem. 9 Araba evin önünde. 10 Bu araba ailemiz için fazla büyük.

### Exercise 4

1i 2e 3a 4h 5g 6j 7b 8f 9c 10d

### Exercise 5

1m 2i 3k 4a 5h 6o 7f 8c 9l 10b 11e 12n 13g 14j 15d
The translations:
1 to do a lesson 2 to watch a film 3 to give a discount 4 to do/wash the dishes 5 to turn off the light 6 to find a solution 7 to send a card 8 to be found/situated 9 to fall asleep 10 to play guitar 11 to go to the shopping centre 12 to go out shopping 13 to catch a train 14 to promise ('give the word') 15 to cook the dishes/food

## Exercise 6

1c 2m 3e 4g 5i 6a 7l 8o 9d 10h 11k 12f 13b 14n 15j
The translations: 1 The children are singing well. 2 Ayşe is going out to do shopping. 3 After I had climbed the stairs, I was very tired. 4 I have to clean the windows but I don't want to. 5 Did your son pass that important exam? 6 During the holiday in Turkey I gained five kilos. 7 We are saving money for a new car. 8 I asked but he didn't answer. 9 First we ate in a little restaurant, after that we went to a club and danced. 10 Hurry, we don't want to lose time. 11 To find a taxi in Istanbul is not difficult. 12 My brother knows Turkish and two other languages. 13 Have you filled in all the forms already? 14 Excuse me, maybe you could give me some information? 15 My mother has to take her medication every day.

## Exercise 7

1 Pop müziğini sevdiğimi biliyor musun? 2 Benim onu yaptığımı ona söyledim. 3 İstediğin bu mu? 4 Politikacının dediğini anlayamadım. 5 Onu sevdiğime inanmıyor. 6 Tebrikler, yeni bir iş bulduğunu duydum. 7 Onların geldikleri için teşekkür etmen gerek. 8 Onun mezun olduğunu bana söyledi. 9 Müzenin Van Gogh sergisinde gösterdiği çok ilginçti. 10 Davranışından çok bıktım!

# Turkish–English glossary

Some Turkish words are accompanied by case markers, such as **-e** or **-den**, which means that they are always used with another word carrying this particular case. For example, **kadar** (**-e**) 'until' is always used with the dative case ending (**-e** or **-a**): **yarına kadar** means 'until tomorrow'.

NB: Words in this part are ordered according to the Turkish alphabet: **a b c ç d e f g ğ h ı i j k l m n o ö p r s ş t u ü v y z**

| | | | |
|---|---|---|---|
| **abi** | older brother | **akıllı** | clever, smart |
| **abla** | older sister | **aklıma gelmek** | to come to mind |
| **acaba** | I wonder | **aklına kaçırmak** | to lose one's |
| **acele** | hurry (*noun*) | | mind |
| **acele etmek** | to hurry | **akşam** | evening |
| **açık** | weak (e.g. tea) | **akşam yemeği** | dinner |
| **açmak** | to open | **aktör** | actor/actress |
| **ad** | name | **alışmak** (**-e**) | to get used to |
| **ada** | island | **alışveriş** | shopping |
| **adam** | man | **Allah!** | Oh god! Gosh! |
| **aday** | candidate | **Allah Allah!** | Oh no! |
| **aday göstermek** | to propose a | **Allah aşkına** | for heaven's |
| | candidate | | sake! |
| **adres** | address | **Allah bilir!** | Lord knows! |
| **aferin!** | well done! | **Allahaısmarladık** | Goodbye |
| **affedersiniz** | excuse me, I'm | **Allahım** | My God! |
| | sorry | **almak** | to buy; to take |
| **ağaç** | tree | **Alman** | German |
| **ağır** | pain, ache | **Almanca** | German (the |
| **ağırlık** | weight | | language) |
| **ağrımak** | to hurt | **Almanya** | Germany |
| **Ağustos** | August | **alo** | hello (on the |
| **ah!** | oh! oh dear! | | phone) |
| **aile** | family | **altı** | six |
| **ait** (**-e**) | belonging to | **altın** | gold |

| | | | |
|---|---|---|---|
| altında | under | aşçı | chef |
| altmış | sixty | aşık olmak (-e) | to fall in love |
| ama | but | aşk | love |
| aman! | my goodness! | at | horse |
| ambülans | ambulance | Atina | Athens |
| amca | uncle (from father's side); old man | atmak | to throw |
| | | Avrupa | Europe |
| | | ay | month |
| Amerika | America, US | ayak | foot |
| Amerikalı | American | ayakkabı | shoes |
| an | moment | aynı | same |
| anahtar | key | ayrılmak | to leave |
| anayol | freeway, motorway | ayrıntı | detail |
| | | az | less |
| ancak | but still, on the other hand, really | az kalsın, az kaldı | almost |
| | | baba | father |
| anlamak | to understand | bacak | leg |
| anlatmak | to tell | bagaj | luggage |
| anne | mother | bağırmak | to shout |
| anneanne | grandmother (your mother's mother) | bahane | excuse, pretext |
| | | bahçe | garden |
| | | bakalım | let's see |
| antrenman | practice | bakan | minister |
| aptal | stupid | bakar mısınız? | can you help us, please? (to waiter in restaurant) |
| araba | car | | |
| arabesk | arabesque | | |
| aralık | December | | |
| aramak | to look for | bakışlar | looks |
| arasında | between | bakkal | grocery store; grocer |
| araştırmak | to investigate | | |
| ardından | after | baklava | baklava |
| arkadaş | friend | bakmak | to look |
| arkasında | behind | baksana! | now look here! |
| armut | pear | balıkçı | fisherman |
| artık | from now on; finally | balkon | balcony |
| | | banka | bank |
| artırmak | to cause to rise | banyo | bathroom |
| artmak | to rise, to go up | bardak | glass (for drinking) |
| aslında | actually | | |
| aspirin | aspirin | bari | at least |
| aşağı | below | basit | simple |

| | | | |
|---|---|---|---|
| basmak | to step, to tread | beraber | together |
| bastırmak | to press | berbat | terrible |
| basun | reporters, | beri (-den) | since |
| mensupları | members of | beş | five |
| | the press | beşik | cradle |
| baş | head | ... Bey | Sir ... |
| başarı(lar) | success | beyaz | white |
| başarmak | to manage to do | beyefendi | Sir |
| | something | bıçak | knife |
| başına gelmek | to run into | bıktım (-den) | I'm fed up |
| | problems | | with ... |
| başında | close to, near | bırakmak | to stop, to leave |
| başka | other | | something |
| başkan | chairperson | biber | pepper, paprika |
| başkent | capital | biçim | way, manner |
| başlamak | to begin | bildirmek | to announce |
| başlayan(lar) | beginner(s) | bile | even, actually |
| baş rolü | main role | bilet | ticket |
| başvurmak | to apply | bilgi | information |
| batı | west | bilgisayar | computer |
| batmak | to sink | bilmek | to know |
| bavul | suitcase | bin | thousand |
| bayılmak | to enjoy, to | bina | building |
| | really like | binmek | to get on (train, |
| bayram | feast | | etc.) |
| bazen | sometimes | bir | one, a |
| bazı | some | bir kere | one time |
| bebek | baby | bir kimse | somebody |
| bedava | for free | bir sürü | a lot, many |
| beğenmek (-i) | to enjoy | bir zaman | sometime |
| beklemek (-i) | to wait | bira | beer |
| bekletmek | to make | biraz | a little, a bit |
| | someone wait | birazdan | in a little bit |
| bela | trouble | birbirleri | each other |
| belediye | state | birçok | a lot |
| belki | maybe | birde | you know, ... |
| belli | certain | birden | suddenly |
| ben | I | biri (or: birisi) | somebody |
| bence | according to me | biriktirmek | to gather, to |
| benzemek | to be like | | save |
| | something, | birkaç | some |
| | resemble | birlikte (ile) | together (with) |

| | | | |
|---|---|---|---|
| birşey | something | cami | mosque |
| bisiklet | bicycle | camları silmek | wash the |
| bitirmek | to finish | | windows |
| bitmek | to finish | canım | dear, love |
| biz | we | casus | spy |
| bizim hanım | my wife | cep | pocket |
| boktan herif | idiot | cesaret | courage |
| bol | full | cevap | answer |
| borç | debt | ceza | punishment |
| boş | empty | ceza vermek | to punish |
| boş ver! | never mind! | cıvıl cıvıl | lively |
| boyamak | to paint | cibinlik | mosquito net |
| boz | grey | cihaz | machine, |
| bozuk | broken | | equipment |
| bölüm | part | civar | surrounding |
| böyle | such | cuma günü | Friday |
| bu | this | cumartesi günü | Saturday |
| bu arada | meanwhile | cüzdan | wallet, purse |
| buçuk | half | çabuk | fast |
| buğday | wheat | çadır | tent |
| bugün | today | çağırmak | to shout, to call |
| bulaşık | dirty dishes | | out |
| bulmak | to find | çağrı aleti | buzzer |
| buluşmak | to meet with | çakı | pocket knife |
| bulutlu | cloudy | çakmak | cigarette lighter |
| burada | here | çalışkan | hard-working |
| buralar | these places | çalışmak | to work; to try |
| buraya | to here | çalmak | to play (instru- |
| buyurmak | to order | | ment, tape |
| | someone in | | recorder), to |
| buyurun! | there you are! | | ring (bell), to |
| | what can I get | | knock (door) |
| | you? | çanta | bag |
| büro | office | çaresizce | inevitable |
| butün | all, whole | çarşı | centre, market |
| büyük | big | çarşamba günü | Wednesday |
| büyükanne | grandmother | çatlak | crack |
| büyüklük | size | çay | tea |
| büyümek | to grow | çaydanlık | teapot |
| C sürücüsü | C-drive | çekiç | hammer |
| cadde | street | çekmek | to draw, to pull |
| cam | window | çene | chin |

| | | | |
|---|---|---|---|
| çenesini | to shut one's | dans etmek | to dance (non- |
| kapatmak | mouth | | Turkish style) |
| çerçeve | window frame | dans oynamak | to dance |
| Çerkezce | Circassian (the | | (Turkish-style) |
| | language) | davet etmek | to invite |
| çeşit | variety, kind, | davranış | behaviour |
| | sort | davranma | action |
| çeşitler | various | dayı | uncle (your |
| çevirmek, çevir | to translate; to | | mother's |
| yapmak | dial | | brother) |
| çeyrek | quarter (¼) | dede | granddad |
| çıkmak | to go out | dedikodu | to gossip |
| çiçekler | flowers | yapmak | |
| Çin | Chinese | defa | time (as in iki |
| çoban | shepherd | | defa 'twice') |
| çoban salatası | shepherd's salad | değerli | valuable |
| | (tomatoes, | değil | not |
| | white cheese, | değişmek | to change |
| | olives) | değiştirmek | to change, to |
| çocuk | child | | turn into |
| çok | very much, very, | deli | crazy |
| | much/many | demek | to say, [that] |
| çorba | soup | | means |
| çöplük | rubbish bin | demin | just now, a little |
| çözüm | solution | | while ago |
| çünkü | because | denemek | to try |
| çürük | rotten | deniz | sea |
| da/de | too, on the other | deniz kıyısı | coast |
| | hand | deri | leather |
| dağ | mountain | ders | lesson |
| dağılmak | to scatter, | devam etmek | to continue |
| | disperse | devamlı | over and over, |
| daha | more, still | | repeatedly |
| daha doğrusu | in other | devir | period, age |
| | words | devlet | state |
| dahil | included | Dış İşleri | Foreign Office |
| daire | apartment, flat | dışarıya | outside |
| dakika | minute | dışında | outside; apart |
| daktilo | typewriter | | from |
| dalmak | to snooze; to | didinmek | to work hard |
| | dive, to | diğer | other |
| | plunge | dikkat et! | watch out! |

| | | | |
|---|---|---|---|
| **dikkat etmek** | to pay attention to, to watch out | **durmak** | to stop, to stand |
| | | **durum** | situation |
| | | **duş** | shower |
| **dil** | language | **duş almak** | to take a shower |
| **dinlemek** | to listen | **duvar** | wall |
| **dinlenmek** | to rest | **duymak** | to hear |
| **direnmek** | to resist | **dükkan** | shop |
| **diş** | tooth | **dün** | yesterday |
| **diş macunu** | toothbrush | **dünya** | world |
| **diş hekimi** | dentist | **düşman** | enemy |
| **dişçi** | dentist | **düşmek** | to fall |
| **doğmak** | to be born | **düşük** | low (price) |
| **doğru** | right, correct | **düşünce** | thought |
| **doğu** | east | **düşünmek** | to think |
| **doğum günü** | birthday | **efendim** | sir |
| **doğumlu** | born | **eğer** | if |
| **doksan** | ninety | **eğlence** | party |
| **doktor** | doctor | **ekim** | October |
| **dokunmayınız!** | please don't touch! | **ekip** | team |
| | | **ekmek** | bread |
| **dokuz** | nine | **ekonomi** | business, economics |
| **dolap** | cupboard | | |
| **dolaşmak** | to wander, to roam, to walk around | **eksersiz** | exercise |
| | | **eksik** | not enough |
| | | **el** | hand |
| **dolayı (-den)** | because (of) | **el feneri** | flashlight |
| **dolayısıyla** | because, consequently | **elbise** | dress |
| | | **elektrikçi** | electrician |
| **doldurmak** | to fill out | **eleman** | employee |
| **dolma** | stuffed pepper | **elli** | fifty |
| **dolmalık** | pepper for stuffing | **elma** | apple |
| | | **e-mail** | e-mail |
| **dost** | friend | **emin** | certain |
| **dostluk** | friendship | **emir vermek** | to give an order |
| **dökmek** | to pour, to sprinkle | **en** | most |
| | | **endişelenmek** | to be anxious about |
| **dönmek** | to return, to turn | | |
| | | **enflasyon** | inflation |
| **dört** | four | **e-posta** | e-mail |
| **dövmek** | to hit, to fight | **eriyip gitmek** | to disappear |
| **dur be!** | hold on! | **erkek** | boy |
| **durak** | (bus) stop | **erkek arkadaş** | boyfriend |

| | | | |
|---|---|---|---|
| erkek kardeş | brother | fotoğraf | camera |
| erken | early | makinesi | |
| ertelemek | to postpone | Fransa | France |
| ertelenmek | to be postponed | Fransız | French |
| ertesi gün | the next day | Fransızca | French (the |
| eski | old | | language) |
| eskiden | in the old days | futbol maçı | football match |
| esnasında | during | futbolcu | football player |
| eş | wife, husband | galiba | probably |
| et | meat | gar | train station |
| etek | skirt | garson | waiter |
| etkilemek | to influence | gayrı | at last, from |
| etli | with meat | | now on |
| etsiz | meatless | gazete | newspaper |
| ev | house | gazeteci | journalist |
| evet | yes | gece | night |
| evlenmek | to marry | gece gündüz | night and day |
| evli | married | gecikme | delay |
| evvelki gün | the day before | geç | late |
| | yesterday | geçe | at ... past ... |
| eylül | September | | (in time- |
| fabrika | factory | | telling) |
| fakat | but | geçen | last, previous |
| fare | mouse | geçiyor | past (in time- |
| fark etmek | to notice | | telling) |
| fark etmez! | never mind! | geçmek | to pass |
| farklı | different | geçmiş olsun! | get well soon! |
| Fars | Persian | gelin | bride |
| fazla | too much | gelişmiş | developed |
| felaket | disastrous | gelmek | to come |
| fena | bad | genç | young, youth |
| fırlamak | to rush out | gençlik | youth |
| fırsat | possibility | Gençlik Parkı | Youth Park |
| fikir | idea | | (park in |
| filan | and so | | Ankara) |
| film | film | genel | general |
| fincan | cup | genelde | in general |
| Finli | Finnish | genellikle | in general |
| firma | company, firm | geniş | wide |
| fiyat | price | gerçek | true |
| form | form | gerçekten | really |
| fotoğraf çekmek | to take a picture | gerek | necessary |

| | | | |
|---|---|---|---|
| gerekli | necessary | grev | strike |
| gerekmek | to be necessary | gri | grey |
| geri | back, backwards | gücü toplanmak | to regain |
| getirmek | to bring | | strength |
| gezdirmek | to walk some- | güç | strength |
| | thing (e.g. a | güldürücü | funny |
| | dog) | güle güle | goodbye (answer |
| gezi | trip, excursion | | to **Allahaıs-** |
| gezmek | to walk, drive, | | **marladık**) |
| | travel around | gülmek | to laugh |
| gibi | as | gülümsemek | to smile |
| giriş | entrance | gün | day |
| girmek | to enter | günaydın | hello |
| gişe | booth; window | güncellemek | to update |
| gişe memuru | person behind | gündem | agenda |
| | the desk | güneş | sun |
| git (ya)! | come on! | güneşlenmek | to sunbathe |
| gitar | guitar | güneşyağı | sun-block |
| gitmek | to go | güney | south |
| giyecek | clothes | güreşme | wrestling |
| giyinmek | to get dressed | gürültü | noise |
| giymek | to wear | güzel | nice, beautiful, |
| gizlemek | to hide | | fine, good |
| gol | goal | haber | news |
| göl | lake | hadi! | come on! |
| gömlek | shirt | hafta | week |
| göndermek | to send | hafta sonu | weekend |
| göre (-e) | according to | hakkında | about |
| görev | function | haklı | right |
| görmek (-i) | to see | hal | market; state, |
| görünmek | to look, to | | condition |
| | appear | hala | just, yet, not yet |
| görüşme | discussion | halı | rug |
| görüşürüz | see you! | halk | people |
| gösteri | performance, | halk müziği | folk music |
| | demonstration | hamam | Turkish bath |
| göstermek | to show | hangi? | which? |
| götürmek | to take (with) | ... Hanım | Madam ... |
| göz | eye | hanımefendi | madam |
| gözkapağı | eyelid | hap | pill |
| gözlük | glasses | hapishane | jail |
| gözlükçü | optician | hareket | departure |

| | | | |
|---|---|---|---|
| **harika!** | great! | **hissetmek** | to feel |
| **hasta** | ill | **Hollandalı** | Dutch |
| **hastane** | hospital | **hoş bulduk** | thank you (said |
| **hata** | mistake | | in reply to **hoş** |
| **hatırlamak** | to remember | | **geldiniz**) |
| **hatun** | woman | **hoş geldin(iz)** | welcome! |
| **hava** | weather, air | **husus** | matters, things |
| **hava yastığı** | airbag | **hükümet** | government |
| **hava yolları** | airways, airlines | **ılık** | lukewarm |
| **havaalanı** | airport | **ısınmak** | to warm oneself |
| **havuç** | carrot | **ısırmak** | to bite |
| **hayat** | life | **ıslak** | wet |
| **hayır** | no | **ısmarlatmak** | to have some- |
| **hayırlı işler!** | have a nice day! | | thing ordered |
| **hayırlı olsun!** | congratulations! | **ışık** | light |
| **hayranlık** | admiration | **içeri** | inside |
| **hayret!** | wow! | **için** | for |
| **hayvan** | animal | **içinde** | within |
| **hazır** | ready | **içki** | (alcoholic) drink |
| **hazır olmak** | to be prepared | **içmek** | to drink |
| **hazırlamak** | to prepare | **idrak etmek** | to understand |
| **haziran** | June | **iflas etmek** | to go bankrupt |
| **hediye** | present, gift | **ihale** | order |
| **hekim** | doctor | **iki** | two |
| **hele** | but first | **ilaç** | medication |
| **hem de** | and even | **ilan** | ad |
| **hem ... hem de** | either ... or ... | **ile** | and |
| **hemen** | immediately | **ileride** | ahead |
| **hemen hemen** | almost | **ilerlemek** | to go forward |
| **henüz** | yet | **ilgilenmek** | to be interested |
| **hep** | all, always | | in |
| **hepsi** | everyone | **ilginç** | interesting |
| **her** | every, all | **ilişki** | contact, relation |
| **herhalde** | probably | **ilk** | first |
| **herif** | idiot, fool | **ilk önce** | first and foremost |
| **herkes** | everyone | **ilk olarak** | in the first place |
| **hesap** | bill | **ilkbahar** | spring |
| **hızlı** | fast | **imleç** | cursor |
| **hiç** | none, never, | **imzali** | signed |
| | ever | **inanmak** | to believe |
| **hiçbiri** | nobody | **indirim** | discount |
| **hikaye** | story | **inek** | cow |

| | | | |
|---|---|---|---|
| İngiliz | English | kadar (-e) | until |
| İngilizce | English (the | kadeh | (wine) glass |
| | language) | kadın | woman |
| İngiltere | England | kafa | head, mind |
| inmek | to get off (a bus, | kağıt | paper |
| | etc.); to go | kahvaltı | breakfast |
| | down (stairs) | kahve | coffee |
| insan | people; human | kahverengi | brown |
| | being | kala | at ... to ... (in |
| inşaat | building, | | time-telling) |
| | construction | kalabalık | busy |
| inşallah | hopefully | kaldı ki | moreover |
| ise | but; however | kaldırım | pavement |
| isim | name; title | kalem | pen |
| İspanyolca | Spanish (the | kalite | quality |
| | language) | kaliteli | of high quality |
| istasyon | station | kalmak | to stay, remind |
| istek | wish | kalkmak | to get up; to |
| istemek | to want | | leave |
| istenilen | required, wanted | kamaşmak | to dazzle |
| İsveçli | Swedish | kamp yapmak | to go camping |
| iş | work, job | kamyoncu | lorry driver |
| işçi | worker | Kanadalı | Canadian |
| işkembe çorbası | tripe soup | kapak | lid |
| işsiz | unemployed | kapalı | closed |
| işsizlik | unemployment | kapanmak | to be closed |
| işte | well ... | kapatmak | to close |
| işveren | employer | kapı | door |
| İtalyan | Italian | kar yağmak | to snow |
| İtalyanca | Italian (the | karanlık | darkness |
| | language) | karar vermek | to decide |
| itibaren (-den) | from ... on | kararsız | undecided |
| iyi | good, splendid | karayolu | motorway |
| iyi günler | hello | kardeş | brother, sister |
| iz | trace | karı | wife |
| Japon | Japanese | karşı | across, the other |
| jeton | token | | side |
| kabak | courgette | kartpostal | postcard |
| kabul etmek | to accept | kaset | tape |
| kaç | how many? | kasım | November |
| kaçırmak | to miss | kaşımak | to scratch |
| kaçmak | to escape | kavga | fight |

| | | | |
|---|---|---|---|
| kavga etmek (ile) | to quarrel (with) | kilo vermek | to lose weight |
| | | kim? | who? |
| kavun | honeydew melon | kimse | nobody |
| | | kira | rental |
| kayakçı | skier | kiraathane | cafe |
| kaybetmek | to lose | kiralamak | to rent |
| kaybolmak | to get lost | kirletmek | to make dirty |
| kaydetmek | to save (files) | kirli | dirty |
| kaymak | to slip | kişi | person |
| kaza | accident | kitabevi | bookstore |
| kazanmak | to win (something) | kitap | book |
| | | koalisyon | coalition |
| kedi | cat | koca | husband |
| kelime | word | kocaman | huge |
| kemerlerinizi bağlayın! | fasten your seatbelts! | koçum! | 'mate' (term of address) |
| kendi kendine | oneself | kol | arm |
| kendisi | (him/her)self | kola | coke, cola, pepsi |
| kent | town | kolay | easy |
| kepçe | scoop, shovel | kolayca | easily |
| kesin | surely | koltuk | chair |
| kesinlikle | for sure | komik | funny |
| kesmek | to cut | komşu | neighbour |
| keşke | if only | konferans | conference |
| kırk | forty | konmak | to be put, to settle |
| kırmak | to break | | |
| kırmızı | red | konser | concert |
| kırpmak | to blink | kontrol etmek | to check |
| kısaca | in short, ... | konu | topic |
| kış | winter | konuk | guest |
| kıyı | coast | konuşmak | to talk, to speak |
| kıymalı et | minced meat | | |
| kız | girl | konuya gelmek | to come to the point |
| kız arkadaş | girlfriend | | |
| kız kardeş | sister | korkmak | to be afraid |
| kızdırmak | to annoy | korku filmi | horror film |
| kızgın | angry | korkutmak | to frighten |
| kızmak | to get angry | korumak | to keep |
| ki | that | koskoca | large |
| kibrit | matches (to light) | koşmak | to run |
| | | koymak | to put |
| kilo almak | to gain weight | koyun | sheep |

| | | | |
|---|---|---|---|
| **köfte** | grilled meat dish, usually with ground lamb | **mahvetmek** | to damage |
| | | **makale** | article (in paper) |
| | | **malzeme** | equipment |
| | | **mama** | cat food |
| **köpek** | dog | **market** | supermarket |
| **köprü** | bridge | **mart** | March |
| **kör** | blind | **masa** | table |
| **körfez** | bay | **mavi** | blue |
| **kötü** | bad | **mayıs** | May |
| **köy** | village | **mektup** | letter |
| **köylü** | peasant | **memleket** | country |
| **kraliçe** | queen | **memnun oldum** | pleased to meet you |
| **kullanmak** | to use | | |
| **kupa** | cup (e.g. in sports) | **memnun olmak** | to be pleased |
| | | **memur** | officer, civil servant |
| **kurbağa** | frog | | |
| **kurmak** | to erect, to put up | **merak etmek** | to worry |
| | | **mercimek** | lentils |
| **kurs** | course, class | **merdiven** | stairs |
| **kurtarmak** | to save | **merhaba** | hello |
| **kusura bakma!** | I'm sorry! | **merkez** | centre (of town) |
| **kuş** | bird | **mesaj** | message |
| **kutu** | box | **mesele** | problem |
| **kuzey** | north | **mevsim** | season |
| **kuzu** | lamb | **meyve** | fruit |
| **küçük** | small, little | **mezun olmak (-den)** | to graduate |
| **kütüphane** | library | | |
| **lacivert** | blue | **millet** | people |
| **laflar** | nonsense | **milli** | national |
| **lahana** | cabbage | **mimar** | architect |
| **lahmacun** | Turkish pizza | **misafir** | guest |
| **lamba** | lamp | **model** | model |
| **lazım (-mesi)** | must | **monden** | worldly |
| **lezzetli** | delicious | **mont** | jacket |
| **lise** | secondary school | **mor** | purple |
| **liste** | list | **muavin** | assistant |
| **lokanta** | (little) restaurant | **muhallebici** | cake shop |
| **Londra** | London | **mutfak** | kitchen |
| **lütfen** | please | **mutlaka** | surely |
| **maalesef** | unfortunately | **mutlu** | happy |
| **mahkemeye vermek (-i)** | to sue | **müdür** | director, manager |

| | | | |
|---|---|---|---|
| mühendis | engineer | o zaman | then |
| müsaade | permit | ocak | January |
| müşteri | customer | oda | room |
| müze | museum | of | oof!, ouch! |
| müzik | music | oğlan | boy |
| müzikal | musical | okul | school |
| nasıl? | how? what kind of? | okumak | to study |
| | | olarak | as |
| nasıl olsa | still, in spite of that, ... | olay | situation |
| | | oldu | OK |
| nasılsın? | how are you? | oldukça | more or less |
| ne? | what? | olmak | to become, be |
| ne haber? | how are you?, what's new? | olimpiyat oyunları | Olympic Games |
| ne kadar? | how many? | on | ten |
| ne var, ne yok? | what's new? | ondan sonra | and then |
| ne yazık ki! | what a pity! | onlar | they |
| ne zaman? | when? | onun için | therefore |
| neden | why?, reason | orada | there |
| nedeniyle | because, for the reason that | oradaki | yonder, over there |
| nefis | tasty | oralar | up there, thereabouts |
| nerede? | where? | | |
| nereden? | from where? | oranla (-e) | compared to |
| neredeyse | almost | orası | there, that place |
| nereli? | from where? | oraya | to there |
| nereye? | where to? | orta şekerli | with (normal amount of) sugar |
| neyse | anyway, well then | | |
| niçin? | why? | otel | hotel |
| nihayet | finally, in the end | otobüs | bus |
| | | otogar | bus station |
| nisan | April | oturmak | to live, to sit |
| niye? | why? | otuz | thirty |
| nohut | chickpeas | oynamak | to play |
| normal | normal | oyuncak | toy |
| not | marks (at school) | oyuncu | player, actor |
| | | öbür | next, the other |
| not almak | to take notes | ödemek | to pay |
| o | that, he/she/it | ödev | homework |
| o halde | in that case | ödünç vermek | to lend |
| o şekilde | that way | öf | ugh!, yuk! |

| | | | |
|---|---|---|---|
| öğleden sonra | afternoon | pembe dizi | soap opera |
| öğrenci | student | pencere | window |
| öğrenmek | to learn | perşembe günü | Thursday |
| öğretmen | teacher | peşinden | after, behind |
| öldürmek | to kill | petrol | gasoline |
| ölmek | to die | peynir | cheese |
| önce | earlier, before | pırıl pırıl | sparkling |
| önemli | important | piknik | picnic |
| önemsiz | unimportant | pilav | rice dish |
| öneri | proposal, | pirinç | rice |
| | suggestion | pis | dirty |
| önümüzdeki | before us | pişirmek | to cook |
| önünde | in front of | pişmek | to boil |
| öpmek | to kiss | piyango | lottery |
| öte yandan | on the other | piyano | piano |
| | hand | piyasaya | to be introduced |
| öyle | such | getirilmek | on to the |
| öyle mi? | really? | | market |
| öyleyse | OK then | plaj | beach |
| Özbekçe | Uzbek (the | plan | plan |
| | language) | polis | police |
| özellikle | in particular | politikacı | politician |
| özen göstermek | to take care | pop müziği | pop music |
| | that | portakal | orange |
| pahalı | expensive | portakal rengi | orange (the |
| paket | parcel | | colour) |
| palto | coat | portakal suyu | orange juice |
| para | money | poşet | plastic bag |
| parça | part, piece | program | programme |
| park | park | program | to run a |
| parti | party (also | çalıştırmak | program |
| | political) | programcı | programmer |
| pasta | cake | radyo | radio |
| pastane | lunchroom | rağmen | in spite of |
| patates | potatoes | rahat bırakmak | to leave in |
| patlıcan | aubergine | | peace |
| pazar | market | rahatsız | upset, not well, |
| pazar günü | Sunday | | ill |
| pazartesi günü | Monday | rahatsız etmek | to disturb |
| peki | all right, OK, | rakı | rakı |
| | well | randevu | appointment, |
| pembe | pink | | meeting |

| | | | |
|---|---|---|---|
| rapor | report | sanal alem | virtual market- |
| rast gelmek | to run into | | place |
| rastlamak | to run into | sancak | flag |
| reddetmek | to decline | sandal | canoe |
| rehber | guide | saniye | second |
| rehberlik | to work as a | sanmak | to believe |
| yapmak | guide | saray | palace |
| rekabetçi | competitor | sarı | yellow |
| renk | colour | satın almak | to buy |
| resepsiyon | reception desk | satmak | to sell |
| reservasyon | reservation | savaş | war |
| resim | picture | sayfa | page |
| rica ederim | I beg you!, | sayı | number |
| | please!, you're | sayıca az | fewer |
| | welcome! | sayın | honourable |
| rica etmek | to ask for | saz | saz (Turkish |
| roman | novel | | lute) |
| röportaj | article, | sebze | vegetable |
| | documentary | seçenek | choice |
| rötar | delay | seçim | election |
| Rus | Russian | seçmek | to measure |
| saat | hour, clock | sefer | time |
| sabah | morning | sekiz | eight |
| sabun | soap | sekreter | secretary |
| saç | hair | seksen | eighty |
| saçmalık | nonsense | selam! | hello! |
| sadece | just, only | sen | you |
| sağ ol! | thank you | sene | year |
| sağanak | cloudburst | sergilenmiş | on display |
| sağlam | solid | seslenmek | to call out, to |
| sağlık | health | | address |
| sahi mi? | really? | sergi | exhibition |
| sahil | seaside | sert | strong |
| sahip | owner | sevgili | sweet, dear |
| sahne | stage | sevgilim | my darling |
| salı günü | Tuesday | sevimli | pretty |
| sallamak | to wave | sevmek (-i) | to love |
| sallandırmak | to rock | seyahat | travel |
| salon | living room | seyahat acentası | travel agent |
| sana ne? | mind your own | seyahat etmek | to travel |
| | business | seyretmek (-i) | to watch |
| | (rather rude) | sıcak | warm |

| | | | |
|---|---|---|---|
| sıfır | zero | sözcük | word |
| sığır | beef | sözleşme | contract |
| sıhhatli | healthy | sözlük | dictionary |
| sık sık | often | spor | sport |
| sıkılmak | to get bored | spor salonu | sports centre |
| sınıf | classroom | sporcu | athlete |
| sırt | back | su | water |
| sıyırmak | to take off, to push away | sularında | about, around (with time) |
| sigara | cigarette | sunucu | server |
| sigara içmek | to smoke | susmak | to be silent |
| sigorta | insurance | süre | period, time span |
| silah | gun | | |
| silmek | to delete; to wash; to wipe out | sürekli | for a long time |
| | | sürmek | to last |
| | | sürü | range |
| sinav | exam | süt | milk |
| sinema | cinema | şahane | great, fantastic |
| sipariş etmek | to order | şaka | joke |
| sivrisinek | mosquito | şans | chance, opportunity |
| siyah | black | | |
| siz | you (*pl.*); you (*sing.* polite) | şarap | wine |
| | | şarkı | song |
| sofra | dinner table | şarkı söylemek | to sing |
| soğuk | cold | şarkıcı | singer |
| sohbet etmek | to chat | şart | condition |
| sokak | street | şaşakalmak | to be confused |
| sol | left | şehir (şehri-) | city |
| son | end | şeker | sugar |
| sonbahar | autumn | şekil | form, shape |
| sonra | after | şemsiye | umbrella |
| sonuç | conclusion | şey | thing |
| sonuçta | in the end | şiir | poem |
| sormak | to ask | şifalı | healthy |
| soru | question | şikayet etmek | to complain |
| sorumluluk | responsibility | şimdi | now |
| sorun | problem | şimdiye kadar | already |
| söndürmek | to extinguish | şirket | company |
| söylemek | to say | şişe | bottle |
| söz etmek | to talk about | şişman | fat, overweight |
| söz vermek | to give the word to | şoför | driver |
| | | şöyle | such |

| | | | |
|---|---|---|---|
| şu | that | tekrar | again |
| şu anda | right now | tekrarlamak | to repeat |
| şubat | February | telefon açmak | to call up |
| tabak | plate | telefon etmek | to call, to phone |
| tabii | of course | telefon numarasi | phone number |
| tadını çıkarmak | to enjoy | televizyon | television |
| tahmin etmek | to guess | tembel | lazy |
| taksi | taxi | temiz | clean |
| tam | exactly, right | temizlemek | to clean |
| tamam | OK | temmuz | July |
| tamamlamak | to finish | tencere | saucepan |
| | something | terbiyeli | well-behaved |
| tamir etmek | to repair | tereyağ | butter |
| tamirci | mechanic | terketmek | to leave |
| tane | piece | | someone |
| tanıdık | acquaintance | tesadüf | coincidence |
| tanımak | to know, to | teslim etmek | to deliver |
| | recognise | teşekkür ederim | thank you! |
| tanışmak | to get to know, | teşekkürler | thank you! |
| | to meet | teyze | aunt |
| tanıştırmak | to introduce | tıraş bıçağı | razor-blade |
| Tanrım | My god! | ticaret | trade |
| taraf | side | tip | character |
| tarife | recipe, | tişört | T-shirt |
| | (time)table | tiyatro | theater |
| tarih | history | toparlanmak | to regain |
| taş | stone | | strength |
| taşımak | to carry | toplamak | to harvest, to |
| taşınmak | to move | | collect |
| tat | taste | toplantı | meeting |
| tatil | holiday, vacation | trafik ışıkları | traffic lights |
| tatlı | sweet, dessert | trafik kazası | traffic accident |
| tavsiye etmek | to recommend | trafik lambası | traffic light |
| tavşan | rabbit | tren | train |
| tavuk | chicken | turist | tourist |
| taze | fresh | turistik | tourist (adj.) |
| tebrik ederim! | congratulations! | turunç | orange (the |
| tebrikler! | congratulations! | | colour) |
| tehlikeli | dangerous | tuş | button |
| tek | only, single | tuvalet | bathroom |
| teklif etmek | to offer | tuz | salt |
| tekne | little boat | tüm | all |

| Türk | Turkish, Turk | üşütmek | to catch a cold |
|------|---------------|---------|-----------------|
| Türk Hava | Turkish Airlines | üzerine | about |
| Yolları | | üzgün | sad |
| Türkçe | Turkish | üzülmek | to be |
| | (language) | | disappointed |
| Türkiye | Turkey | üzüm | grape |
| türküaz | turquoise | vakıf | foundation |
| ucuz | cheap | vakit (vakti-) | time |
| uçak | plane | vallahi | really, I swear |
| uçmak | to fly | vapur | boat |
| uğramak (-e) | to look up | var | there is |
| umarım | I hope that | varmak | to arrive |
| unutmak | to forget | varolmak | to exist |
| usta | master | vatandaş | countryman |
| uyanmak | to wake | ve | and |
| | someone | vejetaryen | vegetarian |
| (ayak) | to adapt | veri | data |
| uydurmak | | vermek | to give |
| uygun | fit, capable | veteriner | vet |
| uyku | sleep | veya | or |
| uyku tulumu | sleeping-bag | vs. (ve saire) | etcetera |
| uymak | to satisfy | vurmak | to shoot, to |
| uyumak | to sleep | | strike |
| uzak | far | yabancı | foreign |
| uzatmak | to pass, to hand | yahni | stew, sauce |
| | over | yakalamak | to catch |
| uzman | excellent | yakın | near, close to |
| uzun | long, tall | yakınlarda | some time soon |
| uzun uzun | for a long time | yakınmak | to complain |
| ücret | fee | yakışıklı | handsome |
| ücretsiz | for free | yaklaşık | about, more or |
| üç | three | | less |
| ülke | country | yalan | lie |
| üniversite | university | yalan söylemek | to lie |
| ünlü | famous | yalı | (wooden) house, |
| üretim | production | | villa |
| üretmek | to produce | yalnız | only; just |
| ürün | product | yalnız başına | by oneself |
| üstelemek | to repeat | yanında | with, at the side |
| üstelik | moreover | | of |
| üstünde | above, on | yanıt | answer |
| üstünde ... var | to wear | yani | so; that is |

| | | | |
|---|---|---|---|
| yanlış | wrong | yeniden | again |
| yanlışlık | mistake | yenmek | to win |
| yanmak | to burn | yepyeni | brand new |
| yapım | task | yer | place |
| yapmak | to do; to make | yeşil | green |
| yaprak dolması | stuffed vine | yeterli | enough |
| | leaves | yetişkin | grown-up |
| yaptırmak | to have someone | yetişmek | to catch (a train, |
| | do something | | etc.) |
| yaralı | wounded | yetmiş | seventy |
| yardım etmek (-e) | to help | yıkamak | to wash |
| yardımcı olmak | to be of help | yıl | year |
| yarım | half | yıldız | star |
| yarın | tomorrow | yine | again |
| yarışma | contest | yine de | still, neverthe- |
| yasak | forbidden, | | less |
| | prohibited | yirmi | twenty |
| yaş | age | yok | there isn't |
| yaşamak | to live | yoksa | or |
| yaşlı | aged, old | yol | road, way |
| yatak | bed | yolcu | traveller |
| yatak odası | bedroom | yolculuk | journey, trip |
| yatmak | to lie down | yolculuk etmek | to travel |
| yaya | pedestrian | yorgan | duvet |
| yayım | broadcast | yorgun | tired |
| yayınlamak | to publish | yorulmak | to get tired |
| yayla | meadow | yönetmek | to govern |
| yaz | summer | yöntem | strategy |
| yazar | writer | yukarıda | upstairs |
| yazık | unfortunately | Yunan | Greek |
| yazılım | software | Yunanistan | Greece |
| yazmak | to write | yüklemek | to download |
| yedi | seven | yüksek | high, tall (not |
| yeğen | nephew | | for people) |
| yemek | food, to eat | yürek | heart |
| yemek yemek | to eat (used | yürümek | to walk |
| | when what is | yürüyüş yapmak | to go for a walk |
| | eaten isn't | yüz | hundred; face |
| | specified) | yüzmek | to swim |
| yenge | aunt, girl! (form | yüzyıl | century |
| | of address) | zahmet etmek | to go to the |
| yeni | new | | trouble |

| | | | |
|---|---|---|---|
| **zahmet olmak** | to be a lot of trouble | **zil** | bell |
| **zannetmek** | to think | **zincir** | chain |
| **zarfında** | during | **ziyaret** | visit |
| **zaten** | anyway | **ziyaret etmek** | pay a visit |
| **zavallı** | poor | **zor** | difficult |
| **zengin** | rich | **zorla** | with difficulty |
| **zeytin** | olives | **zorunda (-mek)** | to be obliged |
| | | **zorunda kalmak** | to have to |

# English–Turkish glossary

| | |
|---|---|
| a little | biraz |
| about | üzerine, hakkında |
| about, more or less | yaklaşık |
| above | üstünde |
| accept | kabul etmek |
| accident | kaza |
| according to | göre |
| acquaintance | tanıdık |
| across | karşı |
| actually | aslında |
| ad | ilan |
| address | adres |
| adult | yetişkin |
| after, later | sonra |
| afternoon | öğleden sonra |
| again | tekrar, yine |
| against | karşı (-e) |
| aged | yaşlı |
| agenda | gündem |
| air | hava |
| airbag | hava yastığı |
| airport | havaalanı |
| alcoholic drink | içki |
| all | bütün, hep, hepsi, her, tüm |
| almost | hemen hemen, az kaldı |
| always | her zaman, daima, hep |
| America | Amerika |
| American | Amerikalı, Amerikan |
| and | ve |
| and even, and ... too | hem de |
| and then, then | ondan sonra |
| angry, to get | kızmak (-e) |
| answer | (verb) cevap vermek; (noun) cevap, yanıt |
| anyway | zaten |
| apple | elma |
| apply | başvurmak (-e) |
| April | nisan |
| arm | kol |
| arrive | varmak (-e) |
| as, in the way of | olarak |
| as | gibi |
| ask | soru sormak |
| assignment, work | ödev |
| at ... to ... (in time-telling) | kala |
| at ..., past ... (in time-telling) | geçe |
| at that/the moment | şu anda |
| at last | artık, gayrı |
| aubergine | patlıcan |
| August | Ağustos |
| aunt (from father's side) | yenge |

| | | | |
|---|---|---|---|
| aunt (from | teyze | beginners | başlayanlar |
| mother's side) | | behaviour | davranış |
| autumn | sonbahar | behind | arkasında |
| awful | berbat | believe | zannetmek, |
| baby | bebek | | sanmak, (in |
| back | geri | | something) |
| (backwards) | | | inanmak (-e) |
| back (part of | sırt | bell | zil |
| the body) | | belonging to | ait (-e) |
| bad | kötü, fena | between | arasında |
| bag | çanta | bicycle | bisiklet |
| balcony | balkon | big | büyük |
| bank | banka | bill | hesap |
| bathhouse | hamam | bird | kuş |
| bathroom | banyo, tuvalet | birthday | doğum günü |
| bay | körfez | bite | ısırmak |
| be surprised | şaşakalmak | black | siyah |
| be used up | bitmek | Black Sea | Karadeniz |
| be born | doğmak | blind | kör |
| be, become | olmak | blue | mavi |
| be closed | kapanmak | boat | vapur |
| be interested in | ilgilenmek (-ile) | book | kitap |
| be afraid | korkmak (-den) | bored, to get | sıkılmak |
| be disappointed | üzülmek (-e) | bottle | şişe |
| be late | geç kalmak | box | kutu |
| be pleased | memnun olmak | boy | oğlan |
| | (-den) | boyfriend | erkek arkadaş |
| beach | plaj | bread | ekmek |
| beautiful | güzel | bride | gelin |
| because | çünkü, | bridge | köprü |
| | dolayısıyla, | bring | getirmek |
| | diye | broken | bozuk |
| become, be | olmak | brother or | kardeş |
| become quiet | susmak | sister (younger | |
| bed | yatak | sibling) | |
| bedroom | yatak odası | brother (older) | abi |
| beef | sığır | brother | erkek kardeş |
| beer | bira | brown | kahverengi |
| before, first, | önce | build up | kurmak |
| earlier | | building, office | bina |
| before us | önümüzdeki | burn | yanmak |
| begin | başlamak (-e) | bus | otobüs |

| | | | |
|---|---|---|---|
| bus stop | durak | chili | biber |
| busy | kalabalık | choose, elect, | seçmek |
| but, if | ise | measure | |
| but still | ancak | cigarette | sigara |
| but | ama, fakat | cinema | sinema |
| butcher | kasap | city | şehir (şehri-) |
| butter | tereyağ | city council | belediye |
| buy | almak, satın | classmate | sınıf arkadaşı |
| | almak | clean | temiz |
| cafe, lunchroom | pastane | clear | açık |
| cake | pasta | clever | akıllı |
| call | çağırmak; | clock | saat |
| | (phone:) | close | kapatmak |
| | aramak, | close to, near | yakın (-e) |
| | telefon etmek | closed | kapalı |
| capable, fit | uygun | clothes | giyecek |
| capital | başkent | cloudy | bulutlu |
| car | araba | coffee | kahve |
| careful! | dikkat et! | coffee-house | kahvehane |
| carrot | havuç | coincidence | tesadüf |
| carry | tutmak, taşımak | coke | kola |
| cat | kedi | cold | soğuk |
| catch | yakalamak; (a | collect, harvest | toplamak |
| | train, plane, | colour | renk |
| | etc.:) yetişmek | come | gelmek |
| | (-e) | come on! | hadi! |
| centre | merkez, çarşı | computer | bilgisayar |
| century | yüzyıl | congratulations! | hayırlı olsun! |
| certain | emin, belli | continue | devam etmek |
| certainly | kesinlikle | | (-e) |
| chain | zincir | cook (noun) | aşçı |
| chairperson | başkan | cook (verb) | pişirmek |
| chance | şans | correct | doğru |
| change | değişmek | country | memleket, ülke |
| chat | sohbet etmek | countryman | vatandaş |
| cheap | ucuz | courage | cesaret |
| check | kontrol etmek | courgette | kabak |
| cheese | peynir | cow | inek |
| chef | aşçı | cup | fincan |
| chicken | tavuk | cupboard | dolap |
| chickpeas | nohut | customer | müşteri |
| child | çocuk | cut | kesmek |

| | | | |
|---|---|---|---|
| cute | sevimli | election | seçim |
| dad | baba | elementary | ilkokul |
| dance (non- | dans etmek | school | |
| Turkish style) | | empty | boş |
| dance (Turkish- | dans oynamak | end | bitmek |
| style) | | enemy | düşman |
| dangerous | tehlikeli | England | İngiltere |
| day | gün | English (the | İngilizce |
| December | aralık | language) | |
| dentist | dişçi | English | İngiliz |
| departure | hareket | (the people) | |
| dial | çevirmek | enjoy | bayılmak, |
| dictionary | sözlük | | eğlenmek, |
| die | ölmek | | beğenmek (-i); |
| different | farklı | | (food:) tadını |
| difficult | zor | | çıkarmak |
| dinner | akşam yemeği | enough | yeterli |
| director | müdür | enter (a | katılmak |
| dirty | kirli, pis | competition) | |
| discuss | tartışmak | enter | girmek |
| discussion | görüşme | entrance | giriş |
| disturb | rahatsız etmek | Europe | Avrupa |
| do | yapmak | even | bile |
| doctor | doktor, hekim | evening | akşam |
| dog | köpek | eventually; | nihayet |
| doll | bebek | finally | |
| door | kapı | everyone | herkes |
| dress | elbise | exactly | tam |
| dressed, to get | giyinmek | exam | sınav |
| drink | içmek | excellent | uzman |
| driver | şoför | excuse, pretext | bahane |
| earlier, before, | önce | excuse me | affedersiniz |
| first | | expensive | pahalı |
| early | erken | extinguish | söndürmek |
| earn | kazanmak | eye | göz |
| east | Doğu | eyelid | gözkapağı |
| easy | kolay | face | yüz |
| eat | yemek yemek | factory | fabrika |
| eight | sekiz | fall, drop | düşmek |
| eighty | seksen | fall in love | aşık olmak |
| elect, choose, | seçmek | family | aile |
| measure | | famous | ünlü |

| | | | |
|---|---|---|---|
| far | uzak | France | Fransa |
| fast | hızlı | French (the | Fransızca |
| fasten your | kemerlerinizi | language) | |
| seatbelts! | bağlayın! | French (the | Fransız |
| fat, overweight | şişman | people) | |
| feast | bayram | fresh | taze |
| February | şubat | Friday | cuma günü |
| feel | hissetmek, | friend | arkadaş, dost |
| | duymak | friendly | dostça |
| ferry | vapur | friendship | dostluk |
| few | az | frog | kurbağa |
| fifty | elli | from where? | nereli |
| fight | dövmek | (origin) | |
| fill out | doldurmak | from ... on | ... (-den) |
| film | film | | itibaren |
| find | bulmak | from now on | artık, gayrı |
| finish | bitirmek | fruit | meyve |
| first | ilk | full of | bol |
| first, earlier, | önce | function, position | görev |
| before | | funny | komik, |
| fisherman | balıkçı | | güldürücü |
| fit, capable | uygun | garden | bahçe |
| five | beş | get off, to (bus, | inmek (-den) |
| flag | sancak | etc.) | |
| flashlight | el feneri | get on, to (train, | binmek (-e) |
| flat, apartment | daire | etc.) | |
| flower | çiçek | get to know, to | tanışmak |
| fly | uçmak | get up, to | kalkmak |
| folk music | halk müziği | get used to, to | alışmak (e) |
| follow | takip etmek | girl | kız |
| foot | ayak | girlfriend | kız arkadaş |
| football match | futbol maçı | give | vermek |
| for free | ücretsiz | glad, happy | mutlu |
| for | için | glass | (water) bardak; |
| for a long time | sürekli | | (wine) kadeh |
| forbidden | yasak | glasses, | gözlük |
| foreign | yabancı | spectacles | |
| Foreign Affairs | Dış İşleri | go out | çıkmak |
| forget | unutmak | go | gitmek |
| form | form | good | iyi |
| four | dört | good morning | günaydın |
| forty | kırk | good recovery! | geçmiş olsun! |

| | | | |
|---|---|---|---|
| good-tasting | **nefis** | help | **yardım etmek** |
| gossip | **dedikodu** | | **(-e)** |
| | **yapmak** | here | **burada** |
| government | **hükümet** | high | **yüksek** |
| grades (in | **notlar** | high quality | **kaliteli** |
| school) | | history | **tarih** |
| grandfather | **dede** | hit | **dövmek** |
| grandmother | **anneanne** | hold | **tutmak** |
| grape | **üzüm** | hold on! | **dur!** |
| great | **şahane, harika!** | holiday, vacation | **tatil** |
| | (as in: I'm | homework | **ev ödevi** |
| | feeling great!) | honeydew | **kavun** |
| | **bomba gibiyim** | melon | |
| Greece | **Yunanistan** | honour | **ödül** |
| Greek | **Yunan** | honourable | **sayın** |
| green | **yeşil** | hopefully | **inşallah** |
| grey | **gri, boz** | horror movie | **korku filmi** |
| grilled (lamb) | **köfte** | horse | **at** |
| meat | | hospital | **hastane** |
| grocer | **bakkal** | hotel | **otel** |
| ground meat | **kıymalı et** | hour, clock | **saat** |
| grow | **büyümek** | house | **ev** |
| guest | **yabancı, konuk,** | housewife | **ev kadını** |
| | **misafir** | how? | **nasıl?** |
| hair | **saç** | how many? | **kaç?** |
| half | **yarım, buçuk** | how much? | **ne kadar?** |
| hand | **el** | huge | **kocaman** |
| handsome | **yakışıklı, güzel** | hundred | **yüz** |
| happy, glad | **mutlu** | hurry | (*noun:*) **acele;** |
| hard-working | **çalışkan** | | (*verb:*) **acele** |
| harvest, collect | **toplamak** | | **etmek** |
| have something | **ısmarlatmak** | husband | **koca, eş** |
| ordered | | I | **ben** |
| have breakfast | **kahvaltı etmek** | I'm fed up | **bıktım (-den)** |
| head | **baş** | with ... | |
| headache | **baş ağrısı** | I'm sorry | **kusura bakma!** |
| health | **sağlık** | idea | **fikir** |
| healthy | **sıhhatli, şifali** | idiot | **boktan herif** |
| hear | **duymak, işitmek** | if | **eğer** |
| heart | **yürek** | if only | **keşke, bari** |
| hello | **merhaba,** | ill, upset, not | **rahatsız** |
| | **selam** | well | |

| | | | |
|---|---|---|---|
| ill | **hasta** | language | **dil** |
| important | **önemli** | last | (previous:) |
| in a little bit | **birazdan** | | **geçen;** (latest:) |
| in front of | **önünde** | | **son** |
| in general | **genellikle,** | last (verb) | **sürmek** |
| | **genelde** | late | **geç** |
| in particular | **özellikle** | later, after | **sonra** |
| in spite of | **rağmen** | laugh | **gülmek** |
| in that case | **o halde** | learn | **öğrenmek** |
| in the old days | **eskiden** | leather | **deri** |
| in the past | **geçmişte** | leave | (something:) |
| in short, . . . | **kısaca** | | **bırakmak;** |
| included | **dahil** | | (someone:) |
| interesting | **ilginç** | | **ayrılmak;** |
| introduce | **tanıştırmak** | | (from:) |
| investigate | **araştırmak** | | **kalkmak,** |
| invite | **davet etmek,** | | **hareket etmek** |
| | **çağırmak** | left | **sol** |
| is that so? | **öyle mi?** | lend | **ödünç vermek** |
| island | **ada** | lesson | **ders** |
| jail | **hapishane** | letter | **mektup** |
| January | **ocak** | library | **kütüphane** |
| Japanese | **Japon** | lid | **kapak** |
| joke | **şaka** | lie down | **yatmak** |
| journalist | **gazeteci** | lie | **yalan söylemek** |
| juice, water | **su** | life | **hayat** |
| July | **temmuz** | light | **ışık** |
| June | **haziran** | lighter (for | **çakmak** |
| just | **hala** | cigarettes) | |
| just now | **demin** | like | **gibi** |
| keep | (protect:) | like this/that | **böyle/öyle** |
| | **korumak;** | listen | **dinlemek** |
| | (hold:) **tutmak** | little boat | **tekne** |
| key | **anahtar** | little | (small:) **küçük;** |
| kiss | **öpmek** | | (few:) **az** |
| kitchen | **mutfak** | live | **yaşamak** |
| knife | **bıçak** | live, sit | **oturmak** |
| knock (door) | **çalmak** | lively | **cıvıl cıvıl** |
| know | **tanımak, bilmek** | living room | **salon** |
| lake | **göl** | long | **uzun** |
| lamb | **kuzu** | look for | **aramak** |
| lamp | **lamba** | look | **bakmak (-e)** |

| | | | |
|---|---|---|---|
| lose | **kaybetmek** | mom | **anne** |
| love | **sevmek (-i)** | moment | **an** |
| low (e.g. price) | **düşük** | Monday | **pazartesi günü** |
| luggage | **bagaj** | money | **para** |
| machine | **cihaz** | month | **ay** |
| Madam | **hanımefendi**; | moon | **ay** |
| | (+ last name:) | more | **daha** |
| | first name | more or less | **oldukça** |
| | **+ Hanım** | moreover | **üstelik** |
| main road | **anayol** | morning | **sabah** |
| make | **yapmak** | mosque | **cami** |
| make dirty | **kirletmek** | mosquito | **sivrisinek** |
| man | **adam** | most | **en** |
| many | **bir sürü** | mother | **anne** |
| March | **mart** | motorway | **anayol** |
| market | **pazar, çarşı** | mountain | **dağ** |
| married | **evli** | mountain | **yayla** |
| married, to get | **evlenmek** | meadow | |
| | **(-ile)** | move (house) | **taşınmak** |
| master | **usta** | museum | **müze** |
| matches | **kibrit** | must | **gerek, lazım** |
| matters | **husus** | | (+ infinitive) |
| May | **mayıs** | My god! | **Allah Allah!** |
| maybe | **belki** | name | **ad, isim** |
| mean (as in: | **demek** | national | **milli** |
| [that] means) | | near, close to | **yakın (-e)** |
| meanwhile | **bu arada** | necessary | **gerek, lazım,** |
| meat | **et** | | **mecbur,** |
| medicine | **ilaç** | | **zorunda** |
| meet | **tanışmak,** | | **(-mek)** |
| | **görüşmek;** | need | **gerekmek, gerek** |
| | (with:) | | **(-e)** |
| | **buluşmak** | neighbour | **komşu** |
| | **(-ile)** | nephew | **yeğen** |
| meeting | (official:) | never | **hiç bir zaman** |
| | **toplantı;** | nevertheless | **yine de** |
| | (date:) | new | **yeni** |
| | **randevu** | news | **haber** |
| milk | **süt** | newspaper | **gazete** |
| minister | **bakan** | next, coming | **gelecek** |
| minute | **dakika** | next to | **yanında** |
| mistake | **yanlışlık, hata** | nice | **güzel** |

| | | | |
|---|---|---|---|
| niece | yeğen | other | başka, öbür, |
| night | gece | | diger |
| nine | dokuz | outside | (place:) dışında; |
| ninety | doksan | | (direction:) |
| no | hayır, yok; | | dışarıya |
| | yooo!; (there | over and over | devamlı |
| | isn't:) yok | own, self | kendi |
| noise | gürültü | owner | sahip |
| nonsense | saçmalık, laf | page | sayfa |
| North | Kuzey | paint | boyamak/boya |
| not | değil | | yapmak |
| not yet | henüz, | palace | saray |
| | hala | paper | kağıt |
| nothing | hiç | parcel | paket |
| notice | fark etmek | part | bölüm |
| November | kasım | party | eğlence; (also |
| now | şimdi | | political:) parti |
| October | ekim | pass | geçmek |
| of course | tabii | past (in time- | geçiyor |
| office | büro | telling) | |
| often | sık sık | pay | ödemek |
| oh dear | aman! | pay a visit | ziyaret etmek |
| Oh, my God | Allahım | pear | armut |
| oil | yağ | pen | kalem |
| OK | tamam | people | insan; (nation:) |
| old | eski | | millet |
| olives | zeytin | pepper | biber |
| Olympics | Olimpiyat | pepper (for | dolmalık biber |
| | oyunları | stuffing) | |
| on the other | ancak, da/de, öte | person | kişi |
| hand | yandan, ise | phone, call | telefon |
| one, a | bir | | etmek |
| one time | bir kere | piano | piyano |
| only | yalnız, sadece | picture | resim, |
| open | (adj.:) açık; | | fotograf |
| | (verb:) açmak | piece | tane |
| optician | gözlükçü | pill | hap |
| or so | filan | pink | pembe |
| or | veya, yoksa | place | yer |
| orange (colour) | portakal | plane | uçak |
| | rengi | plastic bag | poşet |
| orange juice | portakal suyu | plate | tabak |

| | | | |
|---|---|---|---|
| play | oynamak; (instrument:) çalmak | really | ancak, gerçekten; (I swear!:) vallahi; |
| player | oyuncu | | (really?:) sahi |
| please | lütfen | | mi? |
| please don't touch! | dokunmayınız! | recently | yakınlarda, son zamanlarda |
| pocket | cep | recognise | tanımak |
| pocket knife | çakı | red | kırmızı |
| poem | şiir | remain | kalmak |
| policeman | polis | remember | hatırlamak |
| poor | zavallı | rent | (noun:) kira; |
| possibility | fırsat | | (verb:) |
| postcard | kartpostal | | kiralamak, |
| postpone | ertelemek | | tutmak |
| potatoes | patates | repeat | tekrarlamak, |
| pour | dökmek | | üstelemek |
| precisely | tam | repeatedly | devamlı |
| prepare | hazırlamak | republic | cumhuriyet |
| present | hediye | resemble | benzemek (-e) |
| price | fiyat | restaurant | lokanta |
| probably | galiba, her- halde | return | dönmek |
| | | rice | pirinç |
| problem | sorun, mesele | rich | zengin |
| produce | üretmek | right away | hemen |
| product | ürün | right | haklı, doğru |
| programme | program | ring (bell) | çalmak |
| prohibited | yasak | river | nehir |
| pull | çekmek | road | yol |
| punish | ceza vermek | roam | dolaşmak |
| punishment | ceza | room | oda |
| pupil, student | öğrenci | rubbish bin | çöplük |
| purple | mor | run | koşmak |
| put | koymak (-e) | Russian | Rus |
| quarter | çeyrek | salt | tuz |
| queen | kraliçe | same | aynı |
| question | soru | Saturday | cumartesi günü |
| quick | çabuk | saucepan | tencere |
| rabbit | tavşan | say | söylemek, |
| rain | yağmur yağmak | | demek |
| read; study | okumak | school | okul |
| ready | hazır | sea | deniz |

| | | | |
|---|---|---|---|
| seaside | **sahil** | smart | **akıllı** |
| season | **mevsim** | smile | **gülümsemek** |
| second | **saniye** | smoke | **sigara içmek** |
| secretary | **sekreter** | snow | **kar** |
| see you! | **görüşürüz!** | so, that is | **yani** |
| see | **görmek (-i)** | so much | **o kadar** |
| self, own | **kendi** | soap | **sabun** |
| sell | **satmak** | solution | **çözüm** |
| send | **göndermek** | some, a few | **birkaç, bazı** |
| September | **eylül** | some time soon | **yakında** |
| seven | **yedi** | somebody | **bir kimse** |
| seventy | **yetmiş** | someone | **biri (or: birisi)** |
| shape | **şekil** | something | **birşey** |
| sheep | **koyun** | sometimes | **bazen** |
| shirt | **gömlek** | song | **şarkı** |
| shoes | **ayakkabı** | sorry? | **efendim?** |
| shoot, strike | **vurmak** | south | **güney** |
| shop | **dükkan** | speak | **konuşmak** |
| shopping | **alışveriş** | sports | **spor** |
| shout | **bağırmak** | spring (season) | **ilkbahar** |
| show | **göstermek** | sprinkle | **dökmek** |
| side | **taraf** | stage | **sahne** |
| simple | **basit** | stairs | **merdiven** |
| since | **(...-den) beri** | stand | **durmak** |
| sing | **şarkı söylemek** | star | **yıldız** |
| singer | **şarkıcı** | state | **devlet** |
| single | **tek** | station | **istasyon** |
| sink | **batmak** | stay | **kalmak** |
| sir/madam | **efendim** | step on | **basmak** |
| Sir | **beyefendi;** (+ last | still | **henüz, daha,** |
| | name:) first | | **yine de** |
| | name + **Bey** | stone | **taş** |
| sister (older) | **abla** | stop | **bırakmak** |
| sister | **kız kardeş** | story | **hikaye** |
| sit, live | **oturmak** | straight | **doğru** |
| situation | **hal, durum; olay** | strategy | **yöntem** |
| six | **altı** | street | **sokak;** (avenue:) |
| sixty | **altmış** | | **cadde** |
| skirt | **etek** | strike, shoot | **vurmak** |
| sleep | **uyku** | student, pupil | **öğrenci** |
| sleep | **uyumak** | studies | **eğitim** |
| sleeping bag | **uyku tulumu** | study; read | **okumak** |

| | | | |
|---|---|---|---|
| stuffed pepper | **dolma** | Thank god! | **Allaha şükür** |
| stuffed vine | **yaprak dolması** | that/this | **şu** |
| leaves | | that, he | **o** |
| stupid | **aptal** | the day before | **evvelki gün** |
| success | **başarı(lar)** | yesterday | |
| such | **böyle** | the day after | **ertesi gün** |
| suddenly | **birden** | tomorrow | |
| sugar | **şeker** | theater | **tiyatro** |
| suitcase | **bavul** | then, and then | **ondan sonra** |
| summer | **yaz** | then | **o zaman** |
| sun | **güneş** | there isn't; no | **yok** |
| sunbathe | **güneşlenmek** | there you are! | **buyurun!** |
| Sunday | **pazar günü** | there | **orada** |
| supermarket | **market** | there is | **var** |
| surely | **mutlaka** | therefore | **onun için, bu/o** |
| sweet | **tatlı** | | **yüzden** |
| swim | **yüzmek** | these days | **bu günlerde** |
| T-shirt | **tişört** | they | **onlar** |
| table | **masa** | thing | **şey** |
| take | **götürmek** | think | **düşünmek,** |
| take, buy | **almak** | | **sanmak,** |
| take pictures | **fotoğraf çekmek** | | **zannetmek** |
| take a shower | **duş yapmak** | thirty | **otuz** |
| talk about | **söz etmek** | this | **bu** |
| tall | **yüksek** (not for | thousand | **bin** |
| | persons); **uzun** | three | **üç** |
| | **boylu** (for | throw | **atmak** |
| | persons) | Thursday | **perşembe günü** |
| taste | **tat** | ticket | **bilet** |
| tasty | **lezzetli** | ticket booth | **gişe** |
| tea | **çay** | time (as in 'the | **defa, sefer** |
| teacher | **öğretmen** | first time') | |
| teapot | **çaydanlık** | time | **vakit, zaman** |
| television | **televizyon** | timetable | **tarife** |
| tell | **anlatmak** | tired | **yorgun** |
| ten | **on** | tired, to get | **yorulmak** |
| tent | **çadır** | title, name | **isim** |
| thank you (said | **hoş bulduk!** | today | **bugün** |
| in reply to | | together | **beraber,** (with:) |
| **hoş geldiniz**) | | | **birlikte** (-ile) |
| thank you | **teşekkür ederim,** | toilet | **tuvalet** |
| | **sağ ol(un)!** | token | **jeton** |

| | | | |
|---|---|---|---|
| tomorrow | **yarın** | vegetarian | **vejetaryen** |
| tongue | **dil** | very much | **çok** |
| too | **da/de** | vet | **veteriner** |
| toothpaste | **diş macunu** | village | **köy** |
| topic | **konu** | visit | **ziyaret** |
| tourist | **turist**; (adj.:) | visit someone | **uğramak (-e)** |
| | **turistik** | wait | **beklemek (-i)** |
| town | **kent, şehir** | waiter | **garson** |
| toy | **oyuncak** | wake up | **uyanmak** |
| train | **tren** | walk | **yürümek,** |
| train station | **istasyon, gar** | | **gezmek (-i)** |
| tree | **ağaç** | wall | **duvar** |
| try | **denemek,** | wander | **dolaşmak** |
| | **çalışmak (-e)** | want | **istemek** |
| Tuesday | **salı günü** | war | **savaş** |
| Turkey | **Türkiye** | warm | **sıcak** |
| Turkish (the | **Türkçe** | wash | **yıkamak** |
| language) | | watch | (*noun:*) **saat;** |
| Turkish Airlines | **Türk Hava** | | (*verb*, TV) |
| | **Yolları** | | **seyretmek;** |
| Turkish pizza | **lahmacun** | | (watch out!) |
| Turkish | **Türk** | | **dikkat et!** |
| turn into | **değiştirmek (-a)** | water | **su** |
| twenty | **yirmi** | we | **biz** |
| two | **iki** | weak (tea) | **açık** |
| typewriter | **daktilo** | weather | **hava** |
| uncle (from | **amca** | Wednesday | **çarşamba günü** |
| father's side) | | week | **hafta** |
| uncle (from | **dayı** | weekend | **hafta sonu** |
| mother's side) | | welcome! | **hoş geldin(iz)!** |
| undecided | **kararsız** | West | **Batı** |
| under | **altında** | what can I | **buyurun!** |
| understand | **anlamak** | do for you? | |
| unfortunately | **yazık, maalesef** | what | **ne?** |
| unimportant | **önemsiz** | what's new? | **ne haber?** |
| university | **üniversite** | what-do-you- | **şey!** |
| until | **(... -e) kadar** | call-it? | |
| upstairs | **yukarıda** | whatever, | **neyse** |
| US | **Amerika** | anyway, | |
| use | **kullanmak** | when | **ne zaman?** |
| value | **değer** | where? | **nerede?** |
| vegetable | **sebze** | which | **hangi?** |

| | | | |
|---|---|---|---|
| white | **beyaz** | word | **sözcük, kelime** |
| who | **kim?** | work | (*noun:*) **iş**; (*verb:*) |
| who cares? | **boşver!** | | **çalışmak;** |
| why | **niye, niçin,** | | (hard:) |
| | **neden?** | | **didinmek** |
| wide | **geniş** | worker | **işçi** |
| wife | **karı, eş** | world | **dünya** |
| win | **yenmek** | worry | **merak etmek** |
| win | **kazanmak,** | write | **yazmak** |
| | (lottery:) | writer | **yazar** |
| | **vurmak** | wrong | **yanlış** |
| window | **pencere;** (glass:) | yard, garden | **bahçe** |
| | **cam** | year | **yıl, sene;** (with |
| wine | **şarap** | | age:) **yaş** |
| winter | **kış** | yellow | **sarı** |
| wish | **istek** | yes | **evet** |
| with good taste | **lezzetli** | yesterday | **dün** |
| with, at the side, | **yanında** | yet | **henüz, hala** |
| at, next to | | you | **sen,** (*sing.* |
| with | **ile** | | polite) **siz;** |
| within | **içinde** | | (*pl.*) **siz** |
| without stopping | **devamlı** | young | **genç** |
| woman | **kadın,** | youth | **genç** |
| | (derogatory:) | zero | **sıfır** |
| | **karı** | | |

# Index

Printed in Great Britain
by Amazon